ESSENTIALS OF HUMAN RESOURCE MANAGEMENT

D0206620

The field of human resource management (HRM) changes rapidly. Following the recession, new approaches are needed to succeed in a highly competitive global market place, and human resource (HR) managers now draw on disciplines such as business strategy, marketing, information systems and corporate social responsibility to meet the need for functional interdependence.

Essentials of Human Resource Management, now in its sixth edition, uniquely provides a strategic explanation of how established human resource policies can be adapted to meet new challenges. In addition to a thorough exposition of the main policy areas, this comprehensive text offers an introduction to organizational behaviour studies, incorporates relevant aspects of employee relations and presents an overview of employment law.

This new edition shows how HR managers can:

- meet the challenges of international competitiveness through organizational agility;
- develop policies in talent management, total rewards and employee engagement;
- utilize new technology to improve the efficiency and effectiveness of HRM;
- balance business demands with corporate social responsibility.

Written in an accessible manner, *Essentials of Human Resource Management* acts as an introduction to the subject for undergraduate students on HRM courses, as well as for postgraduate students on MBA programmes, and it will also be a valuable reference source for line managers.

A companion website supports this text with further materials.

Shaun Tyson is Emeritus Professor of Human Resource Management at Cranfield University School of Management, UK, and Visiting Professor at the University of Westminster, UK.

ESSENTIALS OF HUMAN RESOURCE MANAGEMENT

SIXTH EDITION

Shaun Tyson

Routledge
Taylor & Francis Group

LONDON AND NEW YORK

First published as *Personnel Management* in 1982
By Butterworth-Heinemann, an imprint of Elsevier

Sixth edition published 2015
by Routledge
2 Park Square, Milton Park, Abingdon, Oxon OX14 4RN

and by Routledge
711 Third Avenue, New York, NY 10017

Routledge is an imprint of the Taylor & Francis Group, an informa business

British Library Cataloguing in Publication Data
A catalogue record for this book is available from the British Library

Library of Congress Cataloging in Publication Data
  Tyson, S. (Shaun)
  Essentials of human resource management / Shaun Tyson. – Sixth edition.
    pages cm
  1. Personnel management.   I. Title.
  HF5549.T958 2015
  658.3–dc23

                                                        2014021400

ISBN: 978-0-415-65583-5 (hbk)
ISBN: 978-0-415-65584-2 (pbk)
ISBN: 978-0-203-07848-8 (ebk)

Typeset in Berthold Akzidenz Grotesk
by RefineCatch Limited, Bungay, Suffolk

MIX
Paper from
responsible sources
FSC® C013604

Printed and bound by CPI Group (UK) Ltd, Croydon, CR0 4YY

CONTENTS

LIST OF FIGURES

LIST OF FIGURES ■ ■ ■ ■

LIST OF TABLES

ACKNOWLEDGEMENTS

We wish to acknowledge with thanks the permissions to reproduce the material from the following works, granted by the publishers and authors:

Chapter 6: The Framework of HRM activities in relation to HRM outcomes and performance page 60, by Jaap Paauwe (2004) from *HRM and Performance. Achieving long term viability*. Granted by Oxford University Press.

Chapter 6: The model Agile organizational capability by Dyer, L. and Shafer, R. A. (1999) from 'Creating organisational agility: implications for strategic human resource management' in (eds) P. Wright, L. Dyer, J. Boudreau and G. Milkovitch. *Research in Personnel and Human Resource Management, supplement 4, Strategic Human Resource Management in the twenty-first Century*. Stanford, CT JAI Press. Granted by Elsevier Publishers.

Chapter 7: The cohort analysis from *Manpower Planning in the Civil Service*. Smith, A. R. (1976) Research Report Series no. 3 *Civil Service Development* (crown copyright), which is printed with the permission of the Controller of Her Majesty's Stationery Office.

Chapter 13: 'The Case Study: MassMutual (Massachusetts Mutual Life Insurance Company'. Larson, B. (2013). 'Custom Careers'. *HR Magazine*. June 54–56. Society for Human Resource Management. Granted by SHRM, Society for Human Resource Management.

I also wish to express my particular thanks and appreciation to Melanie James, associate solicitor with Mills and Reeve LLP, for her extremely helpful comments and advice on the four chapters in Part VII on employment law.

I would like to thank Nicola Cupit of Routledge for her patience and help in the creation of the book.

I am extremely grateful for the considerable help and advice over a long period from Jayne Ashley, without whom the book would not have been possible. Any errors or omissions remain my responsibility alone.

Shaun Tyson
Cranfield, Bedfordshire, UK

PREFACE

Human Resource Management (HRM) is constantly changing, reshaping the field of practice to suit new conditions and new requirements in the evolving context of organizations. For managers with people management responsibilities in Western economies recovering from an acute and lasting recession, this has meant once again developing the capacity to reinvent their roles. For HRM specialists, there has always been a need periodically to reinvent their specialism to ensure relevance and responsiveness. Quite apart from the economic conditions, new technology, demographic change, increased global competitiveness and interdependencies, and a more atomized, time-pressured, rights-conscious society, encourage all senior managers to be aware of the new demands they face. This may require line managers and HR specialists alike to repackage existing knowledge and skills, whilst learning new ideas and techniques.

This is the sixth edition of a textbook on HRM, which has been revised and brought up to date. It aims to give the widest coverage, combined with depth in the key areas of impact on the efficiency and effectiveness of organizations in the way they manage their human resources. The book is intended for line managers and for HRM specialists, and for students of management topics, at undergraduate and graduate levels. HRM is not unique in claiming to be a profession devoted to understanding the human condition, but it is one of the most advanced and diversified professions to do so. This text is intended to be useful for those who are expecting to specialize in HRM, and for experienced practitioners who want a reference text.

The HR function of management, whether performed by line managers or specialists, is context specific. There are, of course, the activities common to all organizations, large or small, whatever their sector, which need to be undertaken, such as recruitment, learning and development, performance appraisal, reward management, and the management of employment relationships. However, there is also a role in translating the effects of contextual changes from the economy and from society into the organization, to help the organization to deliver business outcomes effectively and efficiently. This requires the HR specialist to analyse and to understand how employees can change, and to help them to adapt, to perform and to grow their skills and capabilities in the service of their work.

The purpose in writing the book is to provide in one volume a complete textbook, which covers the fundamental areas of organizational behaviour, HRM strategy, policies and practices, industrial relations and employment law. This is intended, therefore, to be a guide to the whole area of HRM, with a focus on the main topics. Wherever appropriate, there is an account of the historical genesis of theories and management techniques, concepts and management 'fads', so that the reader can analyse the emergence of the topic (for example, employee participation and engagement), in order to understand current issues and thinking, how these have developed over time, and the new relevance claimed for such ideas or theories.

The book is structured into seven parts, starting with Part One 'Understanding organizational behaviour', covering individual differences including motivation and intelligence, groups, teams and leadership, organizations and managing change. Part Two 'The strategic role of HRM' covers HR strategy, planning and the options of a flexible workforce. Part Three 'Recruitment and selection' is about sourcing and selection: covering the principles and the impact of new technology. Part Four 'Developing people' covers performance appraisal, talent management and learning and development. Part Five: 'Rewards' centres on the total rewards philosophy, as well as a thorough exposition of pay systems, and the relationship between corporate governance and executive pay. Part Six: 'Employee relations' looks at industrial relations as it has developed, at conflict, and at the changes in approach towards mediation and settlements. Consultation, participation and engagement all link into the broader agenda on employee involvement and the increasing interest in employee wellbeing. Part Seven: 'Employment law' describes the institutional framework that governs employment law, and makes international comparisons. The three other chapters in this section provide a detailed, up-to-date account of employment law relating to employment contracts, managing diversity and managing trade union relationships. The law chapters underpin much of the discussions on the HR policy areas covered in the other sections.

The book is designed to be suitable for an examination of a particular topic, or to be read as a continuous narrative in each chapter. The book can therefore be useful as an additional text in support of courses that have other set texts. The field of HRM changes rapidly. So also do learning methods and the way people access information. To ensure there are more examples and opportunities to refresh information in the text, and to offer a facility to provide additional information for our readers, there is a companion website, the address of which is www.routledge.com/cw/tyson.

The revisions to a text of this kind could not be achieved without considerable help from many people. In the acknowledgements section I have an opportunity to thank those who have made a special contribution. However, this being the sixth edition, I will mention here also the outstanding contribution from Jayne Ashley over many years and many editions, which has been critical to their success. This text is about outstanding performance by people in organizations, and so it is entirely suitable to mention how one must always remember that, in the field of human resource management, what matters for organizations is the performance of individuals, whose actions make success possible. The task for HRM is to ensure this happens.

PART ONE

UNDERSTANDING ORGANIZATIONAL BEHAVIOUR

1 INDIVIDUAL DIFFERENCES

INTRODUCTION

Human Resource Management (HRM) is founded on an understanding of all aspects of the management of people at work. In this chapter the significance of individual differences between people is taken as the starting point for those who wish to understand the 'human' part of 'human resource management'. In an era when the main source of innovation and creativity is located in the efforts, imagination and application of people at work, there is increasing employer respect for the individual's contribution. The search for talented people as a source of competitive advantage, and the need to find employees who will come to share the values of the organization, who will make a personal contribution, however menial, to their roles, have an important part in human resource strategy.

Almost all aspects of HRM require an appreciation of significant individual differences: understanding what is innate, what is learned, what can change, what motivates people, and what relationships may productively be formed. How to find, to reward, to develop and to elicit the best performance from individuals is very much the subject of HRM, and informs the understanding of relationships at work on a larger scale and provides insights into what constitutes the potential for high performance, and how to make teams and organizations successful.

PERSONALITY

In this chapter, we will take up this theme as the bedrock for the study of HRM. We begin with a consideration of a number of ways to understand individual differences by looking at the concept of 'personality'. Personality is the term often used in everyday language to describe the individual characteristics of people.

When we are dealing with questions concerning individual differences it is useful to consider if we are discussing differences in personality. According to Fonagy and Higgitt (1984: 2): 'A personality theory is an organised set of concepts (like any other scientific theory) designed to help us to predict and explain behaviour.'

Many of the basic ideas about personality derive from early theorists in the psycho-analytic tradition, such as Sigmund Freud, Carl Jung and Alfred Adler. From Freud we have ideas about neuroticism and stability; from Jung theories about the traits that make up someone's personality, and from Adler the notion of complexes, such as the inferiority and the superiority complexes. The theories are intended to be logical frameworks for integrating observations about people, and should help to produce new ideas to explain and understand behaviour. Personality theories describe the characteristic ways in which individuals think and act as they adjust to the world as experienced. These include genetic and unconscious factors, as well as learned responses to situations. Often personalities are described as a series of 'traits'.

Carl Jung defined the personality traits that emerged from his ideas in this theory of individual differences, chief amongst which were the overall attitudes of 'extroversion' and 'introversion'. These traits help to explain how an individual sees and understands the world, how the person processes information and makes decisions, which depends, Jung argues, upon the person's thinking, feeling, sensation and intuition. These ideas have been popularized by the widespread use of the Myers Briggs inventory in occupational guidance, management development and career development.

In HRM, questions about the appropriateness of 'specific traits' or attributes are frequently raised in selection and assessment decisions. We discuss psychometric tests later in the book, but we should note here that researchers have identified a variety of personality traits (McRae and Terracciano 2005). There is evidence that the many individual-specific traits, such as 'warmth' or 'unreliability', can be subsumed under what are known as the 'Big Five' dimensions of personality, these being extroversion, neuroticism, agreeableness, conscientiousness and openness to experience.

These dimensions can be defined as follows:

1 *Extroversion*: extroverts tend to be sociable, relate themselves readily to the world around them.
2 *Neuroticism*: neurotics view the world as a frightening place. Neurotics have anxieties and are self-conscious.
3 *Agreeableness*: the ability to care, to be affectionate.
4 *Conscientiousness*: careful, scrupulous, persevering behaviour.
5 *Openness to experience*: these people have broad interests and are willing to take risks.

These attributes are scales in themselves, for example, extroversion–introversion, neuroticism–stability, and the balance will be a mixture of positions for any individual, along the five *continua*.

Many researchers such as Raymond Cattell have emphasized that the attributes of our personalities are not totally fixed. On the contrary, we are able to adapt and to change according to the situations we face, although it is anticipated any changes in behaviour would be consistent with our personality overall.

INTELLIGENCE

Some of the criticisms of 'personality traits' theories are that these theories imply an embedded set of behaviours, and that traits are described as absolutes, rather than in degrees, and can also be directed against the concept of intelligence. Where the idea of measurement did take hold, there was also the problem of the precise numbers produced being understood popularly as absolute facts. Measures such as a person's 'intelligence quotient', which was originally a measure of development in children in the early part of the twentieth century, suggests a 'scientific', technical way to measure intelligence, through the measure:

$$IQ = \frac{MA}{CA} \times 100$$

where MA = mental age of the child, and CA = the chronological age of the child.

Very often, HR staff are asked by line managers in recruitment activities whether or not a prospective employee is 'intelligent' or not, for example. Just as personality is neither constant nor simply a group of independent traits, intelligence must be judged according to the environment in which the person is being asked to demonstrate it. There is also a view that there are different kinds of intelligence.

Early theorists proposed that there were two factors – general intelligence and special abilities. In the 1920s Spearman proposed that people who possessed good general intelligence (G), often also have special abilities. This line of research has continued, so that Thurstone (1938) believed there were seven factors that described intelligence, including verbal fluency, numbers, memory, speed of perception and spatial visualization. By 1973, Sternberg was considering the importance of cognitive processing as an aspect of intelligence. Howard Gardner (1983) is a modern theorist who has set out a theory of multiple intelligences (MI). He argued there were seven: linguistic, logical-mathematical, spatial, musical, bodily-kinesthetic, interpersonal and intra-personal. He later added existential intelligence (covering knowledge of self) and naturalist intelligence.

Philip Vernon and other researchers concluded that intelligence is best seen as a hierarchical model. This follows Spearman's 'G', as being capable of being broken down into a number of major factor groups, which can be further divided into minor group factors. One conclusion that can be drawn is that intelligence measurement should therefore take account of ability in many fields, not just the IQ test, numerical, logical and linguistic abilities.

Aspects of intelligence are often contained in the attributes measured by the various personality tests. For the HR practitioner, these tests are useful guides in selection, talent management and decisions on promotion, but they are only a guide (see Chapter 11). Whatever analytical perspectives are applied, the important considerations are that the person is considered as a whole individual, not merely as a collection of disconnected attributes.

Emotional intelligence is of the utmost importance in many types of work. There is a need for 'emotional labour' in work that has a personal service element, for example in sales roles, airline flight attendants, and in retail work. At a deeper level, this is taken for granted as a part of some professional roles, where emotional intelligence (EI) is combined with experience, gained over many years, in roles such as school teachers, nurses, and in the legal profession. Many senior managers would also say this is essential in any leadership role.

It is especially important for human resource managers who necessarily spend much of their time listening to the views, proposals, problems and complaints from line managers and their subordinate staff. These aspects of their work also require emotional competencies. This is significant, owing to the expansion of the service sector of the economy: 'Emotional intelligence refers to the capacity for recognising our own feelings, and those for motivating ourselves and for managing emotions well in ourselves and in our relationships' (Goleman 1998: 317).

Intelligence quotient (IQ) and emotional intelligence (EI) are not in opposition, but are different sets of competencies. EI requires knowing one's own emotions, managing emotions, motivating oneself, recognizing emotions in others and handling relationships successfully (Goleman 1996: 43). EI skills can be developed and those who possess such skills are more likely to be effective, having 'mastered the habits of mind that foster productivity' (Goleman 1996: 36).

GENERATIONAL DIFFERENCES

Changing demographics due to longevity and a lower birth rate in most developed economies are encouraging an understanding of the different mindsets of people who were born and educated and worked in different eras, but who are still active in the workforce. These are, of course, perceptions of generational differences.

The four different generations that were working together at the turn of the twentieth and twenty-first centuries created an unusual situation. These were described by the Society for HRM in the USA (2004) as in Table 1.1.

These are very rough classifications, and there have always been generational differences, owing to the different perspectives of the young and the old, which may lead to stereotypical views of the young and the old. The counter to this view is to define generational

TABLE 1.1 CHARACTERISTICS OF FOUR GENERATIONAL GROUPS

Veterans	Plan to stay with the organization long term
	Respectful of organizational hierarchy
	Like structure
	Accepting of authority figures at work
	Give maximum effort
Baby Boomers	Give maximum effort
	Accepting of authority figures at work
	Results-driven
	Plan to stay with organization long term
	Retain what they learn
Generation X	Technologically savvy
	Like informality
	Learn quickly
	Seek work–life balance
	Embrace diversity
Generation Y	Technologically savvy
	Like informality
	Embrace diversity
	Learn quickly
	Need supervision

Source: Burke 2004.

differences in terms not so much of age, but of the shared social and economic experience in different epochs, affecting the lives of people born at different periods of time (Mannheim 1952). There is some evidence that the particular circumstances of different countries (for example in the Far East and in Europe) have created different attributes of the different generations (Parry and Urwin 2011).

For HRM, the significance of different generational values and sources of motivation could be a source of inter-organizational conflict. For example, the SHRM (2004) survey in the USA reported 24 per cent of HR professionals witnessing this conflict on a frequent basis (P2). However, differences between generations may also provide a valuable balance to work teams and points of contact with customers.

MOTIVATION

Motivation may be defined as an inner force that impels human beings to behave in a variety of ways and is, therefore, a very important part of the study of human individuality. Because of the extreme complexity of human individuals and their differences, motivation is very difficult to understand, both in oneself and in others. Nevertheless, there are certain features of motivation that may be regarded as generally applicable:

1   The motivational force is aroused as a result of needs that have to be satisfied. Thus, a state of tension or disequilibrium occurs that stimulates action to obtain satisfaction.
2   The satisfaction of a need may stimulate a desire to satisfy further needs (for example, 'The more they have, the more they want').
3   Failure to satisfy needs may lead to a reduction or a redirection of the motivational force towards other goals seen as more obtainable.
4   The motivational force has three basic elements – direction, intensity and duration in that it is directed towards goals, its force may vary considerably depending on the strength of individual desires and it may last for long or short periods or be intermittently recurring.
5   There are two main sources of human needs:
    (a)   inherited, i.e. all humans share primary physiological needs that must be satisfied for survival
    (b)   environmental, i.e. through the main socializing influences in their lives people acquire attitudes, values and expectations, which lead to learned needs such as status, fame, wealth and power.

Some authorities claim that needs for affiliation with others, creativity and achievement are also inherent in human beings.

Because of its central importance to the study of people at work, motivation has been a subject of continued research since the early years of the twentieth century. In very broad terms, the many theories in existence are of two kinds: they may be based on assumptions by practising managers, resulting from experience and direct observation, or they may be the result of methodical research, usually by psychologists and similar specialists.

MANAGERIAL THEORIES

Traditionally, assumptions made by managers about motivation have largely reflected a 'carrot and stick' approach. Ample evidence of the prevalence of this approach may be seen in the systems of rewards and punishments, applied in both direct and subtle ways, which are characteristic of very many work organizations. Sometimes described as a rational-economic theory, it is exemplified in the ideas of F. W. Taylor (1913) and his followers in the so-called 'Scientific Management School', which introduced methods of time and motion study into work organizations at the beginning of the twentieth century. This theory is based on assumptions that workers are motivated mainly by material incentives. Such assumptions inevitably have a fundamental effect upon the organizational environment, managerial styles, working arrangements and methods. In Taylor's system, for example, time and motion studies were used to maximize efficiency and productivity through payment for results. Workers were regarded as a factor of production. Little heed was paid to the potential influence or importance of human factors upon work performance.

RESEARCH STUDIES

Because of their variety it is not easy to classify theories of motivation without over-simplification. However, for the convenience of a general review, two very broad categories may be distinguished. In one group of studies the emphasis is directed mainly towards the importance of needs as an influence on motivation. Because most of these studies are concerned with higher human needs for creativity and self-fulfilment, they represent a form of reaction to managerial assumptions about the dominance of economic motives. The main authors in this category are Abraham Maslow, Elton Mayo and colleagues, Fred Herzberg, David McLelland and Douglas McGregor.

Maslow's hierarchy of needs

Based on the premise that humans are wanting beings whose behaviour is goal directed, Maslow postulates a catalogue of needs at different levels ranging from the basic physiological and biological needs to the higher, cultural, intellectual and spiritual needs:

1   *Physiological*: these are essential to survival, e.g. food, drink, sleep, reproduction, etc.
2   *Security or safety*: these refer to needs to be free from danger and to live in a stable, non-hostile environment.
3   *Affiliation*: as social beings, people need the company of other humans.
4   *Esteem*: these include self-respect and value in the opinion of others.
5   *Self-actualization*: these are needs at the highest level, which are satisfied by opportunities to develop talents to the full and to achieve personal goals.

Two important assumptions are fundamental to Maslow's theory: first, higher needs do not become operative until lower needs have been met (for example, the hungry professor in prison is likely to be more interested in food than philosophy); second, a need that has been satisfied is no longer a motivating force. Research into the applicability of this system to real situations has indicated that it is an over-simplification. Nevertheless, the classification of needs into categories has provided a very useful basis for subsequent research.

Mayo's theory of social needs

Between 1927 and 1939, onsite experiments were carried out by Mayo, Roethligsberger and Dickson at the Hawthorne Plant of the Western Electric Co., Chicago, which have assumed a classical status in the study of human relations. The initial objective was to study the effect of illumination on productivity, but the experiments revealed some unexpected data on human relations, which had very significant consequences for subsequent research in the behavioural sciences. Very briefly, the main conclusions of the experiments were these:

1   Industrial life has taken much of the meaning out of work and workers are driven to fulfil their human needs in other directions, especially in human relationships.
2   Workers are not solely concerned with economic needs and material comfort.
3   Human factors play a very significant part in motivation and, in this respect, the research work emphasized the importance of social needs and the influence of the work group.
4   Workers are likely to be more responsive to the influence of colleagues (which include workgroup norms and sanctions) than to attempts of management to control them by material incentives.
5   If management styles produce a threatened, frustrated, alienated workforce, worker groups will tend to adopt their own norms and strategies designed to counter the goals of management.

The main lessons for managers that emerge from the Hawthorne data are that the personal and social needs of employees are very important in determining behaviour and that management should not concentrate exclusively on productivity, material and environmental issues, which will prove to be a self-defeating aim. There were also lessons for management about group behaviour, discussed in Chapter 2.

Herzberg's two-factor theory

The two-factor theory is a development of Maslow's system. Herzberg classified two categories of needs corresponding to the lower and higher levels of human goals. He calls one group 'hygiene factors' and the other group 'motivators'. The 'hygiene factors' are the environmental factors in the work situation, which need constant attention in order to prevent dissatisfaction. These factors include pay and other rewards, working conditions, security, supervisory styles, etc. They are essentially factors in attracting employees, and neglect leads to dissatisfaction, but they cannot actively promote satisfaction or motivate workers. Motivation and satisfaction, says Herzberg, can only come from internal sources and the opportunities afforded by the job for self-fulfilment.

According to this theory, a worker who finds work meaningless may react apathetically, even though all the 'hygiene' factors are well looked after. Thus, managers have a special responsibility for creating a motivating climate and for making every effort to enrich jobs. Herzberg's ideas have provoked much controversy, because they imply a general applicability and do not seem to take enough account of individual differences. His insistence that motivation comes from within each individual and that managers cannot truly motivate but can stimulate or stifle motivation is, nevertheless, an important contribution of the study.

JOB SATISFACTION AND MOTIVATION

Herzberg and others have advocated job redesign to make the work itself inherently motivating, through designing the content and nature of the tasks in the job. According to Hackman and Oldham's theory, the five core characteristics that produce psychological states that can result in job satisfaction, motivation and improved performance are, in any one job:

- skill variety (range of different skills demanded)
- task identity (whether work is the whole process or part of the process)
- task significance (impact the job has on others), which together produce the degree of meaningfulness experienced in the job by the job holder
- autonomy (degree of choice, control over the work), which produces experiences of responsibility
- feedback (whether the results of the work itself show clearly the performance level achieved).

The feedback is motivational from the employee's perspective according to the strength of the need for 'growth' required by the employee. All five characteristics combine to produce the 'scope' or complexity of the job.

McLelland's power affiliation achievement model

McLelland's research has identified three basic categories of motivation needs, that is, power, affiliation and achievement, into which people could be grouped according to which need appears to be the main motivator in their lives. Those with a high power need seek positions of control and influence; those for whom affiliation is the most important need seek good relationships and enjoy helping others; achievement seekers want success, fear failure and are task-oriented and self-reliant. These three needs are not mutually exclusive. Many people are well motivated by all three, but invariably one area is predominant. McLelland's research has also indicated that motivational patterns can be modified by specially designed training programmes. The achievement drive, in particular, can apparently be increased by this means. The implications of the theory in practice are that managers can identify employees who are self-motivated, those who rely more on internal incentives and those who could increase their achievement drive through training.

McGregor's theory X and theory Y

McGregor proposed that managers typically make two kinds of assumptions about people, which he calls theory X and theory Y. Theory X is seen as a set of traditional beliefs that people are inherently lazy and unambitious, and will avoid responsibility. The main incentives to work are provided by the carrot or the stick and constant supervision is necessary. Theory X attitudes, in McGregor's view, are the main reasons why workers adopt defensive postures and group together to beat the system whenever they can. Management expects them to behave in this way and they fulfil the prophecy. Theory Y attitudes, on the other hand, take a benevolent view of human nature. Theory Y assumes that work is a natural human activity, which is capable of providing enjoyment and self-fulfilment. According to theory Y, the chief task of the manager is to create a favourable climate for growth, for the development of self-reliance, self-confidence and self-actualization through trust and by reducing supervision to a minimum.

The second category of studies is more concerned with the dynamics of the motivational process. In this group there is much more emphasis on the importance of individual differences, of individual expectancy as a function of motivation, and of the contingencies of different situations.

Lewin's field theory

Believing that behaviour is the result of an individual's reaction with his or her environment (that is, B, Behaviour, is a function of P, Person, and E, Environment), Lewin reached the following conclusions about motivation:

1   Motivation depends upon the individual's subjective perceptions of his or her relationships with his or her environment.
2   Behaviour is determined by the interaction of variables, i.e. tension in the individual, the valency of a goal and the psychological distance of a goal (in other words, the existence of a need, the perception of the possibility of fulfilment and the reality of this possibility).
3   Human beings operate in a field of forces influencing behaviour like the forces in a magnetic field, so that people have different motivational drives at different times.
4   In the context of work some forces inhibit (e.g. fatigue, restrictive group norms, ineffective management), whilst others motivate (e.g. job satisfaction, effective supervision, rewards).

Vroom's valency expectancy theory

Vroom proposes that motivation is a product of the worth or value that individuals place on the possible results of their actions and the expectation that their goals will be achieved. The theory is expressed by the formula: Force (F) = Valency (V) × Expectancy (E). The importance of this approach is the emphasis that it places on the individuality and variability of motivational forces, as distinct from the generalizations implied in the theories of Maslow and Herzberg.

Porter and Lawler's model

This model is in the same genre as the theories of Lewin and Vroom in its concern with the influence of perception and expectancy on motivation. However, it is a more comprehensive account than the other theories. The model is based on the following propositions:

1   The motivational force of an individual depends on how he or she perceives the value of the goal, the energy required to achieve the goal and the probability that the goal will be achieved.
2   This perception is, in turn, influenced by the individual's past experience of similar situations, because this will enable a better self-assessment of the required effort, the ability to perform as required and the probability of achieving the goal.
3   Performance achievement is mainly determined by the effort expended, the individual's understanding of the task requirements and self-assessment of ability.
4   Performance is seen by the individual as leading to both intrinsic and extrinsic rewards, which produce satisfaction if the individual perceives the reward as fair.

This model is probably the most comprehensive and adequate description of the motivational process in its potential practical application. It underlines the need for a system of management by objectives, performance appraisal and very careful attention to the organization's system of intrinsic and extrinsic rewards, as well as the value of training.

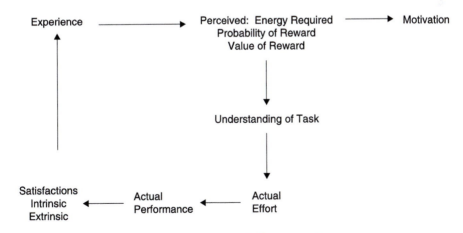

Figure 1.1 Porter and Lawler's variant on Vroom's model of motivation theory

Tyson, S. and Jackson, T. (1992). *The Essence of Organizational Behaviour*. Pearson Education.

Schein's theory of 'complex man'

Schein's thesis is an appropriate conclusion for a survey of motivational 'complex man' theories. His view is that, whilst all theories contain some truths about human behaviour, no single theory is adequate by itself. His position may be summarized as follows:

1   People are driven by nature to fulfil a variety of needs, some basic and some on a higher plane.
2   Needs once satisfied may reoccur (e.g. basic needs); others (e.g. higher needs) are constantly changing and being replaced by new needs.
3   Needs vary, therefore, not only from one person to the next, but also within the same person according to differences of time and circumstances.
4   Effective managers are aware of this complexity and will be as flexible as possible in their approach to their subordinate staff. Above all, they will learn to avoid generalized assumptions about the motivation of others based on projections of their own views and expectations.

Because of the complexity of motivation, managers cannot expect to be able precisely to gauge the various motivational forces that influence their individual subordinates. They can, however, use the available data to broaden their understanding and to provide a framework for analysing the general influences that may interrelate to produce a variety of individual motivational patterns:

1   *Forces within individuals themselves*: attitudes, beliefs, values, assumptions, expectations and needs.
2   *The nature of the job*: extrinsic and intrinsic rewards, component tasks, responsibilities, work arrangements, feedback on performance.
3   *The environment of work*: senior managers and their styles; other colleagues and relationships with them; organizational climate and practices.

QUESTIONS

1   Why is it important to be aware of individual differences? What are they and what effects may they have in behaviour and relationships?
2   Give a brief definition of motivation.
3   What are the distinctive features of the theories of the following authorities: Maslow, Herzberg, McGregor, McLelland, Porter and Lawler?
4   Describe a simple framework for a systematic analysis by managers of motivational factors.

For examples and a commentary on these questions, readers can consult the companion website.

REFERENCES

Burke, M. E. (2004). *Generational Differences Survey Report*. Alexandria VA: Society for HRM.

Fonagy, P. and Higgitt, A. (1984). *Personality Theory and Clinical Practice*. London: Methuen.

Gardner, H. (1983). *Frames of Mind: the Theory of Multiple Intelligences*. New York: Basic Books.

Goleman, D. (1996). *Emotional Intelligence*. London: Bloomsbury.

Goleman, D. (1998). *Working with Emotional Intelligence*. London: Bloomsbury.

McCrae, R. R. and Terracciano, A. (and members of the Personality Profiles of Culture Project) (2005). 'Universal Features of Personality Traits from the Observer's Perspective: Data from 50 different cultures'. *Journal of Personality and Social Psychology*, 88: 547–61.

Mannheim, K. (1952). 'The Problem of Generations' in *Essays on the Sociology of Knowledge*. P. Keckskemeti (ed) London: Routledge and Kegan.

Parry, E. and Urwin, P. (2011). 'The Impact of Generational Diversity on People Management' in E. Parry and S. Tyson (eds), *Managing an Age Diverse Workforce*. Basingstoke: Palgrave MacMillan at 95–111.

Sternberg, R. J. (1977). *Intelligence, Information Processing and Analogical Recording*. Hillsdale NJ: Lawrence Erlbaum Associates.

Taylor, F. W. (1913). *The Principles of Scientific Management*. New York.

Thurstone, C. (1938). *Primary Mental Abilities*. Chicago: University of Chicago.

Vernon, P. E. (1961). *The Structure of Human Abilities*. London: Methuen.

2 GROUPS

The groups of people who work together as teams achieving organizational goals are the bedrock of the organization's structure, and the means through which organizations are run. This chapter is devoted, therefore, to the twin related topics of the psycho-dynamics of working groups, and the leadership roles managers need to adopt in order to elicit high levels of team performance (Harris and Beyerlein 2003: 189).

The main concern of managers about their work groups is that they should work cohesively as teams in order to achieve required results. Their interest in group behaviour is centred, therefore, on basic questions such as what factors make groups work cohesively and what factors cause disruption? In order to find likely answers to these questions we need to examine a series of related questions about the characteristics of work groups. Because of individual differences in personality, interests, characteristics and motivations, formal prescriptions of how work groups should perform are insufficient.

REASONS FOR MEMBERSHIP OF GROUPS AND THE EXPECTATIONS FROM GROUP MEMBERS

When people join work groups a contract is formally drawn up, which makes precise statements about what employers require and what they will give in return. These terms and conditions are invariably expressed in material language. They do not say, for example, that the firm will undertake to satisfy the employees' needs for self-esteem or self-fulfilment. Nevertheless, behind the formal language of the official contract there is always implied what has been described as a 'psychological contract', this being the 'deal' between employer and employee resting upon reciprocal obligations and understandings. This means employers assume that employees' decisions to join organizations indicate a willingness to accept the principle of subordination and to recognize the authority of the organization as legitimate. The employees' perception, on the other hand, is that, since the relationship is voluntary, they have some freedom for the exercise of influential behaviour, which could, if necessary, lead to changes in the work situation.

INTERACTION WITHIN AND BETWEEN GROUPS

Before the research on groups and teams is examined, it would be useful to consider the subject in general terms. Tuckman, for example, has proposed a four-stage model as a general description of the chronology of a group's progress towards cohesive collaboration:

Stage 1 – Forming: the initial stage, when members are tentative about the task, about each other and the group leadership. Extremes of view are usually restrained. Members test each other and draw up rules of conduct. In a leaderless group, leaders may be chosen or begin to emerge. These may be changed in later stages.

Stage 2 – Storming: the members are getting to know each other better and are prepared to put forward their views more vigorously. This leads to conflict between individuals, leaders or subgroups that may have emerged.

Stage 3 – Norming: the conflicts begin to be controlled as the members realize the need to cooperate in order to perform the task. The group produces norms of behaviour, i.e. an accepted code of attitudes and conduct that all the members accept.

Stage 4 – Performing: the group has now developed the required degree of cohesion to work as a team and to concentrate on the problems it has to overcome to attain its goal.

This is only a very generalized model and it may not apply to all types of groups. Nevertheless, the basic principles have a wider application and give a useful insight into the behaviour of groups with a continuous existence and an ongoing task.

Another useful general model of group behaviour is the result of studies carried out by R. F. Bales and colleagues at Harvard University. These data are based on the observation of small discussion groups and, like Tuckman's model, these conclusions would be directly applicable to work groups of a similar nature, such as committees. However, some general principles may be derived to describe the behaviour of people in working groups whose relationship extends over much longer periods. Briefly to summarize Bales's data, he found that behaviour fell into two main categories:

■ task oriented
■ socio-emotional oriented.

His observations showed that, apart from efforts directed towards the task, there was another type of behaviour that concerned the human aspects of the group and its individual members. Bales further distinguished two subcategories of socio-emotional behaviour:

■ emotionally positive
■ emotionally negative.

Emotionally positive behaviour is directed towards enhancing the cohesiveness of the team, and expresses itself in tension-releasing humour, action to support other members of the team, whilst emotionally negative behaviour is egocentric, and expresses itself in the form of antagonism, signs of tension, appeals for help, withdrawal of cooperation, etc. This study also indicated that some people tend to give a lead either in the task-oriented or socio-emotional roles; for example, one person would be primarily concerned with the task and another would be more interested in maintaining group cohesiveness. Occasionally, the two functions might be combined in the same person.

These two general models are not only helpful for providing a broad understanding of group behaviour, but particularly for emphasizing two basic orientations, namely task fulfilment and group cohesiveness. On this basis, we can now look in rather more detail at particular phenomena of group behaviour and the associated problems with which managers have to contend. Certain factors have been identified as fundamental in their influence on the behaviour of groups:

1 *The task*: its nature and the arrangements imposed by management in terms of methods and work conditions.
2 *The group*: its size, composition, relationships and norms.
3 *The leadership function*: styles and their appropriateness to the task and the group.
4 *The environment*: relationships with other groups and the main organization.

The influences of these factors are described below and are illustrated with examples from work situations and data from various research studies.

THE TASK

The nature of the work and the way it is arranged can have a very important influence on either stimulating or impeding group cohesiveness. For example, where the tasks of the group involve prestige and esteem, such as the public display or special service units of the armed forces, there is seldom much difficulty in obtaining recruits to the group, retaining members or developing a high level of group cohesiveness. Similar cohesiveness is found among groups who share dangerous or hard conditions, such as dockworkers, miners and fishermen. On the other hand, where the technology of the task reduces social interaction to a minimum, as, for example, in production lines, then the problem of creating a spirit of group unity may become more difficult.

Some well known and valuable studies have been conducted on the effects of the task upon the group. A team from the Tavistock Institute of Human Relations studied the effects on groups of coal miners of a technological change from traditional short-wall to long-wall methods of mining. Traditional methods had been based on small, highly autonomous, cohesive teams. When new mechanical equipment was introduced, which revolutionized the working arrangements, the traditional small groups were replaced with much larger groups under a supervisor, and divided into three shifts, each performing different stages of the total task. Although the new arrangements were very sound in technical terms, the human consequences were very serious: the former cohesiveness of the small group was destroyed; workers developed feelings of social disorientation; and low productivity became an accepted norm.

Data that underlined the findings of the Tavistock Institute were produced in a classic study of a gypsum factory in the USA by Alvin Gouldner. Here, management introduced a series of new working arrangements into a factory that had a long tradition of highly autonomous working groups and well established group norms. The new broom methods were intended to produce greater efficiency but, in fact, they created much tension, counter-measures and a series of bitter disputes.

Both of the examples quoted above illustrate the potential consequences arising from management's lack of awareness of group behaviour and the influence of the task and working arrangements.

THE GROUP

Relationships within the group are affected by factors such as size, composition, individual personalities of group members and their roles, group norms, etc. Managers need to understand these factors and their influence as a basis for analysing group behaviour. All the evidence suggests that highly cohesive groups are generally more productive than groups that are less cohesive. However, it would be wrong to assume that group cohesiveness necessarily correlates with high levels of productivity. A group may become cohesive as a reaction to and a defence against tactics of management of which it disapproves, or because of perceived threats from other groups.

The size of a group may influence possible patterns of behaviour, and has an obvious relevance to questions of communication. If the group is too large, it may divide into subgroups that may collaborate for reasons other than productive work. In large groups, leaders have problems with the span of control. It is difficult for managers to know their subordinates well, and communication barriers are more likely to occur.

The composition of the group will also influence patterns of interaction. Managers cannot normally be expected to plan or manipulate the composition of their groups to take care of all possible subtle influential factors of personality, experience, values, age, etc. In theory, the greater the homogeneity a group has, the more cohesive it is likely to be. Except for circumstances where there are too many dominant personalities, a blend of personality traits could be as much an advantage as a disadvantage.

Group norms are to a group what the individual perspective is to each separate human being. Thus, a group will develop an identity of its own in terms of common patterns of behaviour and attitudes, as in clubs, gangs and societies that attract people of a like mind. Work groups develop norms about work; for example, internally generated standards, quantity of output and attitudes to management. They may also develop other norms that act, as it were, as the unwritten 'rules of the club', e.g. members of one work group will dislike certain other groups, will read certain kinds of newspapers, will hold certain kinds of political views and so on. Newcomers to the group are expected to comply initially whilst they pass through what is termed 'the socializing process of learning' the expected behaviour. Eventually, they will find that they have unconsciously made the group's behaviour and attitudes their own, that is, they have internalized the norms of the group, or else the group will reject them and they will remain outside the group.

Closely linked with the phenomenon of group norms is the pressure exerted by the group on members to conform. Non-conformists may well be rejected by the group. In extreme cases, this means being totally ignored. A number of studies, especially in the USA, by, for example, Millgram, Asch and Janis (1972), have made special studies of conformity, which have produced some rather disturbing conclusions about the degree to which people may succumb to social pressures to 'conform' and to suppress their real beliefs. Applied to working situations, these data indicate that group decisions, such as those made by committees, may well not be the result of a rational assessment of evidence. Strong pressures within a group to reach consensus can result in the suppression of wiser counsels.

The Hawthorne studies showed how group solidarity – the face-to-face relationships with group members – were more significant to group members than their relationship with managers (Roethlisberger and Dickson 1939).

GROUPS AND TEAMS

From the discussion so far we may conclude that group working elicits behaviours oriented towards the social relations within the group and sometimes encourages 'collective behaviour' between members of the group and towards those who are outside the group. Work groups are often described as teams by managers. An important question for managers is when do work groups become teams? Very often, managers speak of their team, as though because a number of people report to them, this group automatically becomes a 'team'. The idea of a team depends upon a sporting analogy. To be a team, the group should portray the following features in their approach to the work task:

- They are required by their work system to collaborate in the achievement of common goals.
- There are mutual obligations held by group members, who look to each other for specific kinds of support, so there is interdependency.
- Failure or success by a team member has an effect on the performance of the group as a whole.
- Each individual group member brings her/his own abilities to be used in a complementary way in the achievement of the team's task.

The self-confidence of people at work is often derived from their team/group membership, where self-efficacy is developed owing to the regard of other team members, their feedback and concern for performance and support being a shared activity (Bandura 1997; Jaina and Tyson 2004).

In his famous study of team roles, Meredith Belbin (1981) looked at how successful teams make the best use of the different roles people perform in groups. He listed the team roles as:

'Chairman' – Calm, self-confident, welcomes all contributions, strong sense of objectives.
'Shaper' – Highly strung, dynamic, drive, readiness to challenge.
'Plant' – Individualistic, active, intellectual, creative.
'Resource Investigator' – Enthusiastic, curious, contacts people, explores new ideas.
'Monitor/Evaluator' – Sober, unemotional, acts with discretion, judgemental.
'Team Worker' – Socially oriented, responds to people, promotes team spirit.
'Completer/Finisher' – Orderly, conscientious, perfectionist.
'Company Worker' – Conservative, dutiful, organizing ability, practical.

A balanced team ensures these roles are filled. Belbin argues from his research that individuals have a preferred role in groups, but can adopt other roles if necessary for the effective working of the team. For example, the person whose natural preference is to be a resource investigator might slip into the role of the 'team worker' or the 'completer', if this role was not adopted in the group.

This is an account of how individuals can play parts to ensure success in a team by their individual behaviour.

TEAM COMPETENCY

However, there is also the question of whether teams possess collective characteristics, the whole being greater than the sum of the parts. We can see that in sports teams, high performing individuals when grouped together do not necessarily perform well as a team; for example, a World International Cricket XI drawn from the best players in all the major cricketing nations was beaten by the Australian cricket team with a huge margin in 2005. Similarly, the Oxford and Cambridge boat race has often been won by an eight containing many young men only recently introduced to the sport, even when competing against Olympic oarsmen in the other boat. This may be due to 'team mental models':

> Thus, if individual team members have a similar understanding of the task, a similar understanding of their purpose and role within the organization, and a similar understanding of each other's strengths and weaknesses, the overlap between individual mental models could be described as the 'Team Mental Model'.

(Langan-Fox 2003: 328)

TABLE 2.1 THE TEAM COMPETENCY FRAMEWORK (WITH EXAMPLES OF THE TEAM COMPETENCY DEFINITIONS)

Enabling
Communicating
Integrating: This competency is dependent upon those process elements that enable the team to become integrated to an appropriate level to ensure effective task actions.

Adapting
Situational sensing
Creating

Resourcing
Knowing: This is a resource competency that encompasses the shared understanding of that knowledge required by the team to achieve a successful task outcome.

Contextualizing
Evolving expertise
Team wisdom

Fusing
Emotional maturation
Bonding
Openness: This competency enables an environment within the team where members are free to express themselves in an honest and valued way.

Affiliating

Motivating
Committing
Inspiring
Believing: This competency describes those factors that facilitate a sense of team efficacy within the team. This is a type of team belief and team confidence.

To discover how collective competencies help teams to become successful a research project was undertaken by Mills and Tyson (2000), which showed that many different types of teams that were studied (including senior management teams, jazz groups, football teams, virtual teams and project teams) possessed a similar range of team competencies. To be successful, teams have to have competencies in task capability, and within the psychological environment of the team. The task capability competencies were those which enabled the completion of the task, and resourcing the team; whereas the psychological environment of the team depends upon competencies which helped to fuse the team together, and to encourage affiliation, as shown in Table 2.1.

SELF-AWARENESS

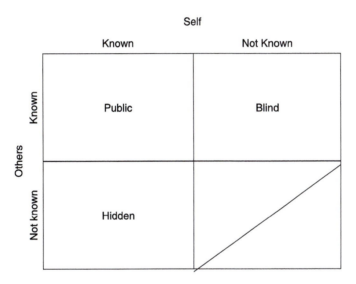

Figure 2.1 The Johari window

The need for and importance of self-awareness has been recognized since the earliest times. The injunction 'Know thyself' was apparently written in gold above the portico of the Temple of Apollo in ancient Greece. Robert Burns addressed the same theme when writing 'O wad some power the gift tae gie us, to see oursels as ithers see us'.

An understanding of one's own capabilities and limitations in terms of knowledge, skills and personal traits is especially important in work. The more insight managers have into their own behavioural traits and the effects on the members of their groups, the more effective they are likely to be, and the less likely they are to alienate the very people they should be motivating. As managerial styles have become more democratic or participative and less authoritarian, so employees are encouraged more than ever before to assess themselves in terms of employment suitability, career paths, work performance and developmental and training needs.

There are two views of individuals. There is the view that individuals have of themselves, and there is the view that other people, who have seen them in various situations, have of them. Obviously, there may often be some divergence in these views. The view of self may conflict with the views others have of us. There may be differences among the external assessors. The main possible variants in assessing individual behaviour have been summarized in the model known as the Johari window (Figure 2.1), named after its psychologist authors, Joe Luft and Harry Ingham.

The window in Figure 2.1 has four panes, described as follows:

1   Known to self and to others (public), e.g. I know that I am lazy and other people think so too.
2   Known to others, but not to self (blind), e.g. I think that I am a caring, sensitive person. Others do not see me in this way. I am not aware that others hold a different view.
3   Known to self, but not to others (hidden), e.g. I know that my lack of moral courage is a major weakness. Apparently others are not so aware of this problem.
4   Not known to self and not known to others, e.g. I am a poor judge of people. I do not realize this and neither do others who know me.

How should self-aware people be described?

■   They realize that their behaviour affects others and that they may need to change in order to achieve effectiveness in performance and human relationships.
■   They take active steps to obtain feedback about their behaviour and performance.
■   They take particular note of any consensus of external views, especially when these diverge significantly from their views of self.
■   They have reached as honest and balanced a view of themselves as is humanly possible.

All this, of course, is very much easier said than done. In real life we find it much easier to list our perceived strengths than our weak points. We do not like unpalatable home truths. We generally prefer to judge other people rather than ourselves. Paradoxically, the achievement of self-awareness depends on awareness of the need for, and importance of, self-awareness in the first place. The person who occupies windowpane 3 in the Johari window may find it very difficult to move to windowpane 1 for the very reasons that placed him or her in windowpane 3.

All of these studies show the significance of group processes for the outcomes achieved. They also reveal that the 'group' or team may be taken as a separate unit of analysis, with its own collective agenda and way of working. Human resource management needs to work with this concept. As discussed later in the book, some of the most important ways in which we can sustain high performance is through the creation of high performing teams; for example, by providing the conditions under which such teams thrive. This means turning the normal processes of group working to positive effect and developing teams, as opposed merely to individual competency.

HIGH PERFORMANCE WORK TEAMS

Since the time of the Hawthorne experiments, how groups are managed has been under-stood to have a powerful effect on organizational performance. Much of the formal work in this area has stressed the way HR policies and practices can help to create high performing teams. Characteristic features of these management practices are high levels of employee involvement in decision-making and problem-solving, with an emphasis on high quality output. In addition, support for these social, intra-group processes by supportive manage-ment practices, such as quality circles, pay linked to performance, and a supportive culture that rewards innovation and high levels of effort.

The idea of autonomous work teams is to encourage team members to take respons-ibility for the completion of tasks and for group maintenance, work allocation and problem-solving. In the field of job satisfaction, there is the thesis that managers design jobs which are inherently satisfying and motivational.

LEADERSHIP AND GROUPS

Leadership has a crucially important bearing on group behaviour. As an influential factor we are especially concerned with different styles of leadership and their possible effects upon groups. Because of its special importance, leadership will be discussed in detail later in this chapter.

Leadership is obviously a subject of extreme importance in management. As modern research has clearly shown, leadership is a part of the study of group behaviour. Leaders cannot operate in isolation, and groups with tasks to perform cannot perform these tasks without leaders. Leaders are members of groups, influencing them and being influenced by them. They are especially concerned with the cohesive development of the group as a prerequisite for the ultimate achievement of the group's goals. If management is defined as a process of making the most effective use of available human and material resources for the achievement of specified goals, then leadership may be described as the component of management that is most concerned with the use of human resources.

Until recently, nearly all the emphasis of leadership study had been concentrated on leaders themselves, usually by examining the careers of well known leaders in history in an attempt to analyse the secrets of their apparent success. Thus, a belief predominated for centuries that leadership was dependent on the circumstances of one's birth. Some became leaders because they had the good fortune to be born into noble, naturally ruling classes; others because they were endowed with certain innate qualities. The idea that leadership is a facet of group behaviour has only emerged in recent times from studies of the human problems of industrial society. It has led to some profoundly important conclusions:

1   Leadership has no meaning outside the context of tasks to be performed and groups to perform these tasks.
2   Studies of leaders as isolated individuals provide little useful insight into the nature of leadership.
3   A deeper understanding can only come by analysing what leaders and groups do in a variety of specific situations.

Studies on leadership published in earlier times invariably included lists of what their authors regarded as the essential traits of a good leader. Whilst these lists naturally coincide in a number of important respects, at the same time they inevitably vary in their total contents, their priorities and their emphases, and these variations clearly illustrate the fundamental limitations of attempts to study leadership on a basis of personal qualities. Such an approach has been shown to provide no means for answering some of the fundamental questions that need to be asked; for example, if there is no consensus on what makes effective leaders, by what criteria are they to be identified, developed and assessed?

The functional approach to leadership as an element of group behaviour has dispelled much of the mystique that formerly surrounded the subject. Above all, it has provided a framework for meaningful analysis and for the systematic selection, training and assessment of leaders. The emphasis has shifted from the study of leaders to leadership as a function of coordinating the efforts of a group to achieve specified tasks. At the same time, it is apparent that there is considerable variation in the nature of tasks and in the composition of groups. From this, certain conclusions may logically be deduced. People can be trained to gain insight into the nature of group behaviour and to develop the interpersonal skills required to accomplish a productive coordination of human efforts; the very wide variety of situations means that certain styles of leadership will be more appropriate to some situations than to others.

After the Hawthorne experiments had aroused the initial interest in group behaviour, serious research into leadership soon followed and has continued ever since. The change of emphasis from the personality of leaders to leadership as a function in a collaborating group had a profound effect during the post-war years, first on the selection and training of military leaders and, subsequently, of managers in general. However, the innovation of the functional approach caused some problems of misunderstanding, because traditionalists interpreted this approach to mean that personal qualities are not important − a view that misrepresents this theory. The personal qualities for effective leadership are not in question. The message of the functional approach is simply that an analysis of personal qualities gives little help in understanding what leadership means in action.

The quantity and variety of research is so extensive that a comprehensive summary cannot be attempted in this brief survey. Nevertheless, the findings and conclusions of some of the most important works merit a brief description because of what they have to say about effectiveness in the management of people. Many of the studies of leadership have been carried out by direct observation of people at work. Others have taken the form of 'armchair philosophy', based on personal experience or the reorientation of previous works. Some of the research has been carried out by university teams and some by particular individuals.

University of Iowa

This was the first serious attempt to study leadership in groups in action. It was based on the activities of boys who were members of a model-making club and were quite unaware that they were being observed for experimental purposes. They were divided into three groups and subjected in turn to three quite different styles of leadership:

1   Autocratic, whereby they were given no scope for initiative and were tightly disciplined.
2   Democratic, whereby the leadership was positive and firm, but allowed participation and freedom of expression.
3   *Laissez-faire*, whereby the boys were allowed to do as they pleased.

The results clearly indicated the superiority of the democratic style for all three groups in terms of general contentment, group cohesiveness and productivity. The other styles produced apathy, disunity and low productivity. It would be dangerous to seek correlations between the behaviour of juveniles in leisure activities and adults at work, but the data of the experiments at least emphasized for the first time the importance of leadership styles.

Harvard Department of Social Relations

The work of R. F. Bales and his colleagues has already been mentioned in connection with group behaviour. Since there is a very close link between the study of groups and leadership, it is not surprising that this research has important messages for managers in their leadership roles, which are:

1   They need to be aware of the equilibrium problem, to balance the demands of the task against those of personal and interpersonal feelings.
2   They need to recognize the main kinds of contributions to a group's work, i.e. task-oriented behaviour and socio-emotional behaviour, and especially to distinguish between the positive (group maintenance-directed) and negative (individually oriented) aspects of this behaviour.
3   The leader's constant task is to move the group in a coordinated way and towards the achievement of its goals, but at the same time to keep relationships harmonious and personal outcomes at a high level (to motivate people who want to retain membership).

4   The two facets are interdependent. In practice, there could sometimes be high-quality work but a rapid turnover of staff, which reduces total efficiency.

Ohio State University

A team from this university carried out an extensive onsite study with employees of the International Harvester Company to study the effects of leadership, which covered a very wide range of different types of behaviour that leaders use in their dealings with subordinates. A statistical analysis of results revealed two broad categories of behaviour: one directed towards fulfilling tasks and goals; the other concerned with group reactions and individual feelings. Applying these categories to different levels of managers, the team found that some managers showed clear preferences for one of the two styles, whilst others exhibited both in fairly equal measure. It was also found that, in general, extremes in task-oriented styles correlated with high grievance rates and that the subordinates of leaders who strongly favoured people-oriented styles had lower grievance rates.

University of Michigan

These experiments took place at the offices of the Prudential Insurance Company and looked at the correlation between work performance and leadership styles. Taking sections engaged in similar work, the team identified those with high productivity and those with low productivity. Next, they established that there were no significant differences in the supervisors of the sections in terms of variables such as age, sex and experience. A study of the supervisory styles produced most interesting results. The supervisors of high-performance groups revealed similar behaviour. In particular, they exhibited concern for their employees, allowed them to share in decisions affecting work and generally established an atmosphere of trust. The supervisors of low-performance groups exhibited opposite types of behaviour and in general were much more concerned with productivity than their subordinates.

Likert's four-systems model

Rensis Likert, also of the University of Michigan, has made a prolonged study of management and, in particular, the effect of leadership styles upon people at work and in consequence upon group cohesiveness, effective performance and productivity. His research has led him to propose four main identifiable styles, which he calls Systems 1–4, described as follows:

System 1 – *Exploitive-authoritative*: managers are very autocratic, do not trust subordinates, motivate mainly by fear and punishment, attempt to communicate only in a downward direction and make all decisions unilaterally.

System 2 – Benevolent-authoritative: managers have a less harsh attitude, but still keep a tight control, especially in decision-making. They motivate with rewards and some-times punishment and allow a limited measure of upward communication.

System 3 – Consultative: managers are much more employee oriented than those of Systems 1 and 2. They motivate with rewards, participation and occasional punish-ment. They allow fairly unrestricted two-way communication. They tend to keep decision-making on major issues mainly to themselves.

System 4 – Participative-group: managers show complete trust and confidence in subor-dinates, who share in communication and decision-making at all levels. They operate with themselves and their subordinates as a group.

Likert's research into actual work situations indicated a clear correlation between the four systems and the managers' success as leaders and the groups' achievement of goals and productivity. System 4, needless to say, was found to be superior to the others, a conclu-sion that closely matched the research data at the Prudential Insurance Company.

F. E. Fiedler's contingency model

Fiedler has made a unique contribution to the study of leadership. He has proposed that there are three critical dimensions for classifying leadership in situations:

1   The leader/group relationship.
2   The ease or difficulty of the task (e.g. structured or unstructured).
3   The leader's vested authority.

He further proposed that in these three dimensions the situation may be favourable or unfavourable for the leader (for example, he or she may not have enough authority to deal with a particular kind of group). Matching favourability and unfavourability with the three basic dimensions, he then produced eight possible combinations, ranging from dimensions 1, 2, 3 all favourable, to dimensions 1, 2, 3 all unfavourable. This is the model for determ-ining the nature of the situation.

Next, he produced a model for categorizing leadership styles. An individual leader's style is determined by scoring a questionnaire designed to reveal individuals' attitudes towards persons that they themselves choose as the work colleague with whom they have had most difficulty in working (designated by Fiedler as 'the least preferred co-worker' – LPC). Each tested subject is then given an LPC rating, in which high scores indicate leaders who are people oriented and low scores for those who are task oriented. The essence of Fiedler's contingency theory is that, in practice, we need to identify the nature of the situation and then select leaders most likely to be suited to a particular situation. Thus, for some situations, a people-oriented leader (that is, high LPC) will be more effective, whilst other situations call for the task-oriented style (that is, low LPC). This theory differs from other theories on leadership in that Fiedler inclines to the view that individuals tend to have preferred styles and that these need to be adapted to situations. Most other authors urge the need for developing flexibility in leaders to meet the needs of varying situations.

Tannenbaum and Schmidt

These authors are concerned with problems of leadership style and with questions such as whether managers can be democratic towards subordinates and yet maintain the necessary authority and control. For purposes of analysis they have produced a 'continuum of leadership behaviour', ranging from authoritarian styles at one extreme to democratic styles at the other, which they call 'boss-centred' and 'subordinate-centred' leadership. Unlike other models that advocate a preferred style, this model attempts to provide a framework for analysis and individual choice. The authors propose three key factors on which choice of leadership pattern depends:

1   Forces in the manager (e.g. attitudes, beliefs, values).
2   Forces in the subordinates (e.g. their attitudes, beliefs, values and expectations of the leader).
3   Forces in the situation (e.g. pressures and constraints produced by the tasks, organizational climate and other extraneous factors).

In summary, their conclusions are:

1   When deciding which point along the continuum represents the appropriate style, leaders need to begin with an analysis of these three factors, but in particular they need to clarify their own objectives.
2   Leaders need to develop skills in reading situations in these terms and then should be able to behave appropriately in the light of their perceptions.
3   No single style of leadership is always right and another always wrong. Successful leaders are neither assertive nor permissive, but are consistently accurate in their assessment and application of where on the continuum they should be.

The Blake-Mouton managerial grid

This is a well publicized system for identifying leadership styles as a basis of training. Following the data of other authors, Blake and Mouton identify two critical basic dimensions: concern for the task and concern for the people. To find the precise location of a leader's style they have produced a grid, with 'concern for people' along one axis and 'concern for the task' along the other. Each dimension ranges from 1 (low) to 9 (high) so that a grid of 81 squares is produced. The extremes are found in each corner:

1   Highest concern for people, lowest for task = 1.9.
2   Lowest concern for people and task = 1.1.
3   Highest concern for task, lowest for people = 9.1.
4   Highest concern for people and task = 9.9.

A moderate concern for both is in the middle of the grid and scores 5.5. The ideal which leaders should aim to achieve is 9.9.

John Adair's functional leadership model

This model was developed whilst the author was lecturing at the Royal Military Academy, Sandhurst. It is based on the research data of studies of leadership and groups, and the author's own experience at Sandhurst. The model is three-dimensional, and proposes that in all leadership situations there are three crucial areas to which the leader must attend:

■   the task
■   the maintenance of team cohesiveness
■   the needs of the individuals.

All three areas require constant attention, but effective leadership depends upon the leader's skill in giving appropriate emphasis to particular areas at particular times. The special importance of this model is its usefulness for training purposes, since activities can be meaningfully analysed and assessed in these terms.

Recent research on leadership has become eclectic. The hangover of the 'great person' theory of leadership still persists, with research into the characteristics of higher echelons in organizations, in terms of their age and background. There are also studies of the process of leadership, in particular the leader's role in managing changes (for example the idea of 'transformational leadership'), leaders as the provider of the 'vision' for the organization, and various forms of collaborative leadership, leaders as coach and learning facilitator, as part of a continuing interest in leadership styles.

Boyatzis and McKee (2005)

In recent years, there has been a return to the notion that leaders should possess particular characteristics to be successful. However, there is also an explicit assumption in these prescriptions that leadership actions have to adapt to the period of rapid economic, political, environmental, institutional and social change through which our societies are passing. Against this background, for example, leaders are exhorted to build 'resonant relationships' with their colleagues and customers, using their emotional intelligence. They should be 'mindful' of self and others, and face changes with empathy and compassion, in an authentic way. The message here is that leaders should create high trust organizations, providing vision and compassion and hope for the future.

Distributed leadership

The idea of semi-autonomous work groups was developed in changing organizations and development programmes. The concept of distributed leadership helps to link the theories of groups and of leadership together. Giving groups more discretion to make decisions, it is argued, encourages more rapid problem solving, and more responsiveness to change. The speed of change leads organizations to introduce various forms of distributed leadership to achieve outcomes. Organization structures that are flatter, and which utilize matrix approaches so that resources are used effectively in project management, have the capacity to restructure and change resources quickly. The growth of professional and specialized occupations has also encouraged a move away from old autocratic, centralized leadership models. Leadership is seen as an activity which is undertaken by many people in the group, rather than as an individual attribute (Thorpe and others 2011).

CONCLUSIONS

One important conclusion we can draw from this multiplicity of research paradigms and methodologies is that the significance of the topic has become so pronounced that leadership is seen to be a critical determinant of most aspects of organizational life. The questions about the relationships between the quality of leadership and organizational success have never been closer to the top of the agenda for researchers and managers alike. For the HR function this raises fascinating questions; for example, how to make top teams effective, how to influence performance and how to manage change are all related to leadership. There are also the associated issues about leadership and employee relations such as partnership approaches, management development, the identification of potential development methods, career planning, succession planning and promotion, recruitment and rewards. We will be addressing these questions in the chapters that follow.

The broad conclusions that emerge from research on group behaviour and leadership (Figure 2.2) are these:

1   Democratic-participative styles are generally likely to be more effective in creating group cohesiveness and productivity than strongly task oriented styles.
2   At the same time, varying situations require different leadership styles, which have to be adapted or selected to suit these different circumstances. The leadership styles that are favoured in the modern era are more distributed and require stronger interpersonal skills, including emotional intelligence, authenticity, resilience and tolerance of

ambiguity, with the ability to manage change and to carry their group or team with them, relying on the trust they engender in their fellow group members.

3   Effective leadership depends upon awareness of the nature of the task, the group and its individual members, the environment, the capacity to analyse and to restructure their teams and, particularly, the self-awareness of the leaders themselves.

Nature of group behaviour
Tuckman's model proposed four stages:

1. Forming   2. Storming
3. Norming   4. Performing

Bale's data includes two areas:

Task oriented; socio-emotional (positive and negative).

Fundamental influential factors are:
Task-nature and work arrangements.
Group-size, composition, relationships and norms.
Leadership–styles and appropriateness.
Environment-relationships with other groups and the organization.

Conclusions

1. Balance between task requirements and team maintenance is essential.
2. Membership of group must be worthwhile.
3. Total organization harmony is paramount. Positive steps are needed to reduce inter-group rivalry.

Nature of leadership

Modern studies emphasize superiority of a functional analysis of leadership in action rather than leaders' personal qualities. Main contributions are:

Univ. of Iowa: study of leadership styles at boys club (autocratic; democratic; laissez-faire).

Harvard (Bales): theory of task-oriented and socio-emotional axes.

Ohio State Univ: data on effects of task-oriented and people-orientated styles at International Harvester Co.

Univ. of Michigan: similar data from studies at Prudential Assurance Co.

Likert's four systems: Exploitive-authoritative; Benevolent-authoritative; Consultative, Participative-group.

Fiedler: Contingency Theory, i.e. matching leaders' LPC ratings with a three-dimensional model (leader/group relationship; nature of task; leaders' vested authority).

Tannenbaum and Schmidt: continuum of leadership behaviour ('boss-centred'-'subordinate-centred').

Blake and Mouton: 9x9 Managerial Grid (concern for task/concern for people).

Adair: Functional Leadership Theory (needs of: task, team, individuals).

Conclusions

In general, democratic-participative styles are more effective.

However, much depends on situational variables. Styles have to be adapted to suit these.

Effective leadership requires awareness of task, group, individual and self.

Figure 2.2 Summary of studies of group behaviour and leadership

QUESTIONS

1   What are the main features of Tuckman's and Bales's methods for analysing group behaviour?
2   What are the main factors that influence group behaviour?
3   What are the group norms and why are they important in the study of group behaviour?
4   Summarize the main conclusions that have emerged from studies of group behaviour and the significance of 'groups' for HRM.
5   What are the significant differences between the former and current approaches to the study of leadership?
6   Briefly summarize the main features and conclusions of the studies of leadership carried out by the universities of Iowa, Michigan and Ohio.
7   What are the distinctive features of Fiedler's theory?
8   What are the reasons for leadership development to be important for HRM?
9   Summarize the main conclusions that have emerged recently from research into leadership.

REFERENCES

Asch, S. E. (1952). *Social Psychology*. Englewood Cliffs, NJ: Prentice Hall.

Bales, R. F. (1950). *Interaction Process Analysis: A Method for the Study of Small Groups*. Cambridge Mass: Addison-Wesley.

Bandura, A. (1997). *Self Efficacy: The Exercise of Control*. New York: W.H. Freeman.

Belbin, R. M. (1981). *Management Teams. Why They Succeed or Fail*. London: William Heinemann.

Boyatzis, R. and McKee, A. (2005). *Resonant Leadership*. Boston, Mass: Harvard Business School Press.

Harris, C. L. and Beyerlein, M. M. (2003). 'Team-based organization: creating an environment for team success' in West, M., Tjosvold, D. and Smith, K. G. (eds) *International Handbook of Organizational Teamwork and Cooperative Working*. Chichester: John Wiley & Sons.

Jaina, J. and Tyson, S. (2004). 'Psychological similarity in work-based relationships and the development of self-efficacy beliefs'. *Human Relations* 57, 3: 275–96.

Janis, I. L. (1972). *Victims of Groupthink* Boston: Houghton-Mifflin.

Langan-Fox, J. (2003). 'Skill acquisition and the development of a team mental model' in West, M., Tjosvold, D. and Smith, K. G. (eds) *International handbook of Organizational Teamwork and Cooperative Working*. Chichester: John Wiley & Sons at 321–60.

Milgram, S. (1963). 'Behavioural Study of Obedience'. *Journal of Abnormal and Social Psychology* 67, 371–78.

Mills, T., Tyson, S. and Finn, R. (2000). 'The development of a generic team competency model'. *Competency and Emotional Intelligence*. 7, 4: 37–41.

Thorpe, R., Gold, J. and Lawler, J. (2011). 'Locating distributed leadership' *International Journal of Management Reviews*.13, 3 Special Issue. 239–50.Figure 2.1 The Johari window

3 ORGANIZATIONS

THEORY AND PRACTICE

Individuals and groups operate within the framework of larger groups, which are loosely described as organizations. Although much of what has already been said about the behaviour of individuals and groups makes assumptions about the organizational context, we need to study organizations because of the complexity of their structure, the interrelationships of their component groups and their relationships with the external environment.

The importance to managers of organizational studies is this: first, when we reach the organizational level of analysis, we are considering the total effectiveness of the organization as a system; second, having considered how an organization does and should control its component elements, we are still left with the very difficult question: how is the organization itself to be controlled? Is it capable of controlling itself? Northcote Parkinson (1958), for example, acquired a special fame for his comments about the uncontrolled ways in which organizations behave and expand: 'work expands so as to fill the time available for its completion'.

The basic problem of size and complexity in organizations is something that everyone experiences sooner or later. It is seen in everyday working life in the difficulties that employees find in describing the organization where they work or in relating to it. Employees usually identify more with smaller groups. When they try to relate to organizations it is as though individual employees are dealing with an unseen, indefinable force that controls their working lives, but with whom they can never come face to face. Nevertheless, HRM as an organizational function is charged with the responsibility of making the organization itself effective.

There has been considerable research into organizations from a number of different perspectives. There is a common thread running through the diversity of particular themes, which is the implicit assumption that organizations as a phenomenon of modern industrial life need to be studied and analysed to understand them and how they affect the people who work in them, and the people (customers, patients, societal members, suppliers, politicians and the many different stakeholder groups) who interact with them. HRM has the opportunity to help to design organization structures and cultures, to manage the boundaries between the organization and society, and to represent the organization in a variety of different ways. How to analyse organizations and to understand what is right and what is wrong with them is an important strategic aspect of the role of HRM.

It is possible to distinguish five broad categories of approach to the study and analysis of organizations, which reflect different emphases in studying the subject:

1   *Structural/Rational*: this includes studies from the so-called classical or traditional school. These are mainly concerned with formal organizations and the related questions such as structural design, the definition of responsibilities and the legitimacy of authority.

2   *Human relations*: those who follow this approach stress the importance of relationships and groups, human needs and reactions to organizational life, and the existence of an informal system of norms and organizational processes which ought to be taken into account when organizations are studied and designed.

3   *Systems theories*: studies included in this category are interested mainly in exploring the systematic nature of the interactions and interrelationships between the component elements of organizations, their functions, the operating systems, and relationship between organizations and their environments.

4   *Contingency theories*: these have links to the structural and systems approaches, but emphasize the intervening variables of institutions, markets, social and cultural factors and the need for onsite comparative studies to find out what organizations are really like, to analyse the interactions of all the internal and external variables and, on this basis, to design organizations to take account of the contingencies of differing situations.

5   *The post-modern approach*: the starting point for this approach is that organizations are not necessarily rational – they only exist in the perceptions of their members and those who wish to deal with them; reality is socially constructed. Our understanding is based on a number of distinct discourses that frequently are in opposition to each other. Language use and power are linked, and power and control are inherent within language structure and use.

Words carry a history; there are different meanings that are part of the language games we play as we define meanings in use. Therefore, human resource management could be understood as a part of the power relations, which seeks to manipulate meanings to suit the needs of those in authority in the organization (Legge 1995; Hassard and Parker 1994).

This categorization is a simplification of a very complex field of study, but is adequate as a basic framework for a broad analysis of the subject. For the purpose of this review, it would be useful briefly to examine some of the important contributions in each approach as samples of the main trends of thought about organizational issues that typically occur, their contributions and applications.

STUDIES OF ORGANIZATIONAL STRUCTURE

The first major study of organizations was made by Max Weber. This work was doubly important because it laid a foundation for subsequent studies and raised the question of authority types:

1   *Charismatic*: authority stems from the personality of the leaders of the organization and is typified in religious, political and industrial organizations by people like Gandhi, Nelson Mandela, Churchill, Henry Ford and Steve Jobs.
2   *Traditional authority*: is based on precedent and custom. The commonest example is a monarchy. In industry, examples are found in family firms, where the leadership is passed from parent to son or daughter, even though initially at least the son or daughter may derive no authority from experience.
3   *Rational-legal*: this is described as a legitimate basis of authority for democratic society and formal work organizations. The main requirement is a hierarchy of levels of authority, which is based on the assumed ability of managers to perform better than their subordinates either through superior professional or superior administrative experience, knowledge and skills, or a combination of all of these. This authority is then incorporated into a set of rules, policies and codes governing the arrangements for work and the conduct of employees.

Weber described the rational-legal organization as a bureaucracy, which he considered to be a superior form of organization. Weber was considering these issues in the late nineteenth century, when in some countries there was widespread corruption and nepotism in governments and 'official' organizations. Its particular virtue, in Weber's view, and hence its name, is that once the roles of office at various levels have been defined, the organization continues to function independently of individuals. A simple analogy would be a long-running play, where different actors join and leave the cast over the years, but the play continues.

Whilst the basic model of the typical bureaucracy is useful for general analysis, it does not take account of the importance of role interpretation. Employees interpret their work roles in the light of their own attitudes, values, beliefs, needs and expectations. Weber has adequately described the formal pattern of organizational behaviour, but beneath the surface there is an informal pattern that is just as important, as the 'Human Relations School' has shown. People interact socially at work and take part in activities not prescribed in the formal system. Nevertheless, the introduction of the idea of authority and legitimacy has made a most important contribution to the study of organizations.

Another significant contribution to the theme of organizational authority has been made by Amitai Etzioni, who was interested in the idea of matching individuals' attitudes and expectations with types of organizations. He identifies three main types of organization, according to their authority base, and three types of employer and member involvement:

1   Organization types
    (a)   *Coercive*: used in prisons, mental hospitals and sometimes in military units.
    (b)   *Utilitarian*: used mainly in industry, related to Weber's rational-legal type and relying mainly on economic rewards.
    (c)   *Normative*: used mainly in organizations where forms of social, values based services predominate, e.g. religious, welfare, and political and professional organizations.
2   Individual types of involvement
    (a)   *Alienative*: members are forced to join and have no psychological involvement.
    (b)   *Calculative*: members join mainly to satisfy economic and similar needs.
    (c)   *Moral*: members place a high personal value on the objectives of the organization.

There is a general correlation between the organizational type and the type of involvement. This model may also be useful when related to the idea of the psychological contract between employer and employee and possible problems of misperception. For example, if an organization that is expected to be essentially utilitarian tries to introduce patterns of authority that are coercive in nature, then an alienative response is likely to be produced. Similarly, if this type of organization expects a moral involvement, such as a heart and soul commitment from employees to the firm and its products, it could be making a psychological miscalculation in asking for more from its employees than it is really prepared to give in return.

THE HUMAN RELATIONS APPROACH

Human relations is the study of the social psychology of organizations, with a particular interest in work groups and the needs and motives of employees. The work group studies discussed in the previous chapter are typical of this approach.

The managerial benefits from discovering more about employee motives are clear. These include the advantages derived from understanding how best to manage different types of groups, relationships within groups, rewards, employee involvement and communication policies. All such studies could bring productivity pay-offs, and information on how to organize groups effectively. The academic benefits from human relations approaches are in countering the deterministic arguments which existed following the 'scientific management' literature, which viewed people at work as simple factors of production that would respond to payment by results schemes in exactly the way desired, as exemplified by F. W. Taylor's studies back in 1913.

The human relations approach therefore brings up an important debate on the extent to which economic theories adequately explain the reasons for the behaviour of people at work. Human relations studies, such as those conducted at the Hawthorne works of General Electric in the 1930s, revealed the significance of employee work norms, and of group behaviour. 'Human relations' offers an alternative view of rationality, which is the rationality of the situation, from the context of the perspective of the person or group being studied, rather than being based on management's rationality. This notion that rationality depends on the perspective of the subject, and is not necessarily shared by all those involved, is a concept known as 'bounded rationality' (Simon 1983).

THE SYSTEMS APPROACH

The emphasis of the systems approach is upon the interactions between the different elements of an organization – the people, the structure, the technology and the environment – which could be seen as a response to the greatly increased changes demanded of organizations and their employees in recent years. These pressures for change derive from new developments in technological, economic, social and political environments.

The studies of coal-mining made by the social scientists of the Tavistock Institute and the conclusions that they reached about the impact of the task upon group behaviour have already been mentioned. Strongly advocating the view that an organization is a complex of interacting variables, two important ideas were established, and the research repeated in other industries such as petro-chemicals, in companies such as Shell and BP:

1   The concept of the *socio-technical system*: this implies that an organization is a combination of two systems: the technology (the tasks, the equipment and working arrangements) and the social system (the interpersonal relationships of employees). The two systems are in constant interaction and each influences the other.

2   The *open-system model*: the essence of this idea is that organizations import resources and information from the environment, which are processed within the organization and then exported to the environment in the form of products or services.

The significance of these ideas lies in their emphasis on the organization's dependence on its environment and on the need to design organizations that take full account of the socio-technical system. A well known example of the systems approach to organizational studies is Likert's theory of overlapping groups and linking pins, the main ideas of which are:

1   The significant environment for a group is composed of other groups.

2   Groups are linked to their environment by people holding key positions and being members of more than one group (e.g. the Head of Department who is also a member of the Organizational Management Committee).

The total system comprises three levels – society as a whole, organizations of similar function, and subgroups within a larger system – which are connected by people in key positions, acting as linking pins. Likert's model emphasizes the importance and the possibly far-reaching consequences of relationships and dependencies.

A theory that is very similar to Likert's in concept, but adds a further important concept, has been developed by Kahn and colleagues. On the basis of Weber's view that organizations should be regarded as a hierarchy of offices and the behaviour of office holders as roles, Kahn proposes that all those with whom office holders have contacts can be described as their role sets. In this way an organization can be defined as a complex of overlapping role sets. The model is useful for analysing organizational problems of relationships and integration. For example, there may be role conflict because members of the role set have different views about the ways role holders should behave; role ambiguity may arise if office holders are not given adequate information to perform their roles; office holders may experience role stress when members of their role set have different expectations of their behaviour, as often happens to supervisors when dealing with the expectations of management on the one hand and those of their subordinates on the other.

The systems approach to organizational study has made a particularly valuable contribution in emphasizing the possible extents of influence, what Rosemary Stewart (1972) has called 'the concept of boundaries'. For example, in studying an organization, we need to think beyond the internal confines of the organization's immediate environment and consider the clientele that it exists to serve and its general social environment. This idea is closely related to the model developed by Blau and Scott (1963), who proposed that an organization's survival and growth depends on its ability to clarify its purpose and to be aware of its beneficiaries. On this basis they propose four categories of organizations:

1 *Mutual benefit* associations – serving their own members (e.g. unions, political, professional and religious groups).
2 *Businesses* – serving their owners, shareholders and the general public.
3 *Services* – serving particular clients (e.g. hospitals, schools, etc.).
4 *Commonweal organizations* – serving the public at large (e.g. police, fire, welfare services, governmental departments).

CONTINGENCY STUDIES

In recent times, there have been developments in organizational research which are different in approach from, but related to, the structural and systems approaches. The authors of these studies have in common that they are especially concerned with the suitability of structures for different organizational purposes, the organization's capacity to adapt to their environment in times of considerable instability and the organizational designs likely to be most effective for various situations. Unlike traditional structural theories, this research has usually been very practical and carried out at work sites in longitudinal studies through direct observation and interviews. The authors are concerned with what working in organizations is really like and what people think they need to do to be effective, rather than only a management perspective.

In the 1950s, Joan Woodward carried out detailed research of a wide variety of firms in Essex UK with reference to certain internal characteristics, for example, the number of levels of authority, the span of control, definitions of responsibilities, communication patterns and divisions of labour, and the effects that environmental variables such as technology have upon work organizations (Woodward 1965). Three types of production technologies were distinguished:

1   Unit and small batch, including self-contained units making products for customer specifications.
2   Large batch and mass, where the technology is characterized by mass production.
3   Process, in which the technology is directed towards an intermittent or continuous flow production, for example of chemicals or food production.

When the internal characteristics of organizations mentioned above were examined, relative to the three types of production, it was found that there was a direct relationship between these types and the technological processes employed. The main conclusions drawn from these studies were:

1   Variables in the environment, and especially the technology used, affect decision-making and the way work is organized, and are fundamental factors in organizational design.
2   It is inadvisable to think of organization design in terms of universally applicable principles, but rather to accept that technology is a driver of organization structure.

A sociologist, Burns, collaborated with a psychologist, Stalker, in a similarly important onsite study of manufacturing firms in Scotland. They were particularly interested in problems of introducing modern electronic technology into traditional organizations. As a result of these studies, the authors have produced a well known model based on the difficulties that different firms experienced in adapting to change. They propose a continuum of organizational structures, with what they describe as 'mechanistic' and 'organic' types of organization at the extremes. The 'mechanistic' organization is typical of Weber's bureaucracy in structure, and works satisfactorily in stable conditions. In unstable conditions, such as those of rapid technological change, the 'organic' type of organization has much more flexibility. Its significant differences compared with the traditional organization are these:

1   Functions and duties are not enshrined in organizational charts.
2   Interactions and communication are not restricted by a hierarchical structure of authority, but depend on the specialist requirements of the situation.
3   There is continuous readjustment to meet changing circumstances.

The impact of technology on organizations has produced opportunities to change the nature of the employment relationship. Changes to size, reporting relationships and contractual relationships are well summarized by the idea of 'post-Fordism' – a post assembly-line, lean production approach, which provides a modern version of Woodward's theory.

A major study typical of the contingency approach has been produced by Lawrence and Lorsch, based on the work of Woodward, Burns and Stalker. These authors studied 10 firms from three different industries in terms of different rates of technological change and the influence of different elements in the environment. They analysed the internal structures of these firms according to two dimensions:

1   The differentiation of different functional departments (differences in objectives, time allocation, interpersonal relationships, etc).
2   Integration (the degree of interdepartmental co-ordination, collaboration and relationships).

Then they analysed the relationships between differences in external environments and differences in internal environments. They found that the internal variables have a complex relationship with each other and with the external variables. In contingency terms, their findings may be summarized as follows:

1   In an unstable and varied environment, the organization needs to be relatively unstructured.
2   In a stable and uniform environment, a more rigid structure is appropriate.
3   If the external environment is very varied and the internal structure is highly differentiated, positive measures need to be taken to ensure integration.

There is a clear similarity in the data from all these contingency studies. These show that organizational effectiveness is greatly influenced by the degree of coherence between the internal and external environments of organizations, and this is a fundamental factor to be taken into account in their design.

A well known principle of organization by Alfred Chandler (1962) is that organization structure follows organization strategy. The divisionalization of organizations arose from diversification strategies by big companies. Diversification gives the opportunity for different divisions to focus on specific products or services, creates centres of expertise and the identity of the division with the product in the market place. Divisionalization may reduce costs owing to economies of scale, improving competitive advantage. Typically, divisions are accountable for types of product, or for sales in a particular geographical area, or by type of customer (retail or business to business sales for example). Divisionalization raises important questions about who is responsible for what? For example, there may be mixtures of responsibility, with head offices responsible for long-term strategic issues, such as senior management development, and rewards, whilst divisions and local units take responsibility for industrial relations. Goold and Campbell (2002) suggest three overall styles of control: strategic planning style, which requires detailed budgets and control, with bargaining between centre and the business units, a financial control style where the centre acts as a banker, and a strategic control style, when control is based on an overall business plan, where the centre seeks to shape the activities without detailed day-to-day control.

A great deal of contemporary research into organizations is concerned to explain the variety of new organization forms, caused by moves away from large bureaucracy, as the most common type, towards federal structures, matrix forms, smaller collegiate structures, flatter organizations and structures that change rapidly in response to market demands.

Matrix structures are much more important in modern organizations. These come in a variety of forms.

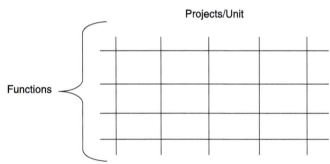

Figure 3.1 An example of a matrix structure

In the 'overlay' form, the person remains largely within the project for example an accountant who has a dotted line relationship to the functional boss, but a day-to-day reporting responsibility to a project or unit manager.

In the coordination form, people work within many projects, and the work is coordinated by project managers (who may be also functional managers). The either/or form has people working on short-term projects within the project teams, but moving on to new projects on completion of their role, to another project (for example software specialists).

POST-MODERNISM AND NEW APPROACHES TO ORGANIZATIONS

Post-modernist explanations are partly a consequence of new technologies which can offer customers flexible specialization (customizing products from a standard range) and stronger lateral rather than hierarchical relationships for organization members, who network and who work in many different teams. The organization subunits now often have considerable autonomy, and there is a return to semi-autonomous work groups as the centre of product output. Taking these trends, together with cost-conscious, de-layered organizations, we have what Peters and Waterman (1982) described as simultaneous 'tight-loose' properties of organizations.

There is a realization that earlier attempts to explain organizations as simply an outcome of rational economic design decisions were inadequate. The effects of a variety of institutional and power pressures clearly affect organization behaviour and structure. Agency theory takes the perspective of the stakeholders, which acknowledges that, for example, managers do not always behave in the interests of the owners, but have their own agendas and power relationships.

The degree of change experienced by modern organizations has also been seen as a consequence of the impact of economic and social forces on organizations. This 'institutional' perspective sees behaviour and organizational choice from a somewhat deterministic viewpoint. For example, Oliver Williamson, an economist, argues that there are two alternative ways in which activities can be organized: as hierarchies (bureaucracies), or as markets. Using transaction costs as the basic unit of analysis he demonstrated that, with the additional behavioural assumptions that managers act with bounded rationality and try to minimize opportunism among organization members, all forms of organization action could be viewed as contractual relations. The notion of the 'internal market' was well illustrated by the reorganized National Health Service, which was changed from a bureaucracy into a market-driven range of transactions, with consequences for organization structures (greater autonomy for general practitioners, 'foundation' status for hospitals and the like).

The relationship between strategy and structure can be illustrated by the way the organization of today has to move beyond the old bureaucratic formula, to be adaptive and to serve many different markets, whilst maintaining systems of integration which permit economies of scale, and an organization direction and control over marketing in an increasingly global context.

The bureaucratic organization form still persists, but is altered in shape and size. Structures are now 'flatter' with fewer levels in the hierarchy, as a consequence of which reward systems have often been 'broadbanded' and there is more flexibility in tasks. Many organizations also see benefits in reducing the size of the 'head office' or top echelon in management. This means divisionalized structures and smaller business units within the larger conglomerate can be managed and run nearer to the customers and the suppliers. At the same time the spate of takeovers and mergers that has seen integration in many industries – including pharmaceuticals, car manufacturing, financial services and retail for example, means ownership itself is less significant to the individual employee. Offshoring and outsourcing have also created a new contractual approach to the different parts of the organization, which hangs together (or not) through interconnecting contracts and mutual interest.

Many of these changes were foreseen by Ashkenas and others (1995) in their idea of the 'boundaryless organization'. They describe the new success factors for organizations as no longer those where key issues were size, specialization and control, but more towards the more flexible, fast moving, innovative style of working, where formal structures were less important than outcomes.

They go on to describe what is now becoming more common – a process-driven organization with a strong internal alignment to objectives and the corporate vision without 'fiefdoms' and organizational silos. They also see the boundaries between the organization and the environment as more permeable, with 'free movement along the value chain', where information, accounting and measurement methods are shared, and customer and supplier relationships are aligned with integrated structures and processes. Networks are becoming more common. These can have marketing purposes (for example Lufthansa's 'Star Alliance', British Airways' 'One World', or even human resource management purposes, for example the Greater London Alcohol and Drug Alliance of organizations which produced an HR strategy for hospitals, charities and the various not for profit organizations established to fight addiction in the capital.

One could see signs of the post-modern approach to understanding structures in the flexible network. We should be clear that a structure may exist, but post-modernist approaches are ways to understand what leads to the acceptance and the legitimation of the structure. However, the need for new organizational forms and the agile approach this requires is a response to broader changes in the business environment. Better use of people has become essential because of the high cost of employment as a proportion of total costs, especially as we move towards the knowledge-based economy in the developed countries. The internet means trading for all is global, and products or services are more likely to be tailored to the customer's needs. It is said that instead of selling millions of products to thousands of customers we are now selling thousands of products to millions of customers. The advent of 3D printing is likely to lead to a direct link between customers and production, involving customers in design and moving the process to an individualized personal transaction.

Organization culture is being seen increasingly as the 'glue' which holds companies together in a world of fragmented and networked structures. Small, entrepreneurial organizations are often admired even after the end of the internet company boom, and even a company such as Amazon.com, set up by an ex-New York banker, was created in a 'garage' to give the impression that it was a new start-up on the same lines as Hewlett Packard. Companies such as 'Innocent Drinks' also demonstrate how small is still beautiful.

For HRM, there is a strong link between brand values and the values sought amongst employees, and a link between brands and talent management as is described in Chapters 13 and 17.

A simple statement from a master baker discussing his craft in the UK sums up the issue: 'Once you try to generate passion through the management structure, you end up with people just doing a job'.

The significance of this strategic shift in HRM is discussed in the next part of the book.

CONCLUSION

Research data have produced the following general conclusions about organizational behaviour and management's responsibilities (see also Figure 3.2):

Structural Studies	Human relations School	Systems Approach	Contingency Approach	Post-modernist and Institutional Approaches (Opposite Approaches)
This group is concerned with types and rationale of organizational structures and raises important questions of authority–legitimacy e.g. Weber's three authority categories: Charismatic Traditional Rational legal Etzioni's three types of organization and corresponding individual involvement:	This group emphasizes the effects of managerial behaviour on working life and especially on motivation: the importance of informal systems of behaviour below the surface of the formal organizational system. The main influences are Mayo, Maslow, Herzberg, McGregor and Argyris.	This group emphasizes the importance of interaction between organizational variables: people, structure, technology, external environment. Important contributors are: Tavistock Institute: Socio-technical theory Likert: Link-pin theory Kahn: Role-set theory	The group is concerned with the suitability of structures for organizational functions and technology, and with capacity to adapt to the environment and change. Data are derived from onsite study. Important contributors are: Woodward Burns and Stalker Lawrence and Lorsch	Institutional ideas deal with the questions of whether new organizational forms are a result of economic and social changes. 'Post-modernist' approaches stress the move from rational towards other criteria for organization structures. Institutional theorists see specific forms of rationality underlying action caused by economic forces. Post-modern theory: Kenneth Gergen Gareth Morgan
Coercive – alienative Utilitarian – calculative Normative – moral				Institutional theory: Oliver Williamson

Conclusions

- Awareness of organizational complexity, the inter-relationship of component elements and the existence and influence of informal system are fundamentally important.
- Organizations, must be specifically designed to suit particular functions.
- Design should facilitate integration of component groups.
- A general atmosphere of trust needs to be established for organizations to function effectively.
- Organizations need to develop a capacity for self-analysis (e.g. organizational development).
- Organizations' form changes rapidly and in response to non-rational dynamics.
- Organizations are determined by economic and social conditions.
- Action in organizations can be measured in terms of transaction costs.

Figure 3.2 Approaches to studying organizations

1   Managers need to be aware of the general nature of organizations, and especially of the complexity of the interactions between the organization's component elements and the external environment.

2   People in organizations need to be able to change structures and processes, to be agile and resilient. The learning approaches of organizations are critical to their survival. This means managers' understanding of the impact of their own performance, and to be able to take responsibility for their own development, aided by 360 degree performance feedback, and an open style in working relationships.

3   Managers need to be aware of the existence and significance of informal systems and their relationships with formal systems in the organization.

4   No universal principles should be assumed in the design of organizations, which should be tailor-made to take account of interactions between internal and external variables. The predominant technology is a fundamentally important factor affecting design.

5   The design should encourage the maximum possible integration of groups and prevent intra-group and intergroup conflict as far as possible.

6   A general atmosphere of trust and openness has to be established, whereby clearly defined objectives are communicated to all employees, and the psychological contract (what the organization can give and what it expects) should be clarified.

7   Finally, in order to survive and grow, organizations need to develop a capacity for self-analysis, whereby diagnosis is possible, and solutions may be proposed. In this connection, 'organization development' (OD) provides a way to keep processes under constant review. The essential objectives of OD are:

   (a) to help organizations to become much more aware of the impact of their own structures and of their internal and external relationships;

   (b) to become more adaptive to change, often in combination with management development strategies;

   (c) to programme a process of continued self-analysis as an integral element of organizational life and to use appropriate knowledge and techniques from the social sciences to create new cultures, structures and styles of working.

QUESTIONS

1   What different kinds of categories of organizational theory can be distinguished and what are the distinctive features of each?

2   Summarize the main conclusions about organization design and behaviour that have emerged from studies of organizations.

3   What are the features of a post-modernist approach to the study of organizations?

4   What is organization development and what are its principal objectives?

For more literature and examples, readers are invited to go to the companion website.

REFERENCES

Ashkenas, R. Ulrich, D., Jich, T. and Kerr, S. (1995). *The Boundaryless Organisation*. Jossey Bass: San Francisco.

Blau, P. M. and Scott, W. R. (1963). *Formal Organisations: A Comparative Approach*. London: Routledge and Kegan Page.

Burns, T. and Stalker, G. M. (1961). *The Management of Innovation*. London. Tavistock.

Chandler, A. (1962). *Strategy and Structure: Chapters in the History of American Enterprise* Mass: MIT Press.

Etzioni, A. (1964). *Modern Organizations*. Englewood-Cliffs NJ: Prentice Hall.

Goold, M. and Campbell, A. (2002). *Designing Effective Organizations*. Englewood Cliffs NJ: Jossey-Bass.

Hassard, J. and Parker, M. (eds) (1994). *Towards a New Theory of Organizations*. London: Routledge.

Lawrence, P. R. and Lorsch, J. W. (1967). *Organization and Environment: Managing Differentiation and Integration*. Boston: Harvard.

Legge, K. (1995). *Human Resource Management Rhetorics and Realities*. Macmillan.

Parkinson, C. N. (1958). *Parkinson's Law*. Penguin Books.

Peters, J. J. and Waterman, R. H. (1982). *In Search of Excellence: Lessons from America's Best Run Companies*. New York: Harper and Row.

Silverman, D. (1970). The Theory of Organizations. London. Heinemann.

Simon, H. A. (1983). *Reason in Human Affairs*. Oxford: Basil Blackwell.

Stewart, R. (1972). *The Reality of Organizations*. Penguin Books.

Weber, M. (1947). *The Theory of Social and Economic Organization* (ed. Talcott Parsons). New York. The Free Press.

Woodward, J. (1965). *Industrial Organisation: Theory and Practice*. London: Oxford University Press.

4 MANAGING CHANGE

Organizational change is now the norm. In this century the pressures for change have accelerated. Driven by economic and technological transformations, the globalization of the major economies, demographic, social and institutional changes, organizations are in a state of flux. Contextual changes of this magnitude produce new opportunities as well as threats. For example, the economic slump and the growth of online shopping, mean new business models have had to be introduced rapidly in the retail sector, and have changed the High Street in the UK and Main Street in the USA for good. A description of the wide range and variety of changes can be found on our companion website.

For those people in employment, and for human resource specialists, organizational change also presents threats and opportunities. The risks of failure hang over all attempts at major corporate change programmes, the failure rate being estimated at around 70 per cent (Beer and Nohria 2000). Organizations rely on a network of stakeholders for their everyday operations, who are concerned at any major organizational change. For employees, the possibility of redundancy, or of changes to place of work, disruption to family and career, changes to status, new conditions and hours of work, new work demands owing to new roles, all generate fear. Some of these are fears of the unknown, and of an uncertain future, but there is also a fear of what the changes might mean for individuals and their families.

In this chapter, initially, individual responses to change are examined, then bearing in mind these effects, the management of planned organizational change is considered, along with the involvement of the HR function in change processes. This will take the chapter into the arena of organization development and therefore into a discussion of organizational learning.

CHANGE AT AN INDIVIDUAL LEVEL

The central objective of organizational change is the need for individual employees to accept and work with the changes proposed. HRM has to gain acceptance by employees to a variety of changes: to contracts of employment, to organization structures and accountabilities, to redundancies if necessary, to new ways of working, and to trade union negotiations. There are often winners and losers in any change situation. Employees may well have too much at stake in their lives to go along with management's view of what should change, without resistance. Nor should the views of employees be ignored. As the people who know their own work the best, who often know more about customers, suppliers and their colleagues, employees are perhaps the most important resource for management to consult in any change, as early as possible in the creation of a strategy for planned change.

The likely effect on individuals when faced with disruption to their lives, such as is found in organizational change, is often represented by the 'transition curve'. This well known diagram describes the negative and positive feelings and attitudes experienced by people when faced with changes that affect them at a very personal level.

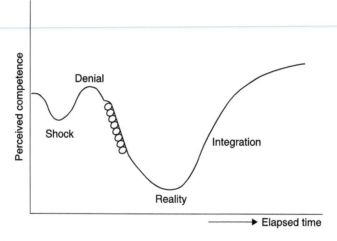

Figure 4.1 Transition curve

The main features of the transition curve as applied to an individual change are listed below:

■ The sudden shock of a major change initiates a series of psychological responses, starting with anger and depression at the realization of the impact of the change on the person concerned and on their family. This is triggered as the damage to the individual's own interests becomes apparent, and the loss of a sense of personal security, the disruption to friendships and any financial losses are anticipated.

- The individual may then go into a form of denial, disbelieving that his or her world has changed in unexpected ways. This may take the form of trying to convince others that this will never happen.
- As the news is confirmed, it becomes apparent this change is going to happen, or has happened, the individual is frustrated and angry, blaming those (often management) for creating this uncomfortable situation.
- The next stage – depression – emerges, where the individual feels deflated, the world seems a joyless place, there is a lack of self-confidence, and feelings of guilt arise (for example an internal dialogue of 'I should have foreseen this . . . I could have acted sooner').
- Eventually, if the person has not given up and left, or remains in a state of worsening depression, he or she will try to experiment with potential solutions, and may find that what seemed a form of competence developing is unfortunately false, and then recycle into the frustration/depression stage. In time, the person may then try to make the best of the new situation and may gradually let go of the past, and move on psychologically.
- Then comes a decision stage: deciding what works and what does not in the new context, the individual begins to come to terms with what has happened.
- The final stage is integration into the new situation.

The transition curve was originally developed by Dr Elisabeth Kubler-Ross in order to explain the way individuals react to bereavement. It shows how people may come through the grieving process, eventually to reintegrate their lives, but for others, who are not able to move beyond the sense of deep personal loss, the depression may take longer, or they may never fully reintegrate themselves into society. One thinks of Queen Victoria, who wore black and mourned for many years after the death of her husband, Prince Albert. For those who are bereaved, 'letting go' could seem to be a betrayal of a loved one's memory, and hence any small attempts to move on in life bring feelings of guilt and further depression.

The application of this framework to changes at work can be criticized, in spite of its popularity amongst change consultants. The psychological processes experienced by people who are suffering from bereavement are not identical to the experiences of those who are going through change at work. Nevertheless, there is high face validity to the framework as applied in a variety of situations. In an organization, employees are susceptible to similar feelings of anxiety and depression, for example when suddenly facing new roles, more insecurity and a real threat to the life chances and the financial prospects of their families.

The benefit of the transition curve is that it directs the attention of those who are responsible for change programmes towards the way they can help individuals to cope with change. At the initial stage, there are benefits in ensuring the people concerned are prepared for the changes by involving employees and their representatives initially. The tone of the announcements, having a plan ready and communicating this clearly, all may help to prevent rumours and to lessen shock and the feelings of anger for those most affected. An understanding amongst management that people gain much of their sense of self-efficacy and social identity from their work, as well as their friendship ties, would be beneficial.

The provision of emotional and social support to the individuals in the fourth phase, with the object of avoiding negative reactions such as depression, anxiety and stress, would help people through to the next phase when they would be looking for solutions to the personal dilemmas that changes can create. This approach calls for coaching and coun-selling skills to be provided, as well as practical help, for example, financial advice, help with relocations if necessary, joint discussions with the spouse if the job is moving to another distant location, or if the person is to be made redundant, with outplacement services.

If, as seems likely, change is to become more common, and that flexible, responsive organizations are now required in order to survive in a turbulent world, there is a strong case for helping both employees and the organization by developing resilience in the workforce.

RESILIENCE

Psychologists have had a long-standing interest in the concept of resilience in people. The question of whether or not certain individuals are more or less resilient than others when faced with stressful situations is worthy of exploration. Whether resilience is a 'trait' or a capacity, or is acquired from experience, is a starting point for considering what can be done by managers in organizations to create a resilient workforce, which will cope well with change. This is discussed further in Chapter 22 when we look at stress and employee wellbeing.

The literature on resilience sees two aspects: the capacity to be resilient and the enabling context that allows this capacity to be used (Barnard 1994; Grotberg 2003). Resilient capabilities are said to consist of:

- social competence (which covers cultural flexibility, empathy, communication skills and a sense of humour)
- problem-solving skills (critical and creative thinking and planning capabilities)
- autonomy (sense of self-confidence, self-awareness, task mastery)
- purpose and belief in a good future (sense of direction, optimism and progress).

It is suggested that everyone could potentially possess these capabilities. However, the extent to which people can use these attributes is dependent upon the particular environ-ment in which they live and work. According to the theory, there are three potentially protective factors in the environment that act as intervening variables, which either encourage resilience or diminish resilience. The intervening contextual factors that allow resilience to grow are:

1   Where there are caring relationships at a personal level, where there is compassion, respect and understanding.
2   Where there are normally high expectations of the individual, there is guidance, challenge and structure.
3   Where there are opportunities for taking part and contributing at work, with valued responsibilities and decision-making.

These ideas suggest that HR can influence levels of resilience by training and development for the employees, and by introducing strategies which aim to establish the contextual conditions in the organization culture where resilience will flourish. There are similarities between the three enabling conditions and the research conclusions from the study of high performing work groups (Chapter 2). In each case the quality of supervision, the importance of challenge and high expectations, visionary leadership, employee involvement in decision-making, and high levels of employee participation are associated with high performance.

SOCIAL SUPPORT

It is known that high levels of stress and uncertainty produce lower levels of job satisfaction and organizational commitment, a low sense of wellbeing and an increased desire of employees to leave their employers. These factors have been found in situations such as mergers, downsizing and when a public sector activity is privatized. Social support mechanisms might help to mitigate some of the negative effects of change.

Support can come from many sources: colleagues, supervisors, HR staff, TU representatives, and from non-work friends and professionals, such as neighbours, lawyers, doctors, as well, and most importantly, from family and partner. Support from colleagues seems to be seen as extremely valuable, since they have a more complete knowledge of the organization, the history, the management and how its practices affect those working in the same roles. In change programmes, HR change consultants sometimes use co-coaching as a way to tap into this rich source of tacit knowledge, so that employees can support each other and deal with issues as they arise. Supervisors are a critical part of the communication chain from senior management, and are usually expected to pass upward concerns about the effects of change on employees. To avoid the possible problems of misinformation arising from long communication chains, an explicit and pre-prepared communication strategy can be devised. For example, the communications at the time of the merger between Lloyds and TSB were all carefully managed by a senior HR director of Lloyds, who insisted that all communications about the merger, and what was to happen subsequently, were through his small communication team, who monitored them for content, style and appropriateness.

Trade union lay representatives may also be helpful. For employees, provided there has been proper consultation prior to the change, they should be in a position to help employees understand what the changes mean. Although there may be management produced information circulating, this may be seen as biased, painting a rosy picture of a future for the business, in order to avoid a high labour turnover. From management's perspective, communications should not be handled only through trade union channels. Instead, parallel routes for communication should be set up, so that both trade unions and employees directly are receiving the same information at the same time, unless there is an agreement to give the information to the unions first during a consultation phase.

These comments on transitions, resilience and social support at the individual level, and the implications for HRM, are intended to inform the discussion which follows on managing organizational change. As the concern here is with changing the way people work, the way they are organized, the organization culture, and sometimes the employees' terms and conditions, it is important to bear in mind that changes of these kinds are dependent for their success upon understanding the psychology of the people themselves.

HRM AND ORGANIZATIONAL CHANGE

HRM is centred on creating effective organizations. The strategic role for HRM is to take a lead in setting-up, changing and adapting organization structures and cultures, designing work systems, jobs and policies that will deliver high levels of performance. Further, HRM must conduct these activities fairly in a way which is acceptable to senior management, and to the work force and their representatives, as well as other stakeholders, including shareholders, owners, customers, suppliers and local communities amongst other stakeholders.

The multiplicity of stakeholders and situations may explain why changes are often said to have failed. Fortunately, HR managers do not usually have sole responsibility for change programmes but they do expect to work as part of the top management team which leads the change. The role of HR in any change process is very dependent upon the kinds of change which are proposed. The most typical representation of change is that by Kurt Lewin, long ago, who described the process of change as being a move from the current (frozen) state, through processes of adaptability, which are described as 'unfreeze', before instituting the new required behaviours (refreeze). The process is often referred to as 'FREEZE-UNFREEZE-REFREEZE'.

HRM is the guardian of the 'freeze' state before the change is initiated. Therefore, one of the difficulties for HRM's involvement in change is the track record of the HR staff in maintaining the *status quo*, through the rules of work and competency and behavioural frameworks. Very often, external consultants are involved, even though HRM may be fronting up any change. Consultants act as advisers on change processes, bringing wider experience of managing change processes than can be found inside the organization.

The contextual demands faced by the organization determine the particular types of change, and therefore the periods over which change will be undertaken. The approach of the change consultants/HR function to the processes of change management can be

TABLE 4.1 CONTEXT AND CHANGE APPROACH

Contextual Demands of the Organisation are for:

Approaches to change	Adapting	Long-term change	Immediate change
Perfunctory	■	■	
Deep but limited scope		■	■
Fundamental change	■	■	

designed to fit how changes could best be delivered in that specific context. The context dictates whether what is needed is a 'slow burn' adaptive approach to new requirements for a need for pervasive changes to which people have to adapt, or a long-term deep change, which is a radical and permanent shift to a new reality, and finally an immediate need to accommodate some new development of a narrow scope. The change consultants/HR function approach to change is adjusted according to the best way to achieve the contextual demand, which is represented by different kinds of programmes.

Table 4.1 shows which approach to change is most likely to succeed according to the contextual demands of the organization. There may be different change needs in a single organization simultaneously. This is not unlikely in larger organizations and, depending upon the degree of centralization, also in planning and organizing change programmes.

DEFINITIONS

Adapting to new requirements/demands: Externally or internally generated change, which is wide but not especially deep and gradual in its effect; medium priority.

Long-term changes: Explicit, deep changes to achieve a long-term objective, wide in scope, important but not urgent needs.

Immediate changes: Enforced by management to meet an urgent and important need, but narrow in scope.

The HR involvement will be dependent upon who is accountable for the different kinds of change: organization development specialists, who may be internal or external consultants, or line managers, or development and training specialists inside or out of the HR function, or sometimes other functions, such as finance or sales, if the need is in one function. There is also the question of whether the development is part of a new business strategy. The strategic HR function would be a natural owner of these programmes, alongside senior line management colleagues as a part of HR and business and functional strategies.

HR ACTIVITIES PRIOR TO THE CHANGE PROGRAMME

The activities which HR managers should undertake when there is a senior management or board decision to introduce a major change are listed below. One should not assume all of these issues have been thought through. That is why the senior HR specialist should explore all the angles as soon as possible by looking at the change requirements in detail. The analysis is intended to decide the best approach to take in order to manage the change:

■ The initial analysis should cover the effects of the changes proposed on the organization's culture, structure, systems, processes and people.

■ A review of the business model proposed should be undertaken, and the consequences for how employees will be asked to add value in the future.

■ A breakdown of what aspects of people management will change is required, in terms of numbers, skills, knowledge, capabilities required and accountabilities. What will this mean for employee relations, and policies such as rewards and development?

■ An outline of the change plan proposed in the light of the three bullet points above. The plan should include the timeframes proposed, the costs, the effects of the changes on customer relationships, the quality of the product or service, and the impact on the organization internally.

■ The plan would need to be reviewed, and checks should be made on whether there is the appropriate communication strategy (internally and externally), and sufficient consideration of the long-term consequences of adopting this change process.

For HRM, the assumptions on costs should be challenged and tested carefully where these involve people costs, and the assumptions on how long it will take to implement the various phases of the change programme should be viewed with a healthy scepticism, bearing in mind the time taken by people to learn new systems and how to use new structures, the time needed to transfer, and how long it takes to recruit new people or make people redundant and to conduct due diligence in mergers and acquisitions.

In their book on strategic change, Balogun and Hope-Hailey (2009) argue that the attributes of the organizational change context, which they describe as a 'kaleidoscope' of different factors, determines the design choices for how the changes will be managed. These attributes include the power structures, the readiness for change, the capacity to change, the scope of the changes and the time frame. However, as the authors acknowledge, each change is potentially different, unique to its historical and organizational context. There is no mechanistic combination of factors which will inevitably result in a particular change design choice. The questions shown above on HR activities are one way to gather sufficient data, and to decide which change processes to adopt.

It is in the strategic fields where strategic programmes deliver against the strategic objectives of the organization that the important role of HRM in change management may be found. These fields include organization restructuring, job design/redesign, quality improvement programmes (Six Sigma, the Balanced Scorecard, International Standardization Organization (ISO) registrations, business process redesign and re-engineering), and other whole organization activities intended to shift the entire approach to work and management in what can be experienced as a revolutionary change. In certain conditions, such as a merger or a major collapse in the business, or a complete change to the business model, the organization-wide impacts require an organization culture change, involving shifts in attitudes and behaviours, perhaps requiring HR to be involved in embedding new corporate values. Of course, large change programmes may require HR to be partnering with line management on any or all of these kinds of strategic programmes.

For HRM, the recent recession in Western economies has brought 'downsizing' – redundancies as a consequence of falling business demand – to the fore. This raises important employee relations issues. There is the proper consultation with trade unions, the efforts to mitigate any adverse effects and also to manage the psychological effects of change on the people themselves, as well as on the 'survivors' of the redundancy programmes. Very often, mergers or acquisitions produce needs to reduce or to change the nature of the employee profile. Here, the HR role goes further, into due diligence on the company which is acquired, or merged, bringing HR into the corporate social responsibility policies, and the legal procedures such as TUPE (see Chapter 26).

ORGANIZATION DEVELOPMENT AND CULTURE CHANGE

Major change programmes often require a change to organization culture. This may be expressly stated or implied, or could be an intended consequence of a large scale change programme. Amongst the formal change programmes that usually lead to culture change, for example 'Investors in People' and 'The Balanced Scorecard', there are attempts to capture a whole way of working with people under the broad umbrella concepts of involvement, participation and the adoption of particular management practices (Mills, Dye and Mills 2009).

Whilst there may be expectations that culture will change as a result of the introduction of the kinds of quality improvement changes above, the HR/change consultant has to reflect on whether culture can really be reconstructed in this way. Ed Schein (1985) defined corporate culture as consisting of three levels. Visible, tangible aspects of culture are seen in the tenets of the company logos, 'vision statements' and the published values. There is a deeper level, where culture becomes apparent from the company's typical ways of acting, preferred management style and decision-making habits, described by Johnson, Scholes and Whittington (2008) as the organization's dominant paradigm, at the heart of what they call the 'cultural web'. This is where there are manifestations of the culture through stories, routines, rituals, power structures, symbols and control systems. The third level is where the values and assumptions drive the preferences, the choices and the ways of behaving that are regarded as acceptable. Organization culture is therefore at a deeper level, and there may well be a number of cultures in the organization – even counter cultures – adopted by those lower in the hierarchy. There are also occupational cultures for example in the professions, such as medicine and the law, as well as in working groups such as manufacturing plants, maintenance workers, in shops, etc.

Making fundamental changes means tackling the drivers of culture at the deepest level. Organization development seeks to make changes that shift the mindset, the beliefs and implicit understandings of employees. In the pre-recessionary period, culture change was often an aspect of major planned change, for example at British Airways, Marks & Spencer and, in the public sector, local authorities and in the Civil Service. With roots in the 'socio-technical systems' view of change these were often attempts to restructure, and to shift the way of thinking, sometimes to introduce new ways of working, applying new technologies, adapting the social system in the organization to fit the new technical system. These were usually management led changes which sought to carry employees with them, rather than be driven from the energy of the bulk of employees, who might well continue with their own subcultures and remain active in opposing the new culture.

Organization development (OD) in its well established form is intended to use social science techniques to create and to manage organizational change, which is seen as an ongoing process. The characteristics of the OD approach, according to French and Bell (1978), were the use of work teams and insights into group behaviour, which were based on studies of group dynamics as processes (see Chapter 2) to foster collaborative efforts in order to gain acceptance of change. Less prescriptive versions of OD began to become popular in the later parts of the twentieth century, when there was an 'action-research method' deployed.

Action research was perceived by Kurt Lewin, its originator, as means to facilitate change through actions and research. French and Bell (1978), developed an organization change version, which moved through six stages:

1   Preliminary diagnosis.
2   Data gathering from client group.
3   Data feedback to the client group.
4   Exploration of what the data mean with the client group.
5   Action planning.
6   Implementing actions.

The main feature of action research is the provision of reviews with the client, on an incremental basis, so that there are opportunities at each stage to adopt a different approach if necessary, and to learn from the process, moving back to cycle through the process.

These early attempts at OD were data-based change. Data are seen as facts, and the actions in collecting the data in themselves may help clients to rethink their interpretations of the situations in their organizations, and to discover new solutions.

However, more recent OD techniques are based on the notion of multiple socially constructed realities, and therefore that there is no one truth about human affairs. Marshak and Grant (2008) argue that there are more recent practices based on these later sociological theories. The four modern practices are based on the idea of constructing a favourable view of the new desired reality in the organization, and a positive view of change should emerge from a more collaborative, consensual process of learning how to operate in the changed state. The change strategies that are adopted under this approach include:

1   Appreciative inquiry.
2   Large group interventions to seek common ground.
3   Changing mindsets to achieve transformational change.
4   Addressing diversity and multicultural realities.

APPRECIATIVE INQUIRY AND CHANGING MINDSETS

The main idea behind appreciative inquiry is that reality is seen as partly socially constructed. This idea is simply the notion that we have to share in each society some sense of what the actions of individuals and groups mean for social life to proceed. These meanings are based on shared understandings and experiences. In appreciative inquiry, those who are involved in change are encouraged to think through their positive experiences of change and the opportunities in the company, and to concentrate upon positive thinking in order to change their mindsets. The methods that can be adopted to do this have been famously summarized as the '4D model'.

Cooperrider's 4D model

Discovery: trying to uncover the strengths of individuals and the organization
Dreaming: envisioning what might be
Design: planning on what could be
Destiny: sustaining what has been achieved.

D. L. Cooperrider (1987)

A similar approach, seeking to change organizational consciousness, has been attempted organization-wide in some cases, where there was an emphasis on changing the leadership approach of senior management, and then cascading the new approach through the company. Leadership transformation would include short programmes on leadership and supporting behaviours, along with coaching and consultancy. Where the changes include changing diversity and multicultural realities, shifting the way people see groups typically discriminated against in society requires a re-educational programme, so that prejudice is confronted and an understanding of how to address one's own preconceptions occurs and hence to change one's mindset.

For some change consultants, the initial goal is to change the predominant discourse about change, to one of acceptance and excitement at the thought of the new opportunities that could be created (Ford and Ford 1995):

> Changing the discourse involves changing narratives, texts and conversations that create and sustain and provide the enabling context(s) for the way things are. This, in essence, adds 'discourse' as an important target and lever for organizational change, in addition to, for example, strategies, structures, rewards and processes'.
>
> (Marshak and Grant 2008: 517)

Large scale change programmes involving the use of a variety of methods to achieve the improvements to organizational effectiveness are likely to be more successful than those that rely on merely one or two techniques. The different methods discussed here are not mutually exclusive.

One would expect in an organization-wide change, new structures, reorganization, new jobs and for HR policies this implies new roles and accountabilities, revised rewards policies, new communications, more autonomy, greater organization-wide financial awareness, a clear vision sold in from top to bottom. This is a time for culture change and more explicit corporate values, connecting the company brands to the employer brand in a coherent offer to employees and recruits, in flatter structures, with more transparency. These are likely objectives for organization-wide change.

THE LEARNING ORGANIZATION

Organization development and organizational learning are two sides of the same coin. In recent years the degree of change through continuous learning is necessary for organizations to survive. This is well expressed in Peter Senge's (1990) book *The Fifth Discipline*, in which he suggested that learning organizations are those that know how to make use of five component technologies, these being:

1   Systems thinking: the notion developed in this book of a systemic approach to learning, seeing the whole as well as the relationships between the parts of the system.
2   Personal mastery: described as 'continuously clarifying and deepening our personal vision', and using our energy to develop ourselves.
3   Mental models: challenging the stereotypes and mental maps that managers carry around them.
4   Building shared vision: leadership through communicating vision and values.
5   Team learning: encouraging team members to think together through dialogue, using teams as the main learning unit.

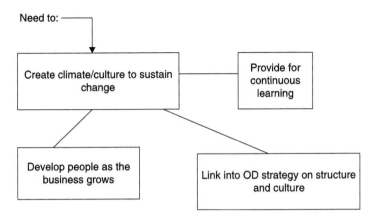

Figure 4.2 Management and employee development strategies and OD

Taylor, Templeton and Baker (2010) argue in their model of the factors influencing the success of organizational learning implementation, that a precondition of successful implementation is a perceived need for change. However, beyond this, a commitment to learning policy, a tolerance of failure policy (to allow experimentation and to learn from mistakes) and a commitment to the workforce are necessary. This latter requires organizational and management support, recognition for organizational citizenship behaviours, and support from the reward system and induction processes for new employees.

Management development is frequently one plank in the change platform, aimed at improving employees through management education, personal development linking these to action learning interventions. Management development has become integral to organization development. The argument is that so rapid is the pace of change that employees need to be highly adaptive, intelligent and educated so that they will know how to learn and will be prepared to go through retraining or re-educational programmes many times in their working lives. This is the point where management and employee development links into OD. See Figure 4.2.

Ultimately all change is about learning. We will discuss the need for organizations to adapt constantly to adapt to new challenges and the implications for HRM in the next chapter.

CONCLUSIONS

In this chapter we have explored the topic of organizational change, first from the individual, and from the organizational and human resource perspectives. This has taken us to the field of organization development, and its variants, and hence to the concept of organizational learning.

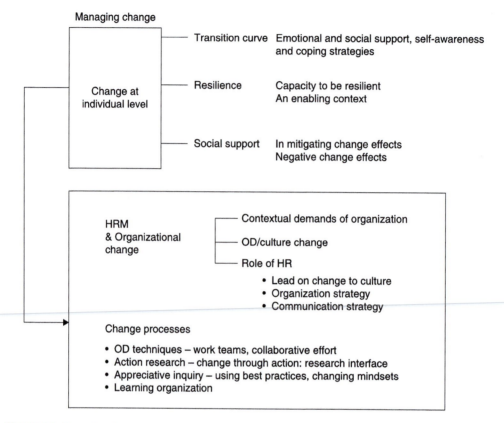

Figure 4.3 Managing change

The role of HRM in these processes is not so much as a 'change agent' but more that of process and policy creation, and implementation consultant. Here we concluded that the way organizations introduce and sustain organizational learning will be the main determinant of success. The processes of learning together with a collaborative approach to change are exemplified by appreciative inquiry.

QUESTIONS

1   To what extent do you think the transition curve adequately describes the feelings and emotional responses of people who are facing major organizational change?

2   Do you understand 'resilience' in people as a personality trait or as a capacity which can be developed?

3   What is the role of HR managers in organizational change management, and how does this role differ from that of line management?
4   What are the strategies that can be adopted to manage large-scale organization change brought about by an economic recession?
5   How does 'appreciative inquiry' differ from other forms of OD?

Readers may wish to look at the companion website for more information on strategic and individual change.

REFERENCES

Balogun, J. and Hope-Hailey, V. (2009). *Exploring Strategic Change*. (3rd edn) Prentice Hall, Pearson Education. Harlow, Essex.

Barnard, C. P. (1994). 'Resiliency, a shift in perceptions?' *The American Journal of Family Therapy*, 22, 2: 135–44.

Beer, M. and Nohria, N. (2000). 'Cracking the code of change'. *Harvard Business Review* May/June, 133–41.

Cooperrider, D. L. (1987). 'Appreciative Inquiry in organizational life'. *Research in Organizational Change and Development*, 1: 129–69.

Ford, J. D. and Ford, L. W. (1995). 'The role of conversations in producing intentional change in organizations'. *Academy of Management Review* 20, 3: 541–70.

French, W. L. and Bell, C. (1978). *Organisation Development. Behavioural Science Interventions for Organization Improvement*. (2nd edn) Englewood Cliffs NJ: Prentice Hall.

Grotberg, E. H. (ed) (2003). *Resilience for Today, Gaining Strength from Adversity*. Greenwood Publishing.

Johnson, G., Scholes, K. and Whittington, R. (2008). *Exploring Corporate Strategy*. Prentice Hall/Pearson Education, Harlow, Essex.

Marshak, R. J. and Grant, D. (2008). 'Organisation discourse and new organisation development practices'. *British Journal of Management*, 19 Special Issue S7–S19.

Mills, J. H., Dye, K. and Mills, A. J. (2009). *Understanding Organizational Change*. Routledge: Abingdon Oxfordshire.

Roden, M. and Williams, S. (2002). 'Individual and organisational stress' in Miller, D. M., Lipsedge, M. and Litchfield, P. (eds). *Work and Mental Health* 47–52. Gaskell and Faculty of Occupational Medicine: London.

Schein, E. (1985). *Organizational Culture and Leadership*. Jossey-Bass: San Francisco.

Senge, P. (1990). *The Fifth Discipline*. Century Business.

Taylor, G. S., Templeton, G. F. and Baker, L. T. (2010). 'Factors influencing the success of organizational learning implementation: a policy facet perspective'. *International Journal of Management Reviews*, 12, 4: 353–64.

PART TWO

THE STRATEGIC ROLE OF HRM

5 DEFINING HUMAN RESOURCE MANAGEMENT

INTRODUCTION

The specialist occupation of human resource management (HRM) has been gradually developing over the last 100 years, reflecting at each stage of its progress the contemporary features of the era. In this chapter we focus on its historical development to discover what defines HRM as a specialist field of management. By looking at how the current models of HRM emerged, we can suggest the future direction of travel of this management specialism.

All managers, whether they are specialists, line managers or with no direct reports, have to be familiar with the skills and techniques needed to manage people. For those with responsibility for teams of people, this is obvious. However, even for positions where the manager is responsible for material rather than human assets, there will be a requirement to communicate and to engage with people in the working environment. Most managers have to motivate and influence the efforts of people at work, a task which is even more difficult where those concerned are not direct reports.

The actions of managers are usually very much concerned with achieving results through other people. Consequently, the interpersonal skills they demonstrate – notably their capacity to engage, to communicate, to receive information, to project a vision of the future, the climate of trust they establish, the degree of enthusiasm they generate, their sense of fairness and their own humanity – will be most significant for organizational success.

We can venture a description of what lies at the heart of managerial work. The essential characteristics seem to be that managers exercise their authority in such a way that it is regarded as legitimate, they maintain the adherence of subordinates to the organization's goals and build teams that are capable of achieving these goals. Human resource management in its specialized sense is concerned to help in the widest possible way with these managerial tasks. The human resource function has organization-wide responsibilities for HR policy, and should be considered as quite separate from the function which all managers carry out when managing people.

The activities of the specialist occupation, now commonly called 'human resource management' (HRM), are concerned with all aspects of the employment relationship – from start to finish of the employment life cycle.

These activities are listed below, covering all the stages of employment.

STRATEGIC FRAMEWORK

The activities referred to above include the following:

- the creation of HR strategy to give effect to the business strategy
- designing organization structures, accountabilities, formal reporting relationships, geographical locations
- setting up workforce planning systems, E-HRM platforms
- creating policies and systems, and rules of work to deliver them
- designing the employee offer/linking employer brand values to marketing strategy
- reward strategy
- employee relations strategy.

ESTABLISHING THE EMPLOYMENT PRACTICES

- recruitment policies/practices
- diversity management policies
- selection
- induction.

TOTAL REWARD POLICIES

- job evaluation
- pay policies
- hours of work/contractual arrangements
- incentive schemes
- pensions and benefits

- working climate
- job design
- team based rewards.

DEVELOPMENT AND TALENT MANAGEMENT

- performance appraisal/identification of potential
- training
- development
- career management
- succession planning
- coaching/mentoring.

EMPLOYMENT RELATIONSHIPS

- TU relationships
- joint consultation
- negotiation procedures
- employee participation in decision-making
- employee engagement
- communication processes
- discipline
- termination procedures
- redundancy policies
- health and wellbeing
- safety and risk assessment.

CHANGE MANAGEMENT

- mergers/takeovers/Transfer of Undertakings regulations
- due diligence
- labour market analysis
- organization development
- employee involvement in change.

Under these broad headings there are subsets of activities such as research on competency frameworks which would inform all the work where assessment of current or future likely performance matters are involved. Matters such as organization culture and employee motivation might be expressly addressed, or be seen as outcomes from policies in areas such as employee engagement and development, and career management processes.

It is because abbreviated lists of HR activities tend to miss purposes of the policies and their essential meaning that there is now a trend towards grouping policy areas under broad umbrella headings. For example, the term 'talent management' is used to refer to competitive areas of individual competence that can be developed to become the corner-stones of organization capability.

The theoretical basis for HRM is also complex. There are multiple theories and fields of knowledge upon which practice has built up over many years, and in response to different societal contexts. An activity such as recruitment depends for its evidential basis upon the theories of individual differences described in Chapter 1, and upon an understanding of labour markets, marketing, psychometrics, developmental psychology, as well as what would be an appropriate 'offer' by the organization, and its culture, and the nature of the work and competencies required. Specialist knowledge of typical careers, qualification structures and what constitutes high potential for the occupations in the organization would also be necessary in most situations.

For experienced practitioners, some of this knowledge may well be so embedded in their consciousness that they cannot always distinguish where the impact of formal training, education and theoretical knowledge are separate from the traditions and contextual effects they have experienced.

Storey (1997) sets out a definition of HRM that emphasizes the strategic role. He sets out a 25 item checklist, differentiating what used to be called personnel management and industrial relations from HRM. The gist of these differences rests on the more individual contract between employer and employee found in HRM, the accent on managing by values and mission and the strong business orientation of HRM. Above all, the management of people strategically is described in terms of human capital, and the optimization of human resources to achieve particular business objectives. We discuss the 'fit' between human resource and business strategy in the next chapter.

It is important to be aware of the many different influences from which HRM as an occupation has emerged, and the resulting contradictions and interpretations that have created a continuing debate about the value of the field and its organizational, societal and economic contribution.

One way to interpret these contrary trends is to appreciate that organizations adopt different HRM strategies according to the threats and opportunities they face in their planning environments. There are also those who regard the term 'human resource management' as merely a glossy label, which attempts to market the same personnel departments as before. Whether or not there is now a new dominant 'paradigm', the degree of change and the effects of the early traditions help to explain how different models have emerged.

For the sake of consistency, we will use the term 'human resource management', or 'HRM', throughout this text.

THE EARLY HISTORY OF PERSONNEL MANAGEMENT UP TO 1914

The industrial revolution that spread throughout Britain during the middle of the nineteenth century was brought about by the application of the principle of the division of labour, combined with the harnessing of steam and other power sources. Concentrations of working people in factories and the related growth of towns led to the helter-skelter existence that we associate with modern industrial life. The rapid increases in population, new markets, new technology and expansion by vertical integration were conditions that helped to create the need for a large-scale organization of resources.

During the first half of the nineteenth century, a ground swell of criticism appeared against what looked like unchecked greed and exploitation of workers by their fellows. Movements for democracy, agitation for the repeal of anti-trade union legislation and for some minimal controls on employers found their expression through the Chartists, the Ten-Hour movement and the Anti-Corn Law League and in sporadic riots and petitions. In the works of Dickens and the later social investigations of Mayhew, Booth and Rowntree, the worst abuses of sweating (excessive hours), child mistreatment and oppression by employers were revealed, and a working-class counterculture was described.

Even among enlightened liberal opinion, public acknowledgement of the reasons for poverty had usually supported the beliefs underlying the 1834 Poor Law, chief amongst which was the view that paupers were the authors of their own misfortunes. There was no understanding of structural unemployment or the effects of a downturn in the trade cycle. The general image of the pauper was of a lazy profligate brought down by his or her own failings, notably excessive drinking. Such a vision was congruent with the middle-class ideology of self-help and the work ethic, which was a celebration of capitalist economics. Management and the owners of business were drawn from the upper middle class, where a high value was placed on individualism, competition and the survival of the fittest. Artisans, supervisors and shopkeepers would also have subscribed to such views. Little had changed for working people in the nineteenth century. Their conditions and life chances had always been poor. As John Clare, the Northamptonshire poet, wrote: 'the poor man's lot seems to have been so long remembered as to be entirely forgotten'.

Pressures for reform and for the protection of working people came towards the end of the nineteenth century, mostly from trade union leaders and members of the labour movement. The extension of the franchise added to these pressures in the last quarter of the century. Active campaigning by individuals such as Rowntree was also effective, and the large Quaker employers set out to provide an example of how good working conditions and profitability could be compatible. What has been called the movement towards 'industrial betterment' came on the fringes of a wider claim for improvement in living conditions. Out of this movement emerged the earliest attempts at welfare policies. One interpretation of the industrial betterment movement is that it was a response by employers to the demand for change in society.

Early welfare workers belonged to the property-owning classes, and at first were concerned only with women. The protection of women was seen as a worthy objective, and even the harshest employer would have found it difficult to oppose these aims openly. Extramural welfare workers visited sick employees and helped to arrange accommodation for women and girls, often including the supervision of moral welfare as part of their work. Welfare workers were usually employed in the newer industries, where women were engaged on light machine work, packing, assembly and similar routine jobs, and it was in these factories that full-time welfare staff were first in service.

The scope of the welfare officer (sometimes called 'welfare secretaries') was allowed to grow in those companies where she could demonstrate a successful integration of welfare and managerial objectives, so that she became concerned with the recruitment, training and transfer of hourly paid female factory hands.

Up to 1900 there were still only a dozen or so full-time welfare secretaries, but their number had grown sufficiently by 1913 for them to seek a recognizable identity by forming the Welfare Workers' Association, this being the forerunner to the Institute of Personnel Management (now the Chartered Institute of Personnel and Development). They often found that managers and supervisors were suspicious of their work, and they were also attacked by the unions as a management device for controlling employees. The problems of being the 'person in the middle' were not unlike the difficulties faced by first-line supervisors. Workers were not sure whether the aims of welfare were altruistic, and felt that there was an element of hypocrisy in the welfare secretaries' actions. Managers saw the possibility of another standard besides economic efficiency being applied, and were antagonized by the thought of any restriction on their power.

The reasons for the development of a welfare movement can best be seen as a response to the wider trend of greater interest and concern for general living conditions. Although it has been argued that Quaker employers such as Cadbury may have been expiating their feelings of guilt by becoming leaders of the welfare movement at a time when they had not yet reconciled the profit motive with Christian ethics, it is more accurate to see in their sponsorship of the welfare movement a belief in good organization, good health, hygiene and a broad mission of pastoral care for their workers. Individual welfare workers probably had mixed motives, but there is no doubt that most of them wanted to help improve conditions for working people and to provide them with some protection.

WHAT WAS THE PURPOSE OF WELFARE WORK?

1   It was an assertion of a paternalistic relationship between employers and their work-force. This outlook was in the spirit of the old guild masters, which meant that employers might expect a reciprocal sense of service from their workers.
2   To grant some form of moral protection over women and children, just as the Factory Acts had sought to provide a form of physical protection.
3   To achieve higher output by control of sickness and absenteeism, and by the early resolution of grievances and problems.
4   To provide sanitary and acceptable working conditions. Much of the early welfare work was in food factories where cleanliness also benefited the consumer.
5   To make the organization of women by trade unions unnecessary through removing the employees' grievances.

From these early days some of the conflict and confusion about HR activities has persisted. In fact, welfare work was always undertaken to meet the interests of management, since ultimately it was a cost met by management. To some degree, the areas of welfare covered by welfare officers, or welfare secretaries, were on behalf of society as a whole, at a time when there was no help from the state.

THE FIRST WORLD WAR 1914–1918

The First World War occasioned a 'step change' in the development of the field. There was a large increase in the number of welfare officers (to about 1300), largely in munitions and war factories, where men were also recruited to oversee boys' welfare. State regulation of employment was instituted through the Munitions of War Act 1915, which, together with its amendments, sought to control the supply of labour to war factories and made welfare services obligatory in these factories.

The extension of controls into such matters as timekeeping, attendance and 'dili-gence' gave the state an unprecedented impact on working life, although it was not until towards the end of the First World War that the controls became well organized and effective. Welfare work was performed on an impersonal, bureaucratic basis.

The government gave direct encouragement to welfare development through the Health of Munitions Workers' Committee, which was the precursor to the National Institute of Industrial Psychology, and which continued the research into the psychological problems of working – boredom, fatigue, monotony, etc.

Women were recruited in large numbers to fill the staffing gap caused by the demand for war-related manufacturing and the recruitment of men from industry into the armed services. By 1915, of the men who remained civilians, one man was expected to do the work of two. The employment of women necessitated agreement with the trade unions on what was termed 'dilution' – that is, accepting unskilled women into craftsmen's work, the abandonment of formal apprenticeship schemes and changed manning levels. Although compulsory arbitration was introduced, there were many bitter wrangles. Lloyd George, as Minister of Munitions, was obliged to go to the Clydeside shipyards to try to resolve a dispute over 'dilutees' and discharge certificates, for example.

After 1918 various forms of joint consultation were proposed. The only enduring form was the Whitley Joint Consultative Committee in the Civil Service, which is still in existence. However, for the first time the state had to open up a dialogue with the trade unions, and a recognizable policy on industrial relations was evidenced in this period.

GROWTH OF EMPLOYMENT MANAGEMENT IN 1920s AND 1930s

Employment management accented labour control, recruitment and discharge of labour and had separate origins from welfare. Labour managers came into being in the engineering industry and in large factories – for example, in process industries – and in some cases developed from more routine jobs such as 'timekeepers' or record-keeping assistants on the works office manager's staff. Often, wages clerks saw job applicants and came to deal with queries over absences, bonuses, piece rates, etc. The employers' federations had industrial relations responsibilities, and employed officials to help settle disputes. In engineering and shipbuilding there were national negotiations of rates, but districts 'plussed up' on these rates according to tradition and the supply of skilled labour. Records of grievances and disputes were kept by engineering employers because of the need to follow procedures within the employers' federation, and therefore specialists in the procedures evolved in some companies.

EARLY PERSONNEL DEPARTMENTS 1920–1939

In the 1920s and 1930s employment managers with various job titles such as 'Labour Officer', 'Men's Employment Officer', etc., were increasingly common. The number of employers' associations that had traditionally fulfilled the major industrial relations role fell from 2403 to 1550 between 1925 and 1936. This was partly as a result of employers wanting to follow an independent tack and because, with the growth in complexity of their businesses, they created their own personnel departments with industrial relations policies. In the large organizations, such as ICI, Courtaulds, Pilkingtons, London Transport and Marks & Spencer, the first specialist personnel departments were formed between the wars.

Specialist personnel management in organizations such as these was a response to the problem of control. Complex organization structures resulted in differing standards and divergent policies unless a central controlling influence was exercised. Mergers, acquisitions and expansions led to the establishment of personnel departments. These were usually in the newer industries, such as plastics, chemicals, mass-produced consumer goods and in multiple retail, whereas there was no attempt to develop employment management as a specialism in industries such as shipbuilding, textiles or mining, which were hit by the slump. This was because employment management addressed itself to the question of staffing control in matters including absenteeism and recruitment with the intention of improving output. In the older industries, the pressing problems were those of structural unemployment, and no techniques such as retraining adult workers, redeployment or work-sharing were considered by managements. The size of the problem (for most of the 1920s and 1930s there was never less than 10 per cent of the working population unemployed), and the worldwide recession, made it unlikely that solutions would be sought by the application of new techniques.

As trade began to pick up, and rearmament began in the late 1930s, the larger companies in the new industries showed an interest in management development and training. Management trainees were recruited, who followed a central training scheme, and in this way the latent purpose of spreading a common managerial philosophy throughout diverse organization structures was ensured when the trainees moved between divisions. Since the First World War the National Institute of Industrial Psychology had begun to develop selection tests and to contribute to the solution of training problems.

In the larger modern companies, the welfare and employment management sections were merged in the later 1930s. Personnel management in all but these few enterprises was a low-level affair until after 1945. The employees covered were usually hourly paid operatives and junior clerical staff. In retail distribution, some moves towards including sales staff and buyers took place in the 1930s, and the Staff Management Association was set up in 1934 specifically to cover the difficult personnel problems of managing staff scattered in small units. Industrial relations was not regarded as the mainstay of personnel work, and was frequently the main responsibility of senior line managers.

THE SECOND WORLD WAR 1939–1945

In the Second World War, personnel management was expanded in its staffing control aspects to virtually all factories, and the designation of welfare and personnel occupations as 'reserved' (that is, those occupying them were exempt from conscription into the forces) shows the importance that was attached to the personnel role. The growth in numbers of personnel officers was again a feature of wartime, as had been the case with the First World War, there being around 5700 by 1943.

The three instruments of labour regulation were 'protected establishments' (for those engaged in war work), the registration of all employment and 'essential work orders'. These gave an expanded Ministry of Labour and National Service considerable power to direct labour, to prevent the call-up of those with special skills and to influence conditions of employment.

Welfare and personnel work were inaugurated on a full-time basis at all establishments producing war materials, and the concept of a total war carried with it the belief that no effort should be spared to ensure high productivity. In addition to the administration of the rules, all aspects of the management of people came under scrutiny, and the government saw specialist personnel management as an integral part of the drive for greater efficiency. For example, the Ministry of Aircraft Production stipulated that specialist personnel management was mandatory in aircraft factories.

The evacuation of large numbers of civilians, the extension of shift working and the problems of training large numbers of women and young people gave welfare and personnel departments the same central place in the organization of production as had emerged during the First World War. Welfare was again part of the rule-governed environment created for large-scale production.

To achieve wartime production targets, strikes were made illegal and compulsory arbitration was introduced. In 1940, three men were expected to cover the work of four, and once again the staffing gap necessitated the employment of women in unfamiliar jobs, such as crane drivers, and in war factories. Of necessity, restrictive practices had to be suspended by the unions, and the state entered into a dialogue with the unions to try to maintain harmony. The linking of productivity improvements with joint consultation made a lasting impression on management thought, and the principles of joint consultation have come to be regarded as important in the training of personnel managers. After 1945, employers and some governments have found various forms of consultation with trade unions, and the TUC necessary, continuing the tradition.

Three significant tendencies deriving from both world wars can be summarized as follows:

1   The belief amongst managers, sustained by research, that output and employment conditions are related, and the development by personnel managers of specific personnel techniques.
2   The integration of employment management and welfare work into the broad function, under the umbrella of personnel management, and the massive increase in the number of people in the occupation.
3   The wars demonstrated that the regulation of employment by the state could produce the desired outcomes in the short term at least, but that this required large-scale controls and could only succeed with the agreement of the workers, who needed a commitment to victory if they were to be convinced of the necessity to relinquish their freedoms.

1945–1968: INDUSTRIAL RELATIONS: CONFLICT RATHER THAN CONSENSUS

Post-1945 industrial relations witnessed an enormous growth in the number and power of shop stewards, and the breakdown of national-level bargaining through employers' federations. Local-level bargaining gave greater scope for personnel staff, and the larger companies preferred to develop their own industrial relations policies that were in tune with their investment plans and their overall corporate strategy. There was a growth in productivity bargaining in the 1960s as employers and unions negotiated about the shares in wealth that were to be gained from improvements in technology: for example, agreements such as those made at ESSO's Fawley refinery. The involvement of line managers in productivity bargaining was essential, both because of their technical knowledge and because they were the managers who had to make the bargain work.

The Donovan Report of 1968 on trade unions and employers was a Royal Commission report that examined British industrial relations in the light of the large number of unofficial strikes that were taking place. The report was particularly critical of what the Commission's members saw as the failure of personnel managers either to cope with the changes that were taking place, to be skilled in negotiation or to plan industrial relations strategy. The immediate *ad hoc* responses that were typical of management's reaction to the disagreements, which so often led to unofficial action, were seen as a failure on management's part to give personnel management a high priority. Donovan failed, however, to offer a solution or a range of techniques which would resolve the problems.

All kinds of organizations (local authorities, hospitals, service industries, for example, as well as manufacturing) were starting to employ full-time personnel staff by the mid-1960s, and the spread of ideas and of specialization within the field began to establish personnel management as an occupation in its own right. The 'consultant problem-solver' role is often the most acceptable one in an organization's authority structure, so there may be greater involvement for line managers in day-to-day negotiation. The research, coordination and back-up activities of personnel officers were often an essential part of the management's control and direction of relationships, however.

The most significant contribution of personnel management to industrial relations was through the creation of conditions under which certain industrial relations policies came to be accepted. Wage payment systems, and conditions of service that created different status groupings, were examples of how personnel systems came to create relationships.

Union leaders were heard to call for better personnel management since personnel managers brought order and were often able to promote good relationships, for instance, through organization development schemes, which started to be prescribed as solutions to difficulties in relationships in the later 1960s. Unions also believed that attention to personnel management might be expected to ensure some minimum standards and to curb the rogue employer.

1968–1979: NATIONAL ECONOMIC POLICY AND GROWTH OF LEGISLATION

In this period there was a boom-slump cycle in Britain. Both Labour and Conservative governments tried fiscal and monetary policies to control the economy. During this time the stability of sterling and the rate of price inflation dominated economic thinking.

State legislation on prices and incomes ranged from voluntary regulations by individual employers to statutory controls maintained by special commissions and boards. Irrespective of the form used, the regulation of wages in accordance with national economic policies entailed the control of wage policies by personnel managers and other senior staff on a company-wide basis. This encouraged the use of job evaluation schemes and incremental scales. Entry to the European Economic Community (EEC) came at a time when multinational companies were expanding, which gave some personnel departments an international dimension and added complexity to the activities.

In addition to prices and incomes policies, the state was extremely active in formulating new employment legislation during the early 1960s. The Contracts of Employment Act 1963, the Industrial Training Act 1964 and the Redundancy Payments Act 1965 were the forerunners of comprehensive legislation on job security, equal opportunity and the position of trade unions. Various state agencies were also set up during this time to encourage good employment practice. One of the major consequences of all this activity was the enhancement in formal authority of personnel departments, and these changes were also a factor in the spread of personnel functions into small organizations.

The burst of legislation coincided with the development of personnel techniques. Management training courses with both educational and vocational aspects expanded (for example the introduction from the USA of MBA courses for business graduates) and theories drawn from the social sciences became popular in the late 1960s to explain motivation to work and organizational behaviour. Communication techniques such as briefing groups were emphasized and greater attention was paid to the social and technical environment of work, largely as a result of the influence of the Tavistock Institute and the 'socio-technical systems' school. The Institute of Personnel Management (IPM) drew heavily on sociology and psychology when restructuring its examination scheme, and the IPM was active in the move to 'professionalize' personnel management.

In the 1970s, staffing planning for larger organizations and in the public sector became more sophisticated, with an interest in computer models. Similarly, record-keeping for large concerns was aided by microfilm and computer storage. Selection tests had been available since the early 1920s, but they began to be used more frequently, often by specialized agencies.

1979–1997: THE THATCHER ERA

The election of a Conservative Government in the UK with Mrs Thatcher as prime minister ushered in a new era for people management. The 1980s were characterized by a political move to the right, ideologically, and the reassertion of managerial prerogatives. The Conservative Party was elected with a mandate to reduce trade union power, following the 'winter of discontent' – a series of crippling strikes in the public sector that reduced services to the public dramatically across the country, and which had helped to bring down the previous Labour government. The new government embarked on a comprehensive legislative programme. There were new laws that outlawed sympathetic and 'political' strikes, increased the liability of trade unions to legal actions in the courts as a consequence of strikes or other forms of protest and laws which increased the power of individual trade union members and sought to reduce the influence of trade unions nationally.

Following the recession of the early 1980s, organizations drove through new approaches to quality improvement and efficiency. Productivity improvements were achieved by new investments and by introducing more flexible working practices: flexibility of time, task and contract. Employers retained a shrinking core of full-time permanent employees while expanding in the secondary labour market of part-time, subcontract, temporary, casual and short-term contract employees. At this time, the use of the term 'human resource management' came to be more common. An import from the USA, the change of title did not immediately come to mean a changed role, but this slowly emerged as a focus on the strategic role of the specialist in people management, concerned to contribute to the business plan and to deliver the appropriate human resources to the organization. The notion that the role was about sourcing and developing human capital was typically introduced at the end of the twentieth century.

During the boom period in the mid-1980s, the skills shortage attracted premium rates. There were 'golden hellos' and signing-on fees for recent graduates. This was a time when deregulation in financial services and the privatization of companies such as British Telecom, British Airways and British Gas gave a considerable boost to HR management in its resourcing and developmental activities. The management of change was seen as the key role, with considerable interest in creating new organization cultures and in organization development techniques, providing a strategic role for HRM.

At the start of the 1990s a new, deeper recession was experienced in the UK. Unusually, this affected the south east of England as much as the north, service industries as much as manufacturing, and substantial redundancies occurred. 'Delayering', restructuring and outsourcing some of the functions previously conducted within the company were organization structure changes that affected HRM, with outplacement as a solution to help the change. These changes brought about a collapse of the career concept and, even in the public sector, the end to 'jobs for life'. Divisional structures and empowerment policies moved the day-to-day decision-making away from large corporate headquarters, which could (in theory) concentrate on strategic issues. Many of the improvements to performance, such as total quality management (TQM) and business process redesign (BPR), originated outside the HR function, but nevertheless increased the focus on people management issues as a likely source of competitive advantage.

1997–2008: EXPANDING SERVICES AND EXPANDING DEBT

In 1997 a new Labour government was elected in the UK, which maintained the same broad agenda on industrial relations and the economy. There was greater stability, with the Bank of

England rather than politicians setting the interest rates, and the low rates of unemployment and of inflation meant the UK was able to maintain a buoyant economy by comparison with its European partners. Growth in the economy was also aided by the globalization of business, through the internet, the expansion of the EU to 25 countries and the rapid growth of economies such as China and India, where low wages and costs attracted investment, so that UK HR managers found themselves frequently with international responsibilities.

Expansion in the labour force in the UK was only possible by immigration and by expanding the number of women returners from maternity leave. Flexibility policies and new legislation to make work more family friendly, and imaginative sourcing, including outsourcing, have been required from the HR function. Smarter working through, for example, laptops, mobile phones and email systems made it easier for people to work from home and to work whilst they travel. There was also a requirement for companies to invest more in training and development, and to find and retain 'talented people'. The expansion, under Labour, of the public sector (especially health and education) also required a professional HRM approach with more HR specialists recruited in the public sector.

We have seen from the description in this chapter that welfare secretaries were the early pioneers who had to deal with male dominated workplaces at a time when men occupied virtually all managerial posts. Men entered personnel management in the 1960s and 1970s, when industrial relations came to be more integrated with other aspects of the personnel role. Men were frequently appointed to the more senior roles in spite of the large numbers of female colleagues who worked as personnel officers and personnel assistants. However, CRANET figures reveal that women have been reaching higher levels since the 1990s.

The demographic changes are potentially the most significant influences on HRM. The large reduction in the number of young people coming onto the labour market in Western Europe, and increasing longevity, meant that organizations had to review their employment policies to attract a variety of people from any age group. Similarly, Britain's multiracial society required HR management techniques that manage diversity. This stimulated interest in equal opportunity policies.

The events of 9/11 in New York and the 2005 London bombings raised security issues for all organizations. HR managers were involved to ensure that measures were in

TABLE 5.1 % OF HR MANAGERS AT THE MOST SENIOR LEVEL BY GENDER, UK

	1995	1999	2003
Males	66	51	39
Females	34	49	61
% University degree	60	60	69

place to ensure their organization could continue to operate whatever the potential interruptions or threats might be, including both physical risks to people and to cyber crime.

HR people may, of course, become directly involved owing to their responsibilities for the health, safety and the wellbeing of employees. This was exemplified on 9/11 by Alayne Gentul, Senior Vice President for HR of Fiduciary Trust International, who was on the 90th floor of the World Trade Center South Tower, and who gave her life trying to help employees out, emptying offices, encouraging and comforting when the first plane hit the North Tower. She was on the 97th floor when the second plane hit the South Tower. She remained 'apparently determined to send everyone down before starting her descent' (Bates 2001: 32) and died when the South Tower fell.

Apart from these direct involvements, HR staff also have special responsibilities for recruitment policies, for example security checks and identity checks, references and matters related to the honesty of employees. Heightened interest in security matters is only one of the many pressures creating a turbulent environment.

The banking crisis of 2008/09 and the following recession was an unexpected shock for many businesses and individuals across the developed and developing economies. Starting as a banking crisis – the direct consequence of excessive debts – and the massive failures in regulations – evident in a situation similar to the 1929 crash – the pervasive nature of the problems underlying the recession affected all sectors of the economy. EU countries as well as the UK and the USA were all drawn into national financial difficulties, because of public debt. The austerity policies that followed in all affected countries had a negative impact on employment.

One of the distinctive features of this recession has been the confluence between the economic and the banking crises and other long-term trends, which signalled a major change in the way people are managed at work. The immediate effects of the recession are shown below.

Labour market effects of the recession

These vary according to the existing state of labour markets in different countries and sectors. Many European countries already had substantial unemployment problems amongst young people, including France and Spain. In the UK, although employment has recovered amongst older people, with a million new jobs created since 2010 (many of them part-time), there are around 900,000 under 24-year-olds who are unemployed. Many of these will be NEETs (not in employment, education or training), reflecting the failures in education and training in the UK, which is a serious problem for UK productivity. There has also been an increase in the number of people who are employed on zero hours contracts, and in various forms of flexible working, which has been encouraged by changes in the law. Most of the redundancies have occurred in the public sector, and the loss in real income consequently will be spread around the UK. In spite of these effects, there was still a war for talent and a shortage of high quality employees with the requisite skills reportedly holding back business performance.

Standard of living issues

Pay freezes imposed for many years in the public sector and low level pay increases in the private sector for many have coincided with rising prices, affecting not just lower level employees but also those in the 'squeezed middle'.

The concept of the 'living wage' as opposed to the minimum wage was created by the 'Living Wage Foundation' as a voluntary movement for employers who agreed to go beyond the statutory minimum, which was seen as neither competitive for labour nor fair. The state regulated national minimum wage in 2013 for employees over 21 was £6.31 per hour, whereas the 'living wage' was £7.65 per hour (the London rate being £8.80 per hour, reflecting the special conditions in the London labour market). According to a KPMG (2013) survey, 5.24 million people were paid less than the 'living wage'.

Reward policies were also tested by the ongoing controversies of high levels of executive pay. The failures in the banking system were partly blamed on the bonus schemes used in the financial services sector where the millions of pounds paid to executives and traders were thought to encourage risky deals. The failure by shareholders to control these bonuses and the 'rewards for failure' issues arising from fat bonuses being given to senior executives of failing companies, such as those awarded to senior executives in the Royal Bank of Scotland failure, led to the EU regulators imposing a cap on bonus payments in financial businesses.

The HR consequences we will discuss in more depth in Chapters 6, 17 and 18, but it is worth commenting here that these trends have encouraged HR specialists to consider questions of perceived fairness, social comparison theory and the corporate social responsibility matters involved, along with their usual reward policy and pay technicalities.

Underlying societal issues

The twenty-first century has brought major shifts in demographics, which are having profound effects on HR policies. In the UK and in other developed economies, there are falling fertility rates and increasing life expectancy. Age discrimination and the use of migrant labour are likely imperatives in the long term for HRM. Fertility rates in the UK fell from 2.4 per cent to 1.8 per cent in 2007. The majority of the populations in developed economies will soon be over 50 years of age, and work force participation rates in the employed populations are increasing (Buttigieg 2011). One consequence is the likely increase in public expenditure as a result of rising pension costs, which stood at 7.5 per cent of GDP in the UK, prompting an extension by the government to the normal retirement age to be around 70 years of age for those in the UK who are in their early 40s now.

For HRM, there are important changes to be made to recruitment, reward and pension policies, to careers, to succession plans, lifetime learning, and to ensure there is no age discrimination.

Institutional change and corporate social responsibility

There are a number of trends that relate to a questioning of the role and calibre of our social institutions. The recession coincided with a movement towards institutional reform, a time when the public lost confidence in the way society operated. These are found in the UK in public disappointment with organizations as diverse and widespread as the church (child abuse cases), the press (illegal activities, phone hacking), the BBC (abuse scandals in respect of some of its presenters and excessive rewards), Parliament (the expenses scandal), the police (reviews of mistakes in some cases and the 'plebgate' affair), local authorities (child protection issues), schools (the quality of teaching) and the NHS (treatment of patients and of mistakes in care of the elderly), to name some recent instances.

In all these cases employees and their managers were seen to be failing in some way. Most of these actual abuses or problems first occurred many years ago, but the public has only recently discovered them, implying that there were cover-ups in some cases. For HR there is the obvious need to improve recruitment, development and training, as well as the significance of the quality of the oversight by the board and senior managers. There is also the need to improve whistle-blowing policies.

Further challenges exist for HR to deal with social integration and to socialize and induct migrant labour into their work forces.

Information technology

The march onwards of new technology developments was not halted by the recession. In many ways, the pressure for improving productivity enhanced information technology improvements.

Developments such as the 'cloud', mobile technology and the rapid advances of social media have revolutionized many aspects of work. Three-dimensional printing and new materials have the potential to revolutionize manufacturing in some industries.

For HRM, the use of eHRM and of social media in recruitment have been most noticeable. Equally, smart phones and mobile working meant employees were no longer tied to their offices or work stations. The possibilities for more flexible working meets a growing social need for improved child care, care of the elderly and family friendly HR policies. Improvements such as Skype encourage communications, video conferencing, webinars and the use of virtual teams.

To quote Ray Wang, CEO of Constellation Research (2011: 40):

The 'cloud' gives you any information from HR data to outside unstructured information. The mobile platform is the access and interaction point to the cloud and the data of choice. Social media will also generate more data, and this is going to drive new analytics.

CONCLUSIONS

In this chapter, we have shown how context affects the development of HRM. As in previous eras, economic trends such as recession have a major impact on organizations, and hence on HRM. Recessions and recoveries affect HRM through the labour market, the impact on rewards and employee relations. Other major social factors have influenced careers, recruitment, benefits and talent management. Some of the greatest leaps in HRM have come as a consequence of the state's interventions, for example in both world wars, and through legislation. New technology promises a revolution owing to the opportunities for new ways of working. The coincidence of the different factors, with some potential problems such as demographic change, may point to where technology might prove to be an important part of the solution.

The strategic role of HRM has developed over time: from the early beginnings in the welfare roles, through the control systems of employment management and on to the wider systematic use of HR techniques and information, in order to impact on businesses strategically. The next chapter takes this further to look at the strategic role and how to discharge it effectively.

QUESTIONS

1   What do we learn about the role of the state in the development of HRM?
2   Which of the main traditions in HRM do you think have influenced the profession the most?
3   What has the HR profession contributed to the creation of a better life for employees, or for the improved performance of companies?
4   What do we learn from the impact of the recessions over the years on the management of people at work?
5   What do you see as the 'direction of travel' for the future of the specialist HR function?

For a commentary on these questions, see the companion website for this book.

REFERENCES

Bates, S. (2001). 'Above and beyond'. *HR Magazine* December SHRM.
CRANET Survey (2003). *Executive Report*. Human Resource Research Centre. Cranfield University, School of Management.
Storey, J. (ed). (1997). *Human Resource Management. A Critical Text*. London: Routledge.
Wang, R. (2011). Quoted in 'The grand convergence', Roberts, B. *Human Resource Magazine* 39–46 SHRM.

6 HUMAN RESOURCE STRATEGY AND ORGANIZATIONAL PERFORMANCE

INTRODUCTION

This chapter locates the HR function as a central feature of business strategy. Human resource management (HRM) exists in order to achieve organizational goals through people resources. People management is perceived by most organizations as a key determinant of success. The changing role of HRM has reflected the growing awareness by senior managers of the importance attached to how people are managed. This is the 'coming of age' of HRM: the recognition that organizational effectiveness and performance outcomes are very dependent on the HR function of management, as discharged by line managers and specialists alike.

This chapter concentrates on three topics. First, we consider the evidence that HRM has an impact on organizational performance. Second, we look at the relationship between HR strategy and business strategy and, finally, we describe the practical processes for creating an HR strategy.

In the previous chapter we described how some of the different traditions of personnel management developed. The variability of organization cultures and the changing environment in which people are managed would lead us to believe that there is no common trend in the development of people management that applies to all organizations. No single model of HR management can meet all requirements. Nevertheless, research in the field rarely differentiates between different industry sectors, organization sizes and the different histories of organizations. The theoretical advances in HRM have been influential, and there are many forces for convergence, including common education and training systems for those entering HR management. In many countries, academic collaboration in research, the growth of multinationals with common policies and similarities in policy agendas as societies and economic systems converge are reflected in European Community rules and laws, in addition to the arrangements in other trade blocs covering laws and regulations. In what follows, therefore, we are making generalizations that will need to be interpreted into the cultures and societies where the organization operates.

HRM AND ORGANIZATIONAL PERFORMANCE

The strategic credentials of HRM depend on there being a consistent, explicable relationship between HR policies and organizational performance. There have been a number of attempts to describe the links between human resource management and organizational goals. The Harvard model of Beer and others (1985) characterizes human resource management as a system that links corporate objectives into societal needs and back into human resource activities. This framework, therefore, describes the integration between business and society. Perhaps the main weakness of this framework is its failure to show corporate or business strategy as a key determinant of human resource strategies and policies.

Other authors, such as Hendry and Pettigrew (1990), have attempted to show human resource management as a process where there are interconnected decisions deriving from the corporate or business strategy, often, for example, originating in the product life cycle stage or in decisions to move into new markets.

One of the difficulties faced by HR researchers was the absence of a theory that would connect HR activities to the purposes of organizations. At the end of the 1980s and into the 1990s, a resource based theory of the firm originating from Edith Penrose (1959) and Barney (1991) became increasingly popular.

The resource based view (RBV)

The resource based view of the firm is a theory which seeks to explain how the internal resources of the firm can provide the company with a competitive advantage. The main feature of the theory is that internal resources and organizational capabilities are firm characteristics which are a source of competitive advantage. These characteristics include, inter alia, the firm's employees, organizational capabilities such as the knowledge of employees, the systems and ways of learning and of interacting with customers, suppliers and logistics. These are ways of operating which are valuable, rare, inimitable, not or imperfectly substitutable (VRIN), which provide a source of competitive advantage. These capabilities could well be a barrier to entry for would-be competitors and, according to the theory, are the attributes that would make the firm highly competitive in its market.

The popularity of the RBV has grown amongst HR and strategy researchers as it gives an emphasis to the strategic importance of resourcing employees, developing competence, knowledge management, the systems and processes that sustain the culture and all the policies such as talent management, appraisal, development rewards and employment relationships which help to sustain organizational capability. HR systems create the human capital pool of capable people, so that they can sustain what Wright and others (2001) describe as 'strategically relevant behaviours'. The RBV also gives HR managers a language and analytical framework which is appropriate for the development of business strategy, and a focus for HR strategy.

The RBV suggests a skills and capability focus for the strategy, so that firms learn faster than their rivals, and protect and enlarge their intellectual capital. As a consequence, companies can generate a human capital advantage owing to the unique capabilities of their employees, as well as an organizational process advantage from their systems, history and ways of working. Mavrinac and Siesfield (1997) have suggested that 35 per cent of an institutional investor's valuation of a company is attributable to the company's non-financial capabilities, such as management credibility and expertise, innovativeness, ability to attract and retain talent, compensation practices, and the quality and execution of the company's business strategy.

Empirical studies of the effect of HR policies on business performance

There have been many research studies into how HR policies can improve performance at the unit or company level. Even F. W. Taylor's 1913 book *Scientific Management* reported on the beneficial results of piece work systems based on time and motion studies, when applied to manual labour. The socio-technical systems theory advocated in the 1950s in the UK presented possibilities for managers to intervene by working on the social system that operates along with the technical system, through better aligning the social and the technical system, especially at the work group or unit level, ideas which were adopted in companies such as Shell and Esso (Standard Oil).

Chapter 2 briefly mentions the attributes of work teams where there is a notion of high involvement work groups, using the energy of the group and their tacit and explicit knowledge and experience in a participative way to solve work problems, and to improve performance of the work group, as well as the technical system as a whole (for example, Appelbaum and others 2000). As discussed in Chapter 2, companies have long used motivation theory and job design principles where jobs are redesigned to be inherently motivational, and utilized group dynamics to improve problem-solving and output, including quality (Hackman, Brousseau and Weiss 1976). All of these studies gave backing to HR policies that could improve performance. However, line managers rather than HR specialists were usually and necessarily the advocates for introducing these management practices.

Interest in empirical studies on this topic was given a boost by Huselid's (1995) research, in which following four national surveys in the USA, it was claimed that results from over 2000 firms showed that small changes to HR systems could bring an increase in the market value of the firm over time. These and similar studies argued that individual HR practices are not sufficient to improve organizational performance; rather, what are often called 'bundles' of HR policies are required which would all need to be consistent in their support for a particular idea (e.g. improved team work). The practices are often in the recruitment, training, reward and appraisal policy areas. Arguably, there is already evidence of HR practitioners bundling up policies, for example in the cases of talent management and total rewards.

Paauwe's Framework

The study of what HR practices 'ought' to be applied to improve organizational performance has been fraught with methodological difficulties, since there are contextual affects, such as organization size, industry sector, type of occupation, trade union relationships, etc., as well as the national context, with its laws, traditions, customs and geographical features. All of these variations make generalization difficult.

Jaap Paauwe (2009) summarizes these problems, following Purcell and others (2003), as the 'black box problem'. The 'black box ' is only an analogy, a way of describing the unknown context and the many variables and the interactive effects of them, which are intervening variables between HR policies and practices and the actual outcomes of a firm's performance.

Paauwe (1998) sets out a framework that seeks to identify the various interactions according to the state of knowledge on this topic. The significance of the model is that, instead of seeking a direct relationship between the HR strategies/policies and practices, and organizational performance HR outcomes such as labour turnover,

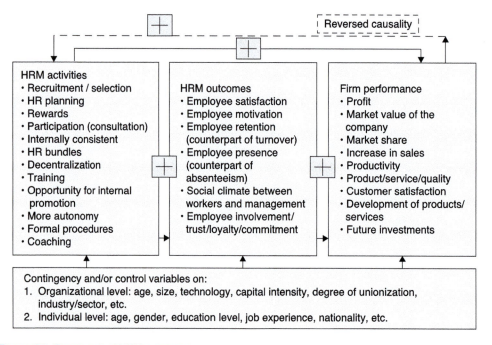

Figure 6.1 Framework of HRM outcomes

Paauwe, J. (2004). *HRM and Performance*. Oxford: Oxford University Press.

recruitment quality and the like are seen as the intervening level, which are measurable, and can be shown in turn to relate to organizational outcomes. One of the potential weaknesses of the model, as acknowledged by Paauwe, is that the model suggests a linear movement, implying causality, whereas there might be a form of reverse causality. In short, financially successful businesses may not be successful because of HR policies and practices but, because they are financially successful, they can afford extensive HR policies and larger HR functions.

BUSINESS STRATEGY AND HR STRATEGY RELATIONSHIPS

Business strategy can be defined as: 'The attempt by those who control an organization to find ways to position their business/organization objectives so they can exploit the planning environment and maximize the future use of the capital and human assets' (after Johnson, Scholes and Whittington 2008).

This definition emphasizes the choices available in the search for competitive advantage, where to position the business, how to exploit the planning environment (that is, the opportunities for the company) and how to maximize the use of capital and human assets in the future. The assumption that employees are assets could be challenged, since clearly some employees might be liabilities.

Business strategy may be created in a variety of ways. Strategy may be imposed, from top down, usually from the main board of directors or the management board, who have accountability for the direction taken by the company, and for the performance of the business to shareholders and to other stakeholders. Public sector boards have a similar responsibility, being accountable as they are for the quality, efficiency, availability and costs of services to local councillors or to Parliament. Strategy may be 'emergent', deriving from actions and choices over time, and sometimes by immediate needs. This may be a form of 'logical incrementalism', where strategy is created step by step. These are two typical approaches, therefore: the more analytical and longer term, driven from the top, or the slower, more emergent approach, where the reconstruction of strategy is continuous, and where input may be from a variety of sources. We should also differentiate between intended and realized strategy. There are many companies where business strategy exists only in PowerPoint presentations, and where much is said about plans, but the ideas are not realized. In this latter case, the benefit to the company may come from the process of consultation, discussion and general agreement on the direction of the business going forward, rather than any specific plan with timelines and measurable objectives.

Research has shown the complexity of the relationships between corporate and human resource strategies. The term 'corporate strategy' is taken to mean the strategy pursued by a corporate board, which includes the portfolio of interests it wishes to acquire or retain, together with the financial ratios (such as return on capital employed, ROCE) the company uses to measure the corporate performance of its various businesses. Human resource strategies should not be confused with human resource or personnel policies. HR strategies are typically a series of policies and practices, overall programmes of action designed to meet business objectives (Tyson 1995). These policies may, for example, be a mixture of recruitment and reward policies, and job satisfaction/job design work, together with succession planning and career management, which are intended to ensure the company manages talent successfully.

Different types of 'fit' between HR and business strategy

By business strategy here we mean the strategy of a particular business or business unit, which has a strategy to achieve its objectives, in which there are people management aspects. There are three distinct types of fit:

1   The fit between the HR strategy and the business strategy. The purpose of the HR strategy is to give effect to the business strategy, and to ensure the strategic object-ives of the business are achieved. This is the fundamental rationale for the HR func-tion. If the function is not helping the business to operate its business model effectively, the very existence of the function would be questioned. This type of fit, therefore, is a priority.

2   The fit between the different policies and practices (the bundles of policies) in the HR strategy, so that there is an overall coherence in the HR objectives and the HR policies and practices. This enables a clear vision and a more easily understood direction to the strategy, helping to communicate and to embed the strategy with line managers and employees alike.

3   The fit of the HR strategy to the organizational context. We know that the economic, the social and technological context change rapidly. HR has to play a boundary span-ning role at the boundary between the organization and its legal, economic, social and technological context. New employment laws, changes to labour markets and to rewards and benefits, social changes such as demographic shifts, attitudes towards marriage and to child care and care of the elderly exemplify strategic input to the HR strategy.

These three types of 'fit' are not mutually exclusive, but it seems likely that organizations will focus on different types of fit according to the situations they face. For example, the fit to the business strategy may not be so important when the organization is in the process of chan-ging the strategy if, for example, it does not seem to be working. 'Fit' to ensure cohesion is less likely to be top priority when there is an intention to devolve policy creation to local business units in a conglomerate organization, or may be seen to be inappropriate because management does not want to retain the same approaches to reward in a company where to do so would encourage trade unions to bargain for a wider group of employees. Similarly, when the context is changing in significant ways, HR will wish to respond with new approaches, and the context becomes of superordinate significance.

Dynamic capabilities

It follows from the ideas in the RBV theory that companies are always striving to remain competitive by adopting management practices (including HRM practices), which maintain their competitive advantage, through their VRIN capabilities. Competitor organizations are also seeking to do so, and therefore firms must constantly seek to maintain their advantage, especially when the context changes. Just such a contextual change was initiated by the 2008/09 financial collapse, and the ensuing recession. The recession spread like wildfire from the USA and the UK to Europe and beyond. This became a time for economic and financial reform, and institutions were under the spotlight, leading to institutional reviews and changes. At the same time, societal, technological and organizational changes were also continuing, creating a 'perfect storm' for managers who were expected to adapt their organizations to change (Moyo 2011; Parry and Tyson 2014). This raises questions about the processes that can help organizations to change.

The idea had already been proposed that firms needed adaptive processes in order to remain competitive and the concept of 'dynamic capabilities' was attracting the interest of researchers. Dynamic capabilities were defined by Teece and others (1997: 516) as: 'The firm's ability to integrate, build and to reconfigure internal and external competences to address rapidly changing environments'.

Because of uncertainty in the economic, political and social environment the strategic planning horizon for most organizations was already shifting from five years down to three or even two years. Capital intensive businesses (such as manufacturing, power generation) will typically plan over a much longer period than labour intensive businesses (such as retail, financial services). Very often, there is a long-term statement of strategic intent, with a short-term plan for the next one or two years.

There are enormous international pressures for change owing to increased competition, and from rising customer expectations, globalization and customer demands for improved quality, technology innovations, demographic and social change. Organizations are changing as part of a dynamic aimed at making both private sector companies and the public sector more responsive, with a strong capability to change. Acquisitions, joint ventures, mergers and demergers are producing a great variety of organization structures, including network and federal structures. This organic approach means organizations are more fragmented, and less inclined to favour stability, rigidity and rationalistic formal relationships, as we described in Chapter 3.

The capabilities that are thought to be necessary for firms in the dynamic environment we experience are described by Bowman and Ambrosini (2003) as those which aid in the tasks of reconfiguring organizations (for example reorganizing organization structures to be more responsive to customer needs), leveraging (for example ensuring best practice from one unit is adopted at other similar business units), improving learning systems (for example by ensuring learning is a continuous process and is adopted in all parts of the business), creative integration (for example looking for synergies across the business, and investing in new ideas or products based on the new insights this brings). Dynamic capabilities could be summarized as organizational attributes:

- change capability
- learning capability
- innovative capability.

Firm processes which derive from the capabilities and impact on firm performance are:

- integration
- review
- reconfiguring
- renewal.

In their summary of the literature on dynamic capabilities, Ambrosini and Bowman (2009) point out that the literature differentiates between the dynamic capabilities themselves and how they are enabled in the firm, i.e. how these capabilities are brought into existence and sustained in the firm, which is seen as a managerial task.

Human resource strategies which seek to put in place processes are 'ways of working' akin to the old ideas of 'stratagems' or ploys to achieve particular ends, rather than the ends themselves. For example, we can conceive of organizational cultural strategies that aim to set up a style of working in support of certain values. These processes themselves are typical of the kinds of process advantages that are referred to in the RBV. There is often an *ethos* in a company or partnership that competitors find difficulty imitating, for example in John Lewis retail stores in the UK, in McDonalds restaurants around the world, in Rolls Royce aero engine manufacture and in Mercedes Benz car manufacturing.

Fit between business and human resource strategies can be achieved not only through policies designed to drive the business strategy forward, but also by adopting a style of working, or an organization culture.

In a knowledge based society, organizations need to be able to take forward the ideas and new products from the people who work within the organization, and to adapt quickly and take in ideas from the whole society. For example, whilst the research of Watson and Crick on DNA resulted in the genome project, it is the adoption of these ideas within the pharmaceutical and related industries that eventually produces advances for society. Cell phones, tablet computers and all the latest electronic and telecommunications technology derive from inventiveness and the conversion processes into products and services.

THE AGILE ORGANIZATION APPROACH

One capability all organizations wish to develop is the capacity to manage change well and naturally and to be adaptable to the fast moving markets where they operate. As the chief protagonists (Dyer and Shafer 2003: 7) of this approach argue: 'Dynamic organisations compete through marketplace agility. Marketplace agility requires that employees at all levels engage in proactive, adaptive and generative behaviours, bolstered by a supportive mindset.'

The challenge is to find ways of changing organizations in a responsive way, so that instead of seeing change management as a specific campaign to move an organization from one position to another, the objective is to create an internal dynamism whereby organizations adjust at all levels to new circumstances and conditions as required. Agile organizations are 'self-organising systems', which have 'the capability to be infinitely adaptable without having to change' (Dyer and Shafer 1999).

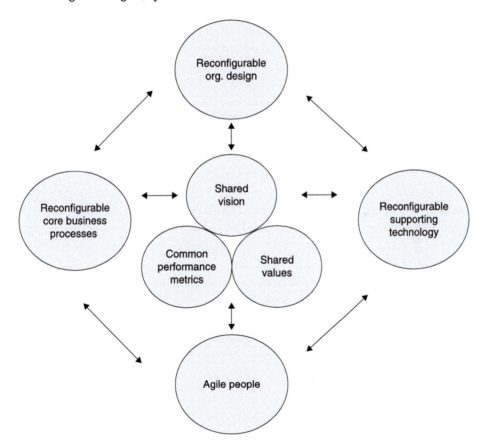

Figure 6.2 Agile organizational capability

Source: Dyer, L. and Shafer, R. A. (1999). Creating organisational agility: Implications for strategic human resource management, in eds. P. Wright., L. Dyer, J. Boudreau and G. Milkovich, *Research in Personnel and Human Resource. Management, Supplement 4, Strategic Human Resource Management in the Twenty-first Century.* Stanford, CT: JAI Press, 145–74.

The paradox is that, in order to change, some aspects of organizational existence must remain the same. Hence, at the heart of the agile organization are a shared vision and shared values, together with a general understanding of performance metrics. Where organizational agility exists, this enables organization redesign, and the reconfiguration of technology and business processes to occur, and to support agility in employees who can rely upon a core of high quality staff. There are advantages in the organization renewal context for this approach, which promises a duality in strategy so that it is possible to optimize adaptability and efficiency simultaneously, as demonstrated by the strategic approach taken by companies such as GlaxoSmithKline. The central feature of all these examples is the organization culture, which expects change to be a norm and to be constant. This type of culture has been described as a 'gazelle' culture. The characteristic features of such a culture are informality and networking, with only the budget as a powerful constant which is immutable, strong values associated with flexibility and a market orientation, combined with a 'can do' philosophy and strong loyalty to the products and to the company. This is a very focused culture; there is a challenging atmosphere, where intellect and flair are valued.

The culture thus described is found in companies with a strong marketing orientation such as the French/international cosmetics, hair care and skin care company, L'Oréal. The brands and the brand values dominate the thinking, there is extensive innovation and new ideas frequently come from the staff. People move around the company and undertake a variety of roles in their careers. The organization as a whole seeks to learn constantly about the work and to improve the company's routines through feedback. HR staff in such a culture are expected to spend much of their time on development and career management, and to work closely with general managers as business partners.

Agility could be said to be driven by the RBV. There are three specific competencies that need to be fostered: reading the market, mobilizing a rapid response and embedding organizational learning. Learning is developed to the point where all are involved in generative double loop learning, learning about the processes as well as the content. This helps to eliminate defensive routines.

We can see that the idea of organizational agility as a self-adjusting system is consistent with the work on dynamic capabilities.

In this model, HR should be building the dynamic capabilities into the firm strategy, which will enable the firm processes of integration, review, reconfiguring and renewal, which is the platform for organizational performance and for creating and maintaining a competitive advantage.

THE PROCESSES FOR CREATING AN HR STRATEGY

Where is HR strategy created?

The answer to the question of where HR strategy should be defined and produced depends upon both the organization structure and on the involvement of stakeholders in the process.

Organizational structure variables, such as whether or not there is a transnational structure, influence the degree of complexity required in the process, as would divisional structures. Industry sector, as mentioned earlier, affects the planning time horizon. Differences in control and budget systems between public sector and private sector organizations also influence the planning process. Often, the strategy needs to be designed to meet mixed requirements from seeking to fit the needs of a number of managers in different parts of the organization (see Chapter 3) and, consequently, only the overall strategy captures the totality of all the HR activities in the years ahead. The strategy could deal with the following allocation of responsibilities:

Head office: HR planning, organization structure, organization development, due diligence, senior level recruitment, promotion development and rewards.
Division: manager recruitment, development, rewards/pay structures, HR policy, the broad terms and minimum standards, communication in the division.
Business unit: employee relations, policy implementation, recruitment and selection, training.

The fit to the business plan

Irrespective of the level at which the HR function is located or the unit for which the function has responsibility, the starting point for the HR strategy is the business plan, again irrespective of its format. The HR director or the specialist HR strategy unit needs to tease out the key issues, for example looking at the priorities and the people management implications of the business model. The business model is the structure of the product or service flows of work and information, covering issues such as how the business operates to deliver its service or to manufacture its product and to generate sales/revenue. Here, the issue to explore is how those involved expect the existing model to change over the coming planning period? The business strategy may have already articulated important potential contributions from HR to the achievement of the business objectives.

As we described earlier, there are different types of fit, including a fit to the business plan, which might be both a business unit plan and a divisional plan, and a broader corporate plan, containing items such as proposed mergers or acquisitions and potential divestments.

HR interventions

However, the HR function legitimately has its own agenda. There may be issues related to employee motivation and involvement, levels of job satisfaction, communications and employee perceptions held of the organization, organization culture, employment relationships, reward structures and the external labour market changes, new contractual forms and labour costs, the types of benefits including pensions and services to staff, which have significant cost implications for the business. New employment laws sometimes require organization-wide responses, for example changes to laws about discrimination, such as age discrimination legislation, which affect not only recruitment, but also development, rewards and benefits such as pension plans. In addition, the HR function is likely to be involved with senior line management in programmes to improve efficiency and to undertake development and training initiatives.

One of the competency areas that HR specialists need to develop is how to make effective interventions, such as those which are concerned with change management, using for example organization development techniques and organizational surveys to determine what is happening in the organization and why?

The improvements in computing which allow businesses to use large scale data sets such as attitude data from an organization-wide survey in conjunction with other data sources such as absence statistics and data on stress or other occupational health information, for example, using a 'private' cloud, provides HR with powerful tools to ensure that people management issues are on the strategic agenda of the organization. This raises important questions about the extent to which employees are to be consulted and involved in HR strategy creation.

Involving employees is not a new approach. A good example of this method was when a European institution, employing nationals of all Member States, found itself in difficulty with its own staff, who had set up an in-house trade union, encompassing all levels of staff. The terms and conditions of employment were extremely generous, and there were considerable difficulties experienced when trying to put new appraisal and career management policies in place. The solution adopted was to arrange an organization-wide survey in which the in-house union had an involvement, and where the results were all fed back to the staff by the president of the organization. By tackling the dissatisfactions alongside the need to change as a whole, new policies were implemented with the full agreement of the staff and their representatives.

HR strategies can only be created and agreed where the often tacit issues about the power of the different organization leaders have been sufficiently addressed for action to proceed. Whether or not there is HR recognition at main board level, there is likely to be a dominant coalition or a powerful network of senior managers who 'call the shots'. Much will be down to the personal credibility and the track record of the HR director. Successful HR directors will have established a good working relationship with the dominant coalition as a natural part of their working relationships.

The HR strategic plan

The following documentation is commonly found in organizations with an HR strategy:

- HR plan, separate – showing all the HR initiatives, with targets and milestones
- a business plan, with consequential HR initiatives and strategies integrated
- an operational plan, perhaps designed using an existing framework, such as the EFQM
- a balanced scorecard type of plan.

The more fully integrated plans imply a joint approach with line management ownership of the plan, alongside HR.

For the last few years there has been an interest in the idea of the 'balanced score-card', originally from Kaplan and Norton's 1996 book of that name. This takes the idea of linking value creation with the notion of stakeholders. The RBV is also drawn upon in this framework, which sees capabilities, learning and growth as the foundation upon which internal business processes are based, and that these processes should serve the customer's needs, which produce financial performance.

Simple frameworks such as lists of business objectives and the HR implications (expressed as programmes of work, with key performance indicators (KPIs) milestones, and outcome performance measures) are sufficient. There are more elaborate models such as the EFQM framework, which is used in a quality competition, with points awarded by peer group assessors, resulting in Europe-wide winners. This recognizes that there are different but interlinked groups of people involved in strategy achievement – including suppliers, customers and shareholders, as well as employees (see Figure 6.3).

Stakeholder models of HR strategy show the KPIs for each stakeholder in regard to each HR objective or programme, as illustrated by the example from a large retail mail-order business.

Stakeholders are looming in organizational thinking for several reasons:

1   Shareholder power is more apparent because of the free movement of capital, through their non-executive director representatives on boards and the growing demand for remuneration committees to exercise more control over top pay, and for more transparency and disclosure to produce less generous top pay rewards. Public sector shareholders, the taxpayers, are even more likely to be concerned about strategy.
2   There is a demand for more transparency generally, and for more accountability by companies to their customers and to the public.
3   The requirement for the employee voice to be heard as a means to improving organizational effectiveness, means explicit stakeholder relationships with clear KPIs are needed.
4   The notion is gaining ground that organizations have to be seen to be socially responsible to satisfy 'green' investors, local communities and central government, and to retain their employees' commitment. All these reasons argue for a stakeholder place in the corporate objectives, with KPIs for each stakeholder.

THE PROCESS FOR CREATING HR STRATEGIES: A 10 POINT PLAN

1   Agree corporate vision/mission/values.
2   Establish HR vision or philosophy of management.
3   Produce business objectives and business strategy (maybe in the form of KPIs).

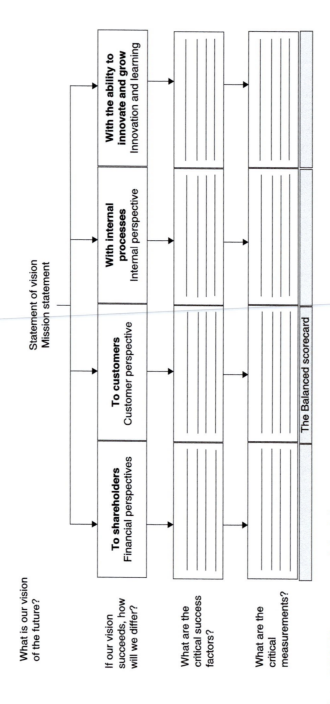

Figure 6.3 Linking measurements to strategy

4   Analyse what is happening inside the organization.
5   Agree HR objectives which fit the business objectives.
6   HR proposes long term HR objectives which support the mission/values.
7   Agree HR strategies for achieving 5 and 6 above, including policy changes.
8   Set measures of achievement.
9   Agree an outline timetable with HR milestones and responsibilities for each element.
10   Set out implementation strategies, feedback, monitoring and evaluation.

There is no one way to write HR strategies or business plans. They will usually consist of a number of people management objectives (the achievement of which will be measurable), together with the policies and actions which are thought necessary to achieve them. The statement may also include express reference to any assumptions made (for example about the availability of budget, or if a sales forecast is to be met, etc.). For example, a business objective to which HR might contribute might appear as set out in Figures 6.4 and 6.5.

Business Objective

Improve efficiency in paint spraying department by reducing overall labour costs by 3% p.a. whilst maintaining current levels of output and quality

HR Strategy

Reduce labour turnover from 20% p.a. to 8% p.a. (thus reducing overtime, training costs and recruitment costs) by

1. Improving selection using specially designed selection test
2. Providing realistic job previews for candidates
3. Improving induction process (new course, involving supervisors)

Figure 6.4 Example of a business objective to which HR might contribute

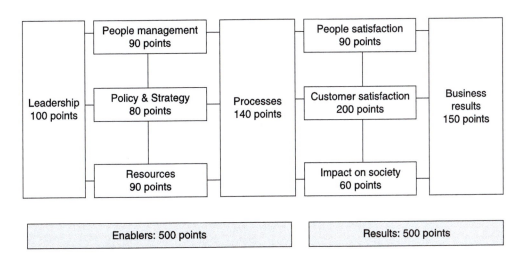

Figure 6.5 EFQM model

There should be timescales and cost/benefits associated with this strategy. Any assumptions made should be stated explicitly. For example, efficiency savings anticipated as a consequence of redundancies.

Even if the HR strategy is fully written up with the business strategy there are advantages in identifying separately the HR policies to see if they are consistent. The grouping of policies together can have a significant impact on performance as we discussed earlier.

Figure 6.6 shows how HR strategy is typically dealt with at different levels in a divisional structured company.

Strategic planning processes require a cascade of objectives, which typically follow a series of iterations, starting with the company vision, or mission, down to an implementation plan, but a review at each stage, shown by the feedback arrows on the left side, as set out in Figure 6.7.

The role of HRM in creating an HR strategy is to work at the heart of the strategic decision-making in the organization. This is an ideal opportunity for HR managers to adopt the business partner role and to exercise the skills of the internal consultant. As discussed in the previous chapter, analytical skills and organizational behaviour knowledge will need to be combined with an understanding of the business, financial acumen, and an awareness

What issues are dealt with at different levels?

Typically

Head Office	HR strategy
	Top people's talent management
	High potential's development
	Management development oversight
	Senior level rewards
	PR
	Due diligence/corporate governance
	Appeals from divisional level
	Oversight of legal issues
Division	Input to HR strategy
	Management recruitment
	Manager development/promotion of unit managers
	Rewards/pay structures
	Policy – broad terms and minimum standards
	Divisional oversight of performance management
	Communications
Business Unit	Industrial relations
	Policy implementation
	Recruitment/selection
	Training
	Unit level performance management
	Junior promotion/recruitment
	Unit level health, safety, welfare.

Figure 6.6 Creating HR strategies

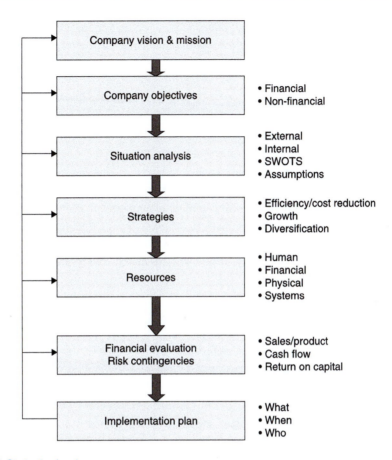

Figure 6.7 Strategic planning processes

of the many different fields such as corporate taxation, operations management, financial reporting, accounting, corporate social responsibility and marketing.

In the following chapter a more detailed discussion covers the topic of workforce planning. These activities are essential first steps in the detailed HR plans which flow from the HR strategy.

AUDITING THE HR STRATEGY (SEE THE COMPANION WEBSITE)

There is a requirement when creating or updating the strategy to know the questions to ask and the kinds of data to collect, as well as how to write up the strategy. The following 10 point plan is an audit instrument for this purpose.

Readers are recommended to work through the questions, using appropriate chapters in the book for a guide in the process and to consult the companion website.

The main headings of the 10 point plan can be used as a prompt to audit whether you have HR strategy development or review needs, and what HR strategies you should be putting in place.

1. Agree corporate, mission/vision/values

1   Do you have a mission/vision/values statement? (Whose values are they?)
2   What do your customers think of the statement?
3   Is it remembered by employees?
4   Do members of the organization care about the mission/vision/values?
5   Is it clear, up-to-date and representative of what your organization seeks?
6   If you do not have a statement of mission/vision/values do you want one?
7   What do your key stakeholders think about your mission/vision/values?
8   Are there specific aspects of the mission/vision/values which affect or should affect the HR strategy?

2. Establish an HR vision/mission/values/philosophy of management

1   Do you have a vision for the HR function?
2   Do you want your employees/potential employees to identify with your employer brand?
3   What are the characteristics of your employer brand as seen by employees?
4   What should be the employee experience of working for you?

3. Produce business objectives and business strategy

1   Where is the business/organization strategy created (group, or division, or company level or at other levels)?
2   What is your role in creating the business/organization strategy (are you a member of the board/committee responsible for this)?
3   How are the business objectives expressed (e.g. key performance indicators, balanced scorecard, etc.)?
4   Is there a written business strategy/plan showing how the objectives are to be achieved.
5   What is your role in creating the HR strategy (working with the top team, or producing first draft yourself, or as part of a planning unit, etc.)?
6   Are the HR implications of the business plan clearly spelt out?
7   Do you have to infer the HR implications, separately from the business plan?
8   Are there significant changes to organization structure, and/or location forecast?
9   Are there predicted changes to the workforce, e.g. expansion, contraction, changes to skill/knowledge.

10   Are there to be improvements to productivity, or changes to working methods, systems/technologies?

4.   What is happening inside the organization?

1   What are the significant changes to internal labour markets? (i.e. labour supply), e.g. age profiles, labour turnover, absenteeism, productivity, skill levels, qualifications, experience levels, supervisory and management skills, succession plans.
2   What are recent attitude survey results?
3   Are there any issues revealed in grievances, industrial disputes, discipline cases, appraisal information?
4   Are there effects known or likely to become important for existing policies from forth-coming legislation (e.g. age discrimination)?

5.   Agree HR objectives which fit business objectives

1   What timeframe do the business objectives assume or mean for HR objectives?
2   Do these affect strategically significant groups of employees?
3   Are the business objectives reasonable, and achievable in HR terms?
4   Can measurable HR objectives be decided which will satisfy the various stakeholders?
5   What are the effects on costs and the quantifiable benefits to come from the object-ives being achieved?
6   Do these objectives affect the coherence of the HR vision/corporate values, employer brand etc?

6.   HR proposes long term HR objectives

1   What HR policy changes are needed to deliver the HR vision?
2   What are the cost: benefits of these objectives?
3   Auditing of existing HR policies e.g. recruitment, reward, development; are they deliv-ering value for money, are they achieving the desired objectives?
4   What can be done to make the vision coherent, clear, communicated?

7.   HR strategies agreed for achieving 5 and 6 above

1   Bring the data together from 4, 5 and 6.
2   What strategies are needed to achieve the business objectives and to deal with existing issues?
3   What changes to HR policies and practices will be needed?
4   How will these be introduced (e.g. consultation, training, communication, etc.)?

8. Set measures for achievement

1   What practical, measurable targets can be set?
2   Who is responsible for achieving these – project groups, etc.?
3   What procedures will be put in place in order to make this measurement possible?

9. Agree an outline timetable

1   What timeframe is to be used for each strategy?
2   How do these strategies interact and what pressures on resources (managerial/HR, etc.) will be imposed by the timetable?
3   Who are the members of the HR department to be involved?
4   What resources are required in HR or elsewhere to achieve policy changes?
5   What HR systems/technology changes are required?

10. Implementation strategies, feedback, monitoring

1   How will the various projects be monitored and reported to TU, workforce, to senior management.
2   What review procedures are in place? (frequency, who is involved, etc.).
3   Are there to be evaluation projects to test the assumptions made in the strategies?
4   Are there to be major change strategies? If so, is this to be handled as OD?
5   How much employee involvement is to be encouraged in strategy implementation?
6   Are there to be action/research/collaborative change methods?

REFERENCES

Ambrosini, V. and Bowman, C. (2009). 'What are dynamic capabilities and are they a useful construct in strategic management?' *International Journal of Management Reviews* 11, 1: 29–49.

Applebaum, E., Bailey, T., Berg, P. and Kalleberg, A. (2000). *Manufacturing Advantage: Why High Performance Systems Pay Off*. Ithaca, NY: ILR Press.

Barney, J. (1991). 'Firm resources and sustained competitive advantage'. *Journal of Management* 17, 1: 99–120.

Beer, M., Spector, B., Lawrence, P. R., Quinn Mills, D. and Walton, R. E. (1985). *A General Manager's Perspective*. Walton: The Free Press.

Bowman, C. and Ambrosini, V. (2003). 'How the resource based and the dynamic capability views of the firm inform competitive and corporate level strategy'. *British Journal of Management* 14: 289–303.

Dyer, L. and Schafer, R. A. (1999). 'From human resource strategy to organizational effectiveness, lessons from research on organizational agility'. *Research on Personnel and Human Resource Management*. Supplement 4 at 145–74. Stanford Ct.: JAI Press.

Dyer, L. and Schafer, R. A. (2003). 'Dynamic capabilities: Achieving market place and organizational agility' in R. S. Peterson and E. A. Mannix (eds). *Leading and Managing People in Dynamic Organizations*. Mahwah, N.J: Lawrence Erbraum Associates 7–40.

Hackman, J. R., Brousseau, K. R. and Weiss, J. A. (1976). 'The inter-action of task design and group performance strategies in determining group effectiveness'. *Organizational Behaviour and Human Performance*. Vol 16 at 350–65.

Hendry, C. and Pettigrew, A. (1990). 'The model of strategic change and human resource management'. *International Journal of Human Resources* 1, 1: 26.

Huselid, M. A. (1995). 'The impact of human resource management practices on turnover, productivity, and corporate financial performance'. *Academy of Management Journal* 38: 635–72.

Johnson, G., Scholes, K. and Whittington R. (2008). *Exploring Corporate Strategy*. (8th edn). Harlow: Prentice Hall/Pearson Education.

Kaplan, R. and Norton D. (1996). *The Balanced Scorecard: Translating Strategy into Action*. Boston, MA: Harvard Business School Press.

Mavrinac, S. and Siesfield, G. A. (1997). 'Measures that matter: An exploratory investigation of investors' information needs and value properties'. Ernst and Young Center for Business Innovation.

Moyo, D. (2011). *How the West Was Lost*. London: Allen Lane.

Parry, E. and Tyson, S. (2014). *Managing People in a Contemporary Context*. Abingdon, Oxford: Routledge.

Paauwe, J. (1998). 'HRM and performance: the linkage between resources and institutional context'. *RIBES Working Paper*, Erasmus University, Rotterdam.

Paauwe, J. (2004). *HRM and Performance*. Oxford: Oxford University Press.

Paauwe, J. (2009). 'HRM and performance: Achievements, methodological issues and prospects'. *Journal of Management Studies* 46, 1: 129–49.

Purcell, J., Kinnie, N., Hutchinson, S., Swart, J. and Rayton, B. (2003). *Understanding the People Performance Link: Unlocking the Black Box*. London: CIPD.

Teece, T. J., Pisano, G. and Shuen, A. (1997) 'Dynamic capabilities and strategic management'. *Strategic Management Journal* 18: 509–33.

Tyson, S. (1995). *Human Resource Strategy*. London: Pitman Publishing.

Wright, P., Dunford, B. B. and Snell, S. A. (2001). 'Human resources and the resource based view of the firm'. *Journal of Management* 27: 701–21.

7 WORKFORCE PLANNING

Workforce plans are produced following the overall strategic planning and the HR planning processes, which set out the specific quantitative plans and details of how the capability needed for the future realization of the corporate goals will be acquired and retained. The HR strategies discussed in the previous chapter provide the context, the firm's posture on competitive advantage, the direction of travel, and the assumptions and the reasoning behind the strategy. Workforce planning puts the facts and the figures on how the people who are part of the plan will achieve the objectives, and the options for developing and finding capability, and for using different kinds of contractual arrangements to bring this capability into the service of the organization.

All management is about decision-making in an environment of risk and uncertainty. Effective management aims to reduce the risk and uncertainty as far as this is possible in an imperfect world by the acquisition of the best available information and the use of a system. Improved HR information systems mean there is no reason why data driven decisions on HR planning should not be the basis for assessing risks, as we argued in Chapter 5. The expanding range of options available to organizations in the workforce profile widens the scope of workforce planning from the simple question: how many people do we need? to the more fundamental question: what capability does the organization need to remain competitive in the future period under review?

The first part of the chapter explains the workforce planning processes and for reconciling the forecast need ('the demand') for capability with the forecast supply of labour/capabilities. There seem to be two meanings to the term 'workforce planning'. It is used to describe the practical processes needed to ensure the people required are in place throughout the planning period. That is the subject of this chapter. The term is also used to mean the acquisition of capability, whatever its source, and the cost-effective utilization of labour through appropriate workforce strategies, shift systems and the allocation of people to tasks, adjusting the contractual relationship to the firm according to efficiency and effectiveness criteria. The flexible working issues raised are the subject of the next chapter.

The specific issues for workforce planning to examine are:

1   *Balancing the cost between the utilization of plant and workforce*: this involves comparing costs of these two resources in different combinations and selecting the optimum. This is especially important when costing projects.
2   *Determining needs for capability*: an essential prerequisite to the process of recruitment is to avoid problems of unexpected shortages, wastage, blockages in the promotion flow and needless redundancies. The company will also be aware of the pace of change, and the uncertainty of the future, and may therefore place a premium on workforce flexibility, encouraging the consideration of the non-standard type of employment contract, and other sources of capability, such as franchise arrangements, subcontracting, and the like.
3   *Determining training needs*: this is fundamentally important to planning training programmes, for which it is necessary to assess the types of skills, experience and attributes required in the future workforce, including not only quantity but also the quality of the skills required.
4   *Talent management and development:* a succession of trained and experienced personnel is essential to the effectiveness of the organization, and this depends on accurate information about present and future needs, careers and ways to identify and develop talented people.
5   *Productivity:* the business plan will, of necessity, make assumptions about productivity, and the human resource implications of mergers, acquisitions and divestment decisions will have an impact on the organization's employment relationships. In addition, there are some significant decisions and assumptions to be made about costs, including pay and benefit costs, the terms and conditions of service and the alternative ways of finding and using capability.

In this chapter we will concentrate on the demand and supply of labour and problems arising from the process of reconciling these factors. Any workforce planning system has to be based on analyses of demand and supply and the plans and decisions that follow these analyses.

A SYSTEM OF HUMAN RESOURCE PLANNING

Below are the main elements contained in the 10 point plan (as described as the end of the last chapter), when we establish what expansion, contraction or redeployment of people will be required over the planning period. The aspects of the HR strategy we are concerned with here, therefore, are:

1   Assessing future requirements to meet objectives (demand).
2   Assessing current resources and availability of resources in the future (supply), and applying a cost:value model to decide the most cost effective way to meet the need.
3   Producing and implementing the plan in detail, i.e. balancing forecasts for demand and supply, related to short-term and/or long-term timescales.
4   Monitoring the system and amending as indicated.

Figure 7.1 shows how workforce planning and human resource strategies can be devised. Strategic planning requires the planners to assess the national/international political, economic, social and technological trends (a PESTEL analysis), and to look at how their own organization is responding. The planners will also wish to assess the likely challenges and opportunities available – perhaps through using a SWOT analysis – looking at the strengths, weaknesses, opportunities and threats to the organization. Strengths and weaknesses are usually internal, whilst threats and opportunities are external.

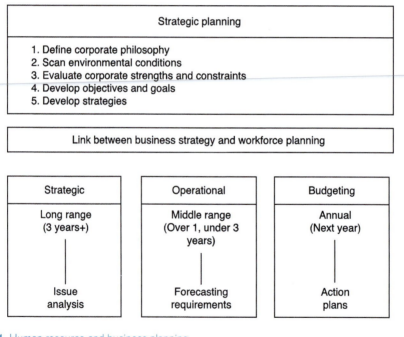

Figure 7.1 Human resource and business planning

IMPLEMENTING BASIC REQUIREMENTS FOR HUMAN RESOURCE PLANNING

Sound HR planning needs to be based on the following principles and actions:

1   It has to be fully integrated into the other areas of the organization's strategy and planning.

2   Senior management must give a lead in stressing its importance throughout the organization. Organizations are great store houses of information. The systematic collection of relevant data is now made easier by the use of new technology (see below), as stated earlier.

3   In some larger organizations, a central workforce planning unit responsible to senior management may be established. The main objectives of this unit could be to coordinate and reconcile the demands for human resources from different departments, to standardize and supervise departmental assessments of requirements and to produce a comprehensive organizational plan. In practice, the HR department would normally play a leading role in the task. In smaller organizations these responsibilities would probably be carried out by a senior member of staff, and could be by the person responsible for a particular business unit, such as the manufacturing manager or the production manager.

4   The time span to be covered by the plan needs to be defined. Because of the abiding problem of making forecasts, a compromise is often adopted in which a general plan is produced to cover a period of several years, and a detailed plan produced for the first year. If the system is operated as a continuous, overlapping plan, the three or five-year period of general forecasting could be maintained, and each first year is used in turn for purposes of review and revision for the future. The high degree of uncertainty in our environment has already been mentioned, arguably, this calls for attaching more importance to forecasting and scenario planning, even if the outcome of the exercises is the preparedness of the organization to respond quickly to new circumstances.

5   Forecasting for long periods ahead in the face of uncertainty results in a requirement for agility and versatility within HR strategic planning. Long term HR planning has been replaced by a move to the more flexible use of labour, and a preparedness to outsource and to invest in cheaper labour markets. A second response is to be more attentive to 'weak signals' from the business environment: to have a sensitivity to any signs in order to pick up new trends quickly.

Although the more capital intensive organizations may plan for longer periods, in most cases there are broad statements of strategic intent, with detailed plans for 12 months and increasingly generalized plans as each year goes out. For many situations, organizations find themselves 'muddling through'.

Planning techniques

The strategic plans are overall guides, but in our rapidly changing economic conditions, companies are moving from defined strategies, which are fixed for the period, to strategic options.

Whatever the approach to strategic planning, what matters is that the business strategists, involving the HR function, develop the list of key options for the business, along-side the HR implications. From this stage, specific strategies have to be selected. A number of techniques can be applied to help determine which strategy is most suitable. All require that the key criteria for success have been identified.

■ Ranking the options, whether or not they all have equal weight, allows the strategists to set out a priority order for actions, possibly keeping as many options still open for as long as possible.

■ Decision trees rank options by eliminating those which do not meet the criteria already predetermined.

■ Scenario planning helps managers to select options by matching them against prob-able future scenarios. Scenario planning is especially useful for uncertain environments.

Scenario building is not just based on a hunch, but tries to build plausible views of different possible futures for the organization based on groupings of key environ-mental influences and drivers of change which have been identified. The result is a limited number of logically consistent, but different scenarios which can be considered alongside each other.

Johnson and Scholes (1997: 103)

The scenarios examined could be, for example, the consideration of what the organization and the business model would look like in the event of any of the following happening:

■ major shifts in market conditions, such as a return to high inflation rates, or another euro zone crisis

■ the merger or acquisition of the company or of one of its competitors

■ relevant new technological developments, such as 3D printing

■ conflicts in areas which affect the business, for example wars in the Middle East.

The scope and details of the plan have to be determined. For large organizations, separate plans and forecasts may well be needed for various subsidiary units and functions. In smaller organizations one comprehensive plan will probably suffice for all employees. Where partic-ular skills or occupations are strategically important, in recruitment or development, special attention may be needed.

Workforce planning is reliant on data from the Human Resource Information System (HRIS). The advances in information technology now make more complex analysis possible, for example determining the likely causes of labour turnover, an analysis of applicant profiles to determine recruitment failures, the relationship between sickness absence and job satis-faction data, and the probable effects on labour turnover. The availability of cloud computing, such as 'private clouds' and of big data sets, has helped in this regard. HRIS can make a difference because organizations always collect lots of data, but in the past have not had the facility to bring the data together and to use it.

Glossary of terms

Cloud computing

The overall definition of 'cloud' is as a computing architecture, in which information can be accessed as a network. 'Cloud computing' is also used to mean a number of computers connected through a real time network.

Software as a service (SAAS)

The term 'cloud' also sometimes refers to a networked based service where the customer can use a provider's applications running on a 'cloud' infrastructure, accessible from a number of devices through a web browser.

Platform as a service

This is where customers pay a subscription to use a service and a platform for hosting applications and to produce new applications.

THE GAP ANALYSIS

The next stage is to make comparisons between the most probable situation required for people management in the planning period or at least the next two years, and then the present situation. The time period chosen is a function of the industry sector and the degree of volatility in the business environment, and the present situation. This looks at the gap between the current and the future needs (looking at hard to fill vacancies, talent management, strategic issues of long term capability and competitiveness, for example).

From this analysis, an understanding of the size, the profile and the key issues in the future requirements should emerge. The results should be expressed in both the likely numbers of the groups and of the capabilities needed. The results will be fed into the workforce plan and the strategy documentation. It is desirable to include those outcome measures that are to be used to determine the success of the plan.

Effectiveness measures can be defined as the extent to which HR policies and practices will give effect to the organization's objectives. Efficiency is the cost of the actions needed to do so.

RISK ASSESSMENT

Risk assessments can also be undertaken. An example of a risk assessment matrix is shown below in Table 7.1.

The severity of the risk is multiplied by the probability of the event occurring, to produce a score, where any total in excess of 6 is an unacceptable risk.

The value of the matrix is dependent upon whether those using it have a clear and commonly understood notion of what 'minor' and 'major', etc. mean, and on what basis the probability of the forecasted circumstances happening is assessed.

TABLE 7.1 RISK ASSESSMENT MATRIX. PROBABILITY OF CIRCUMSTANCES HAPPENING X SEVERITY OF RISK

Severity of risk	Extremely Improbable 1	Extremely Remote 2	Remote 3	Probable 4
Minor 1	Acceptable 1	Acceptable 2	Acceptable 3	Review 4
Major 2	Acceptable 2	Review 4	Review 6	Unacceptable 8
Severe 3	Acceptable 3	Review 6	Unacceptable 9	Unacceptable 12
Catastrophic 4	Review 4	Unacceptable 8	Unacceptable 12	Unacceptable 16

FORECASTS OF FUTURE REQUIREMENTS (DEMAND)

This task is concerned with estimating the quantity and quality of human resources needed to meet the objectives of the organization. Several methods of forecasting are in regular use, some of them simple and non-technical, others sophisticated and involving specialist statistical knowledge and skills. These include:

■ estimates based on managers' experience, opinions and calculations
■ statistical methods
■ work-study methods
■ forecasts based on measures of productivity.

In practice, these methods are often used in combination, especially in larger organizations. The essential features of each type are briefly summarized below:

1 *Estimates made by management*: this is the simplest method of assessment and is, therefore, the commonest method in use, especially in small organizations.

Assessments of this kind are provided from two main sources: the estimates submitted by individual line managers and the estimates produced by senior management, advised by the HR department. Since these forecasts rely entirely on personal judgements, they have an obvious potential weakness of subjectivity. However, this can be mitigated in the following ways: first, in submitting assessments, managers should include explanations, justifications and the strategic reasons to support their claims; second, these assessments 'from the bottom up', should be compared with those prepared by senior management, perhaps by an *ad hoc* staffing committee with the purpose of discussing and reconciling discrepancies.

2 *Statistical methods*: a number of statistical techniques are now used for forecasting, which vary in their degree of sophistication. Some of the techniques most often used are: simple extrapolation, which attempts to predict growth or decline of a variable or set of variables for a period of time; regression analysis, based on assumptions about the stability of certain relationships; and econometric models, in which past statistical data are studied on the assumption that relationships between a number of variables will continue in the future.

3 *Work-study methods*: work study is a systematic analysis of working methods, covering the people, skills, materials and machines, and in particular the work hours needed per output unit to achieve maximum productivity. Work-study data may be used to forecast productivity, detailed production schedules for specific periods of time within the plan, and to estimate the total numbers needed to achieve production targets within a specific period, with a given level of technology in use. The production schedules may comprise the following details: product quantities; production methods; machinery needed and available; times for individual operations; and quantity and quality of labour needed and available. Work-study techniques are particularly appropriate for estimating human resource requirements for work that is directed towards end products. Where the product mix and the forecast changes are too complex to use this approach, a simple added value method can be adopted (Example 7.1).

ASSESSMENT OF CURRENT RESOURCES AND AVAILABILITY OF RESOURCES IN THE FUTURE (SUPPLY)

Current resources

As a basis for estimating the future supply of people, an accurate account of the current situation is needed. Each organization has to decide for itself the quantity and quality of information it needs, but some broad bases can be established for analysing existing resources, namely, operational functions, occupations, status and skill levels, and other specific categories (for example, qualifications, trainees). Understanding the potential

EXAMPLE 7.1

Using an added value approach where the added value (at constant prices) has to be increased from £12 million per annum to £14 million per annum, what is the effect on the demand for employees?

Clearly a number of assumptions are made, about existing working practices, etc., but we can build in changes to our calculation:

Year 2013
Added value for the year = £12,000,000
Average no. of employees = 400 people
No. of weeks worked per annum = 46 weeks
Average hours per week = 35 hours
Total hours, per worker per week

$35 \times 46 = 1610$ work hours

Total work hours per annum

$400 \times 1610 = 644,000$ work hours

Productivity

$$\frac{£12,000,000}{644,000} = £18.633 \text{ per work hour}$$

Year 2018
Planned added value = £14,000,000
Productivity increase 5% = £19.564 per work hour
Required work hours

$$\frac{£14,000,000}{19.564} = 715,600.08 \text{ work hours}$$

No. of people required

$$\frac{£715,600.08}{1610} = 444.5 \text{ people}$$

However, if working hours are reduced further by one hour per week, and holidays increased by one week per year, the work hours change to the following amount, which changes the forecast numbers as shown:

$34 \times 45 = 1530$

$$\frac{£715,600.08}{1530} = 467.7 \text{ people}$$

effects of retirements can be enhanced by age profiles. However, age discrimination legislation reminds us that decisions based purely on age are no longer legally acceptable.

Operational functions

An initial count of all employees is made, based on divisions into functional units (for
example, sales department, store's branch, repair workshop, etc.). Specific categories
produced by subsequent analyses may be related to these units, if desired.

Occupations

Employees are categorized according to occupational groups. These categories may
usefully be related to strategically significant occupations and anticipated recruitment problems. Although broad homogeneous groupings will normally suffice, for certain key occupations detailed and specific categorizations may well be needed. In order to facilitate and
standardize the task of occupational analysis and definition, the Office of Population and
Censuses publishes the *Standard Occupation Classification* (*SOC*). The broad groupings
conventionally used for occupational analysis are managers, supervisors, professional staff,
technical staff, clerical staff, manual and other staff (skilled, semi-skilled and unskilled). For
the service sector, it may be better to keep to occupational titles, e.g. airline pilot, geolo-
gists, economists, etc.

Status and skill levels

To a certain extent, the categorization of employees by occupation also implies a categorization by status and level of skills. This kind of analysis is especially relevant to the task of
producing data for planning succession to senior levels.

Other specific categories

In addition to the basic kinds of analysis described above, it is normally necessary to
produce other types of information, especially for critical groups and occupations, such as
the qualifications of employees, and records of employees at the various stages of
development.

Apart from the purposes of workforce planning, an organization may be expected to
have detailed records of its employees, showing their qualifications, experience, particular
skills and aptitudes, which are relevant to its functions and objectives. On this basis the
organization can assess the strengths and weaknesses in its general pools of skills and
experience in particular areas, and will be in a good position to plan for recruitment and
selection, transfer or promotion, training, retirements, etc.

For the period to be covered by the plan, the analysis will project the flow of numbers
of employees passing through all forms of training programmes, both internal and external.

LABOUR TURNOVER

As human resource planning is an exercise in projecting likely future situations based on past trends, it is important to obtain information about those trends which indicate any significant changes. These data are invaluable as a background against which the forecasts produced by other methods already described may be finally assessed. The changes that are likely to be significant in workforce planning, and value analysis, are those that affect shifts in the relative numbers of employees in the various categories represented in the HR information system. A well known problem in organizations with high-cost operational goals, for example, is the tendency for administrative and supporting staff to grow disproportionately to the relatively small number of operational staff.

Labour turnover (wastage) has traditionally been calculated by the following formula:

$$\frac{\text{Number leaving in a year}}{\text{Average number of employees}} \times 100 = x\%$$

This index can be considerably distorted, however, by untypical features in the organization's employment pattern. For example, redundancies, acquisitions, and there is a value in researching voluntary turnover as an indicator of other problems. A significant element of wastage may be limited to a specific category, which may give a false impression of movement in an otherwise stable labour force. A commonly used guide to predict labour turnover in one part of the labour force is the Labour Stability Index, which is calculated by the formula:

$$\frac{\text{Number of employees exceeding one year's service}}{\text{Number of employees employed one year ago}} \times 100 = x\%$$

Even more sophisticated results can be obtained by the use of the actuarial/statistical techniques known as cohort and census analysis. In the same way that life expectancy for age groups can be actuarially assessed, a so-called survival curve can be graphically plotted to enable predictions to be made about the relationships between employees' length of service or age and rates of wastage.

Labour turnover is service and age specific. Hence we would expect a higher amount of wastage amongst new starters than within a stable work force.

Table 7.2 gives an example of a cohort analysis, drawn from the Civil Service, using the 'Markovian' wastage rate, which is calculated as follows:

$$\frac{\text{Number of leavers during the year}}{\text{Number of staff present at start of year}} \times 100 = \begin{array}{l}\text{probability that} \\ \text{staff will not be} \\ \text{present at year end}\end{array}$$

TABLE 7.2 AN EXAMPLE OF COHORT ANALYSIS

Length of service (completed years)	Survivors at start of period (I)	Leavers	Central wastage rate (M)	Markovian wastage rate (Q)	Mean strength
0	1000	113	0.120	0.113	943
1	887	161	0.200	0.182	806
2	726	144	0.220	0.198	654
3	582	55	0.100	0.095	554
4	527	31	0.060	0.059	511
5	496	24	0.050	0.048	484
6	472	18	0.040	0.038	462
7	454	13	0.030	0.029	446
8	441	13	0.030	0.029	433
9	428	13	0.030	0.030	420
10	415	12	0.030	0.029	408
11	403	12	0.030	0.030	396
12	391	391	(2.00)	1.00	195
13	0	0	0	0	0
Total		1000			6712

Expectation of service = 6712 ÷ 1000 = 6.7 years

Half life = 5 years (approx.)

Population surviving for 2 years: 73 per cent

Population surviving for 5 years: 50 per cent

Population surviving for 10 years: 42 per cent

Source: Smith and others (1976: 58).

Apart from wastage as a factor complicating human resource planning, any internal variations in working conditions, such as a reduction or increase in working hours or retirement age, will affect the situation.

Finally, there are external factors that also need to be taken into account when the availability of human resources is being considered. They may be categorized as macro- (national) or micro- (local) influences. At the macro level the commonly significant factors are:

1   The intervention by the state in the field of employment as a user and protector of the labour force in the form of employment legislation, regional development schemes, governmental and related agencies.

2   National trends affecting the working population such as, for example:

   (a)   the higher percentage of older people

   (b)   changes to the school leaving age

   (c)   the percentage of people pursuing courses of higher education, and the types degree or diploma courses

(d)   the variety of contractual arrangements available (part-time, job-sharing, etc.) is a reflection of the need for part time and flexible working arrangements

(e)   welfare and benefit policies, and those designed to reduce unemployment.

3   International recruitment possibilities (e.g. the recruitment of nurses for hospitals in the UK from outside the EU and from mainland European countries).

The important factors at micro level are:

1   The nature of the local population: numbers, growth or decrease, reserves of skills, availability of part-time labour, etc.

2   The level of unemployment and its location.

3   The competition from other employers.

4   The costs of labour, local premia and the ease of travel to the locations.

5   The attractiveness of the area to live in and the degree of development of the area, such as: accessibility, schools, medical facilities, costs of housing.

6   Plans of central and local government and other organizations that may significantly affect the area.

7   Types of transport links.

8   The reputation of the organization and how this is sustained.

THE PLANNING STAGE

The last stage, in which the plan is produced, is based on the information that the preceding stages have provided. This involves:

■   matching the forecasts for supply and demand

■   identifying key areas essential to the achievement of objectives

■   making plans to minimize the effects of possible shortages or excesses of staffing considering whether the best use is currently being made of the organization's human resources.

As we described earlier, situation planning is a technique that helps senior management to understand the various alternative possibilities by looking at the consequences of following different policy options. There are now a number of computer-based approaches with software available to represent the options graphically, such as those developed by the Institute for Employment Studies, which examine staffing systems – building in the variables that influence the numbers employed in any given hierarchy of positions and showing how variations, for example in labour turnover or in recruitment rates, influence the numbers employed in the different grades. The rates of change are sometimes called 'flows' and the numbers employed in the grades or jobs 'stocks'.

The simplified example of a bank's system shown in Figure 7.2 illustrates this. (In practice, there may be many different levels, not just three, and also cross-overs to other systems. The computer models can handle much greater complexity than is shown here.)

The flows (or rates) can be varied to show the effect on stock sizes or the stock sizes may be held constant to show the effect on the flows (rates) over the planning period. By varying such factors as these, and by introducing proposed policy changes within the planning exercise, such as age at retirement, the likely consequences in terms of the main policy options can be discovered before the organization is committed to any change.

Until the preliminary analyses have been made and the final plans formulated, no meaningful plans can subsequently be made for recruitment and training of staff. Finally, it is worth emphasizing once again that planning cannot guarantee any particular levels of success in ensuring that the right number of employees of the necessary quality will be provided to meet an organization's requirements. The most important benefits from HR planning are that any staffing restrictions on future operations can be avoided, and the

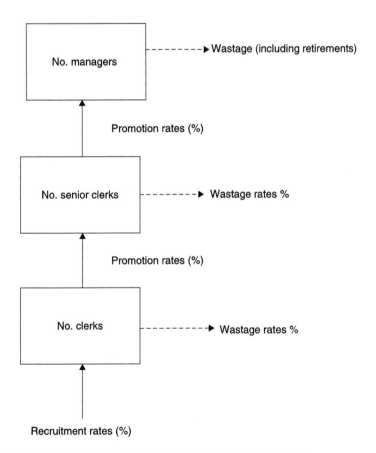

Figure 7.2 Computer models – forecasting based on a systematic relationship

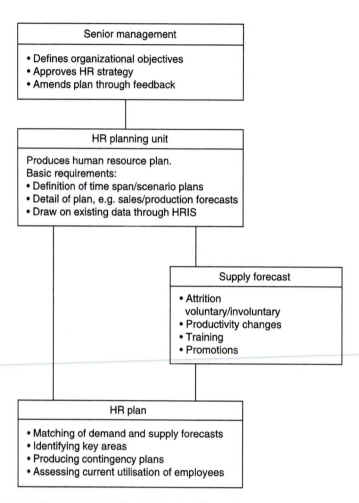

Figure 7.3 Summary of main elements of a system of workforce planning

strength of the organization's capabilities can be taken into account in the strategy (Figure 7.3). There should be a regular review at various periods throughout the life span of the plan. This review could be incorporated into an annual general review of corporate objectives, achievement, budget planning, etc., in accordance with the system for a running, overlapping plan, as already discussed.

QUESTIONS

1   The wastage (turnover) rate for a group of your sales representatives is high (25 per cent) whilst the stability index is low (5 per cent). What conclusions do you draw about this group of sales representatives? Do you have a major problem or not?

2   From a SWOT analysis, what do you see as the current risks facing your organization? How do you assess the work force planning risks deriving from your analysis?

3   Name the methods of forecasting demand commonly used, and comment on the advantages and disadvantages of each one described.

4   What are the main stages in producing the HR plan, comment upon how these plans are integrated with the overall business strategy?

REFERENCES

Johnson, G. and Scholes, K. (1997). *Exploring Corporate Strategy*. London: Prentice Hall.

Smith, A. R. and others (1976). *Manpower Planning in the Civil Service*. HMSO.

8 FLEXIBLE WORKING

One of the options facing those preparing an HR strategy is how to meet the economic and social challenges of the twenty-first century, where survival depends upon remaining responsive to a highly competitive market place, which is global in scope and subject to rapid change. In this chapter we examine flexibility strategies as one approach employers adopt to meet these challenges. These strategies are examples of the HR function creating a 'fit' between the business strategy, including the particular business model adopted by the company, and the HR policies and practices used to source the capability the company requires.

Economic challenges in the form of high employment costs in Western companies, compared to the large newly developed economies of China, Brazil and India and the rapidly developing economies of countries such as Indonesia, Turkey, South Korea and other Far Eastern countries mean there is a constant pressure on costs. New technology improvements have made it possible to service markets in high price areas of the world from economies where the labour supply is plentiful and relatively cheap. The UK and other high cost countries in the EU are also exposed to competition from European countries where wage costs are lower, but the quality of the work is as high as it is domestically. Arguably, in some countries, such as India and China, the quality of both manufacturing and services is better than in the West in some industries.

There are societal changes which also drive improvements demanded by customers – the 24/7 society, the desire for needs to be met quickly and expectations from customers of high quality. The range and innovation in goods and services puts continuous pressure on businesses to change.

Employers are therefore always looking for ways to reduce costs and to create a workforce capability that matches the needs of customers in the availability of products and services, and the needs for speed and customization. These aspects of competitiveness can only be delivered by smarter working practices, a flexible work force and innovativeness, often enabled by developments in new technology.

At the same time, some of the social changes are providing a need for a more flexible work/life balance on the part of employees. Women now constitute a larger proportion of the work force than before (excluding the Second World War). The UK economy would not be able to continue without a large workforce. More flexible working suits both men and women with child care responsibilities. Demographic change has put further demands on those who are working to care for elderly relatives for longer periods of time, a difficulty exacerbated by the fact that even if the state were able to provide this care itself, the costs of the provision would drive up taxes, so that both partners in a relationship would have to work more time to survive. There are also generational differences (Parry and Urwin 2011). The so-called 'Generation X', born 1965–1980, and 'Generation Y', who are sometimes called the 'Millenials', or the 'Nexters' are less interested in saving, and seek instant gratification, like informality. They seek a good work/ life balance, learn quickly, and are at home with the latest technology. These generations, one might anticipate, are more interested in task time than clock time, are more prepared to do two or more part-time jobs simultaneously, are flexible in their attitudes and expect flexible opportunities in the labour market. For HR, there would always be a need for flexibility in policies and working arrangements, without the financial crash. These employees are, of course, also the customers of companies; they need flexible working in their dealings with others, in an online society.

FLEXIBLE WORKING

Flexibility policies can be viewed as being of strategic importance, in so far as sourcing, customer relationships, responsiveness to new demands and to new technologies, and new business opportunities are concerned. Sourcing is affected by the capacity to recruit from different labour markets, for example by being able to recruit women returners to work after maternity, and to reflect social diversity in the organization. Customers increasingly demand service at weekends and at later hours, or to be available over holiday periods. New technology offers employers and employees opportunities for flexibility of location, and of time. Contractual flexibility, including part time working and franchise and subcontracting arrangements, provide new business opportunities and different cost platforms. There is therefore flexibility of time, of task, of contract and of location.

HOURS OF WORK

The hours of work for any job are a result of tradition, collective bargaining, technical necessity, convenience for management control and for communication needs. There are some people, such as sales representatives, for whom there may be no normal hours of work.

The distinction should be drawn between 'basic hours' and the normal hours worked, which may include overtime. For some of the major industries, the basic hours are subject to negotiation between employees and trade unions at a national level. When thinking of basic hours, we have to be sure of what is included: for example, does the time include tea breaks, lunch breaks, time for starting machinery, for cleaning up, etc?

Overtime is more common in the UK, where until recently around 16 per cent of employees worked more than 48 hours a week, which is more than in other European countries. As a way of bolstering earnings in low-paid jobs it is clearly an unsatisfactory approach by which whole occupational groups and management come to rely on longer hours. The tendency to use overtime as a common way to flex labour in response to changes in demand is diminishing, in preference for changed working time arrangements.

There is legislation in the UK covering the permitted hours of work for women and young people, and for occupational groups such as drivers, for health and safety reasons. There is also European-wide legislation on hours of work. A summary of the main rules is given below.

The Working Time Directive came into force in the UK on 1 October 1998. This stipulates a 48 hour week, four weeks' paid holiday per year, weekly rest periods of at least 24 consecutive hours every seven days, a daily rest break of at least 20 minutes during a working day of six hours or more and a daily rest period of 11 consecutive hours in every 24 hour period.

The rules about working times are complex. Air, road and seafaring workers are excluded from the rules. All those on a contract of employment are included, but a minimum of 13 weeks' service is required and the genuinely self-employed are excluded. Exemptions are few. For example, partners are exempt (but not solicitors), as are very senior autonomous workers. Under Regulation 21 certain provisions are excluded in specific circumstances, for example, where there is a need for continuity of service or production, such as hospitals, prisons or the media.

The calculation of the average weekly hours is over a 17-week reference period. If an employee or employer opts out of the 48 hour week, for special reasons, the employer or the employee must keep a daily record of the hours worked. Night workers cannot opt out, and their average normal hours should not exceed eight hours for each 24 hour period. Night workers are entitled to a free medical assessment.

Holiday pay may be accrued and paid at the termination of employment. The regulations only deal with minimum leave entitlement. Regulations are enforced through employment tribunals.

There are many variations in hours, according to industry, occupation and, of course, where there is shift working or where flexible hours or zero hours contracts are used. These three aspects of hours are worthy of special attention.

DEFINITIONS: FORMS OF FLEXIBILITY

Flexibility of time

Weekend work – working Saturday and/or Sunday.

Shift working – working one of a set of consecutive periods into which a 24 hour working day is divided.

Overtime – extra time beyond employees' normal time, added on to a day or shift.

Annual hours contract – agreement to work number of hours annually.

Zero hours contracts – on call arrangements with an employer, where employees are only paid if they work.

Part-time work – hours of work defined as part-time by employer or legislation.

Flexi-time – some working hours may be determined by employees, around a fixed 'core' time.

Compressed working week – totals a standard number of hours compressed into a reduced number of shifts.

Flexibility of contract

Temporary/casual – workers employed on a temporary basis for a number of hours, weeks or months.

Fixed-term contracts – workers employed for a fixed number of months or years.

Home based work (flexibility of location, hours and contract) – workers whose normal workplace is home but who do not have permanent electronic links to a fixed workplace.

Teleworking (technology based) – workers who can link electronically to a fixed workplace.

Flexibility of task and of time

Job-sharing – dividing up one job between two or more employees.

Flexibility of task

Job enrichment – including performing some of the work of the supervisor in the work of the employee, sometimes by acting in the other's role when the other is away.

Job enlargement – taking a broader range of skills into the job, so the employee can cover more different types of work. Taking in work from those in similar roles or in less skilled work as well as own skilled work.

SHIFT WORKING

Shift working is introduced to make more efficient use of machinery, to increase production, or because the customers, the service user's market or the technology require continuous staffing. There are five main types of shift working, as shown in Table 8.1

TABLE 8.1 EXAMPLE OF SHIFT-WORK PATTERNS

Shift type	Hours per shift	Typical start times and finish times	Cycle
Double day	8 hours per day	06.00–14.00; 14.00–22.00	2 groups of workers rotate each week, early/late shift
Day and night alternating	10 in 24 hours	08.00–18.00; 22.00–08.00	2 groups of workers alternating weekly or fortnightly, with rest days in between
Permanent nights	11 in 24 hours	18.30–05.30	2 groups of workers, 2-week cycle, with rest days: 3 rest days after 1st week, 2 rest days after 2nd week
3-shift discontinuous	8 in 24 hours	06.00–14.00; 14.00–22.00; 22.00–06.00 Monday to Friday inclusive	Weekly or fortnightly for the 3 groups of employees
3-shift continuous	8 in 24 hours	As above, but 7 days Monday to Sunday inclusive	4 groups of employees' cycle for 3–24 weeks. 1. Traditional pattern: one week of each type for each person, with rest days; 2. 'Continental' pattern: 2 or 3 shifts of the same kind, with rest days in between

In addition to these shift patterns, there are different forms of part-time working used, and mixtures of the systems outlined in Table 8.1; for example, one part of a factory may be working, say, permanent nights, whilst another part operates a 'twilight shift' from 16.00 to 22.00.

Shift working leads to problems with domestic and social life for many employees, and may give rise to health worries. Most of our lives seem to be structured to a working existence where 8.00 to 17.30 is the norm. In the provision of children's schooling, travel and services, the assumption of daytime working is made. There are trends towards more 24 hour shopping, and telephone banking, which are gearing people's lives to a different style. Although there may be compensation in being at home when others are at work, partners and children can be upset by the irregularity of hours and absences in the evening. The change of the shift cycle from days to nights, and then back again, disturbs the bodily functions – the circadian rhythms of heart, respiration, body temperature, blood pressure and digestion. 'Stress' manifested in sleeplessness, digestive disorders and even depression may therefore be felt by some shift workers.

The research on the effects of shift work on health is inconclusive so far, but it is possible that some people are better able to accept the disturbance of different shift cycles than others. The extent to which the shift worker's family accepts the pattern of the hours, and whether or not the worker is psychologically prepared to accept the changes, may be the key factors.

There are also managerial problems with shift work. Communications between the members of each shift are often inaccurate; the night-shift personnel may feel left out or come to regard themselves as a separate unit. Friction between the shifts can arise from apparently trivial incidents, such as the cleaning up of machinery or failure to report a new technical problem. It follows, therefore, that management must make a special effort in:

- training managers in the special problems of shift work
- attending to shift workers' communication problems, for example, by working along with shift supervisors and using written communications
- the provision of welfare, occupational health and catering facilities, such as canteens, social clubs, etc., which cater for the needs of the shift worker.

CLOCK TIME AND TASK TIME

Hours of work are not important to those whose activities are directed towards the accomplishment of tasks, irrespective of when they occur. To use Berne's terms, we can distinguish between 'clock time' and 'task time'. Attendance at work at particular times may be essential for jobs that provide a service to others, but for other posts where there is an amount of work that has to be completed, quite apart from the time, attendance can be more flexible. It may also be possible only to pay people when 'called out' to work – that is, to employ them on zero hours contracts. The development of a more flexible approach to working hours stems from the desire of employees to avoid rigid time-keeping and for employers to meet the needs of customers and to overcome the difficulties that employers have in recruiting and retaining staff in some areas.

New technology in the form of laptops and online facilities has revolutionized the way work is done and, just as significant, where work is done. Home-working and flexible contracts fit together well for some people, where work may be completed in the evening or at weekends at home without any loss of efficiency. There are potential gains – by working at home and avoiding wasteful journeys to and from work, more productive hours are available and capable staff whose contribution would otherwise be restricted through childcare, care of the elderly or through disability are able to work, and creativity is encouraged. However, home-working does potentially reduce the socializing benefits of congregating with fellow workers and, in spite of teleconferencing, makes meetings less easy to attend and to run. Home-working for managers who also go to the office may create a situation where work becomes intrusive in the home.

FLEXIBLE WORKING HOURS

The basic principles of flexible working hours have been described by Baum and Young (1973: 19) as: 'The essential aim of the flexible working day is to replace the traditional fixed times at which an employee starts and finishes work by allowing him/her a limited choice in deciding his/her starting and finishing time each day.'

A 'core time' (see Figure 8.1) is established by the employer when attendance is required – usually the middle period of the day, excluding the meal break. The start and finish times are variables on either side of this. The contract between the employer and the employee fixes the number of daily contracted hours, which are assessed over periods of from one week to one month. The employee thus starts and leaves work at times that are convenient for him or her, times which can vary day by day to suit his or her own circumstances. When an employee works longer than the contracted daily hours a credit is carried forward or, if he or she works less, a debit. The period over which the employee is expected to balance debits and credits is known as the 'accounting period', and can be a week, two weeks, four weeks or a calendar month. The idea was pioneered in Germany, but has now spread to the UK, where there are a number of different types of flexible working hours (FWH) schemes in operation. Electronic recording equipment is used because of the necessity for large numbers of accurate records to be processed.

As an illustration of the variety of schemes, we can note that there are those that have flexibility over the lunch break, and there are different approaches to the amount of core time, the total debits and credits allowed to accumulate, the length of the accounting period and the methods of calculating holidays and overtime.

In the case of Figure 8.1, the employee may start any time between 7.00 and 10.00, and the time of leaving is flexible from 16.00 to 18.00. He or she must take at least half an hour for lunch between 12.00 and 14.00.

A further refinement is used where the employee can carry credits over to the following accounting period, and these can be put towards holiday entitlement. The company would need to have agreed a formula for credit leave units, which could be half or whole days based on the number of contracted hours per day.

A company policy on the 'core time', the accounting period and how credits and debits will be dealt with should be thought out well in advance. Questions about how overtime is to

7.00	8.00	9.00	10.00	11.00	12.00	13.00	14.00	15.00	16.00	17.00	18.00
				Core time				Core time			

Figure 8.1 An example of a flexible working hours scheme

be calculated, what to do about domestic crises, the problem of part-time staff and explanations about the equipment on which records will be kept must be dealt with early on in the planning. Communication about the scheme needs expert handling with extensive consultation beforehand, and the role of the first-line supervisor is crucial in this process.

The overriding constraint on FWH schemes is the needs of the business, and there will be many occupations where it is not practical. Flexible working hours schemes seem to be most used where there are large numbers of administrative staff, such as in national and local government departments and large insurance companies, and the benefits of the scheme for recruitment in tight labour markets are clear.

Flexible working hours should be distinguished from agreements made between employers and trade unions to work a total number of hours per year, the precise start and finish times to be decided by management. Such annualized hours contracts allow organizations to match closely the amount of labour to market demands. This is helpful, for example, so that there is sufficient labour to meet the peaks in a seasonal demand. Annual hours agreements give control to management over working time, the flexibility is at their discretion, whereas flexible working hours are (within limits) under the control of the employee.

ZERO HOURS CONTRACTS

Zero hours contracts create an 'on call' arrangement between the employer and the employee. Under this arrangement, there is no obligation on the employer to provide work for the employee. The employee agrees to be available for work as and when required, so that no particular number of hours or times of work are specified. The employee is expected to be on call, and receives compensation only for the hours worked.

National Minimum Wage regulations require staff to be paid the minimum wage for the time they are at the work place, even if there is no work to do. Although there is no guaranteed work, employees on these contracts may be required to obtain permission from their employer before obtaining other work.

There has been considerable growth in the numbers of people on this type of contract. The CIPD reported in August 2013 that 1 million workers (around 3–4 per cent of the workforce) were on zero hours contract. UK employers such as McDonalds, Sports Direct and J D Wetherspoon are said to make extensive use of these arrangements. From the WERS survey in 2011, around 8 per cent of employers used these contracts.

STRATEGIC USE OF FLEXIBILITY

An analysis of the data on flexible working practices reveals a number of associations between the data, from which we may see patterns in the use of flexible working and bundles of practices which are associated together (Croucher and Mills 2004):

- non-established workers – part time, job share, temporary or casual, fixed term contracts
- extended hours – weekend working, shift work, overtime
- flexible hours – job share, flexi-time, compressed work week
- remote working – home based, tele-working.

These factors, which emerged from a factor analysis, showed that employers adopting one practice in the bundle have a high probability of using the others in the bundle, implying that there are distinct labour market strategies, which may, of course be dictated by specific contextual conditions. Atkinson proposed in 1984 that flexible strategies would revolve around a core of permanent, stable employees, so that employers could flex their labour in accord with demand. The evidence here suggests that employers adopt a range of flexible strategies owing to a mixture of demand led and sourcing needs.

HOLIDAY ENTITLEMENT

Employees now have a right to four weeks' paid holiday a year. The main difference is between rules under which the employee has to build up his or her entitlement first, by working for the full 'holiday' year, and schemes where the employee can anticipate his or her completion of a year's service.

The holiday entitlement year is the year during which entitlement is built up. This may be the same as the calendar year, or based on 'financial', 'accounting' or other 'years'. Factory shutdowns were common in some industries for the whole holiday period, for example, the 'Wakes Week' in northern England, and where there are localized traditional days such as the 'Glasgow Fair'. There are often good technical reasons for a total shutdown, which provides time for essential overhauls and maintenance on the factory buildings. Shutdowns also avoid difficulties where the work is so interlinked that staggered holiday arrangements would not be practical.

OFFSHORING

The growth of international business operations has introduced further levels of complexity to workforce planning and a new set of choices about where and by which organizations tasks are performed. The choices of 'offshoring' and 'onshoring' are also the result of cost pressures. There are opportunities not previously available to build a competitive advantage where the business is in a high wage area, while its workforce is located in a low wage area.

Definitions are important to help understanding in this field. We will draw on the work of Rilla and Squicciarini (2011), where they helpfully review the research on this topic.

Offshoring

This is defined as activities that are moved or relocated to a country other than the company's home country. This is also known as 'outsourcing abroad' by the OECD. This usually requires moving tasks and having capability, and working in a coordinated way across national borders.

Outsourcing

Increasing efficiency by moving some work to other businesses who have specialized capability.

Captive offshoring

Work which is undertaken by vertically integrated affiliates, or by partner companies that are located in another country.

Insourcing

'Goods supplied by the parent firm to the foreign subsidiaries – or vice versa – on an inter firm basis' (Jahns and others 2006), as quoted in Rilla and Squicciarini 2011: 396.

The reasons often quoted for offshoring are:

■   to reduce costs
■   as an alternative to purchasing products from outside providers
■   inability to find or attract the talent needed from the home labour market
■   research and development offshoring and outsourcing in locations where there are innovators, sources of capability and technology.

Companies that are involved in outsourcing need to be supportive, with appropriate information technology systems and processes involved, to be skilled at organizing international teams, and to have senior managers who are enthusiastic about offshoring strategy.

TEMPORARY ORGANIZATIONS

An option which is available to consider when planning a work force is the creation of a temporary organization. The main characteristic of a temporary organization is its time-bound nature, where people are employed to achieve specific and particular outcomes which are in a separate structure. These temporary types of organizations are becoming more common. Examples include (inter alia) film-making, entertainment events, sports events (such as the Olympics), but also in software development, advertising, television broadcasting, fashion, theatre, the construction industry and consultancy (Bakker 2010).

For HRM, the teams involved must be able to work in harmony quickly, and leadership is critically important. Leaders must be able to create 'quick trust', and to have authority to act swiftly. They need to be purposeful, well organized and skilled in project management.

The benefits of temporary structures for the workforce plan are that specific time-bound work can be accomplished by a dedicated group, in a separate structure with no commitment to continued employment beyond that task, provided they are dedicated to the task and have high quality leaders and a clear goal. There are, however, potential problems with the connection back into the host organization, so that budget control and the robustness of the common culture and values will be very significant for success. The down side of flexible working is discussed in Chapter 22.

There is evidence of the growth of 'non-standard' working arrangements (including hours of work), across Europe. A recent EU report shows the range of these arrangements on a continuum from the informal sector, to the very atypical arrangements (short-term, fixed-term contracts), part-time, zero hours and on call work, through to self-employed and to the 'standard', indefinite, full time contract. Depending on the definition used the 'non-standard' type of employment may account for around 30–40 per cent of employment in the UK. Different forms of non-standard contract are to be found in the various countries in Europe. The countries where these arrangements are prevalent and well embedded were Austria, Germany and the UK. Additionally, around 10.5 per cent of the workforce in the UK were on short-term, part-time work. Zero hours contracts were used for around 5 per cent of the workforce in the UK (IES/European Working Conditions 2010).

If the self-employed and the many other forms of non-standard working arrangements are taken into account, there are now almost as many on non-standard contracts as there are on standard ones. This has major implications for HRM. The options for using different contractual relations have never been greater, which also assists in creating flexible, agile organizations. This changes the world of work fundamentally.

QUESTIONS

1   Which forms of flexible working are suitable for different kinds of business?
2   What are the benefits and the disadvantages for the main types of non-standard, flexible working arrangements, for the company and for the employee?
3   Which HRM policies are affected most by the move to flexibility of working?
4   How do you anticipate changes to technology over the next decade will affect the types of flexible working offered?

For further evidence and discussion on Flexible Working Arrangements, consult the companion website to this book.

REFERENCES

Bakker, R. M. (2010). 'Taking stock of temporary organization forms: A systematic review and research agenda'. *International Journal of Management Reviews*, 12, 4: 466–86.

Baum, S. J. and Young, W. E. (1975). *A Practical guide to Flexible Working Hours*. London: Kogan Page.

Croucher, R. and Mills, T. (2004). 'Trends in time and locational flexibility in British organizations'. 1989–2004. *Paper for Department of Trade and Industry*, London.

IES (2010). *European Working Conditions Observatory*. Document ID: TN08120195. Institute of Employment Studies/Eurofund. 5 March 2010.

Jahns, C., Hartmann, E. and Bals, L. (2006). 'Off-shoring: dimensions and diffusion of a new business concept'. *Journal of Purchasing and Supply Management*, 12: 218–31.

Parry, E. and Urwin, P. (2011). 'Generational differences in work values: A review of theory and evidence'. *International Journal of Management Reviews*, 13: 79–96.

Rilla, N. and Squicciarini, M. (2011). 'R&D (Re) location and offshore outsourcing: A management perspective'. *International Journal of Management Reviews*, 13, 4: 393–413.

PART THREE

RECRUITMENT AND SELECTION

9 JOB ANALYSIS: DEFINING PERFORMANCE

Defining what employees need to do in order to perform their work effectively, and hence to make a contribution to the achievement of organizational aims and objectives, is of fundamental importance for managing human resource systems, which exist to locate and engage the resources needed. We saw in the previous chapters that HR strategy depends upon an understanding of what is meant by effective performance to meet objectives. The definitions of effective work performance provide the criteria or standards against which recruitment success, development success and the employees' rewards, promotion and personal success are measured.

This chapter is concerned with the answers to the following three issues:

■ How to conduct an analysis of jobs in order to reveal what is required for high performance, in terms of the competencies which underpin the firm's dynamic capabilities?
■ How to identify the enduring competency requirements, which are central to the company's culture and identity?
■ How to express competences using behavioural terms that are measurable?

The techniques applied in job analysis are expected to help determine what competences are needed in the company now and in the foreseeable future. This helps to establish how the requirements for effective performance should be expressed in job advertisements, and which applicants appear to meet these requirements.

This will also be useful data to help newly appointed employees in the induction stage to meet the firm's requirements.

THE COMPETENCY APPROACH

The term 'competences' has come to be used to describe the attributes necessary for effective performance. Competences can be purely role-related, or be a mix of personal and job attributes. In the case of the connection of personal and current job attributes, competences can be used to assess the potential for future roles. Competences can be highly specific, as we suggest here, for use in a person specification, or they can be generic, that is, general for certain types of work (for example, managerial work at different levels) for an organization. Many companies use competences as the touchstone for talent management and for the whole human resource system so that recruitment, appraisal, training and development are all based on a common standard of effective performance.

In a series of 51 HRM audits, Tyson and Doherty (1999) found that 95 per cent of organizations used competency systems for their managerial staff, around 80 per cent for clerical level staff and 75 per cent for manual staff. These schemes were in all cases used for development and training, in around 88 per cent of cases for performance appraisal, 80 per cent for recruitment and in 58 per cent of cases for rewards.

DYNAMIC CAPABILITIES

In our discussion on HR strategy, we identified three dynamic capabilities as being critical for organizations to be successful in the current highly competitive market place. These are:

- change capability
- learning capability
- innovative capability.

These capabilities are organizational, but are, of necessity, also part of employees' attributes, as employees provide the impetus to influence corporate performance. Just as human capital can be seen as an individual phenomenon, or as an organizational attribute, so competency is both individually and collectively manifested.

Change capability we described as being achieved through the agility of the organization. The competences employees need in order to make organizations agile are not particular skills but are more associated with attitudes or states of mind. Reed and Stoltz (2011) express something similar in their idea of the 'mindset' of potential employees as being of the greatest importance. From their research they describe the top 20 qualities that companies look for in employees, which include in the top 10 qualities such as honesty and commitment, but also adaptability, accountability and flexibility. Employers have long valued the attitudes of employees who can be relied on to do their utmost, in whatever job they are given. This is found in the often quoted maxim of 'recruit for attitude, train for skill' – implying that skills can be acquired through the training system, but the overall attitude to work cannot.

Employee attributes we would expect to find in the agile company employee include resilience, flexibility in attitude and the classic organizational citizenship behaviours of willingness to exert discretionary effort and being an enthusiastic advocate for the company in dealings with others outside the business. Of course, agility is concerned with organizational capabilities, especially a passion for the products and services offered by the company and a strong desire to be as close to the market place as possible, to adapt swiftly to changing customer requirements.

Learning capability and innovative capability are linked as, indeed, are change and learning capability. Organizational learning derives from amassing knowledge from outside and from inside the company. The RBV argues that competitive advantage is gained from firm attributes such as systems and processes of working which integrate, review and reconfigure the organization, helping the firm to renew itself in the face of constant challenges from a global market place. This requires learning capability, which will both bring new knowledge into the firm, from exploration of the field of knowledge, and learning to work smarter, to improve routines and processes, by exploiting existing assets and tacit knowledge within the firm more effectively. Bringing knowledge into the firm requires a capability to innovate and use new ideas. Exploiting existing knowledge is also part of the change capability, since it means leveraging experience and expertise. In this way learning is a dynamic capability, which should be manifested in the competency of employees who have the opportunity to influence competitive advantage (Easterby-Smith and Prieto 2008).

The speed of learning is related to the level of intelligence of staff. However, as we discussed in Chapter 1, there are many different kinds of intelligence – emotional, spatial, practical, and so on. Competency clusters used in determining high performance will inevitably major on the intelligence required to perform work at a high level, whatever type of intelligence this uses.

MANAGERIAL COMPETENCIES

Managerial competencies usually consist of lists of competences (sometimes devised from research within the organization, sometimes from a focus group or from the executive) with accompanying definitions. The following list, drawn from a large retail bank, illustrates managerial competences:

- achievement motivation
- complex thinking
- customer-service orientation
- developmental ability
- delegation
- technical expertise
- flexibility

- initiative
- interpersonal sensitivity
- organizational awareness
- relationship-building
- self-confidence
- self-control
- team leadership.

Competence can be defined at different levels. Taking the competency 'delegation' from the above list, there were four levels defined (1 low to 4 high), as in the following example.

EXAMPLE 9.1 DELEGATION

Definition: Allocates tasks to others, making full use of resources and skills available. Knows to whom can delegate and how best to delegate, to ensure delivery to expectation. Makes objectives and expectations clear to others.

Levels:

1 Delegates discrete tasks with clear rules on how they should be completed. Gives clear instructions, telling the individual exactly what to do. Sets a specific deadline and reviews process at regular intervals when the task has to be completed over time.

2 Delegates discrete tasks with some discretion over how they are completed. Sets achievable short-term objectives for others, clarifying the standards required and setting the time parameters for the work. Makes occasional checks on progress and formally reviews at key milestones.

3 Delegates complex tasks that need further delegation. Defines the problem for others, and explains the context and surrounding issues. Sets the priorities to attend and be attended to and then leaves the individual to complete the task as appropriate.

4 Delegates complex and problematic issues to be resolved by others, first having agreed the issues to be tackled through discussion and consultancy. Delegates some account-ability, keeping an overview through management information.

Competences can be used to produce different role profiles. For example, a large pharmaceutical company produced a job profile and a spidergram (Figure 9.1) for sales management roles, showing where the individual's competences matched those required and where they were deficient.

There are software systems that produce the competency clusters and plot a spider-gram for each individual, based on appraisal and other data stored about each person's competence.

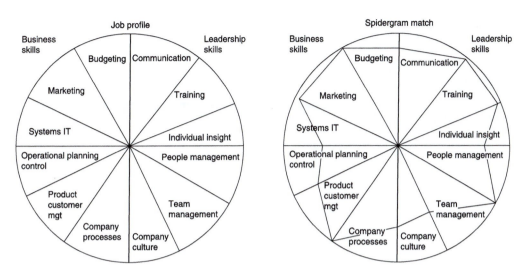

Figure 9.1 Job profile showing competencies for a sales manager in pharmaceuticals

If any job, no matter how simple or complex, is analysed, it will become apparent that the requirements for effective performance can be described in four interdependent, overlapping categories, which are: knowledge, skills, attitudes and personal attributes. Whilst skill and knowledge are necessary, they are not sufficient for success. High performance that is sustainable requires appropriate attitudes, traits and motives. For example, the effectively performing lawyer could be said to need knowledge of the law and court procedures and customs, skills in relating to a variety of people, particular skills in advocacy; together with attitudes and personal attributes such as honesty, integrity, conscientiousness, care, patience, calm temperament, etc.

Competence in performance sometimes tends to be considered mainly in terms of professional aspects, that is, knowledge and skills. But the personal qualities that an employee brings to a job may make all the difference between success and failure, as we discussed in regard to emotional intelligence. Of what use to an employer, for example, is the employee who is professionally the most proficient member of the work group, but at the same time has a disruptive influence because of an uncooperative attitude and surly demeanour, and is a constant source of friction with colleagues and clients? In researching within the organization to establish the competences, and the definition, the best practice is to examine low, average and high performers' behaviour, to show precisely what succeeds in the organizational context. For example, team leadership could be taken from the bank's list above, as follows in Example 9.2.

EXAMPLE 9.2   TEAM LEADERSHIP

Definition: The desire and ability to take on responsibility and the role of leader. Values team-working as a means of achieving objectives; the ability to develop team effectiveness by encouraging team members' participation, creating an environment of integrity and profession-alism; communicating and being supportive; setting an open climate and engendering pride.

Average performer

Clearly communicate goals. Provides clear accountabilities, and empowers the team. Invites all the team members to contribute their ideas. Gives specific feedback, and praises individuals and the team as a whole.

Star performer

Identifies any sources of conflict and facilitates resolution. Sets an example, by actions, as well as words. Congratulates and publicly takes pride in the team's achievements. Creates an open climate, which encourages change.

The criteria for effective performance are established by the process known as job analysis. Job analysis can be conducted for a variety of reasons. First, it can be used to establish what is required for recruiting purposes; second, as part of a development programme, to discover competences and attributes of high performance and, third, as part of job evaluation, to determine rewards. Sometimes the same definition is known by different names. Semantic distinctions are unimportant, however. For selection, two specific-ations are required: one to describe the job, its component tasks and competences; the other to describe the requirements for effective performance in the kind of personal terms mentioned above (this may well be a combination of competences/personal attributes). We shall call one 'the job description' and the other 'the person specification'.

For managerial-level work, the role requirements are likely to be mostly personal. For lower-level jobs the tasks are more likely to be significant (as in the National Vocational Qualification approach), which means a more person-centred approach for senior roles and a more task-centred one for others.

The lists below are intended to give a general guide to indicate the kind of information that job analysis needs to provide as a basis for the various functions of HR management.

JOB DESCRIPTION

1   *Basic data*: Exact title and grade (if applicable). Numbers engaged in the job. Location(s).

2   *Purpose*: Objectives and relationship to the aim of the organization.

3   *Tasks*: Main tasks and key areas. Occasional tasks. Secondary duties. Hours of work.

4   *Measurable targets:* For achievement.

5   *Competencies*: These combine standards for effective performance of tasks, the criteria indicating that tasks have been effectively performed with levels of knowledge, skills to perform the tasks.

6   *Responsibilities/accountabilities*: Position of job in organization structure. Managers/ supervisors to whom job holder is accountable. Subordinate staff for whom job holder is responsible. Responsibilities for:
    (a)   finance
    (b)   materials, equipment, etc.
    (c)   information.

7   *Physical and social environment:* Particular features of work environment (e.g. sedentary, static, indoor–outdoor, mobile, dirty, hazardous, etc.). Contacts with others (e.g. small/large groups, isolated, external contacts, etc.).

8   *Development/education:* Training planned to bring new job holders to required levels of performance (e.g. induction programme, job rotation, visits, external courses, etc.). In-job training and educational courses normally associated with the job.

9   *Advancement opportunities:* Opportunities open to job holders for promotion and career development.

10 *Conditions of employment:* Salary and other emoluments and benefits such as pension schemes. Possible overtime requirements. Sickness schemes. Welfare, social and other facilities. Leave entitlement. Any special employment conditions applying to the job.

11 *Job circumstances:* Aspects of the job commonly accepted as pleasant or unpleasant, easy/demanding.

PERSON SPECIFICATION

1   Competences required, including knowledge, skills, attitudes and personal attributes.

2   Specific qualifications (if any are needed).

3   Previous experience (if any is needed).

4   Health (general and specific requirements/ demands, reasonable adjustments that could be made).

5   Special conditions (e.g. travel, unsocial hours, etc.).

Any requirements included under the heading 'health' or fitness may vary considerably from one organization to another. In some occupations, such as the armed forces and the police, the standards of health required are necessarily stringent and high. Health is also an issue in occupations such as drivers of passenger and heavy goods trains and vehicles, airline pilots, sports teachers and many others. If we include 'stress resistance', a massive range of occupations could also be included.

The job description and the person specification are both necessary and complementary definitions. Of the two, however, the person specification is immediately important, since it provides the criteria for assessing effective performance affecting, as we have already seen, the main functions involved in the management of people at work, and in particular is the basis for job advertisements and candidate details. The job description has a wider, longer term applicability and can be used in various formats, for appraisal and objective-setting, development reviews, etc., and with some additional information for evaluation exercises.

Because all jobs in various ways require knowledge, skills, appropriate attitudes and personal attributes, it may be useful to use these headings as the initial basis for analysing the job, to produce the person specification. The information that this analysis reveals can then be adapted to suit preferred formats. Starting the analysis on this basis is systematic and logical and has the following advantages:

1   Attention is focused immediately on the essential requirements for effective performance.
2   This approach provides the criteria for defining and assessing standards of potential and actual performance. For example, a candidate for employment may reveal during the selection procedures an insufficient level of knowledge defined as necessary for effective performance, but may be accepted nevertheless, because the deficiency could be remedied by training. An employee whose performance is being appraised may reveal attitudes that hinder effective performance and require counselling as a possible remedy.
3   It helps to review whether the formal qualifications and experience often associated with a particular role are, in fact, required. In some jobs, specific qualifications are obviously essential, e.g. medicine, law, accountancy, etc. In others they may be desirable but not essential.
4   Now that managers are asked to guard increasingly against unfair and discriminatory practice, it is especially important to produce person specifications that truly and fairly state what the job requires, and to be cautious about using personal characteristics that are thought to be associated with high performance, unless there is unequivocal proof of the association.

An illustration of how job analysis based on these lines has been applied to an actual job is provided in Figure 9.2. The job description and person specification refer to a training administrator, employed at a training centre which provides courses and consultancy work, in the UK and overseas, in management and related subjects. This job is demanding not only on account of the responsibilities implied in the job description, but especially because of the crucial importance of human relationships. Effective performance of the job depends greatly on the job holder's ability to communicate successfully with a very diverse range of people, the various levels of staff at the centre, external sponsors and agencies, external

JOB DESCRIPTION
Training Administrator
Training International

Location: 9–10 Sheffield St, London WC2A
Purpose of job: To provide all supporting services necessary for effectively
                       organized courses.
Responsible to: Course Director.
Responsible for: Clerical staff allocated to courses.

Tasks
Before courses
• Corresponding (letter, telephone, email, fax, etc.) with:
  1 Sponsoring agencies, overseas nominating authorities, course applicants.
  2 External course tutors.
  3 Centres to be visited.
• Preparing of nominal rolls.
• Arranging for any visits during courses travel, accommodation, special diets, etc.
• Arranging for training accommodation (class and syndicate rooms), training
  aids and materials (e.g. books, hand-out articles, etc.).
• Preparing of course statement of accounts (income and expenditure).

During courses
• Working in close collaboration with Programme Consultant and Course
  Director to meet their requirements.
• Confirming and checking arrangements made above.
• Meeting, liaising and collaborating with external contributors.
• Attending to various needs and welfare of course members (liaising with
  British Council, sponsors, embassies, etc.).
• Maintaining course statement of accounts and keeping Programme Consultant
  informed.

After courses
• Collating final report on course provided by Course Director and course
  members' individual assessment reports.
• Finalizing statement of course accounts for Programme Consultant.
• Ensuring that accounts of expenditure on the programme and income are
  recorded, invoices are authorized.

Standards
See person specification and schedule for performance appraisal.

Working environment
The training centre is located in a completely modernized 18th century listed building
characteristic of the area. Offices and classrooms are very large, well lit and equipped
with modern equipment.

Training and development
Induction training; on-job training as required; external training as appropriate;
development by job rotation.

Figure 9.2 Job description   (Continued overleaf)

Advancement opportunities
Opportunities may occur for suitably qualified and experienced staff to be promoted to senior administrative posts or occasionally, to be appointed as Programme Consultant or Course Director.

Conditions of employment
• Salary £30,000–35,000, subject to annual review.
• Contributory pension scheme available.
• Interest-free travel loan available.
• Luncheon vouchers provided.
• Leave: 25 days per annum plus public holidays.
• Working day: Monday to Friday, normally 0900–1700. Unsocial hours occasionally required.

Person specification
General requirements

Knowledge
• Work and organization of the training centre and associated agencies.
• Contacts in regular collaboration with external tutors, centre, etc.
• Purpose and contents of courses and consultancy projects.
• Office procedures and equipment.
• Training methods, resources and materials.

Skills
• Office administration, organization and procedures.
• Use of office equipment (word processors, copiers, etc.).
• Interpersonal–communicational.

Attitudes and attributes
• Sympathetic to nature of the work of the organization.
• Conscientious.
• Able to stand pressure.
• Equable and calm in temperament.
• Patient and tolerant.
• Cheerful, cooperative, willing.
• Able to relate effectively with very wide variety of people.
• Able to use initiative.

Specific requirements

Appearance	Smart and tidy
Health	No history of recurring illness likely to affect performance.
Qualifications	(1) Education to GCE A level or equivalent.
	(2) Recognized certificate/diploma in Business Studies, Office Administration, etc. (not essential but desirable).
Experience	Previous employment relevant to this job, e.g. office administration, training support (flexible).
Special conditions	Occasionally required to work away from home (e.g. during residential courses away from the training centre or for overseas projects).

Figure 9.2 (Continued)

tutors, speakers and consultants, course members from the UK, Europe and other countries, covering a very wide variety of cultures and customs.

JOB ANALYSIS IN PRACTICE

Job analysis may be carried out in two ways. It may be for managers and job holders to discuss and agree among themselves, or it may be carried out by HR staff of the employing organization or by external consultants or some mixture of these. Whether it is carried out by managers and job holders or others will depend on the nature of the organization, the jobs in question and the preferences of individual organizations.

Cost-effectiveness is a major consideration. For a large organization, in which there are groups of identical jobs, it may be worthwhile to employ the personnel staff or external consultants to carry out a comprehensive analysis. For other organizations, which are small or where a number of jobs are unique, it would probably be impracticable to incur the time and expense of a comprehensive, in-depth analysis. There is another important consideration: jobs are changing all the time, affected by technological and by economic and social factors. Therefore, job descriptions need constant revision and amendment.

Job analysis carried out through discussions between managers and job holders can be an important part of the appraisal review. Before considering the performance of the person and what future action may be needed, it is obviously necessary to enquire whether the tasks in the job and criteria for effective performance are the same before drawing any conclusions about performance. When job analysis is carried out by HR staff or outside consultants, the following methods are often used:

1   *Direct observation*: here the analyst observes actual work in progress and makes notes as necessary under the various headings of the job description. These notes can be used as a basis for subsequent questions that the analyst may wish to ask. The advantages of seeing a job performed for oneself are obvious, but the method has the following limitations:
    (a)   It is very time-consuming. A great deal of time would be needed adequately to observe a number of jobs. All jobs need to be observed over a period of time which is representative of the typical work in order to appreciate the fluctuations between, for example, the quieter and busier periods, avoiding any seasonality effects. A brief observation can very easily produce a distorted view.
    (b)   There is no substitute for personal experience of the job and the evidence of observations can be very misleading. Special skills expertly applied may make jobs seem easier. Skilled workers could make jobs seem more difficult if they chose to do so.
    (c)   Behaviour that is formally observed is inevitably influenced by the act of observation, unless this is done without the knowledge of those being observed, (which would raise ethical questions). All the research data confirm this

phenomenon (often described as the 'Hawthorne effect' from the studies carried out at the Hawthorne plant described earlier).

(d) There is a great difference between observation of manual and managerial jobs. It is unlikely that an observer can obtain any kind of accurate picture or evaluation of the mental energy expended, personal pressures, contemplative and planning activities or the subtleties of interpersonal relationships, which form a large part of the managers' and supervisors' work.

2 *Interviews*: these should be carried out with the job holders themselves, their immediate managers and any others who can give useful information. The interview is a necessary and potentially useful method in job analysis, enabling the job analyst to raise questions, to gather the evidence of observation and to compare the perception of one job holder with others. The caveats that need to be made about the use of the interview in job analysis are these:

(a) As in all other interview situations considerable skill is needed. The interview has to be systematic and purposeful, and conducted with particular empathy, tact and sensitivity.

(b) For reasons already explained, however cooperative the job holders may be, the job analyst has always to deal with personal biases and perceptions of jobs.

(c) The interviewer needs to be careful to distinguish fact from opinion.

(d) Interviews provide especially useful data on topics such as what responses/ attitudes about work challenges seem to be necessary (for example the interviewer could use the critical incident technique, see below), for example in jobs such as teaching, nursing, selling and interacting with the public.

3 *Diaries*: using this method, the job analyst provides job holders with the areas of the job description about which information is required. Job holders then analyse their own work over a period of time, recording information systematically in diary form under the required headings and the time spent on each item. The advantages and disadvantages of the diary method are these:

(a) Self-recorded data of this kind can be made over a longer period and thus provide a more reliable picture of the nature of the job.

(b) The data can be used as valuable bases on which to conduct interviews.

(c) The data are an obvious means of saving some of the time that prolonged direct observation of jobs requires.

(d) Like the other methods, diaries are inevitably affected by factors of subjectivity. Moreover, because the information is self-recorded there is no means of verifying accuracy.

(e) To be of real value the diary has to be kept accurately, conscientiously and regularly. This approach can soon become a chore, especially if job holders are not in sympathy with the job, in which case it might be perfunctorily fulfilled or neglected.

4 *Questionnaires*: here the job analyst compiles a series of questions designed to elicit the maximum possible useful information about the jobs under analysis, and distributes

these with careful instructions about the completion of the form. The advantages and disadvantages of questionnaires are:

(a) They enable the job analyst to put standard questions to all the job holders taking part in the survey.

(b) If there are large numbers working, random samples and larger numbers of people can be covered.

(c) Specialized skill is needed in devising the questionnaire and framing the questions. For example, attractive as the prospect of open questions may seem to be, it is probably better to require the respondent to choose from a range of answers that best fit particular situations, which also facilitates analysis. Skill is also required in the analysis of responses.

5 *Critical incident reviews*: as the term implies, this method uses examples of real events at work as a means of eliciting what the criteria for effective performance should be. The component tasks of a job are systematically analysed with job holders, who are asked to cite actual examples of typical incidents that could have had a significant impact on their performance, from their experience of the job, and how they dealt with them.

It is unlikely that any one of these methods will be adequate by itself. In practice, therefore, a combination of techniques is usually employed and adapted to meet the needs of particular situations.

JOB ANALYSIS

There are many examples and proprietary systems of job analysis documentation. These can be called position analysis questionnaires or schedules. The questions normally found in these types of documents can be used as a basis for interview. Examples are given below:

Job title.

Purpose of job: what is the purpose/objective?

For what specifically is the job holder personally accountable?

How does this job relate to the unit (department/office, etc. objectives)?

Provide a brief organization chart, locating the job in relation to those roles with which it interacts.

Summarise the main activities of the job and the performance standards used.

What are the duties/functions of the job? (noting frequency, cycles of work, significance or weighting attached to each activity).

What is the responsibility for materials? (equipment, materials).

What is the responsibility for money? (amounts)

What is the responsibility for people? (managerial/supervisory duties, activities related to training, day by day, supervision, coaching, career and professional development).

Specify any additional duties performed in the job (e.g. key account management, project group membership, etc.).

What experience is required to perform the job? (include time, months, years, etc.)

What knowledge, skills, abilities are necessary?

Are there any special licences, qualification requirements?

What educational, professional qualifications are essential?

Are there any particular hazards, environmental conditions associated with the job?

The output from this process will be a detailed job description. Such a description may be for training, recruitment or reward purposes. Clearly, the above schedule could be modified according to the job in question. There are also sample job descriptions for a variety of roles available on the internet.

A summary of the main elements of job analysis is shown in Figure 9.3.

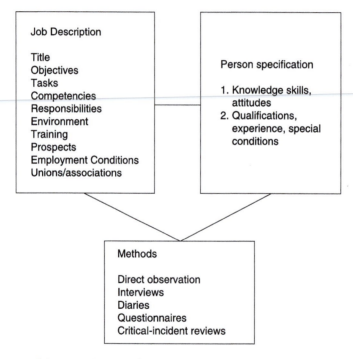

Figure 9.3 Summary of the main elements of job analysis

QUESTIONS

1   Why is the definition of effective performance fundamentally important to the whole system of HR management?

2   How would you define competences? Are there fundamental attributes that are important for high performance?

3   Name and describe the methods commonly used in job analysis.

4   After reading Chapter 25, list the possible issues relating to discrimination which might arise in a job analysis exercise and how to avoid them.

REFERENCES

Easterby-Smith, M. and Prieto, I. M. (2004). 'Dynamic capabilities and knowledge management: an integrative role for learning'. *British Journal of Management*, 19: 235–49.

Reed, J. and Stoltz, P. G. (2011). *Put Your Mindset to Work*. London: Portfolio Penguin.

Tyson, S. and Doherty, N. (1999). *Human Resource Excellence Report*. Cranfield/*Financial Times*.

10 SOURCING

How many goodly people are there here!
How beauteous mankind is! O brave new world,
That has such people in't.

William Shakespeare *The Tempest* Act V Scene I

The people who work in organizations are the human capital that are the source of activity and creative energy. Recruitment is arguably the most important of human resource functions. All our successes and all our failures in HRM stem from the quality of the people in the organization. Recruitment is the activity that produces candidates, which helps to establish the employer brand and, through recruitment policies, has a major impact on the organization's culture.

The purpose of all sourcing and the recruitment of people is to find suitable candidates to meet organizational needs, in as cost-effective a way as possible. We are therefore distinguishing between recruitment and selection. In practice, then, the objective of a recruitment procedure is to attract genuinely suitable candidates and examine their credentials carefully, in order to produce a short list for further investigation in the selection procedures. Apart from the methods used and the general administration of the task, the achievement of the objective will depend very much on how efficiently workforce planning and job analysis have been conducted and applied.

Recruitment has taken on a wider significance, and is now subsumed under the broader heading of 'sourcing'. There are three reasons why we must look at sourcing as more than the mere routine (and important) vacancy filling procedure:

1   Sourcing implies we can find skills and knowledge from a variety of sources to assist in the continuous struggle to gain or maintain a competitive advantage.

These resources may come from outsourcing, sub-contractors, and other non-standard contractual employment relationships, so allowing the company to access a variety of labour markets and service providers.

2   Developments in new technology, especially web 2, and any similar points of contact, have introduced social media and mobile devices, such as iPhones into the sourcing agenda. This enables organizations to access a wider range of candidates, to engage with them at an earlier stage and to obtain information about them not previously available.

3   The consequence of being able to reach wider audiences on the internet and social media means that sourcing has to become aligned with the organization's marketing strategy, so that corporate brands can be exploited, and the corporate image can be sold to the public. Although this might be more important to some types of companies than others, where there are opportunities, for example in retailing or public services. However, back selling (selling the brand to end users) and building brand awareness are possible in other industries. For example, Rolls-Royce aero engines are sold to aircraft manufacturers, who in turn sell their aircraft to airlines, which have to sell tickets to passengers. The brand has justifiable prestige and worldwide acclaim for technical excellence and safety, which is attractive to airlines and to customers, and is a source of pride for employees. This makes any vacancies there, such as apprenticeships, eagerly sought and entry to the company highly competitive, resulting in only the best applicants succeeding. This, in turn, feeds into the quality of the products and the brand, in a virtuous circle.

One consequence of the three points mentioned above is that organizations are now more likely to take a coherent approach to marketing and to understand the importance of corporate identity in finding suitable employees, sub-contractors and customers alike. Employees and their friends and relatives might fall into all of these categories, for example.

The efficient recruitment of staff may be described as knowing what resources are required, what resources are available, and where and how they may be found cost-effectively. The recruitment system can be considered under the following headings:

1   Determining the vacancies.
2   Sourcing strategy.
3   Recruitment policy.
4   Recruitment methods.
5   Preparing and publishing information.
6   Processing applications.

A flow chart showing the sequence of the recruitment process is shown in Figure 10.1.

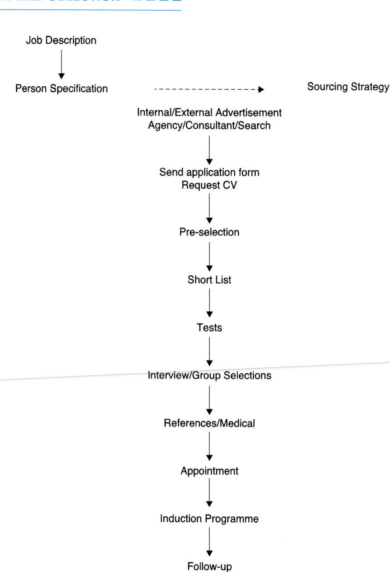

Figure 10.1 Flow chart of recruitment process

DETERMINING THE VACANCIES

The first stage is concerned with the question of what resources are needed, that is, the demand. Details of requirements will emerge from the compilation and regular revision of the workforce plan. In practice, job vacancies may occur when an organization or work unit is set up *ab initio*, when there is expansion, when any reorganization takes place through changes of policy, technology, location, mergers, acquisitions, demergers or, most commonly, when employees leave the organization and need to be replaced. Because of the subtle changes that are continuously taking place in work organizations, when line managers declare there is a vacancy, the existence and type of job vacancies should not be accepted without question.

One of the most important roles the HR function can perform is to ensure there is a review of the need for skills and to discuss with line managers how work is being organized efficiently. Labour turnover offers the chance of making adjustments to structure, analysing work processes, perhaps to decide that there is no need for recruitment, or that the competences required are different from those of the previous employee. It is helpful to think in terms of capability and the competencies necessary for successful performance, rather than the 'job' as being a fixed set of activities, as though it were a tangible object. Jobs are a collection of tasks, which change very often according to the incumbent, and as new systems, products, services and technologies are developed.

Increasingly, organizations consider employing people with non-standard contracts that depart from full-time, normal working hours. This allows the organization to access new labour markets, and to make efficiency savings. Variations include short-term, part-time job-sharing, working from home, term-time working, annualized hours, compressed work hours, twilight shifts and zero hours/call-out contracts, amongst a variety of other working time arrangements (see Chapter 8). At the same time, franchise operations and subcontracting arrangements provide opportunities for work to be carried out without the employer bearing many of the costs and risks of traditional recruitment and employment.

SOURCING STRATEGY

This stage is concerned with general questions about the supply and availability of resources and the particular avenues through which these are likely to be obtained. The workforce plan is designed to provide general information about the factors that influence the supply of labour at macro and micro levels. Here the situation is similar to that which the manufacturer has to face in ascertaining in advance what the limits of the available market are, what competition and other constraints obtain and what, therefore, the share of the market is likely to be. In considering possible sources of recruiting employees, it is easy to assume that these are inevitably external. Even when it is possible and feasible to fill job vacancies from within the organization, the transfers and promotions which this usually involves will more often than not produce a vacancy at the end of a chain reaction, necessitating external recruitment. Nevertheless, the possibility of filling vacancies internally should always be considered for the following reasons:

■   Existing employees are known to the organization and are generally familiar with the working environment, the products, customers, organization culture and the predominant management style.

- The costs and the time that external recruitment, selection and induction procedures consume can be significantly reduced.
- Internal recruitment to fill vacancies may be used as a means of career development, to widen opportunities and stimulate motivation among existing employees.
- There are fewer risks in recruiting from within for the reasons stated above. However, there are also fewer opportunities to bring new ideas and talent into the organization, to refresh the talent pool.

RECRUITMENT POLICY

Recruitment policy is largely a matter of making choices, within a framework of legal rules and requirements. The laws relating to discrimination in employment, which we describe more fully in Chapter 25, are now comprehensive. The legal frameworks in most Western democracies cover the need to prevent racial, gender, religious, age and disability discrimination, as well as rules regarding ex-offenders and references, amongst other areas. This affects choices of recruitment methods, advertisements and the processes used.

Recruitment policy choices are decisions about sourcing. The first issue is the central question discussed above, of whether or not the organization recruits internally or externally. There are three archetypical recruitment policies (Tyson and Fell 1986):

Although these are 'ideal types', in reality there may be a mixture of these, for example with fast track graduate entry careers, and with specialists entering at higher levels even in a single tier entry. Decisions on recruitment policy have a big impact on career management, and organization culture. Two tier structures encourage a 'them' and 'us' approach, and produce two value sets, whilst this does encourage rapid development for management. Single tier recruitment (for example typically in the police, fire service, school teachers, etc.), produces a strong culture. Here, HR manages a sophisticated internal labour market, with a need for extensive policies covering recruitment, appraisal, development and reward. Multiple tier policies encourage new blood to enter the organization, but there are no promises of promotion, and jobs are all advertised externally, putting the spotlight on reward policies.

The second main policy issue concerns the degree of flexibility there will be in responding to recruitment demands. There are broader policy issues raised by part-time employment, job sharing, term-time working and so on. Apparently creative solutions to recruitment difficulties which involve the organization in new employment contracts, suggesting for example flexibility of contract, or flexibility of time or of task, commit the organization to costs and precedents that continue for years to come. Value:cost analysis is a methodology for determining if there are advantages to the business in outsourcing a service or activity, and whether this is the best value for the organization (see Chapter 16). We discussed flexible working in Chapter 8.

Third, there are numerous linkages between recruitment and other policies, so consistency is essential, for example with reward policy where there may be a stipulation that recruitment will be at the upper quartile in pay.

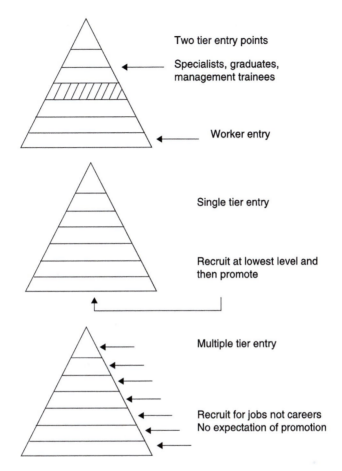

Figure 10.2 Three archetypical recruitment policies

A formal recruitment policy facilitates understanding in large or widely dispersed organizations. Given the importance of line managers in recruitment, a common policy encourages a wider understanding of the anti-discrimination policies, the significance of recruitment for the organization's culture, and of policies which have wider organization significance, such as talent management, graduate recruitment, internships and inter-departmental transfers.

RECRUITMENT METHODS

When the organization has to use external sources, there are a number of ways of conducting the search for employees:

■ Through employment consultancies and agencies. These include specialist agencies and 'head-hunters' as well as public agencies such as Jobcentre Plus, and private commercial agencies of varying kinds.

- By contacting potential employees directly through advertisements online, on the corporate website, in newspapers, journals, posters (for example in their own premises), on radio, on television and other media outlets.
- By using social media, such as Twitter, Facebook and LinkedIn.
- Recommendations from existing employees, and from customers and suppliers.
- Institutional agencies, such as universities, colleges and schools, and from armed forces resettlement, and local employers (for example, as part of their outplacement services following closures, and redundancy).

A combination of these media will typically be used, depending upon the labour market, and the levels of unemployment and availability of the skills and abilities sought. A brief evaluation of these different methods is shown below.

Employment consultancies and agencies

Agencies can provide a rapid and helpful service, especially if they know the organization well for whom they are recruiting staff, in particular the organization culture, the kinds of people who have been successful there in the past and they can answer questions about some of the practicalities of working there.

As they are independent of the prospective employer, their opinion will carry weight with potential applicants. The sort of questions the applicants will ask are: is this a reputable employer, what kinds of fellow employees would the applicant work with, how easy are the travel arrangements, is there a track record of new staff being quickly accepted into the organization, does the organization promote from within, how good are the facilities such as restaurants, canteens and so on.

Agencies are useful for finding temporary staff quickly, and for finding people who are able to work in the industries where they may specialize. Similarly, administrative, sales staff, drivers and warehouse personnel are often recruited this way. Many businesses believe in direct applications, for example Network Rail believes it can bring substantial savings in terms of the costs of using third parties and the time and money saved by finding the right candidates.

Recruitment consultancies and 'head hunters' are frequently used for managerial and senior executive staff recruitment. At the more junior levels, these are akin to the agencies described above; however, a recruitment consultant should visit the employer and analyse the job, write a specification and agree with the client the competencies and attributes required before the vacancy is advertised. They will carry out initial interviews and tests where appropriate, and produce a short list. At a senior level, the consultancies are more likely to be head hunters, much of their work is conducted by means of an informal network of contacts, and they keep records of career profiles of people likely to be in constant demand. In addition, they use contacts extensively and will do all the preliminary screening for the employer, producing a short short-list often for the employer to meet informally first and to engage in a series of conversations until it becomes clear that the person wants the role and the company wishes to employ her/him, or that either side has serious reservations. They work in a confidential way, bringing both sides together, so that either party can withdraw without a 'loss of face', and to ensure there is a cultural fit and that the terms and conditions for the role are acceptable.

Agencies are relatively cheap and quick but, of necessity, do not draw on a wide field of candidates. They may conduct an advertising campaign for the employer, which adds to the cost, and the success all depends on the agency understanding the role and the needs of the employer. Head hunters are expensive, their fees being multiples of the starting salary package and, although they may know the vacancy and the candidate well, they may spend a great deal of time trying to produce something similar to an arranged marriage between the two parties, only for it all to fall apart at the last minute. If going down the recruitment consultancy/head hunter route, the critical issue is the experience of the industry sector, and the typical senior roles in it, as well as the ability of the consultant engaged to help.

Advertisements online and corporate websites

This is the most common method employers now use to find suitable staff. Very often, companies will use advertisements, either online – for example on mobile devices or through jobs boards, or in the press to drive applicants to their website, where details of the vacancy can be found. Jobs boards, for example in the case of HR jobs, such as 'Changeboard', provide the platform for advertisers, which may be the company with the vacancy, or very often a consultancy to whom applicants can apply, with details of the vacancy, application details and the like.

Clearly there are differences in the type of advertisement that can be placed in a newspaper, and online, for example on an iPhone. In 2013, Cisco reported that the number of mobile devices would exceed the number of people on the planet by the end of the year, at an estimated number of 7 billion mobile devices. It is not surprising, therefore, that smartphones and mobile devices are a preferred way to find and apply for a job (*The Recruiter Magazine* January 2014: 6). The article also points out that those recruiting will need a mobile optimized version of their desktop site to improve the experience of applying on smartphones.

One of the benefits of advertising, wherever it appears, is the possibility of attracting the passive job seeker. On that basis, apps may not be the best way to find candidates, as it will not be the subject of a search.

Recruitment through social media

The advent of social media (so-called web 2.0) in the form of social networks online and easily accessed, containing large quantities of personal job-related information, has introduced the option for companies to search such sites methodically for potential employees, and to put their job vacancies on the sites through their own pages. This has also given organizations the chance to put their job opportunities before passive job seekers.

Networks such as LinkedIn, Twitter and Facebook have interest groups that facilitate the analysis of the large amounts of data contained in them. In the case study on ITV, Parry and Tyson (2014: 81) describe how ITV relies heavily on social media for its recruitment: 'The functionality of LinkedIn means that members entering the ITV careers pages will automatically be directed to the page that is relevant to their work experience (based on an analysis of the information in their profile)'.

The UK fashion company Lyle and Scott used Twitter to hire its CEO in 2013, who had no experience of the industry or the top level of management. Twitter was used by the recruitment consultants as a source of candidates because the company wanted applicants with characteristics which they believed would be found by members of Twitter.

There are clearly benefits recruiters can gain from social media, the immediacy of the medium, the lower costs, the availability of extensive data on potential candidates and a medium which is in tune with a wide group of passive job seekers, who are more likely to use this medium than any other.

Recommendations from employees

This is a method which is as old as employment itself. The benefits are clear: existing employees know most about the company, and are able to see whether any of their acquaintances would be successful.

However, there are also potential problems with this source of candidates. If the employee fails, the sponsor will be embarrassed, and could leave also. The relationship with the sponsor and the recruited person could mean that the person recruited feels he or she 'owes' the sponsor, with all the dangers of an inappropriate relationship – for example in covering-up mistakes.

However, if appropriate safeguards are in place (for example, those concerned should be in a different department, and not in a manager/subordinate relationship), there are advantages for this approach. Some companies create an alumni association to encourage employees to remain in touch when they leave, so that they could easily return if they wished. Returning to the virtual world, one company is known to have created a 'Second Life' pavilion, where current and previous employees can 'meet' and network (Libert and Spector 2008).

Institutional agencies

Several different kinds of agencies are included under this heading. The features they have in common are that they are all agencies set up by particular organizations to help their own members or ex-members find employment and that they are generally non-profit-making. The agencies of this kind that employers are likely to need and use most regularly are:

Career services of academic institutions: universities and similar institutions maintain a full-time careers advisory service.

Employment services of professional institutions and trade unions: a number of professional institutions, such as those representing accountants, engineers, linguists, etc.

and a number of trade unions, have an employment advisory service whereby a register is kept of members seeking employment and information is collected from employers seeking staff.

Resettlement services of the armed forces: all three services have full-time officers and non-commissioned officers with a specialized knowledge of employment opportunities.

Job centres and careers advice provided by the state: for example, Jobcentre Plus, and careers advice in schools, and attendance at open days for employers.

PREPARING AND PUBLISHING INFORMATION

Recruitment advertising is a specialist area that is often best left to advertising agencies and the consultancies in the field. The principles are simply stated.

The advertisement must be:

■ Succinct and yet give a comprehensive and accurate description of the job and its requirements.

■ Attract the attention of the maximum number of potentially suitable candidates (i.e. is published through the right media).

■ Give a favourable image of the organization in terms of efficiency and its attitudes towards people, including the values of the organization, its products or services.

■ Not contravene employment laws concerning all the areas of discrimination as described in Chapter 25.

The preparation and publication of the advertisement should be based on two simple questions that any applicant would normally ask:

1   What are the details of the job – what kind of job, in terms of competencies, skills, duties, opportunities, rewards, conditions and its location? (In short – a summary of the employee value proposition; see Chapter 17).

2   How should applications be presented, and are there deadlines for applications?

The preparation of the information needed to answer the first question is based on the data produced by the job analysis, in particular the person specification. There is not much point in waxing eloquently, as some job advertisements do, about the personal qualities needed. This is best left to the assessment of the personnel selectors. Self-assessment has its place, but without a full understanding of the role and the organization, it would be difficult for the candidate to do more than express an interest in taking the application further.

On the other hand, it could well be relevant to mention any special features, such as aptitudes that are important to the job, for example, 'ability to read music at sight is desirable', or 'extensive travel throughout the UK and some evening or weekend work is an essential part of the job'. Selection is as much a choice by the candidate as by the organization, ultimately. The key to preparing good job advertisements is to see the advertisement through the eyes of potential applicants.

The part of the advertisement advising applicants on the presentation of their applications varies in practice. Sometimes a personal letter covering the applicant's *curriculum vitae* (CV) is the only form of application required. More frequently, the employer provides an application form together with information on requirements for testimonials and referees' reports. Most employers will require the application to be made online.

A letter of application or a CV is sometimes used as a kind of selection device. There is certainly something to be said for giving applicants a free hand to state their own cases without inhibition, especially for more senior roles, but there are some important caveats that have to be made about this method. The CV has the disadvantage that this usually contains the information the applicant wants to give to the prospective employer, rather than the information the employer wants to know in order to make a decision. Second, for automated sifting and responses, applications would have to be on the same type of form, to make comparison between applicants possible.

THE JOB ADVERTISEMENT

The advertisement needs to cover information derived from the job description and person specification in seven broad areas:

1   *The work organization*: its activities, function and location.
2   *The job*: its title, location, key responsibilities, accountabilities.
3   *Education, qualifications and experience* (both those which are necessary and desirable): professional qualifications, experience, aptitudes, etc., at least a broad indication.
4   *Rewards and opportunities*: basic pay or an indicator of starting salary, and benefits.
5   *Training and development provided*: in the job, long term development
6   *Conditions*: any special factors and circumstances affecting the job.
7   *Applications*: form of application; closing date, email address, telephone number for any queries.

The companion website to this volume contains some examples of types of advertisements.

THE APPLICATION FORM

The design of an appropriate application form will clearly depend on particular situations and needs, but there are some basic principles that are universally relevant. Different forms may be necessary for different kinds of work. For all appointments the same general background details will be needed, for which a standard format is possible. Additional sections can be added, specifically designed to cover the range of jobs, if necessary. The items that will normally need to be included in application forms are:

- job title/reference number; application arrangements
- applicant's full names
- address and telephone number
- nationality (see section below on eligibility to work rules)
- education (full-time, part-time, training courses)
- academic qualifications
- professional qualifications
- present employment – details of present post, duties, accountabilities, skills used, numbers supervised
- previous employment in chronological order, with details of achievement in each post, name, address of employers, dates of employment
- main current interests, pursuits and achievements outside work
- health (including any serious illness or disability, past or present)
- court convictions if any (other than for spent convictions; see Chapter 23)
- additional information (any information not covered in the form, which the applicant considers significant to the application)
- referees
- source of information about the vacancy.

ELIGIBILITY TO WORK

Employers in the UK should check that employees from abroad are entitled to work in the UK, since employers are liable for employing anyone illegally, and can be prosecuted. This entails checking documentation, to ensure any permissions have not expired; identity checks on passports or birth certificates; checks that any visa granted covers the type of work the applicant will be doing if successful; and checks on the number of hours they are permitted to work. The certificate of the right to abode is only valid if it is in a correct, valid passport. Employers must make checks with the UK Visas and Immigration (UKVI) checking service, to see if the individual has the right to work in the UK, if the applicant is unable to provide the right documents (see the UKVI website). These checks could be initiated from the next stage (short-listing) onwards.

PROCESSING AND ASSESSING APPLICATIONS

When all the applications have been received by the due date, the next task is to select those applicants who, on the evidence available, appear to be the most suitable as future employees of the organization and, therefore, worth the time and cost of further examination in the selection procedures. This task will be based on the published requirements for the job and involves a painstaking and scrupulous study of the information provided by applicants, a comparison of this information with those job requirements and, finally, a decision whether to accept or reject at this stage.

To systematize the process, it is normally useful to carry out a preliminary sift to produce three categories of applicants: suitable, not suitable and marginal. With this method, the main effort can then be concentrated on deciding which of the doubtful applicants should be accepted and which rejected. When there are constraints on acceptable numbers, which is the usual circumstance, and a choice has to be made between applicants of apparently equal merits according to the essential requirements, a careful consideration of the list of desirable requirements may provide the weighting needed to assist the final decision. A simple description of the sifting task such as this could make it seem a disarmingly mechanical process. It is, in fact, anything but this, and a number of important points need to be made about the general approach to the task and methods used.

To start with the general approach, those responsible for processing applications need to be very aware throughout, first, that they have a responsibility to their employers to be as careful and thorough as possible in selecting the most suitable of the applicants and, second, that they have a responsibility to the applicants themselves to examine their applications conscientiously and fairly. A short concise note should be made and kept by HR against unsuccessful candidates showing the reason for rejection at this stage, so that the company can follow an 'audit' trail if challenged. Since the task is virtually part of the selection procedure, it has very important implications for the choice of staff to perform the task. Biodata, which can be automated, and provides a good prediction of the likely success of applicants, is a useful way of handling large numbers of applicants, but requires a regular recruitment requirement to be cost-effective – as in the case of the Inland Revenue.

Biodata or sometimes more complete data can be used to show the key characteristics of the applicants as compared to the requirements of the role, so that there can be automated sorts of large numbers of applicants.

A further important point that has to be made concerns the need for flexibility in making the final decisions about acceptance or rejection. This relates to the previous comment on the problems of making decisions solely on the basis of documentary information. To illustrate by example – if a job demands a heavy goods vehicle (HGV) licence as an essential requirement, then all applicants who do not have this qualification could be rejected immediately, no matter what their other qualifications may be, but if, say, at least five years' experience in the type of job in question were included as an essential requirement, it might be very short-sighted to rule out an apparently otherwise excellent candidate whose experience happened to be only four years.

There is no way of confirming from written evidence whether the four years' experience of this applicant is not, in truth, superior in quality and value to the longer experience of other applicants. It is best not to be stubbornly inflexible or over-precise about matters such as length of experience, in the first place. When job requirements are being established, room must always be left to decide individual cases on their merits, as we balance and weight various attributes.

NOTIFYING SHORT-LISTED APPLICANTS

The final step is to notify the chosen applicants of the arrangements for the selection procedure, and the rejected applicants that they have not been chosen. The letter to the successful applicants will need to give full details about the arrangements for the selection procedures, i.e. time and place, together with other administrative information such as travel, expenses, etc. At the same time it is often very helpful to point applicants to the corporate website, where more can be discovered about the organization and its work. In this way a number of questions that candidates might otherwise wish to ask, for example, about locations, opportunities to travel, career opportunities in general, educational, training, social, sporting, welfare facilities, etc., can be anticipated.

Letters or emails to unsuccessful applicants should be brief, courteous and sympathetic, but not curt. We must bear in mind the need for maintaining the corporate image. Many organizations will provide verbal feedback to candidates who were not successful. All letters informing applicants of the results of applications should be sent as soon as possible. Apart from the natural tensions and anxieties that most people experience when waiting for the news of any decisions that affect them personally, they have a special need for speedy information that concerns the planning of their working lives, and other applications.

ADMINISTRATION OF THE RECRUITMENT PROCESS

The responsibility for administering and supervising the task of recruitment belongs to the HR staff. They act as the representatives or agents of their employers and are a link between the managers of the organization who require staff, the external sources for finding employees and the people who respond to the advertisements and apply for employment. The main elements of the task are:

1   *Acting as the focal point for coordinating the organization's needs for staff*: in this function they use the data of the workforce plan and job analysis. HR has a responsibility to determine whether there is a need to recruit. Could reorganization obviate the need for someone new?
2   *Providing specialist knowledge about factors affecting the availability of required staff, and of current legislation affecting recruitment for employment*: in this context they may also make recommendations about recruitment policies that the organization should adopt. HR staff often need to drive new policies against discrimination through the organization.
3   *Using specialist knowledge to decide what sources are likely to be most fruitful in the search for suitable staff*: here it is particularly important that the HR staff establish and

maintain harmonious relationships with those agencies and consultants who are most likely to satisfy the recruitment needs of the organization, and keep up-to-date on labour market, educational and economic trends.

4   *Formulating and administering the details of the recruitment procedures, related to the publication of information, processing of applications and notifying applicants*: HR will use a tracking procedure on which candidates can check the progress of their applications from their computers, laptops, etc., and HR staff need to liaise closely with line managers in the various stages of the recruitment process. The phases of the recruitment procedure when consultation between HR staff and line management are most likely to occur are the publication of the advertisement for the job vacancy and the processing of applications. Line managers should be asked to verify that advertisements accurately reflect requirements before advertisements are finally released for publication. They should be closely involved when a short list of candidates is being produced.

5   *Maintaining records and data on what happened*: to satisfy any research or audits on equal opportunities, and to check the most cost-effective selection source.

See Figure 10.3 for a summary of the recruitment process.

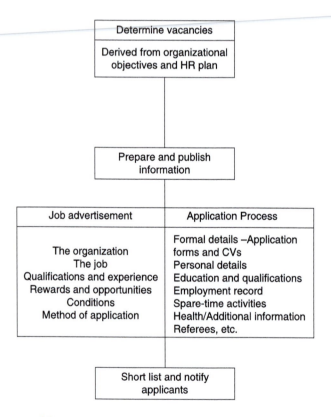

Figure 10.3 A summary of the recruitment process

QUESTIONS

1   What are the main types of recruitment policies that organizations can adopt, and what are the advantages and disadvantages of each, from the perspective of the firm's competitive advantage?

2   How would you rate the different sources of recruits, in terms of cost-effectiveness?

3   What sources of recruitment would you use to find a field of candidates for (a) external sales roles, (b) for production roles, and (c) for senior management roles?

REFERENCES

Home Office (2012). *The Summary Guide for Employers on Preventing Illegal Working within the UK*. Home Office: The UK Border Agency.

Libert, B. and Spector, J. (2008). *We are Smarter than Me*. USA: Pearson Education.

Parry, E. and Tyson, S. (2014). *Managing People in a Contemporary Context*. Abingdon: Routledge.

The Recruiter Magazine (2014) January.

Tyson, S. and Fell, A. (1986). *Evaluating the Personnel Function*. London: Hutchinson.

11 SELECTING EMPLOYEES

In this chapter attention is focused primarily on the selection of people from outside the employing organization. These may be employees, contractors or capabilities taken into the organization under a variety of contractual arrangements. The systematic approach to the selection of employees may and also should apply to people who are already employed by the appointing organization, for example in promotion decisions and in the clarity of criteria required to subcontractors. Two basic questions provide the foundation for an effective system:

1   What are the criteria for effective performance against which selectors and other decision-makers judge the suitability of candidates for appointment or to provide services?
2   What methods are most likely to reveal the evidence needed to make judgements and decisions about the suitability of candidates and any other person applying to provide the capabilities?

The crucial importance of selecting people who can meet the requirements prescribed in the job description and person specification is apparent to all experienced managers. It is equally evident that mistakes in selection decisions can have very serious consequences for corporate effectiveness. Such mistakes may well adversely affect output quality and quantity, as well as cause difficulties for colleagues, subordinates and clients. Incompetence may lead to costly mistakes, loss and waste of valuable resources, accidents, avoidable expenditure on training, stress on staff and reputational damage.

There are important strategic issues which impinge upon selection. HR strategy is designed to match the business strategy. Much of the purpose in selection is to fulfil the requirements for organizational capability. In the climate of economic uncertainty which is now part of the 'new normal', companies are interested in the efficiency as well as the effectiveness of selection.

POST-RECESSIONARY SOURCING AND SELECTION

During the post-recessionary era, the issues of cost reduction are likely to continue. In order to retain talent during the recession, part time employment expanded, which at least retained talented people who could probably be returned to full time when demand warranted this. One of the main concerns is to avoid mismatches between demand and supply. Flexible working is now the norm, often satisfying the needs of employers and of employees for family friendly policies. Such flexible working practices may also attract different kinds of candidates, and the selection system should be family friendly also – with interviews which are at times possible for those with responsibilities for dependents, and tests of a kind which do not discriminate against such groups.

In the previous chapter, flexible sourcing was discussed, including zero hours contracts, casual work, 'permanent' temporaries (a cadre of temporary staff, known to the Company who can come in to help when needed). In this category, short-term contracts, secondments and exchanges, for example between public sector bodies and the private sector, are all potential solutions to recruitment difficulties, but which still require some selection decisions.

CULTURAL FIT

In the previous chapter, the significance currently accorded to finding employees who will easily adapt to the organization's way of doing business and the organization's culture, which is often simply described as the 'way we do things around here', was emphasized. The cultural fit could derive from a high level of employee adaptability, or from a match between the employee's values and world-view, and that of the company and organization.

Selection methods which help to establish cultural fit include those which seek to attract employees and assess them 'in situ', within the role they will play should they join the company. These include internships, temporary workers who can become permanent, trial periods, probation and realistic job previews.

Internships have grown in popularity on both sides of the Atlantic, extending from 'work experience' into fully-fledged interns who are usually recent graduates, performing actual roles, even if these roles are providing assistance to staff, without specific account-abilities themselves. In the UK, there is no legal definition of internship, but HM Revenue & Customs draws a distinction between volunteers and work people. Short-term activities, without set duties and hours can be classified as being performed by volunteers, whereas those who are working for months and are expected to bring some knowledge or skill to set duties are workers, who must be paid the minimum wage. At one time in 2013, there were said to be around 100,000 unpaid interns in the UK (Waller 2013, quoting the Institute for Policy Research).

In the USA, there are also formal federal restrictions on 'unpaid' internships, unless the interns were working for charities. In the USA around 63 per cent of 2013 graduates held internships during their undergraduate studies. The benefits for the interns on both sides of the Atlantic are perceived to be the advantages of gaining experience, if possible with well known companies, which is believed to help their job prospects. For employers, 'Internships are seen as a probationary period where the student is evaluated as a potential full-time hire and treated that way' (Meinert 2013: 26). This is exemplified by Intel, which hired 48 per cent of their interns to permanent jobs.

In many cases, there are learning agreements between interns and their employers. The interns in companies are often managed through a centralized programme, which coordinates their activities. It is, of course, in the interests of employees to give interns a positive experience with the company, as they wish to attract them, or at least, to present a good image of the company, and may see interns as potential customers.

Internships and probation or trial periods are similar approaches. Apprenticeships are formal processes for learning, but also offer something equivalent to a trial period. Apprenticeships are also 'rites of passage', stages through which a craft can be learned, and the person becomes a skilled worker. There are some companies using 'apprentice style' selection processes, as seen on the TV programme: 'The Apprentice'. The selection process is a series of tests, where the applicant could spend two weeks on the selection process. The idea of a trial where the applicant must pass each one in turn is similar to a tournament.

In organizations where there is a vital need to ensure the long-term fit between the employee's and the organization's values, selectors' take their time to be sure they have made the right choice. This also reflects the amount of investment in training that will be required. Examples include the armed forces, the civil service and companies where employees must take risks as part of their work, which requires them to have good judgement. Examples here include Goldman Sachs, where applicants can have as many as eight meetings with 10 interviewers in each meeting, so that applicants see, and are seen by, a large number of managers, before the decision is taken. Similarly, MI5 takes up to six months, where the successful candidates go through an 'assessment day', which is a 'day in the life of an intelligence officer', before the final interview (*People Management* July 2013: 25).

Realistic job previews can now be aided by videos, using e-recruitment technologies, including webcasts and video links online between applicants and existing employees, websites through which company alumni can keep in touch, and rejoin if a suitable vacancy occurs.

THE SELECTION PROCESS

Selectors face an inevitable dilemma. They have to carry out a vitally important task, but one that is at the same time fraught with problems to which there are either no answers or no easy answers. The abiding problem is the dependence on subjective judgement. The essential problem can easily be seen by reference to the idea of the person specification. When considering the attitudes and personal attributes identified as necessary for effective performance, how can the selectors identify these requirements in a person whom they do not know and have only met in the short acquaintance of the selection process?

Selection is all about how to minimize the risk of making mistakes, and doing what is possible in the time available to find enough evidence from the candidate of his or her suitability for the job. One of the advantages of the human element is that management is a social process, and so the inherent subjectivity of selection exposes the candidate to this social reality in the organization to see if both sides, candidate and employer, are happy with the relationship.

In view of the importance and difficulties of the task, employers need to take it most seriously. Appropriate investment at this stage can and will be cost-effective if it avoids the possibly enormous and incalculable costs that faulty selection may produce. Effectiveness in employee selection depends upon:

1   An awareness of the essential nature of the task and its inherent problems.
2   Clear and comprehensive definitions of the criteria for effective performance by job analysis.
3   An understanding of the implications of the concept of reliability and validity for employee selection.
4   An awareness of the range of possible selection methods, their potential value and predictive capabilities.
5   A recognition of the need for training for selectors to make them aware of the inherent problems and to develop the necessary skills for effective practice, for example training in interviewing skills.
6   A follow-up system to check how well the predictions made in the selection process have turned out in practice, in order to correct any systematic errors in the system.

The selection task, as we have already seen, is difficult enough with all its inherent and unavoidable limitations. In the absence of the systematic approach described above, the possibilities of selection becoming a free for all, governed only by self-interest, bias and an opportunity for those in power to select people in their own image.

There is one final important point that needs to be made in discussing the selectors' task. The definitions of effective performance, contained in the job description and person specification, are prescriptions for total effectiveness of performance. There can be few jobs, if any, where the job applicant would be capable of meeting these standards initially or in their entirety. They would normally only be achievable after work experience and training. The selector's task, therefore, is to assess candidates' potential to meet the prescribed performance criteria.

The first of the main questions described above, concerned with the definition of criteria, has already been thoroughly explored in the chapter on job analysis. The remaining part of this chapter will, therefore, deal with the second main question, which concerns the methods available to produce the necessary evidence of potential.

METHODS OF EMPLOYEE SELECTION

Reliability and validity

In choosing methods of employee selection, the selectors need to find methods which are practicable enough to be used in the short duration and restricted environment of the selection process and which provide the closest possible correlation between the predictor and the criteria for effective performance of the job. Before we look at the range of possible methods in any detail, there are fundamental requirements by which the effectiveness of all selection methods have to be judged. These requirements are known as reliability and validity.

Reliability

Reliability here means that the selection methods, tests and ensuing results are consistent and do not vary with time, place or different subjects – that is, test and retest reliability. Thus, a ruler is reliable as an instrument for measuring dimensions whether the subject is wood or cheese, and whether the measurement is done in summer or winter, in Russia or Africa. By this criterion, human selectors of employees are inherently not reliable because standards may vary between selectors and within one selector over a period of time. The issue is the degree of unreliability. This may be reduced by using a variety of measuring devices (tests, interviews), by training assessors and using more than one assessor.

Validity

A valid method or test is one which truly measures what it purports to measure. For example, to ask a candidate at interview to define the requirements for effective management might be a valid measure of knowledge. It is certainly not a valid measure of the candidate's performance potential. The answer could not be of any use in predicting how successful the candidate might be in practice as a manager.

Criterion-related validity is the extent to which the test measures what it is intended to measure, for example, whether the results of the test do predict job performance or the attribute in question. This requires validation of the performance by some independent means, and a statistically significant relationship between performance and the test results for the population involved.

Content-related validity and *construct-related validity* are issues about the technical construction of the test. Content-related validity is the extent to which the content domain is tested by the method chosen. Construct-related validity explores the independence and presence of the psychological construct or trait, and the validity of the test in finding this.

There are three aspects of validity that selectors need to understand:

1 What are the criteria for successful performance, and are they being assessed in the selection process? (The criterion problem)
2 Are the criteria being used valid and reliable (i.e. consistent) measures of behaviour, experience or personality, which predict the performance of candidates?
3 Do the tests actually used predict what they are purported to predict?

The answers to these questions, therefore, are:

1 Agree in advance what constitutes a desirable range of attributes, or competencies, which are required for successful job performance. If possible these should be established by research into the job attributes of successful employees of the organization.
2 Operationalize these into attributes, such as skill levels so they can be tested.
3 Decide, after research, which tests or methods that will accurately predict the possession of these attributes or competencies.

The search over many years for methods that may provide the evidence needed for decisions has produced a wide variety of tests. These tests could be categorized in various ways, but in broad terms they may be conveniently divided into two main types according to their purpose. They are designed to assess candidates' potential to fulfil the requirements of the job in terms of:

■ knowledge, skills and attitudes which already exist
■ knowledge, skills and attitudes which might be developed after training and experience in the job.

In other words, in a comparison between the test situations and those actually occurring in the job, prediction may be based on evidence derived from actual past behaviour, and/or from a calculation of potential future behaviour.

To illustrate the difference with a simple example, let us suppose we are told that a particular job requires the ability to speak Japanese fluently. Having first determined what we mean by speaking fluent Japanese and the criteria by which it is to be assessed, we could make a direct test of all the candidates who claim to speak the language fluently and then assess their abilities against our predetermined standards.

However, if there were a shortage of easily recruitable Japanese speakers, we might decide to invest in training suitable candidates to the standards required. In this situation, we would need to devise some test designed to show whether candidates with no knowledge of Japanese have the latent ability to learn to speak the language fluently in a given period of time. This alternative test clearly could not be a test in Japanese itself, but it would have to be some kind of aptitude-revealing test. We might decide, for example, that proven ability in other languages would be a sufficient indicator of the skills required, but to assume a correlation between, say, the ability to speak French fluently and a potential ability to speak Japanese fluently (for example knowledge of Japan, its customs, etc.), would be unwarranted. This is also an illustration of the need for specialist guidance, because any aptitude test devised would have to be based on a very careful analysis of the factors that seem to be important in speaking Japanese fluently. Furthermore, the reliability and validity of the test would need to be proved by confirming that an acceptable number of people chosen by this method have, in fact, become fluent speakers of Japanese. This kind of proof takes time to obtain, and the original test may well need regular modifications before the employing organization is finally satisfied with its predictive qualities.

To give some idea of the variety of methods used in Europe, Table 11.1 reports on the percentage of use in the countries shown. In the practice of personnel selection, there are many different methods that may be used, as listed below:

(a)   *Ability tests of achievement*: these are designed to test what the candidate already knows or can do, relative to the requirements of the job (e.g. skills in driving, keyboard skills, foreign languages; knowledge of the law, antique furniture, etc.).

(b)   *Ability tests of aptitude*: these are designed to predict latent potential to meet job requirements, which can be developed to required standards by training and experience. Aptitude tests may include intelligence tests, or more specialized tests, designed to indicate particular aptitudes, e.g. mechanical skills. There are numerous ability tests, covering a wide range of aptitudes.

Nevertheless, a well known example of the use of these kinds of tests is worth quoting to illustrate their practical applicability and potential efficacy. Because the training of pilots to fly aircraft is enormously expensive, it is particularly important that selectors should make as few mistakes as possible in selecting potential pilots. However, because selectors are faced with the central problem of predicting future success they need predictors which are as reliable and valid as possible, i.e. where the test data have the highest possible correlation with the performance criteria for flying, and the correlations are statistically significant. Over a number of years aptitude tests have been developed, which have been validated in practice and can be shown to be very good predictors of the success rates in flying training. When tests of this kind are used in combination, as they are in selecting aircrew, they are known as a 'test battery'.

Personality traits undoubtedly have a very important effect on the performance of work, and especially any kind of managerial work, where judgement, and influence on and

TABLE 11.1 INTERVIEW METHODS USED FOR MANAGEMENT (% ORGANIZATIONS)

	UK	France	Germany	Sweden	USA
Panel interviews	77.1	22.1	56.6	59.3	59.6
One-to-one interviews	51.0	92.1	60.0	72.1	68.5
Application forms	65.8	75.7	13.8	33.9	59.2
Psychometric tests	47.0	23.6	6.3	66.3	10.0
Assessment centres	26.4	12.9	22.5	13.1	7.3
Graphology	1.1	19.3	1.6	2.9	0.4
References	78.7	46.4	45.3	84.9	64.6

Interview methods used for professional/technical jobs (% organizations)

	UK	France	Germany	Sweden	USA
Panel interviews	64.1	7.1	47.5	41.5	51.2
One-to-one interviews	52.5	88.6	65.6	77.3	73.8
Application forms	69.5	63.6	22.8	36.8	64.6
Psychometric tests	32.6	16.4	1.6	34.2	8.8
Assessment centres	18.7	4.3	14.7	3.4	7.3
Graphology	0.9	7.1	0.3	1.0	1.2
References	77.5	36.4	32.5	82.2	66.2

Interview methods for clerical jobs (% organizations)

	UK	France	Germany	Sweden	USA
Panel interviews	43.6	5.0	39.1	30.3	23.8
One-to-one interviews	60.2	85.0	65.0	78.9	76.2
Application forms	72.9	58.6	25.3	37.6	69.2
Psychometric tests	15.0	11.4	0.9	18.0	6.2
Assessment centres	6.4	2.1	5.6	1.3	9.2
Graphology	0.9	2.9	0	2.6	0.8
References	74.9	25.7	23.1	80.4	58.5

Source: CRANET Survey 2003.

relationships with others, are crucial (see Chapter 1). A number of tests have been developed and used by psychologists over the years in an attempt to determine personality characteristics as a basis for predicting likely future behaviour at work. Various methods have been designed, for example:

(a)   *Projective tests*: a method in which the subject is required to react freely and spontaneously, usually to visual stimuli. Reactions are then interpreted by the tester as indicators of personality traits, interests, etc. The best-known examples of this kind of test are probably the Rorschach Ink-Blot Test (interpreting responses to ink-blot shapes) and the Thematic Apperception Test (interpreting responses to a series of pictures). The interpretation of the results of these tests is a task for specialists.

(b) *Inventories*: with this method subjects are required to respond to questionnaires normally concerned with how they feel about certain subjects and situations. Well known examples of these kinds of tests have been produced by Cattell (16 PF), Eysenck and Saville and Holdsworth (the Occupational Personality Questionnaire, the OPQ for example). Some inventories are designed to be administered and scored by anyone using the instructions and key provided. With others the tests have to be administered by people trained in their application and interpretation.

(c) *Group situational tests*: in these tests, candidates are observed by the selectors over a period of time as they perform a variety of tasks as a team, sometimes with and some-times without an appointed leader. Tests of this kind first became well known during the Second World War. They began in the UK with the War Office Selection Boards (WOSBs) and are now widely used by the armed forces, governmental and private sector organizations for the selection of potential leaders. The tests are designed to reveal data about the personality traits and interpersonal skills required in managing or cooperating with others in the performance of actual tasks. They provide useful insights into candidates' behaviour as members of groups in a way that no other individual selection method can do. Nevertheless, they represent behaviour measured by the personal, subjective interpretations of human observers in artificial circumstances and are, therefore, open to question in terms of their reliability and validity.

(d) *Interviews*: whatever other tests could be used, the selection process invariably includes an interview. Quite often it is the only method used, and in various ways. There may be several interviews covering general and specialist aspects of the job, and interviews may be conducted by individual interviewers or by a board of inter-viewers. Apart from the information obtained at the interview, interviewers also make use of accounts provided by candidates themselves in the form of completed applic-ation forms, CVs, letters, etc., and by others competent to comment on the candidates in the form of open testimonials or confidential reference reports.

It is vitally important to the effectiveness of the system that results should be followed up. This means that the selectors need to have a regular flow of feedback from line managers reporting how effectively selected employees are actually performing. These data can then be used to trace and remedy weaknesses in the selection process. Formal validation studies are rare, but some organizations do analyse labour turnover, and sometimes appraisal assessments, to check the effectiveness of selection decisions.

ASSESSMENT CENTRES

During the 1980s, organizations increasingly used assessment-centre type approaches, especially for the selection of young graduates and for those organizations where there was likely to be a group or cohort entry. Sometimes this rather expensive method is adopted where although only one post is involved, selection decisions are seen to be especially sensitive, given the likely consequences of error.

Assessment centres are not necessarily physical places – the term is used to describe the collection of assessment methods, including group situational tests, applied to a cohort entry where there are specifically designed tests and exercises applied to all applicants (sometimes based on the competencies researched within the organization which are associated with effective entry level or higher level performance). The activities may span several days and include assessment by senior line managers and informal discussions, as well as psychometric and other tests conducted by psychologists and other experts.

At the end of the exercise, judgements are recorded on each candidate and, of necessity, there must be a final discussion between the assessors, after the exercises are over, to determine an overall rating. The following principles apply to the establishment of assessment centres:

1   They are costly, and need expert assistance to design. Therefore, they are only really cost-effective if there is a large repeat demand for the job in question (e.g. graduate management trainee).
2   The assessment-centre exercises must be researched to establish validity and reliability in that particular organization.
3   The observers/assessors must be properly trained and must have practised observation.
4   The administration of the centre must be professional, with suitable accommodation available, and documentation prepared well in advance.
5   Candidates must be advised in advance that this is to be an assessment-centre approach.
6   Candidates, whether successful or not, should be given expert feedback on their performance, and reasons for selection or non-selection.
7   Confidentiality must be maintained with data, apart from in 6 above. However, training plans for successful candidates should address any needs revealed.

THE SELECTION INTERVIEW

The selection interview has already been briefly discussed above in the general survey of selection methods. However, because it is the one method that is always used, and is of proven and demonstrably limited value as a predictor, it merits a separate, detailed examination. This examination will cover why its value is limited and, since it has to be used, what steps can be taken to give maximum possible effectiveness. How can a limited instrument be used to best advantage?

For many years the selection interview has been the subject of research in order to determine its value as a method. In general, the research has produced a pessimistic evaluation of the selection interview, but has also indicated that its value may be significantly enhanced when interviewers have been trained. If the interview is analysed in the light of the general problem of human communication and of the particular requirements for reliability and validity, it is not difficult to see why it has inherent barriers to success as a selection method. The selection interview is not reliable for the following reasons:

1   The instrument of measurement is human.
2   No two interviewers will interpret and assess information in the same way.
3   The same interviewer will reveal fluctuations in interpretations of data and assessments over a period of time.

The interview on its own cannot be a valid test of candidates' suitability for employment for the following reasons:

1   It is a contrived, interrogative conversation, involving a meeting invariably between strangers and seldom lasting for more than about an hour. It is, therefore, an artificially distorted and entirely stressful situation, no matter what efforts the interviewers may make to reduce the tension. The larger the number of interviewers the greater the tension is likely to be.
2   It cannot possibly test the important areas that add up to suitability for employment, i.e.: competence effectively to perform the professional requirements of a job over a period of time; the personal disposition to relate cooperatively with future work colleagues in groups and within the organization as a whole; the capacity for self-development and the potential to assume wider responsibilities.
3   The interview may indicate that a candidate is presentable, fluent or quick-thinking under the conditions of the interview, but to suppose that the pattern of interview behaviour would be repeated in the very different circumstances of work in the organization over a long period of time would be a quite unwarranted assumption.

The only kind of validity that the interview can confidently be said to have is to test whether people can cope with the special and unusual conditions of the interview. Nevertheless, it is often very difficult to persuade selection interviewers that much of the evidence that they require about a candidate's potential for effective work performance cannot be properly tested by the interview.

It is pertinent to ask why the interview is so widely and prominently used if it is a method with such demonstrable limitations. The reasons are these:

1   It has a high face-validity, i.e. both selectors and candidates have long been accustomed to its use and appear to have much greater faith in its efficacy than the research evidence warrants.
2   Sooner or later there has to be a meeting between the employer and prospective employee, if only so that a number of routine checks may be made on both sides and

to give the employer an opportunity to amplify and clarify information provided by application forms and any other documents. It is also an opportunity for the employer to inquire into any inconsistencies, and to explore the evidence. In this way, the interview can be combined with other methods to examine the value of other sources of evidence, and to hear the applicant's views.

3   The candidate has a need also to be able to present his or her views and explanations about his/her career history, the reasons for success or failures that he/she has come to see as the public narrative of his/her career. The need for the selection process to be seen to be fair by the candidate, with opportunities for candidates to present their views, is also significant for the corporate image.

4   Despite continuous research and the introduction of possibly promising advances in new directions (e.g. assessment centres), a method that will solve the basic dilemma of accurately forecasting future behaviour in employment has yet to be found.

Since the interview is likely to continue to play a major role in the selection process, it seems sensible to adopt a realistic approach, which means making the best possible use of the interview. This is the really important question to which attention needs to be given. As the research data have shown, anyone who is likely to have responsibilities for personnel selection needs to be trained.

There is sometimes a particular problem in training senior managers. Having interviewed without any formal training perhaps for many years, they inevitably develop confidence in their own styles and methods, and often come to believe that seniority and experience are the main requirements for making decisions on suitability for employment. They may find it very hard to accept that the selection method that they have been using for years is a very fallible instrument, (and one which was used to select them) or that they lack system and skills. Training courses can have a particular value in helping to overcome problems of insight and sensitivity in unskilled interviewers. Trainees can participate in selection interviews that are very close to reality. Discussion with observers and tutors, supported by video replays of the interview, can demonstrate the inherent problems of the interview itself and the methods that are likely to be effective in practice, in ways which no amount of lecturing or reading could ever achieve. The skills used in interviews, such as question technique can be broken down, and taught as a distinct topic.

VARIATIONS IN PATTERNS OF INTERVIEWS

The following variations are possible in the patterns of interviews:

1   A single one-to-one interview.
2   A series of one-to-one interviews at the end of which, interviewers compare evidence and discuss final conclusions.

3   A board or panel interview with a group of interviewers.
4   A combination of one-to-one and board interviews.

There are arguments for and against each variation. The main criteria to be considered in assessing the merits and demerits of a particular interview pattern are:

1   Acquiring the best possible evidence on which to base judgements and decisions.
2   Giving candidates the fairest possible opportunities to provide the most accurate account of themselves in the difficult circumstances of the interview.

If we assess the possible variations in the light of these criteria, we could draw the following conclusions:

1   A single one-to-one interview is likely to be the least stressful, but has the disadvantage that the acquisition of evidence, judgements and decisions rely on one person only.
2   A series of one-to-one interviews overcomes the problem of the single interview and has the advantage of providing a range of views and judgements, helping to avoid biases.
3   Board interviews are potentially more stressful for the candidates than one-to-one interviews because the candidate is faced with several interviewers at the same time, and questioning can seem relentless. The board interview has the advantage that all interviewers are provided with the same evidence, but are able to make independent interpretations and judgements. There is research evidence to show that boards are more likely to make successful selection decisions than the single one-to-one interview.

Because of the perceived stress inherent in board interviews, it is very important to keep the number of interviewers to the absolute necessary minimum, for example, three or four members at the most. Interview boards of large numbers of interviewers are not only likely to intimidate many candidates, they are also much more difficult for the chairperson to control. The number of interviewers also has an effect on the length of the interview.
        The main requirements for an effective interview are listed under three headings.

PRE-INTERVIEW PREPARATORY PHASE

1   Use the data of job analysis to determine the requirements for effective performance in the job and the criteria by which these may be identified and assessed. These data provide the foundation for the whole selection process.
2   Determine acceptable entry levels for new staff vis-à-vis the job requirements for fully effective performance.

3   Consider and, whenever practicable, use, other tests and information to supplement the evidence provided by the interview. Any of these other selection methods used need to be validated, i.e. shown to improve the predictive quality of the process.

4   Decide on the number of interviewers. When an interview board is used, the membership should be the smallest number necessary to fulfil the task.

5   Pay particular attention to all important environmental details such as time, place and setting to enable candidates to feel at ease.

6   Produce a coverage plan designed to provide the maximum possible significant information. One plan that is the simplest and likely to be most effective is a systematic, chronological survey of the important areas of the life history. Equally, areas critical to success in the job can be used as a framework, e.g. relevant skills, knowledge, experience, knowledge of the industry sector, how to apply skills, development, education and training received.

7   When interview boards are held, discuss and agree the objectives, criteria, the coverage plan and the areas that each board member will cover. The leadership of this discussion is a major responsibility of the chairperson.

INTERVIEW-COVERAGE PLAN

The criteria for assessing applicants' suitability for employment are contained in the person specification, which is a definition of the knowledge, skills and personal attributes needed for effective performance. Applicants may already possess some of the required qualifications or have the latent ability to develop others with training and work experience.

Following the broad chronological, systematic coverage plan throughout helps to ensure a comprehensive coverage. Deviations are likely to create gaps in the plan.

PROCESSING APPLICATIONS

Recent survey evidence shows that 92 per cent of employers with more than 20,000 employees are using hiring technology, such as software which tracks applications, grades applicants, administers tests and sends out letters automatically. Even in the case of employers with less than 5000 employees, 54 per cent use some type of online tool according to the Towers Watson HR service delivery survey 2012, quoted by Robb (2013). Even for some manufacturing jobs, USA employers responding to the large numbers of applicants coming forward owing to the economic climate, used online tools to screen applications. In those companies where there are large number of applications, candidates are screened, there is an automated application system and assessment to identify high risk candidates, and following job interviews, behavioural and characteristic tests.

To create automated systems, processes mapping is the first step. This is a valuable step in any case to improve efficiency.

TABLE 11.2 THE SEVEN-POINT PLAN AS A MODEL FOR A SELECTION PROCEDURE FOR POTENTIAL AIRCRAFT PILOTS

	Essential	Desirable	How identified
Physical	100% fitness		Comprehensive range of medical tests
Attainments	Specified subjects and grades in A levels and GCSEs	Degree or equivalent qualifications	Documentary evidence amplified by interview
General intelligence	Levels specified in terms of psychometric tests		Ability tests of education/intelligence supplemented by interview data
Special aptitudes	Coordination, mechanical comprehension, speed of reaction, handling rapidly changing information		Special ability tests of aptitude related to success in flying training
Interests	Aviation and related subjects	World affairs	Documentary evidence amplified by interview
Disposition	Equable temperament, sociable and co-operative		Documentary evidence amplified by interview
Circumstances	Mobility		Documentary evidence amplified by interview

Social media is often used now to make checks on applicants, such as Facebook, LinkedIn and similar networks. CIPD research (PM Today Online 9 December 2013) shows that two-fifths of companies look at the candidate's own online activity when making decisions (what the person says about himself/herself, the contacts they have and their non-work activity). It would be good practice to advise candidates that these checks are being made.

EMPLOYMENT LAW AND PERSONNEL SELECTION

Relevant employment law is discussed in detail in Chapters 24 and 25. However, we need to stress here the importance of legislation about discrimination on grounds of race, gender, marital status, age, religious belief and disability. Current legislation and codes of practice require employers to take all possible measures to ensure that there is no direct or indirect discrimination in their job descriptions, person specifications, advertisements and selection procedures.

Direct discrimination (for example, white males only) is blatant. Indirect discrimination (for example, asking women but not men questions about the effects of domestic commitments on employability or specifying requirements such as physical height which are not necessary for the job but which would discriminate against women) is more difficult to combat. It is usually the result of long-established attitudes, and selectors are often not alert to their own unfair discriminatory practices.

The training of all selectors along with more general management training in anti-discrimination practices and policies, is essential. Recognizing the inherent tendencies to discriminate in many people is an important part of any such programme.

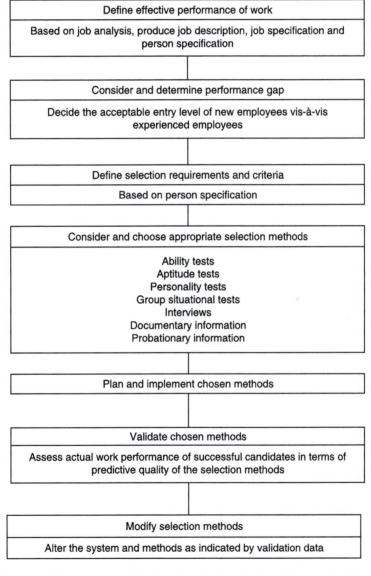

Figure 11.1 Summary of the main elements of a system for the selection of new employees

QUESTIONS

1   How can selection decisions be made with the minimum bias?
2   What are the steps that can be taken to ensure tests for selection are reliable and valid?
3   What is the role of assessment centres in the selection process? Why is this method used?
4   What are the main problems with the selection interview and what can be done to mitigate these?

REFERENCES

Meinert, D. (2013). 'Fresh faces'. *H R Magazine*. November 23–28. *Society for Human Resource Management*.

People Management (2013). 'The world's toughest recruiters'. July 25.

Robb, D. (2013). 'Better hiring through technology'. *H R Magazine*. June 46–52. Society for Human Resource Management.

Waller, D. (2013). 'Intern or employee?' *People Management*. July 34–38.

PART FOUR

DEVELOPING PEOPLE

12 PERFORMANCE APPRAISAL

This chapter examines appraisal systems, and the attendant policies which link into development. The fundamental importance of defining the criteria for the effective performance of work has already been stressed in previous chapters. The assessments of performance, potential and development needs involve eliciting evidence of past and recent achievements and shortfalls which are related to the criteria as a basis for judgements and decisions. This puts managers and HR in a position to provide answers with reasonable confidence to important questions arising from assessments, for example:

■ Are employees meeting the criteria for effective performance?
■ If not, why not, and what action needs to be taken (e.g. training, further work experience, counseling, change of job or changes to the current role)?
■ What does the evidence of assessment show in terms of potential for promotion and advancement and the development needs of the individual?
■ What does it show in terms of the rewards that are merited?

The 'psychological contract' is the term used to describe the 'deal' between employer and employee, not the legal contract, but the bargain implicitly struck about what each party can expect from each other, and about the obligations each has to the other. Performance appraisals are not just about performance: they are also a window onto how the employee value proposition is perceived. The employee experiences the reality of the promises made when discussing career and other issues in the appraisal. The central features are the notions of 'exchange' and the reciprocity of a personal relationship. When we assess performance we enter into the debate about the bargain at an individual level on topics such as the promotion opportunities available and the challenges and developmental aspects of the work. Some employers are reluctant to promise careers, but can offer learning opportunities, which improve the employee's chances of employability, and they can sometimes offer flexibility in working arrangements. In return they may expect flexibility and commitment on the part of the employee.

The desire for feedback is a part of the human condition. There are a variety of reasons, which are summarized by Anseel, Lievens and Levy (2007). These feedback needs are associated with our own human needs:

Self-assessment: to reduce uncertainty, to know how well you are doing.

Self-improvement: to improve performance, to acknowledge personal goals, to master a performance or role.

Self-enhancement: to protect one's ego, to cope with stress, to avoid threats to the self-concept.

Self-verification: to locate the self, and to preserve identity in social and and personal situations.

(adapted from Anseel, Lievens and Levy 2007)

Performance management approaches are specific to particular cultures. Although in this chapter the Anglo-Saxon approach is described, and is likely to be found in many large businesses, one should keep in mind there may be other approaches taken elsewhere. How performance is judged depends on the way managers are regarded, who decides the ratings, the way criticism is normally understood in each culture, and the extent to which feedback from others is sought or provided in certain cultures.

Examples here include the importance of 'saving face' in Far Eastern cultures, so that the more direct approaches to feedback might be unacceptable, and has to be delivered in a more subtle way. The importance of group performance to managers in other cultures, such as in Japan, may mean managers in these countries are uncomfortable attributing success or failure to individuals (Clause and Briscoe 2009). One consequence of cultural differences is that HR practices in multinationals are not always transferred successfully between countries.

THE REQUIREMENTS FOR EFFECTIVE APPRAISAL SYSTEMS

The main requirements for effectiveness in systems of staff assessment are:

1   The purpose of the scheme should be very carefully defined and published. This indicates the organizational philosophy and determines the nature and details of the scheme to be used in practice, and the way the psychological contract is intended to be acted out.

2   The details of appraisal schemes should be carefully explained to all newly appointed employees during induction interviews, following discussions of their roles, objectives and careers.

3   Formal arrangements, which are simple and not excessively bureaucratic, should be established for the effective implementation of appraisal schemes and to ensure adherence to agreed criteria. Wherever possible, avoid complex 'point scores' type schemes and reduce the number of forms to the minimum necessary to produce consistency of data gathering.

4   All staff involved in appraisal schemes should be given training in the requisite know-ledge, skills and attitudes. This will be the best way to ensure the performance criteria are applied fairly. Training should include purposes, details and requirements of the schemes in use in the organization, an analysis of the problems of assessment and the accepted means of mitigating these problems, the skills required for effective practice and practical exercises to illustrate what is required.

The assessment of work involves three types of review: performance appraisal, potential and reward reviews. These reviews are closely interrelated and linked by the main theme of assessment but they serve different purposes, require different methods and cannot all be undertaken by a sole manager. All three reviews have a major impact on the psychological contract. Assessing work performance of an employee in a particular job is clearly the responsibility of the line manager concerned. Reviewing potential has long-term implications. It needs to take into account all available information about performance over a period of time in a variety of jobs, and may require the use of specialist techniques and methods for the assessment of potential. Potential assessment has to be seen in an organizational context, related to organizational needs, objectives and opportunities. For these reasons it is a task for senior management and HR staff, who, by definition, have an overall view of the organization's future needs. Reward reviews would normally be carried out by line management, but will typically involve HR staff. The latter will needed to work on the application of scales, the overall costs of recommendations and to administer any reward schemes, such as performance or merit payment schemes.

These three aspects of the assessments of staff are discussed below.

THE DEVELOPMENT OF PERFORMANCE APPRAISAL IN PRACTICE

Historically, performance appraisal in this country originated mainly in the public sector of employment, for example: the armed forces and the Civil Service. Now, formal approaches to performance appraisal are widely used in the majority of work organizations in both public and private sectors. The details of these formal schemes vary considerably depending on the purposes and cultures of individual work organizations. These differences are reflected in the format of reports, the degrees of confidentiality and openness rendered, who conducts the appraisal, the level of participation by those being appraised, the nature of appraisal discussions between those appraising and those being appraised and how the information is used, for example in rewards, promotion and training decisions.

In the development of performance appraisal schemes, two broad approaches are discernible. For convenience of description and comparison we will label them as Theory X and Theory Y, after McGregor's thesis on managerial attitudes. The essential difference between the two is that, in a Theory X scheme, managers produce assessment reports on their subordinates but in a Theory Y scheme assessment reports are the product of joint discussion between managers and their subordinates. A Theory X performance appraisal scheme has the following typical features:

1   Managers are the sole judges of work performance.
2   There is an apparent confidence in the manager's ability and authority to judge and, therefore, no training is given to appraisers for this task.
3   Assessments are based on numerical ratings of abstract qualities, e.g. initiative, drive, energy, reliability, intelligence, loyalty, integrity, etc.
4   The appraisal includes a narrative report made by the manager, which is often not divulged to the appraised subordinate and is open to personal bias, to misunderstandings of meanings and sometimes even to sarcasm.
5   There are minimal formal provisions for feedback to, or discussions with, those being appraised.
6   The main purpose of the appraisal is to identify those seen by management as good or bad performers.
7   There is little or no attention paid to the developmental needs of employees.

A Theory Y approach to performance appraisal has objectives which are quite different from the Theory X approach, these being:

1   To provide feedback to the employee on his/her work performance, and an opportunity for the employee to talk about perceptions of progress.
2   To identify and remedy problems in the job itself, in respect of job satisfaction, and the extent to which there are motivational aspects of the role.
3   To identify strengths and weaknesses in performance as a basis for future action.
4   To identify needs for training, development, further experience and suitability for advancement.
5   To develop constructive manager/subordinate relationships.
6   To develop the individual's capacity for self-assessment and self-awareness, for seeking ways to solve his or her own problems and to find ways for self-improvement.

The Theory X approach to performance appraisal in its extreme form, as described above, is prevalent in organizations where styles of management are generally more authoritarian. In recent years there has been a visible move towards the Theory Y end of the continuum. Nevertheless, vestiges of a Theory X approach to performance appraisal still survive. In some organizations it remains very much in its traditional form. In others, whilst their schemes may reveal noticeable changes in the direction of a Theory Y approach, for example, more openness in discussion between managers and their subordinates, they still retain some of the essential features of Theory X attitudes. For example, in spite of the demonstrable and proven problems of defining and measuring abstract qualities, and the obvious advantages of concentrating on the objectives and tasks of the job, in some appraisal schemes, managers are still required to give marks for abstract traits (e.g. initiative, reliability, etc.). Again, although open discussions may be held between managers and their subordinates, these may in practice amount to little more than attempts by managers to justify their own views and marks, which are already recorded in the reports and are not likely to be affected by anything that appraised subordinates may say during discussions.

The main difference between these extremes is the limitations of the one and the opportunities afforded by the other. All the evidence of academic research and practical experience strongly emphasizes the advantages and potential effectiveness of performance appraisal schemes based on a Theory Y approach. We can now examine in more detail the general requirements for an effective system that applies this philosophy in practice.

THE REQUIREMENTS OF AN EFFECTIVE SYSTEM

The requirements described below are based on the premise that a Theory Y philosophy applied to performance appraisal is likely to produce the most effective system, because it emphasizes, in particular, the importance of helping individuals to improve their performance, to develop their abilities and to encourage their commitment.

The first step is to define the requirements for effective performance in order to provide the criteria without which sound and systematic judgements cannot be made.

Many performance appraisal schemes have, at their heart, an objective setting process. This often requires the classic cascade of objectives downwards, so that at each level the objectives of the individual are incorporated into the objectives of the organization as a whole. This raises a number of issues:

1   Are the objectives decided by the manager, the subordinate, or is there a process by which both come to agree them? There may be some objectives which are preset, where the department has little choice, for example sales targets already agreed in the budget, whilst other targets may be open to adjustment (for example the frequency of sales calls according to the type of customer).

2   Are the objectives sufficiently challenging or too difficult to achieve? If the objective is a 'stretch' target, it may be ideal for some individuals, but a step too far for others, who will be demotivated by being asked to work beyond their capacity without training.

Without challenge, and expanding intellectual horizons, some individuals will seek more learning opportunities elsewhere.

3   Is the difficulty of objectives consistent for all people at that level or do some people have particularly difficult tasks, and others have easy targets to achieve? Managers need to be careful that they balance the objectives for each individual according to their subordinate's capacity and capability. This can be an important issue if there is a linkage of appraisals to promotion and reward.

4   Setting objectives in matrix structures is much more difficult than in a more traditional bureaucratic structure. The matrix role interdependencies create complex priorities and varying demands. It is often impractical to involve all the people involved in the goal setting process. Apart from the number of people potentially involved, objectives and priorities can change rapidly. A workshop format may be useful here, for all the parties formally to come together on a quarterly basis say, to thrash out difficulties, to gain common perceptions and standards, and to set priorities. Some organizations use the acronym 'SMART' to give managers a memorable shorthand for describing best practice in objective setting. Objectives should be: Suitable, Measurable, Achievable, Realistic and Timely. Suitable objectives will be those which come from the objectives and plans for the unit, cascaded down. Measurement of objectives is important, otherwise no one will be able to say the extent to which the objectives have been achieved. Unless objectives are achievable, employees will not be motivated to try to achieve them. Objectives must also be realistic, have a real impact on the work of the employee and be subject to a time dimension for their accomplishment.

Next, the purposes of the scheme should be defined and published as a basis for effective practice, e.g.:

- to assess whether defined requirements and objectives of work are being met
- to identify strengths and weaknesses and to take any appropriate subsequent action
- to help employees to develop themselves by self-awareness, self-analysis, self-confidence and by finding solutions to their own problems
- to identify employees who are performing well or badly for purposes of retention, advancement, rewards, inefficiency or development procedures
- to develop and improve communication and relationships between managers and their staff.

The purposes and details of the appraisal scheme should form an important part of the induction interview between managers and new employees. Managers should adopt and explain the following measures to be taken in practice:

1   Performance appraisal is a continuous process involving a joint assessment by managers and individual members of staff. It should not be an annual ritual in which managers make confidential judgements about their employees.

2   Managers and their members of staff need to make regular agreed notes about performance, e.g. successes, failures, reasons, suggestions for remedies, etc.

3   Managers and their staff should meet regularly for discussions about performance and any problems in achieving the agreed objectives, so that any action needed is taken there and then. There is no point in delaying such necessary action until a formal annual performance takes place. For example, an identified training need requires immediate attention. The annual performance appraisal is not the place to spring surprises on the employee.

4   A periodic review (for example annually, or six-monthly) should be held to conform to organizational policy and practice, to summarize the appraisal discussions that have regularly taken place and to plan for the future.

5   Before the periodic review takes place, managers and members of staff who are being appraised need to confirm the time, place and agenda for the appraisal meeting.

6   The details of the agenda will naturally vary with different situations, but the broad outlines for appraising performance by means of joint discussion between managers and their staff should cover the following headings and questions:

   (i)   *The role:* the role description, objectives, component tasks, methods and resources. Are these up to date, are they relevant, are these problems identified with any of these? What changes are indicated? What precise action is recommended by whom, and how and why?

   (ii)   *Work performance*: what are the objectives that have to be met and the tasks to be fulfilled? Have these been achieved? What is the actual evidence from work performance, indicating success or failure? What are the reasons for success or failure? How far have any failures been within or outside the job holder's control? What does the evidence of past performance show about strengths and weaknesses in the knowledge, skills and attitudes of the job holder? What precise action is recommended by whom, does it show how and when to build on strengths, to remedy weaknesses and to develop the individual by means of training and further work experience?

   (iii) *Summary of action proposed*: what action has been agreed to be taken by whom, how and when?

Before the appraisal discussion takes place, the manager and individual member of staff separately work through these headings to answer the main questions, using any notes that they have made throughout the period under review. This exercise is the crux of the process and of the philosophy underlying this approach, because it emphasizes and concentrates on:

- joint assessment, involving both managers and their staff
- the key issues – the job, performance and future needs
- observable, measurable evidence from actual work rather than abstract qualities.

Having made their separate notes and assessments, the manager and the individual meet to compare their views, to find out how far they agree or disagree, to explore reasons for any disagreement, to try to find constructive solutions and to decide what action is needed for the future to resolve problems in the job and to meet the individual's development needs.

The manager leads the discussion and is, therefore, responsible for seeing that it systematically follows the agenda in order to achieve its purpose. At the same time, it is very important that it should be conducted in an atmosphere that is as informal and relaxed as possible. The manner in which the discussion is conducted is extremely important. The manager is 'in the chair', but if performance appraisal is intended to help to improve perform-ance, to develop individuals and to improve communication, then the discussion needs to be an open two-way exchange of perceptions and not a managerial monologue. Thus, managers should try to find out how far perceptions coincide, where and how they differ and what any differences of views might imply. They need to stimulate people to think, to encourage them to analyse, to become more self-aware and to put forward constructive proposals.

In practice, this requires managers to start by asking questions and listening. Having noted what those being appraised have to say, they are then better placed to make helpful comments, to give their own views and any advice or instructions that they think appropriate.

At the end of the discussion, the main points covered and the action agreed need to be summarized, recorded and, above all, followed up. These decisions will be the first items on the agenda of any subsequent appraisal discussions. The record of the meeting should be mutually agreed, and retained on the employee's file.

BEHAVIOURALLY ANCHORED RATING SCALES (BARS)

'Bars' are numerical scales which identify the specific behaviours which are evidence of good performance in the role under consideration, and the range of behaviours which could be expected to be found in the role. The appraisal shows the degree to which the beha-viours of the person concerned correspond to the scales, giving a numerical score.

This method represents yet another example of the move away in recent decades from unprofitable attempts to assess abstract qualities and to focus attention on actual perform-ance and behaviour, for example, considering not whether an employee shows initiative, but what he or she actually does that indicates 'initiative' or lack of it.

Scales and ratings are produced through discussion, observation and analysis (for example, critical incident technique) by managerial and HR staff. The first task in this process is to identify key categories of performance, that is, core competencies, as described earlier. Scales of behaviour, derived from actual experience of the job, are then produced for each category, ranging from definitions of the most efficient to the least efficient behaviour and performance.

For example, a key category for a manager might be training and development of staff. The highest rating on the scale might be 'is totally committed to the training and develop-ment of staff and makes effective use of on-job and off-job methods'. The lowest rating might be 'does not understand the importance of training and development of staff and takes no action in this direction'.

It is as yet a matter for debate whether BARS represent a significant advance in performance appraisal. The identification of comprehensive and detailed criteria, based on actual job requirements, is undoubtedly an important contribution to improved quality of judgements. On the other hand, experience of the scheme indicates that the production of the categories and scales tends to be a time-consuming and expensive process, needing to be regularly reviewed as job descriptions change.

As we have already emphasized, criteria are vitally important as the first stage in any judgemental process. But so is the task of producing valid evidence, and in any open joint system of appraisal this could sometimes result in unresolvable differences between the manager and the employee being appraised. If the recommendations for effective practice based on a Theory Y approach described above are put into practice, this will logically be reflected in the details of formats used for performance appraisal. Ideally, therefore, the format should:

- be based on the definition of criteria for effective performance, as described in the job description and person specification
- require the need to produce evidence related to the criteria
- require the need to produce judgements, based on a comparison of evidence and criteria, followed by recommendations for future action
- require completion by managers and employees being appraised as a joint exercise
- be simple, easy to understand and accompanied by explanatory notes based on organizational policy, purpose and required practice
- be uniformly applied throughout the organization.

PROBLEMS OF PERFORMANCE APPRAISAL

Whatever scheme of performance appraisal is used, there will always be fundamental, inev-itable problems. In essence, performance is a human judgement which, as we have already seen when considering personnel selection, suffers from problems of reliability and validity. Human judgement depends on the unique genetic and environmental influences that form each individual's values, attitudes, expectations and perceptions.

The questions addressed by managers before conducting the appraisal are:

■ What does the job require?
■ What does the job holder have to do to perform effectively?
■ What evidence from work performance would indicate effective performance?
■ What does the assessment of evidence of performance indicate about future actions required?

These questions are systematically interdependent. Each requires a judgement that affects the next question in the sequence.

An approach that seeks to make use of a wider range of relevant opinions is 360 degree feedback.

360 DEGREE FEEDBACK

There has been an increase in the use of 360 degree feedback processes in the assessment of people. The notion of 360 degree feedback is that employees benefit from feedback from those who are colleagues, customers, their manager and their subordinates: from all 'directions', below, above and at the same level.

Feedback is designed to build confidence, to reinforce desired behaviours, clarify problems, improve self-awareness, give recognition and, ultimately, to improve performance.

The process usually follows a procedure whereby competencies having been established and defined, individuals are asked to nominate up to, say, six significant others (who could be described as stakeholders in the organization) whom they know within the categories (subordinate, colleagues, manager, customer, etc.) to whom feedback forms are sent asking for the respondent's opinion of the subject on the competency dimensions. The respondents may well use a rating scale. These are returned to HR and will usually be given to the employee, who discusses the responses with his or her line manager. This latter stage could be optional, but it is important that there are discussions about the meaning of the feedback to the individual, and what future development the person would find helpful in their work performance. This discussion can be successful if there is coaching or development counseling available, so that the evidence from the 360 degree feedback can be used in a future development plan.

For example, one large organization introduced eight main competencies, which were broken down into their component definitions, and rated by respondents in terms of the importance of the competencies to the job, and the individual's performance (effectiveness). Thus, for example, the competence of 'making things happen' included 'establishing and maintaining contacts in all areas of the organization', 'balances day-to-day operations with important projects', 'encourages collaborative working' as well as seven more parts of the competence. Each part is rated on the performance scale and the importance scale (see Figure 12.1), for example: 'balances day-to-day operations with important projects'.

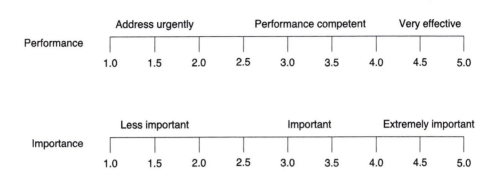

Figure 12.1 Example of performance scales

Averages of the data can be taken, and improvements over time can be plotted. The reports of all the respondents are usually grouped together for each individual, showing how respondents in general rated each competence. Taking these ratings, individuals are encouraged to share the data with their manager (although this is not mandatory) and to discuss what the feedback means. From the discussion, a personal development plan can be drawn up.

The HR department usually runs the scheme, but the data is 'owned' by the individual in most 360 degree systems. This means confidentiality is preserved, although clearly there are sensitivities involved. Respondents are anonymous as far as the subject is concerned, and if the subject chooses to share the data with his or her manager or colleagues, it is usually the subject's own decision.

THE NEED FOR TRAINING

Because a system is only as good as the people who operate it, managerial staff at all levels need training in performance appraisal to make it effective in practice.

The objectives of training should be:

1   To standardize practice across the organization, in the interests of fairness. This is particularly important if rewards or promotion decisions are affected by the appraisal decisions.
2   To explain the organization's system and give opportunities for staff to discuss and question.
3   To identify general requirements for effective practice.
4   To provide practice in the important skills, such as giving and receiving feedback, assessing and discussing performance.

Details of potentially effective training exercises are outside the scope of this chapter. However, they should simulate reality as closely as possible in the following ways by requiring those on the programmes:

1   To make assessments of real, but unidentified, job holders, so that the discipline of the appraiser's approach may be analysed, i.e. defining criteria for effective performance, making sound and fair conclusions.

2   To carry out role-play discussions, based on credible scripts, in order to practise the general performance appraisal agenda described earlier and the necessary skills.

The learning opportunities provided by simulated role-play exercises will be significantly enhanced by the use of video recordings for purposes of analysis and discussion.

THE LINKAGE TO TALENT MANAGEMENT

Performance appraisal is a basic building block for talent management, where career management, succession planning and management development are all brought together in the strategic purpose to build capability for the organization for the future. We go on to look at this in Chapter 13, where we explore talent management.

QUESTIONS

1   Why do organizations usually set up a process and system for conducting employee appraisals?

2   What kinds of data can be gathered from the appraisal process, and how could (a) line managers and (b) HR departments make use of this?

3   What are the advantages/disadvantages of the 360 degree performance appraisal approach?

4   What should the employee gain from a performance appraisal review with their manager?

REFERENCES

Anseel, F., Lievans, F. and Levy, P. E. (2007). 'A self-motives perspective on feedback-seeking behavior: linking organizational behavior and social psychology research'. *International Journal of Management Reviews* 9, 3: 211–36.

Claus, L., and Briscoe, D. (2009). 'Employee performance management across borders: a review of relevant academic literature'. *International Journal of Management Reviews* 11, 2: 175–96.

13 TALENT MANAGEMENT

WHY IS TALENT MANAGEMENT IMPORTANT?

The term 'talent management' came into prominence in 1997, when the consultancy firm McKinsey and Company referred to the 'war for talent'. The term has been used increasingly over the last decade. This represents an awareness of the importance attached to the recruitment and development of high quality employees for the success of an organization. There are many definitions of talent management. For some commentators, the whole of HRM is devoted to talent management, which indicates that the management of people touches on every aspect of HRM. For others, talent management is concerned with fostering and watching over the talented few in the business, who can make the biggest strategic contribution now and in the future.

One fundamental issue for the organization to decide is whether talent is to be sought at every level in the business, from cleaners to directors, or is talent a term which describes special characteristics, unusual abilities, not easily developed or found in the labour market? In addition to the universality versus specificity debate, there is the question of whether talent management is an overall management approach, or is it a convenient way to 'bundle' policies together because they are all concerned with development? The following table helps to show the implications of each approach.

In this chapter, the way talent is managed and developed will be the main topic. The apparent dichotomy in Table 13.1 can be resolved by taking a broader, more strategic approach to talent management. The strategic argument is based on the need to manage human capital as an organizational capability, since these strategically important assets are a source of competitive advantage (following the ideas of the 'resource based view' (RBV)).

TABLE 13.1 DIFFERENT APPROACHES TO TALENT MANAGEMENT

Talent Management:

	Applies universally	Applies to specific roles
HR belief/values/stance	All employees, everyone has an equal chance of success.	All senior staff and certain specialists.
TM development policies	All appraisal and development and educational programmes are open to all.	Policies applicable, changes with needs/and business case.

With this in mind, the time and resources spent acquiring, protecting and developing human capital is well spent. This means there is a need to lay down medium to long term plans to ensure the organization can recruit the talented people it needs, who are much in demand, and that the development of these strategically important people is undertaken so that capabilities are embedded in the business which will provide the business with a competitive advantage. From the RBV perspective, the processes of development are also significant. By developing talented people, who can be available to take on bigger jobs as they flourish, the organization is establishing a valuable hedge against risks such as unwanted losses of staff, and the process involved itself is an inimitable, organization specific attribute, which gives the company a competitive advantage.

Talent management is based, therefore, on the assumption that superior organizational performance derives from high quality skills, knowledge and the attitudes of its employees. Even if the approach is to ensure these attributes are only needed amongst strategically important roles, rather than for all employees, the principles remain the same. The human capital approach encourages managers to see development as an investment, and the decision to create a pool of talented people means managers at all levels have a part to play to ensure there is a return on the investment. HR managers in particular have a responsibility. The Bank of America/Merrill Lynch suggests that HR managers should be seen as investment managers of human capital (Seig 2012).

In addition to the human capital and RBV theories, there are other reasons why talent is seen as important in the current business climate. As technology advances and as international competition becomes ever fiercer, all types of work seem likely to require higher levels of education in the future. Even apparently straightforward jobs are subject to pressure to become specialized, and to acquire a set of more advanced capabilities. For example, crane drivers now operate cranes at the docks and container terminals using computer systems to move containers quickly from the incoming ship to precisely the right place on the docks where they can be transferred to another ship, to be transshipped to another destination. This is a routine where minutes are important because of the costs of remaining in port, perhaps missing a tide, costs which have to be acceptable to shipowners who would otherwise choose another route next time.

In the service sector the quality of the people who are providing the service, conditions the response of the customer and hence the opportunities for repeat business, for building up a customer base and for remaining competitive. Although it may be possible for competitors to copy the technology of superior performing businesses, being able to replicate the quality of the service they provide is a more difficult human resource management issue.

TALENT MANAGEMENT POLICIES

With the objectives of talent management clear, we should now consider the HR policies that help HR to achieve them. In Figure 13.1, the four major approaches to talent management are set out.

The main issue in the universal approach is whether all talent management policies are used for all employees. Even in the most egalitarian companies, it is unlikely that all employees will go through development centres, and whether there would be identifiable career paths for all. However, the move to use new technology in a self-service mode, so that individuals can go as far as they like with their own development, perhaps pausing and picking up development programmes later on, makes it possible for high levels of involvement for people, without any corporate commitment to promotion or careers. Nevertheless, the values embedded by the universal approach may suit the business strategy and do bring additional benefits that indicate corporate cohesiveness and fairness, which should produce some exceptional individuals whose talent would otherwise have been neglected.

In a specific view of talent, policies will probably be more extensive, and those people identified as high potential may be put on a fast track to development and promotion. There is no ambiguity, and there is an open and honest approach, employees know what to expect, there will be clarity about what an employee has to do to improve his or her position, and there is a clear narrative on how talent management fits into the company philosophy.

Where organizations have a pragmatic HR approach, there may be a coherent set of policies, of a limited or extensive nature, which are either applied to all under the universal approach, or are applied to specific roles and individuals. The decision about what policies are applied will be pragmatic, and may change rapidly over time, according to circumstances. Talent management is driven entirely by the work force needs at that time.

The policy areas that are used in talent management include:

■ identification of potential
■ fast track development
■ career management
■ identifying people for promotion
■ succession planning
■ assessment of general potential
■ career interviews.

THE IDENTIFICATION OF POTENTIAL

Performance appraisal inevitably leads to discussion on careers and potential. In practice, the review of potential serves two main purposes: the identification of those who appear to be suitable for promotion, and the assessment of the general potential of individuals in order to decide how their abilities may best be employed in the interests of the organization and of the individuals themselves.

We cannot be certain that those employees who are performing well now will necessarily be high performers at the next level up and beyond. The well known 'Peter principle' may apply, that is, people who perform well continue to be promoted until they reach a level where they are working beyond their capacity, and they are no longer recommended for promotion. In this way, people are promoted to their level of incompetence.

If we are planning our people resources effectively we can see where to categorize people according to their performance and potential ratings, acknowledging always that these are two axes along which considerable variation is possible over time, and that ratings have a strong subjective element.

There are policy choices about how to manage these various groups of employees. The 1:2 low performers with no potential should be replaced unless the performance lapse is temporary (assuming new starters are not included in this grid). The high performers with little potential should be retained and managed to deliver results on a continuing basis. Those whose performance is low but whose potential is high should be developed, and the

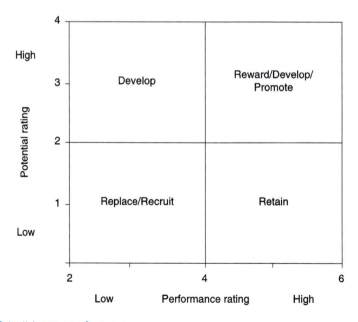

Figure 13.1 Potential versus performance

stars with high potential and high performance should be rewarded, developed and promoted.

Some companies take a harsh view of the low performers. For example, General Electric under Jack Welch fired the lowest 10 per cent performers every year, thereby raising the bar, and rewarded the high performers 'in the soul and the wallet'. These decisions are dependent upon labour market conditions. If the low performers are working in specialisms where recruitment is difficult, even if they have low potential, a company might decide to spend more resource on improving performance. Those with modest performance but with a high potential could be well worth long-term investment. When there is a 'war for talent' and high performers are much in demand in a tight labour market, the HR challenge is in retaining the high performers, irrespective of their potential.

FAST TRACK DEVELOPMENT

In fast track recruitment and development schemes, potential is assessed before the person joins the organization. The risks are obvious, since the organization is committing itself to the appointment of individuals into long-term careers, such as the civil service, and into large corporations, without evidence of performance within different roles in the organization. The other main risk is the opportunity cost of making wrong selection decisions. Typically, recruitment into fast track schemes is for a limited number of people, once a year, for example recruiting graduates on the 'milk-round' from universities. High potential candidates will be the object of competition between recruiters, and if the selectors' judgements turn out to be wrong, another graduate will miss out, and a place will have been wasted. Risks can be mitigated by asking candidates to go through a battery of selection tests, assessment centre type exercises, interviews and realistic job previews. There are also often reviews in the first 12 months, designed to pick up any problems.

CAREER MANAGEMENT

The changing nature of careers is one reason why talent management is such a dynamic field. In Chapter 3, 'boundaryless' organizations were discussed. Careers also have a boundaryless quality, and few individuals will spend their working life in one organization. The shifts in employment patterns, with more short-term roles, greater flexibility and the rise and fall of corporations, with mergers, acquisitions and public sector reorganization and contraction mean the old 'linear' careers are gone for the vast majority of working people. There are now what Hall and Moss (1998) called 'protean' careers, where people change their career direction frequently in their working life, and in many cases will have no career concept at all. Even in the civil service, at senior levels and with specialists, people are brought in for short periods, and civil servants leave to work in other organizations. Careers are built between organizations and the individual is expected usually to take responsibility for his or her own career. The growth of professions (the professionalization of occupations), in number and variety, encourages professionals to look to their specialism as the source of their career identity, for example, whether they are engineers working in the oil industry, technicians in the film or television industry, or teachers, lawyers or IT specialists, they see themselves as being in charge of their own destinies.

However, if we give the career concept a wider meaning, more as the journey people take through their working life or their profession, there is much that HR staff (who also may regard themselves as professionals, temporarily residing in an organization) will need to do. To engage the high quality people required to obtain and sustain a competitive advantage, the management of the organization's human capital is more important than ever, but also in view of the changes to the career concept, more difficult. Providing career management policies is therefore as much about ensuring there is a corporate voice in the career decisions, as it is about making decisions for the corporation about its talent.

One way in which organizations can bring together the parties interested in potential and career management is through career development panels. In such a system, the data on high potentials is gathered (often through the appraisal process) and is fed into the HR department, which prepares the papers for a panel of senior managers with accountability for key roles in the organization. The panel then makes decisions based upon the perceived development needs of individuals, their motivation and intentions, the opportunities available and the needs of the business.

Such systems often operate internationally, with country managers submitting data to the head office HR function. In this way the 'cream rises to the top' and the high potentials from around the world can become known to senior management, who will ensure the sequencing of opportunities for learning as far as this is possible, and appropriate development programmes are undertaken. Such schemes may be operated in conjunction with career workshops, personal development guides and succession planning. Organizations such as Kodak, 3M, BP Exploration, Amoco and many others conduct such schemes, often with innovative approaches and tools to help individuals take responsibility for their own careers. The degree of centralization or devolvement to business units and to individuals for career planning varies. Sometimes, there is a support service to individuals with personal career plans, coaches or mentoring, workshops and software to help people make decisions, to understand what they can do and what is available. A good example is shown in the case of Massachusetts Mutual Life Insurance Company (see below).

IDENTIFYING STAFF FOR PROMOTION

The selection of staff for promotion is, in essence, the same process as the selection of new employees. Everything that has already been said about the problems of selecting new employees, the limitations of predictive methods and especially the interview, apply equally here and need not be repeated. A job vacancy has to be filled and there is usually a field of several candidates. The requirements and criteria for effective performance at the higher level need to be defined in exactly the same way as for recruitment and selection: the task and problem of the selectors is to predict the candidate's likely behaviour in a new job situation.

However, there are some significant differences between recruitment and promotion situations. In the former situation the employing organization is dealing with unknown people. When selecting staff for promotion, it already has a store of information both formal and informal about candidates. Furthermore, there are important areas in which prediction is not necessary, namely, compatibility with the organizational culture and relationships with colleagues. Nevertheless, examples regularly occur of employees who are very effective at one level, but prove to be far less successful at a higher level, as if to confirm the well known 'Peter principle' that people eventually are promoted to the level of their incompetence (beyond which they will not be promoted because they are failing).

The methods adopted by organizations for the promotion of staff vary considerably. In some cases, promotions may be made virtually by the unilateral decision of heads of companies or departments on the basis of demonstrated work competence. This method is more likely to occur in the smaller private sector companies. In the public sector and in larger private sector concerns there are formal procedures for selecting candidates for promotion. Since most of these also have a system of formal performance appraisals, these are often used as the basis for decisions about promotion. They provide a picture derived from a series of reports on performance in a variety of jobs and situations by a range of managers. Since appraisal reports also suffer from the same difficulties of subjectivity as the selection procedures themselves, the problem is in fact compounded, hence the importance of ensuring that the system of staff reporting is as accurate as it can possibly be.

SUCCESSION PLANNING

Succession planning is a part of the career management system. Instead of identifying specific individuals and developing them for particular posts, the more effective method is to develop a pool of talented people, with appropriate capabilities, and to provide them with the experience to be suitable candidates when a vacancy arises. Therefore, the organization is not reliant upon one person to be promoted, who may leave at a time which is inconvenient. This practice depends upon there being a sufficient number of high quality candidates who can develop a large enough range of skills and abilities to be potentially appointable to the likely roles which may become vacant. If those in the pool are able and are prepared to move elsewhere, they will also be targets for 'head hunters', or may not be around for other reasons at the critical time when a vacancy occurs.

In preparation, it is sometimes possible to give them roles acting up to the next level, or for them to take on high profile roles (for example in subsidiary companies), so that there is both a chance to see how they perform at a more senior level and to give them experience and interesting challenges prior to their eventual promotion. This tactic may also keep the individuals sufficiently engaged so they avoid the blandishments of head hunters and the attractions of external offers.

ASSESSING GENERAL POTENTIAL

The essence of this task is to assess whether employees have the potential to perform the types and levels of work that are likely to be available in the future (at least as far as the end of the business planning period). This assessment has to be based on the evidence available from the HR records, including, performance reviews, development and education records, which are centrally maintained and coordinated by the HR staff. These records cover a period of several years and extend beyond the confines of the present job. Since the assessment of the general potential of employees is set in the wider organizational context, often the review is carried out jointly by the responsible HR and line managers.

Attention has already been drawn to the responsibilities of individuals for self-development, but people cannot usually take a detached view of their own potential. They may easily overestimate or underestimate their own capabilities. Personal interests, past conditioning or narrowness of experience may also play a part in restricting individuals' capacities to assess their own potential. Nevertheless, it is very important that individual employees be fully consulted in any review of their potential in order to help them see themselves as the organization sees them, to enable them to put forward their own views and wishes, and to develop their commitment to any plans for their future employment. This can be achieved by means of a schedule of career-development interviews, in which HR staff use the history of past assessments and the career record to date as a basis for joint consultation with employees about their potential and the opportunities for employment and development that are or may become available.

Examples of this approach include the World Bank where specialists who were often on varying contractual terms, when they came to the end of a contract, could go through a series of tests on their career preferences, and could access details of the available vacancies. This was followed, if they chose, by a meeting with an independent career counsellor (not part of the HR function), who could discuss the results of the tests, the career options and the vacancies in the light of the information the individuals had gained about themselves to facilitate their decisions about their next career moves.

One popular theory that is often helpful for individuals to use comes from Professor Ed Schein. He developed the notion of career anchors. A career anchor is 'a combination of perceived area of competence, motives, and values that you would not give up, to represent your real self' (Schein 1993: 1). He identified eight different career anchors: 'technical/functional competence', 'general management competence', 'autonomy/independence', 'security/stability', 'pure challenge' and 'lifestyle'. The 'pure challenge' career anchor is one when the intellectual challenge is the motivating force, such as for some engineers and consultants. The 'lifestyle' career anchor is concerned with balancing family needs, work needs and personal needs, in an integrated way. Career anchors are one way of describing the values people have about work, and provide a starting point for a career discussion.

THE POTENTIAL REVIEW/CAREER DEVELOPMENT INTERVIEW

This type of interview is very similar to the performance-appraisal interview in the basic framework and general approach that are appropriate to the situation. The three phases of the interview should be planned and conducted in the following way.

Pre-interview preparation

1   As with the performance appraisal, members of staff to be interviewed need to prepare themselves by considering their personal career objectives and by analysing their own strengths and weaknesses, training and educational needs and employment preferences.
2   Those managers conducting the interviews need to study the relevant personnel records, i.e. career histories, staff reports, performance-appraisal summaries and training records. They will usually need to consult responsible line managers to ascertain whether any changes have occurred since the last report and generally to amplify information about current performance and potential.
3   Finally, they will need to determine the specific objectives to be achieved in each particular situation.

The interview

1   The interview should be based on the following broad plan:
    (a)   Explanation of the general purpose and scope of the interview.
    (b)   Discussion of the individual's career to date in terms of perceived strengths and weaknesses, likes and dislikes, employment preferences (e.g. 'career anchors'). Data from 'life line' or other such exercises may be helpful.
    (c)   Discussion of the future in terms of the potential revealed by past performance, the opportunities that the organization is able to provide and the individual's needs for training and education.
    (d)   Summary of agreements about action required.
2   Like the performance appraisal, this is essentially a problem-solving, counselling situation, and the prerequisites for its successful conduct are basically the same. However, there are some special aspects of this interview which are worth stressing.

First, because of the fundamental problems associated with the subjectivity of human perception and the individuals' natural pursuit of personal objectives, the task of the career or HR staff in this review is not only to assess potential, but also to help to reconcile organizational and individual perspectives.

Second, because a joint commitment and agreement between employer and employee is necessary for success, the general purpose to be pursued by HR staff in this kind of review is to help individuals in the following ways: to make as realistic an assessment as possible of themselves and their own potential; to adopt realistic expectations of what is achievable and available; to understand that, whilst the organization has a duty and a vested interest to provide all possible opportunities for growth, individuals must accept responsibility for their own personal development.

Post-interview action

Immediately after the interview, managers should produce a brief summarized report of the interview, the main points of discussion and agreements reached, for retention in the personnel records, and liaise with line managers.

Assessment centres

We discussed assessment centres in the previous chapter on selection. However, assessment centres are also used for promotion and development purposes.

Increasing use has been made of assessment centres for assessing the potential of candidates for employment and that of existing employees. They are used mainly for identifying staff, especially managers, who show potential for advancement to senior positions. These centres may be established internally by the organization, or they may be external, offering an assessment service to all organizations that wish to send staff for testing. Internal organizational centres will normally be staffed by senior managers of the organization, trained in the methods of the centre, and by occupational psychologists. External organizations providing this service will often be staffed by occupational psychologists.

The problems of predicting future behaviour at work have already been discussed in the chapter dealing with selection procedures. The main advantage of assessment centres lies in the opportunity to give candidates a chance of demonstrating skills that they may not yet have had a chance to exhibit in their work. Because centres are run by trained specialists, the predictions produced are likely to be considerably more reliable and valid than those of untrained managers and a further benefit comes from training managers to make valid assessments. A possible disadvantage is cost. The costs of establishing a 'centre' include the research and development necessary into the behaviours of successful applicants, and devising and validating tests that will predict those behaviours. Only very large companies could afford the expense of setting up their own centres. In any case, organizations have to make a cost-benefit analysis. They have to ask whether the results justify the outlay. In view of the costs of promoting staff to senior posts, who later prove to be incompetent, it may well be worthwhile investing in improving predictions, which could avoid serious managerial problems in future years.

On the basis of the model already described for making systematic judgements, the first task of the assessment centre is to define the required competencies. For example, a process for assessing managerial potential might be based on the following criteria:

1 *Personal attributes*: self-confidence; emotional stability; resilience; breadth of vision; flexibility and adaptability; sociability and cooperativeness; sense of humour; tolerance and patience; balanced views; personality, which can make an impact; moral courage; management ability and readiness to learn.
2 *Competence in practice*: analytical and reasoning powers; problem-solving and decision-making skills; identification of priorities; planning and organizing abilities; team membership skills; leadership and communication skills.

The methods commonly used to test and reveal these attributes and competencies are:

■ psychometric tests of intelligence, aptitude and personality
■ group situational tests involving problem-solving and decision-making exercises
■ leadership and team membership role-play exercises
■ presentations to group members
■ individual, written and oral problem solving exercises
■ exercises to test mental, emotional and physical characteristics. These could include outdoor exercises.

CASE STUDY

(from Larson, B. (2013) 'Custom careers' *HR Magazine*. June. 54–56. Society for Human Resource Management)

MassMutual (Massachusetts Mutual Life Insurance Company)

THE CAREER RESOURCE CENTER-BACKGROUND

This mutual company had 6800 employees, with revenues in 2013 of US$26.7 billion. The company reorganized in 2009, in order to take the opportunity of the economic downturn and recession, so that it would emerge stronger, leaner and having gained efficiencies. It restructured to be a flatter structure, after delayering, which increased the spans of control and put the customers closer to the top executives. A 2010 employee survey showed employees wanted more opportunities to advance, and clearer career paths.

The company responded with a desire to provide employees with opportunities to achieve as the main driver; the company wanted their employees to feel inspired.

A team was established of 10 HR and communications professionals tasked with rethinking and redesigning their career strategy. The idea was to introduce a new career concept where people would not see their career in terms of promotions only. Instead, the intention was to show the positive aspects of moving sideways, to gain valuable skills, to improve the person's employability and to provide them with new experiences.

They sought to give employees the chance and the tools to explore their talent, their potential and their opportunities. The career development was enhanced by the following:

The career resource center. This is a self-assessment tool which helps employees to discover their interests, values and strengths.

The competency model and development guide. Each job description has a list of competencies, and employees use the guide to inform them of relevant courses to study; there are useful articles and books listed to read to improve their knowledge of particular competences, and tips on how to gain related experiences.

Mentoring tools. This tool gives employees a simple way to locate advisers or mentors.

Job framework. This framework shows the different jobs across the company, by function, by job family, by title and level. There are 28 categories of job function and 136 job families (related groups of jobs).

Job explorer tool. Users can see detailed information for each job, the required professional competencies and technical skills needed.

The feedback showed the system had been extensively used – after six months, about 4000 employees had visited the career resource, 2086 had taken courses to improve competencies and 438 had completed profiles in the mentoring tool. Employee affinity groups continued to be enthusiastic.

SUMMARY

This chapter has 'unpacked' the talent management concept. Talent management is a system: the selection of employees, identification of potential, career management, and policies such as fast track development and succession planning, are all tied together and are interdependent in the system. Provided a common language of competencies can be created, and the variations in jobs and qualifications required can be set out, there are possibilities to convert the system into a self-regulated approach, as indicated in the MassMutual and the World Bank examples cited in this chapter.

Clearly, computer based systems are now making this a reality for all organizations. The real benefit is in the handling of information. Talent management is about obtaining, codifying and presenting timely information on which people can make decisions about the future.

However, one should not be taken up too much with the technology. These talent management activities are about human decisions, and career counselling will always be needed, whether from one's partner, parents, friends or from coaches, mentors and professionals in the field. This is where advice is valuable, to put the data together, and to interpret it into the individual's own career concept, or even more widely, into how the person wants to live his or her life in the future. That is ultimately how the human capital created comes to be valuable for the organization.

QUESTIONS

1   How should 'talent management' be defined?
2   What approaches to talent management do you believe improve corporate perform-ance, and why?
3   How would the different types of career management discussed in this chapter relate to emerging concepts of 'organizational career'?
4   What part should line managers and HR specialists play in talent management?

REFERENCES

Larson, B. (2013). 'Custom careers'. *HR Magazine*. June. 54–56. Society for Human Resource Management. Alexandria VA. USA.

Schein, E. H. (1993). *Career Anchors*. Pfeiffer, San Francisco.

Seig, A. (2012). 'Beyond war for talent: investing in human capital through benefits'. *H R Magazine*. June. 82. Society for Human Resource Management. Alexandria VA USA.

14 LEARNING AND DEVELOPMENT

THE FOUNDATION FOR EFFECTIVE PRACTICE

Developing employees to become effective in their jobs is a fundamental aspect of people management and links into the talent management field. Employers depend on the quality of employee performance to achieve organizational aims and objectives; employees have motivational needs for development, recognition, status, achievement and improved reward, which can and should be met through job satisfaction and performance achievements. Learning and development is one of the policy areas that supports the capabilities central to the RBV.

There are many different definitions of the activities covered by learning and development, including 'training' and 'Human Resource development'. As the common denominator of all of these terms is learning, it is better to see training as a learning process, as defined below, rather than to engage in debates about semantic differences. However, we do accept some learning (which may be termed 'developmental') is undertaken with long term and imprecise objectives in mind, whereas learning to perform specific tasks may be seen as training to perform a particular role.

There is no adequate, all-embracing term to describe this process, although 'work-directed learning' comes close to the view taken here. In the meantime, the word 'development' will be used in discussing the process in the widest possible context, starting with the following comprehensive definition as a foundation for effective practice.

Development and training in work organizations concerns the learning process in which learning opportunities are purposefully structured by managers, HR and training staff, working in collaboration or through external agents acting on their behalf. The aim of the process is to develop in employees the knowledge, skills and attitudes that have been defined as necessary for the effective performance of their work. The aim is to accomplish the achievement of the organizational aims and objectives by using the most cost-effective means available.

The importance of using a comprehensive definition as a basis for practice is that it focuses attention on the main aim of development, that is, effective long-term performance, and leads logically to certain important conclusions and questions arising from the definition that determine the degree of effectiveness in practice, which can be summarized under the heading of how development is typically organized.

HOW IS DEVELOPMENT TYPICALLY ORGANIZED?

Development is always a means to an end and not an end in itself. Unless it leads to the effective performance of work, it inevitably raises questions about costs and time spent, and therefore the waste of valuable resources. Definition of the requirements for effective performance in terms of knowledge, skills and attitudes by means of job analysis is of fundamental importance. Because it is directed towards effective employee performance of work, development must be seen as an integral and vital part of the whole culture and work system. This is not, for example, an extraneous activity for which training staff are largely responsible.

Since managers are responsible for the effective performance of work to achieve the organizational aims and objectives, they logically must have the responsibility for ensuring that employees have learned how to do this. Management must take the initiative in setting up, resourcing and monitoring the effectiveness of the learning and development system and its provision in practice. Whilst management bears the main responsibility, all staff in the organization are involved in learning. Effective practice requires the collaboration of managerial, HR and learning and development staff. In addition, employees are expected to take some responsibility for their own learning. The purpose may be achieved in a variety of ways, e.g. by planned work experience in a series of different jobs, by planned experience within one job, by formal training at the workplace or at training/development centres. The sole criterion for choice of method is that which is most likely to achieve the business aim cost-effectively.

The development of an organization's human resources applies to all its employees from the most senior to the most junior. When training is defined in traditional narrow terms, it tends to be directed towards junior and middle grades of employees. However, all employees are likely to need 'training' or development of some kind throughout their working lives. It surely could not be assumed that senior staff, on whom so much depends, have no need for further learning, especially in view of the demands of economic, social and technological changes. Because of the vital contribution that employee development makes to the creation of organizational capability of human resources, all those responsible for learning – the learning and development staff (L and D staff) – irrespective of the form it takes, must themselves be prepared for the task.

COST-EFFECTIVE LEARNING AND DEVELOPMENT: A SYSTEMS APPROACH

How is cost-effective learning and development to be achieved? It is achieved by applying basic principles for cost-effective management to the specific situation of training, assuming that effective systems of job analysis and performance appraisal have been established so that performance criteria are defined and assessable. The steps are as follows:

1   Identify training needs – who needs training and what do they need to learn?
2   Taking account of how people learn, design and provide development to meet identified needs.
3   Assess whether training and development has achieved its aim with regard to subsequent work performance.
4   Make any necessary amendments to any of the previous stages in order to remedy or improve future practice.

This process is commonly known as the systems approach to training (SAT). It has been successfully applied for many years by many organizations in the private and public sectors as one main way of achieving cost-effective learning and development. There is a continuum in the way that the training and development processes are devised. At one end, the SAT approval can be rigidly construed, with precise learning outcomes and subjects for learning broken down into small modules in order to improve the learning process. Another model is a more educationally based approach to long-term development, which is at the other end of the continuum. This stresses the development as a basis for developing adaptability in employees. An 'action learning' approach is also possible. However, all these have some notion of systematically determining what development is needed.

The SAT is so-called because it is a series of interdependent systems, functionally linked together and integrated into the whole work system. The interdependence of the stages is crucial, since the malfunction or neglect of any one of them inevitably affects the others and the total system. Thus, if job analysis has not defined the criteria for effective performance, training needs cannot be identified by performance appraisal. If needs have not been properly identified, it is not possible to design and provide needs-related training, or to assess ultimate effectiveness in terms of subsequent work performance. The above explanation of SAT shows that, in its 'purest' form, the approach is best suited to a steady state organization, rather than to organizations that are going through rapid change.

LEARNING THEORY

Since development is essentially a learning process, all those who are in any way involved in changing behaviour, attitude, skills and in development need to have an understanding of learning. Because learning is a continuous human activity, it has always occupied an important position in psychological studies. The main questions to be discussed here are what learning is and how do people learn? There is a general consensus about the first question, but much more debate about the second.

Learning may be defined as a process which results in a more or less permanent change in behaviour, which occurs as a result of the influence of external, environmental stimuli on the inherent, genetic disposition of the individual. In the context of training it is useful to consider learning and behavioural change in terms of knowledge, skills and attitudes needed for effective performance. In formal learning situations, this change is demonstrated and assessed by examinations or tests. In everyday life it is ascertained by observable changes in behaviour patterns; for example, an employee without commitment demonstrating through behaviour that he or she is now hard-working and conscientious. Since learning and development is directed towards the effective perform- ance of work, ultimately this is when learning or behavioural change really matters and needs to be demonstrated. There is no point in such changes being shown at the end of a programme if they are not transferred into observable changes in practice in the real work place.

There are a number of theories about how children learn, but most ideas about the process place experience as a critical aspect of all theories. How adults learn has been the subject of continuing discussion and some controversy for many decades. Much of the evidence leads to the conclusion that, irrespective of our age, we mostly learn from experience. Kolb's (1984) learning cycle (Figure 14.1) suggests a cyclical process of continuous learning.

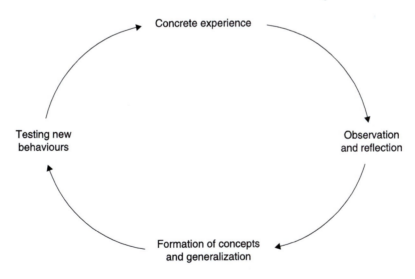

Figure 14.1 Kolb's learning cycle

Figure 14.1 demonstrates the role of experience in learning where we generalize from our experience, and experiment with new ideas, as a consequence of what we have learned, taking into account the feedback we have received from significant others. The challenge for development processes is to find ways of creating learning environments where new behaviours can be tested, and where there is assistance with observation and reflection, to facilitate the learning process.

From the theories, it is possible to distil some basic, simple, general truths about learning, which are fundamentally important to those responsible for the design and provision of learning and development, which we can summarize as follows:

1   People must be motivated to learn. They must see a beneficial outcome for themselves. They must see how training could help them to perform their work effectively. They must see a personal need for this to happen and to accept the methods chosen to achieve the training objectives.

2   Feedback is important for motivational and learning reasons. People need to have feedback on their learning achievement.

3   Because learning depends on motivation, it is a mixture of individual and group processes that may stimulate motivation to learn (for example competitive pressures, and forces for such as 'group think'). People will learn, if they want to, in their own preferred ways and at their own pace, depending on a variety of genetic and environmental factors.

4   People learn from experience and therefore from example and by imitation. As a consequence, they may demonstrate behaviour that could be regarded as socially unacceptable or not conducive to the effective performance of work. In other words, people may easily acquire bad habits and practices and regard these as good.

5   Learning can only take place through the human senses. All senses may contribute to the learning process, but the visual is the most powerful and, to a lesser degree, the auditory.

What implications does the individual orientation of the learning process have for L and D staff and line managers?

■   Development is a learner- and not a trainer-orientated process.
■   L and D staff are essentially a catalyst in the learning process. As Galileo is reputed to have said, 'You cannot teach people anything. You can only help them to learn'.
■   In the practice of employee development, L and D staff must: (a) show why people need to learn, how it will help them, how their learning fits into a total picture and the relationship of parts to a whole; (b) make development as experiential and active as possible, i.e. using real work as the learning medium; (c) see that people learn from good examples and practice as far as possible; (d) use an imaginative approach, involving interesting, varied and stimulating methods for learning, using a variety of techniques; (e) be interesting and stimulating themselves through their own presentational skills; and (f) structure learning so that people have regular assessments of their performance

and achievement. Although tests are an obvious means of providing feedback, they can be given informally by the skilful choice of participative and active methods.

IDENTIFYING LEARNING NEEDS

An analysis of training needs is an essential prerequisite to the design and provision of effective learning and development. This is the first main stage in the problem-solving process that characterizes the SAT, that is, the diagnosis that precedes prescription. The purpose of this diagnosis is to determine whether there is a gap between what is required for effective performance and present or required future levels of performance. If any deficiencies are revealed, the causes and remedies may be various, and development is only one of a number of possible solutions.

Needs arise at three levels, these being the organization, group and individual levels. They are interdependent because the corporate performance of an organization ultimately depends on the performance of its individual employees and its subgroups.

The corporate needs of the organization and its groups may be identified in the following ways:

■ *The evidence from human resource planning*: this provides information about the demand and supply of human resources and the possible implications for development needs. Thus, a forecast of a possible difficulty in recruiting people with required entry levels in knowledge and skills could affect recruitment and training policy, compelling the organization to recruit at lower levels and then to provide development to fill the performance gap.

■ *The introduction of new methods*: whenever new methods of work, e.g. new systems are introduced, this changes the requirements for effective performance, creates a performance gap in knowledge and skills (and in some situations, in attitudes also, perhaps), and hence a training need.

■ *Collective evidence from performance appraisal and formal methods for needs assessment*: information emerging from the performance appraisal of individual employees, including aggregated data from appraisal reports or from formal methods such as meetings, interviews or questionnaires, in which line managers, learning and development and individual employees are involved, may reveal needs for development that are common throughout the organization or to groups of employees.

This systematically acquired information is valuable for seeing what centrally provided development is needed. Accurately diagnosing the specific training needs for individuals requires the following system:

1   Job analysis to determine:

(a)   the objectives and component tasks of the job

(b)   the knowledge, skills and attitudes required for the effective performance of these tasks.

2   A gap analysis by line managers and individuals, based on a comparison of present and planned requirements.

3   The specification of learning and development needs indicated by this comparison.

4   The specification of the forms of learning and development needed to satisfy the identified needs.

The joint participation of line managers with L and D staff, and their individual employees, to assess development needs is very important. It is more likely to produce a comprehensive and systematic analysis, and commitment on the part of the individual. It is also an opportunity to encourage employees to assess their own needs and possible solutions as a part of their development.

It requires time and conscientious effort to make a thorough analysis of jobs and their specific requirements and then to set up formal arrangements for assessing needs, but there is no other basis for designing and providing the learning and development that is really needed. Specific needs for individuals may arise at any time during their working careers. However, there are particular occasions when a formal assessment is needed, based on the system described above, that is:

1   *Starting employment*: new employees will invariably need some development to fill the gap between their present levels of knowledge and skills and those needed for effective performance of work. The assessment of training needs is best undertaken at the stages of selection and induction of new employees. Formal induction programmes are discussed below.

2   *Appraising performance*: in performance appraisal, recent performance is compared with required levels. If the comparison regularly reveals deficiencies and needs, these should be remedied by training and development.

3   *Changing jobs*: people changing jobs are in a similar situation to those starting employment. The requirements for the new job may well create a performance gap that needs to be filled by learning and development.

When organizations change there are often significant changes to jobs. One way to assess whether people can be transferred into different roles is to give the person a 'trainability test'. An example shown below is drawn from an airline which wished to transfer staff from non-customer facing roles into the check-in teams. Each individual was given a short training session on the various routines and ways to behave with customers. There was then a series of role plays where candidates were given the chance to deal with different kinds of customers. This was intended to show the candidate's potential, and his or her natural aptitude for the new role, in the assessor's judgement, and therefore how the candidate would respond to learning and development in the new role. (See the companion website for more details of this example.)

Apart from the specific needs described above, individuals have continuing general needs for learning and development in the broad developmental sense. They may need to develop their experience within particular roles. This is the responsibility of line managers, who must determine these needs by careful observation of performance and regular discussions with their staff, and who need to provide the necessary opportunities by informal methods such as delegation, job rotation, etc. People often also need the wider experience that comes with a variety of jobs. It is the responsibility of L and D staff, and the HR function in their career development role to ascertain these developmental needs and to meet them by career planning, as far as operational demands will permit.

THE DESIGN AND PROVISION OF NEEDS-RELATED LEARNING

This question is the second stage of the problem-solving process. The first stage was diagnostic, that is, to determine what the needs are. The second stage is prescriptive, that is, to decide what action is most likely to meet the identified needs. This requires generating and analysing a range of options in the light of objectives to be achieved and the economic use of available resources. As we have already seen, options available to meet the requirements of work (to fill the performance gap) could well cover a wide range, and development is only one of these possibilities. When learning and development is the selected option, the same problem-solving principle applies – the next step is to determine in detail what form of development is most likely to meet identified requirements cost-effectively. In the light of a broad interpretation of development, the range of possible options is wide. Making these choices raises questions such as who should provide development, of what kind, where and by what methods? The answers to these questions will be determined by the learning objectives.

LEARNING OBJECTIVES

Producing clear objectives is crucial for learners and L and D staff alike. Objectives should specify what participants have learned and can demonstrate they know and understand by the end of training. Without learning objectives it is impossible for anyone concerned with the learning process to evaluate the success of the programme.

Learning objectives should meet the following criteria. Objectives should be:

- expressed in learner-oriented terms: e.g. 'By the end of the programme delegates should be able to demonstrate specified knowledge and skills'
- as specific as possible about performance, standards required and attendant conditions: e.g. 'By the end of the course, the individual will be able to use the computer to

create a project plan showing the resources, the time lines, the review stages, and to calculate and explain the main risks in the project'

- as measurable as possible and capable of achievement in the time allowed
- expressed in language that clearly states what the learners have to do.

Learning objectives that fail to meet these criteria are still regularly seen in published programmes. For example, an objective for a management development programme might be expressed in something like these terms: 'To familiarize students with the principles of effective management'. In no way could any objective such as this be used as a criterion for measuring learning achievement. If the objective had said 'By the end of programme students should be able to define the principles of effective management and support their answers with real examples drawn from practice and personal experience', the assessment of learning is then possible.

In fairness, it is much easier to produce objectives that enable learning achievement to be confidently assessed for some subjects than it is for others. It is a relatively straight-forward practical task to define objectives in measurable terms for specific activities such as computing skills, driving, flying, playing musical instruments, carpentry, plumbing, cooking, etc. It is much more difficult with a broad conceptual subject, such as economics or finance. The task is simpler for specific managerial activities such as chairing meetings, and interviewing, etc. Here the criteria for effective performance can be reflected in the objectives and used to measure learning achievement. The solution to more abstruse topics is therefore to break the topic down into parts, with objectives that can be measured.

Once learning objectives have been defined, it is possible to address the next stage in the process and to consider questions such as: Who will provide the development? What form will it take? What will be the contents? Where will it be held? What methods will be used?

For development requirements in less structured environments, some of the approaches that can be created are examined below.

THE LEARNING ORGANIZATION

In recent years the degree of change in organizations has encouraged the view that organizational change through continuous learning is necessary for organizations to survive. This is well expressed in Peter Senge's (1990) book, *The Fifth Discipline*, in which he suggested that learning organizations are those that know how to make use of five 'component technologies', these being:

- *Systems thinking*: the notion developed in this book of a systemic approach to learning, seeing the whole as well as the relationships between the parts of the system.
- *Personal mastery*: 'continuously clarifying and deepening our personal vision' using our energy to develop ourselves.

- *Mental models*: challenging the stereotypes and mental maps that managers carry around with them.
- *Building shared vision*: leadership through communicating vision and values.
- *Team learning*: encouraging team members to think together, through dialogue, using teams as the main learning unit.

Management development is frequently one plank in the change platform, and the notion of continuous development, aimed especially at improving employees through personal development, has gained ground. The two classic management development strategies for dealing with discontinuous, unpredictable change are personal development and action learning. Management development strategies are therefore now integral to change strategies, the argument being that the pace of change is so rapid that employees need to be highly adaptive, intelligent and educated so that they will know how to learn and will be prepared to go through retraining or re-educational programmes many times in their working lives. This is also consistent, when applied as a principle throughout the organization, with the notion of empowerment, devolving responsibility to work teams and to individuals.

This is the point where management and employee development links into organization development (OD). OD programmes are conducted when the organization requires people throughout the organization to change their behaviours (see Chapter 4). The process for doing so might embrace a range of 'interventions' or activities. Amongst these, 'evaluative or collaborative inquiry' are methods by which employees become involved in the change as active participants in creating the new structures, or roles as they are produced.

'Evaluative inquiry is a means for fostering individual and team learning about complex organizational issues' (Preskill and Torres 1999: 17). Relationships between people in the

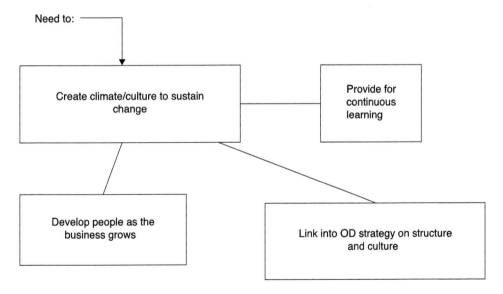

Figure 14.2 Learning and development strategies and OD

project or learning teams assist in the transfer of knowledge and as they share their learning, the organization itself changes and learns. Evaluative inquiry necessarily requires discussion and reflection, and joint working on problems. A feature of the approach is a focus on the team processes (often drawing on research on group behaviour; see Chapter 2) from which learning also comes.

MANAGEMENT DEVELOPMENT

There are some special features of development for managers that warrant a separate mention. Management development has grown as an activity with the growth in the number of managerial, professional and administrative roles. Management education, in the form of MBA and Doctor of Business Administration (DBA), has expanded rapidly. In the last decades of the twentieth century and more recently, specialist masters programmes in management subjects such as finance, logistics and HRM have become popular. In addition, organizations see a benefit in the creation of tailor-made programmes delivered either in-house or at a training centre, in a business school, via a consultancy, etc. The benefits from these in-company courses include the tailored materials with case studies and exercises from their own company, or from the same industry sector, and real time issues from the course delegates to work on. Alongside this expansion in management education needs, a more European or US focus to learning is often sought. International experience for employees could be through being moved into international roles in the company, or through taking a largely international programme (for example in the USA, at European business schools or INSEAD).

PERSONAL DEVELOPMENT

The other way management development is changing is through a concentration on personal development. Skills training is easier to justify and so, although such courses may be ostens-ibly about developing skills, in practice there may be deep level work taking place using psychometric or occupational psychology resources. Personal style and individual beha-viour are now seen to have an impact on performance, which legitimates personal develop-ment interventions. These programmes not only provide skills and techniques but also self-confidence, and MBA style courses assist in the person's attempt to set up his or her own network. Networks are very important at the top, where the internal networks as well as the external networks are often integral to business success. Team building at a top level draws on the interpersonal relationships, for example, and how to make them productive.

COACHING

Coaching as a technique has become extensively used, this being consistent with the focus on personal development skills and performance issues. The business coach role at a senior level will best be undertaken by an external coach, but for middle managers and more junior managers, internal coaches would be acceptable, as long as those concerned have the right skills. The concept of a personal coach draws on a growing convergence between the language of sport and the language of business. The very idea of a team is drawn from sport. Coaching is a necessity for sports stars and for novices alike. In this sense, executive coaching with boards of directors as with sports coaching, is not seen as a sign of weakness, but of strength, because those involved recognize that constantly honing skills, reviewing performance and learning from the situations they face is a powerful way to remain at the top of their game.

PROGRAMME DESIGN

The view that development should be viewed as an integral part of work, requiring the involvement and collaboration of all employees, leads to the logical conclusion that all the staff of an organizations are concerned in the development process. Organizational staff may be involved in providing development in a variety of ways, for example, managers or their deputies, who provide or supervise on-the-job training, coaching or open and elearning methods at the workplace, or management development advisers, who give formal presentations and facilitate learning at training centres or assist line managers in the design, provision and supervision of development at the workplace.

APPROPRIATENESS OF METHODS

Training and development methods and locations can be discussed under three broad headings, i.e. at the workplace, at organizational or external centres (off-job training and development, including educational courses) and a combination of development at the workplace and at separate educational or training centres. In addition, the methods adopted might be through online learning or through developmental activities, including personal development or separate broader educational or vocational courses. At all locations a variety of methods are likely to be used. The choice will be determined by whatever is assessed as most likely to achieve the objectives of providing for the person's needs and work by the most cost-effective means.

DEVELOPMENT IN THE WORKPLACE

Development in the workplace may take a variety of forms. In its very broadest sense it may be identified with career development and the acquisition of required knowledge, skills and attitudes from the continuous experience and opportunities provided by work itself. Here, the HR department has the key role in the supervision and direction of career paths to enable employees to widen their horizons and to develop their capabilities to assume wider responsibilities for the future. Line managers also obviously have the main responsibility for developing their own staff at the workplace. They may do this in the course of normal work by delegation, job rotation, attachments and visits to related work units, placing individuals under the tutelage of selected, experienced employees (mentoring), or through the use of formal workplace methods such as coaching and elearning.

As a result of the ever-increasing emphasis on cost-effectiveness, there has been a trend for much of the training that was formerly given off the job to be now carried out at the workplace. The rapid development of elearning, which is now used to replace many of the traditional methods, means new ideas, new technologies, processes and information of all kinds are available. To the generation now taking up work roles, access to the internet or a corporate L and D website on mobile devices, such as iPhones, tablets and their own laptops is routine. L and D roles include the creation and design of elearning materials and trainers are tending to be increasingly employed as consultants to local managers in the design and provision of training at the workplace and less in their traditional presentational and instructional roles. The cost-effectiveness of this approach is already well established, in terms of saving the very high costs of central training and in improved performance.

For the increasingly market-oriented organizations, which have an agile HR strategy, there is also the benefit of customer feedback, as a source of improvement ideas, which includes improvements to development activities. Shortfalls in customer expectations, and data on the aspects of the company offering which attract them, gives HR and senior managers ideas about how to gain and retain a competitive edge. Many of these improvements will be incorporated into the various opportunities for development found in all kinds of development events – away days, customer service improvement webinars, as well as into new procedure training as and when it occurs (Fox 2013).

APPRENTICESHIPS

Those responsible for the development of young people, new to the workplace, have a particular responsibility to ensure they learn good working habits. The number of unemployed people under the age of 24 has been rising across Europe. In the UK, the 'NEETs' – not in employment, education or training – also consisted of a large number who claimed they did not have the confidence or the basic education or skills to enter the labour market. Youth unemployment was around 900,000 16 to 24-year-olds at the end of 2013.

Following the Richard Review, which recommended more academic rigour for apprentices, the UK Government announced a new 'improved' apprenticeship scheme, to which 60 organizations (including companies such as Microsoft, Tesco, National Grid and Barclays Bank) had signed up in October 2013. The new apprenticeship lasts a minimum of one year. Employers will design the learning and development plans, there will be more academic assessments in English and mathematics and participants will be graded by measuring achievements against the requirements in full-time education. Participants will receive a minimum of 20 per cent off the job training (Churchard 2013). The National Apprenticeship Service has seen a rise in the number of apprenticeships generally, but demand outstrips the supply of apprentice vacancies.

INDUCTION

The induction of new employees is such an important topic that it merits special consideration. The induction of the person is not only into a new job, but also a new culture. Regular analyses of labour turnover statistics show there is a higher turnover during the first few weeks and months of employment. The wastage curve looks like something on the lines of Figure 14.3 below. This phenomenon is known as the induction crisis.

The causes of the induction crisis are usually one or more of the following:

- Newcomers may experience difficulties in being accepted into work groups because of strong group norms, which they either do not understand or may not, at least initially, agree with since these are so different from those they are used to (see Chapter 2).
- Group cohesiveness may be seen as antagonism to the newcomer, which might also stem from the fact that the newcomer has a lower level of output initially, and requires help and some practical training from the other members of the group, thus affecting their own work output. Similarly, the newcomer may seem to pose a threat to the

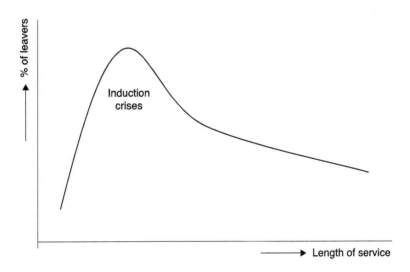

Figure 14.3 Wastage curve

existing social structure of the group, and is unaware of the history of existing relationships in the group.

■ The psychological contract may be a problem, for example, the job may have been oversold at the time of recruitment, and for whatever reason, may not meet the newcomer's expectations. This applies to matters other than the work itself as well; for example journey to work time, facilities and evidence from employees of the reality of promotion prospects.

There is clearly a responsibility of the line manager, and of L and D staff, to help the person to settle in, to feel welcomed and to have a structured plan for induction and development, using the data already collected at the time of selection, when strengths and weaknesses would have been identified.

The induction programme should not overwhelm the newcomer with information or assume that he or she is familiar with all the formal and informal processes and the culture of the organization, from its acronyms in use, to its procedures or the rituals and norms surrounding meal breaks, dress codes, nicknames and so on.

An example of an induction programme outline is on our companion website.

OFF THE JOB TRAINING

Most people are familiar with formal methods of learning and many organizations use either their own centres, or hire hotel and conference accommodation for off the job events, such as away days for a department, or courses for groups of employees. Here, the development activity is conducted by full-time staff, assisted as necessary by occasional lecturers and tutors. L and D staff usually work in groups, and the methods commonly employed are lectures, discussion groups, case studies, simulation, role-play and exercises of various kinds, supported by multimedia presentations. The content usually covers subjects where needs are identified that are common to groups of employees of similar grades or jobs.

Although this kind of development is costly and requires people to leave their places of work, it is necessary and essential for some forms of learning, especially in managerial and related subjects. Here people need to work in groups and to learn from each other in a residential setting. One of the consequences of this type of programme is a kind of bonding amongst the delegates, often including the specialist development staff, which helps to encourage interdepartmental relationships, friendships and wider understanding of the organization. This latent function of the method strengthens organization cultures, helping to create bonds across organizations where people are employed all around the world, facilitating a common understanding and vision. Just as line managers need the assistance of central learning specialists to plan local programmes, so the specialist developers must design central training in collaboration with line managers to ensure that it provides what they and their staff need for effective performance of work.

LINE MANAGEMENT AND TOP DOWN DEVELOPMENT

The drive for cost-effectiveness, the widespread use of the systems approach and elearning have all added a new dimension to the design and provision of training. The combination of workplace and centrally driven initiatives takes two forms: a series of modules; and e learning methods. The use of a series of modules has proved to be a very effective means of facilitating learning for subjects such as management. Instead of cramming all the activities into a few weeks, the subject is broken down into component topics. Thus, a course on management might comprise modules such as marketing, strategy, operations management, project management, problem-solving and decision-making; time management; human aspects of management; interpersonal skills of management; financial management; and include perhaps an in-company project as a way to summarize and consolidate the learning.

Open and distance methods of learning were pioneered by the Open University through television. This is now a part of a common approach used where there are teaching materials consisting of textbooks, online content and projects at the workplace, with continuing learning and webinars at home. Here again, progress is supervised by learning specialists and line managers who can monitor progress centrally, and use feedback and a dedicated website to maintain contact. In recent times, these methods have been used with conspicuous success in cost-effective terms in both the public and private sectors. By combining learning through seminars, and interpersonal skills courses with elearning (sometimes called 'blended learning') there is the best of both worlds. This combination approach to training has a number of potentially significant advantages:

■ It uses the advantages of the individually oriented workplace and the benefits of group-oriented development methods.

■ It is very flexible.

■ There is no pressure to cram learning into a short period of time because of the demands of work or the costs of central training. Development can be extended as long as is necessary, e.g. over several months, to cover subjects in the required depth and breadth.

■ There is a continuing achievement-oriented partnership between line managers, delegates and development staff.

■ The crucial importance of line management and the integration of work and learning is very apparent.

■ When development is extended over longer periods and is directly work oriented, the assessment of learning achievement is more valid.

■ It is especially useful for management development, which can never be satisfactorily encompassed by short central courses.

■ It is likely to be more cost-effective than other methods.

TRENDS USING TECHNOLOGY TO IMPROVE LEARNING

The use of online communications has, of course, revolutionized management processes. Global collaboration is itself used as a way of learning. Global virtual teams are geographically dispersed groups that use internet communications in collaboration on common interests or projects, where the very interaction across boundaries and cultures becomes a way of learning about culture and differences, and of generating new ideas and better problem-solving approaches.

Learning is now undertaken on the move, reflecting the 24/7 society that is now the new normal. A study of 40 large companies in 2011 by the Boston based 'Aberdeen Group' revealed that mobile devices were used by 55 per cent of companies for internal communities and forums, by 48 per cent for informal learning activities and development, and 42 per cent for formal learning and development. Both forms of learning, mobile devices such as smart-phones, tablet computers and iPads are adopted by the majority of people (Roberts 2012).

Video gaming is being applied to learning content, including video tutorials, the interactions facilitated by new technology foster more peer to peer learning, for example co-coaching, and online mentoring, including 'blended mentoring', using the telephone or Skype, as well as emails (Murphy 2011). Individuals can create their own personalized learning approaches. For companies, these devices make updating new instructions easier, helping businesses to manage change faster.

The need for better educational development has business consequences, because of the pace of development, and the inequalities of educational provision in some countries. One solution that is developing is a movement towards 'massive, open online courses' (MOOCs). These are free, non-degree online courses with open, unlimited access for anyone, irrespective of their educational level. There is a complete range of topics available, which consist of lectures online by famous professors from top universities. These are very helpful for low income and student populations, and fit in with the idea of democratizing learning. However, there is no accreditation or certificates awarded, and participants do need free, high-speed internet access.

EVALUATING LEARNING AND DEVELOPMENT

Assessing how far the investment in development has been worthwhile is the 'bottom line' for the L and D staff. The main question is, has development had the effects on individual and corporate performances that it was intended to have?

Evaluating learning is notoriously difficult. This is especially true of management development, where outcomes are less easy to determine. There are a number of principles we should follow in evaluating any training or development activity. Following the ideas of Hesseling (1966), we need to be aware of the different stakeholders in the organization and to evaluate the effects of training and development in terms of the outcomes for participants, managers, staff, customers and any other groups who are involved. Similarly, we should not just evaluate the development or training process (so often evaluated by the 'happy sheets' – the responses from participants at the end of the programme) but also we should evaluate the content and the objectives of the development, or training.

Data sources for evaluation include:

- questionnaires to participants and their managers
- 360 degree feedback before and after the events (i.e. over a one-year period at least) showing any improvements
- surveys of morale, climate, attitudes with appropriate questions (again, before and after over a one-year period)
- feedback from customers/suppliers
- data on improvements, changes to output, service quality or similar performance data before and after
- tests, examinations of trainees at the end of programmes and later to evaluate learning retention
- interviews with trainees, their managers and their staff and customers, to judge what improvements have been achieved.

A form of triangulation of the data is to be recommended, with several independent data sources used to confirm any changes. Development is often seen as more difficult to evaluate than practical training. The training need analysis sets out clear training objectives. However, it is not easy to evaluate unless one can perform a before and after study. It is also important to have measurable learning objectives. In the case of development, the notion here is of some change to the self, rather than purely skill or knowledge acquisition. The difficulties are in knowing how interventions have produced specific outcomes, because there is so much other 'noise' in the system. Development also takes time, and changes to the participants' self-image, and to their sense of mastery may take years to come to fruition.

There are some well known evaluation frameworks. For example, Kirkpatrick's (1994) four level framework, where he suggests there are four levels of analysis in the evaluation of training: trainee perceptions of learning, learning achieved, trainee performance and ultimate impact. In a study by Tyson and Ward (2004), a framework was created with three areas of enquiry, with a focus on outcomes:

- Process (what the participants thought about the process of learning. Did this facilitate learning what was intended?)
- Content (what was learned in the sessions, or processes?)
- Objectives (whether what had been learned achieved the objectives intended?).

For example, if the objective was to ensure that delegates could speak French to a standard that would enable them to negotiate deals with customers in France, that would be tested by their interactions with customers, whether their French was up to a good negotiating standard, and whether they understood the social norms and customs surrounding negotiation in France. The content of the teaching would be tested by their knowledge of how to speak French fluently, and the process by whether the way of teaching was helpful to those trying to learn.

The second element in the model takes account of the different stakeholders. As with the areas to be evaluated these are specific to the context, but would usually include the management who wanted the development undertaken, the delegates themselves, those teaching or responsible for the learning design and delivery, the line manager of the individual person and in the case above, the customers. Each might have a view on the success or otherwise of the development process.

These stakeholders are recorded for each of the three areas of enquiry, namely objective, content and process, to form a matrix of areas for which evidence would be sought to populate the matrix:

Stakeholder	Process	Content	Objectives
Delegates			
Organization			
Internal customers			
External customer			
Staff			

Figure 14.4 Evaluation matrix

The evidence can then be evaluated horizontally, by stakeholder, to arrive at the aggregated view, and by evaluation level to assess the stages or parts of the development process that worked well, as well as those parts that needed some improvement.

This technique can be applied to most areas of HR activity.

When programme delegates/trainees return to their work on the completion of a course, there also needs to be a constructive, systematic discussion with their line managers. The main purpose of this discussion is to ascertain the delegates' views of training, but especially to plan how line managers may help their staff to develop, through their jobs, the knowledge and skills that they have learned in the learning process they have undertaken. It is a very demotivating experience for people to return to work from a development activity with an awareness of their needs for improvement, and stimulated to put their new learning into practice, only to be ignored and sometimes even discouraged by the attitudes of their line managers.

The second stage in the assessment of training effectiveness for individuals after a lapse of time is the ultimate verdict. It is very easy after a lapse of time, when people are caught up once more in the toils of work, to forget about recent training. A formal system is essential, therefore, to impose the necessary discipline for action and to standardize organization practice. This assessment is of particular concern to line managers and those who should have benefited from the development, and should be automatically included in a formal scheme for performance appraisal. It is also very important for the training and development staff to receive feedback. The questions to which answers are needed are:

1   How far has development met the specific needs of work for which it was designed?
2   What changes need to be made, if any, in future development activity, i.e.:
    (a)   Was any material included that has subsequently proved to be of limited or no value?
    (b)   Was any material omitted that has subsequently proved necessary?
    (c)   How appropriate were the methods for learning purposes?

Finally, it is necessary to estimate the cost-effectiveness of development from an organizational point of view and whether the investment of human and material resources made a justifiable contribution to the achievement of organizational aims and objectives.

The problems of assessing the effectiveness of training become even more complicated at organizational level. A whole range of factors may contribute to an organization's success or failure. The admitted difficulties of organizational assessment cannot be an excuse for neglecting or avoiding making the best possible attempt. As always, since sound judgements can only be made if criteria have first been defined, each organization must decide for itself what the appropriate criteria for assessing the cost-effectiveness should be and what evidence should be acquired. The kinds of criteria that might be used, for example, are productivity, profits, customer satisfaction, levels of complaints, labour turnover, accident rates, mistakes at work, wastage of materials, etc.

The ultimate responsibility for providing and assessing cost-effective learning and development rests with management, and especially with senior management responsible for central direction of policy and practice.

QUESTIONS

1   What are the purposes of learning and development?
2   What are the basic ideas behind the SAT approach to learning?
3   What are the main ways to undertake a needs analysis?
4   Are there types of learning situations where SAT is less useful?
5   How do management development programmes differ from other kinds of programmes?
6   Why is coaching so popular as a learning method?
7   What techniques can be used to evaluate learning?
8   How has new technology transformed the way learning and development is delivered?

REFERENCES

Churchard, C. (2013). 'Apprenticeships reforms will give training "kudos" says Cameron'. *People management online* 28 October 2013.

Hesseling, P. (1966). *Strategy for Evaluation Research* Rotterdam: Van Gorcum and Company.

Kirkpatrick, D. (1994). *Evaluating Training Programs: The Four Levels.* San Francisco: Berret-Koehler.

Kolb, D. A., Rubin, L. M. and McIntyre, J. M. (1984). *Organizational Psychology: An Experimental Approach.* Englewood Cliffs, New Jersey: Prentice Hall.

Murphy, W. M. (2011). 'From e-mentoring to blended mentoring: increasing students' developmental initiation and mentors' satisfaction'. *Learning and Education* 10, 2: 606–22 Academy of Management USA.

Preskill, H. and Torres, R. T. (1999). *Evaluative Inquiry for Learning in Organizations.* London: Sage.

Roberts, B. (2012). 'From e-learning to mobile learning'. *HR Magazine.* August 61–65 Society for Human Resource Management USA.

Senge, P. M. (1990). *The Fifth Discipline.* New York: Century Business.

Tyson, S. and Ward, P. (2004). 'The use of 360 degree feedback technique in the evaluation of management development'. *Management Learning* 35, 2: 205–23.

PART FIVE

REWARDS

15 JOB EVALUATION

In this chapter we are concerned with how pay structures can be created that are competitive in the labour market, which are seen as fair by employees, and which reflect and support the performance intentions of the company, or unit concerned.

DEFINITION

The purpose of job evaluation techniques is to measure the relative worth of jobs so that the relationship between the jobs can be expressed in salary and wage scales, based on a logical, ordered system. 'Job evaluation' is a term used in a general way for a number of techniques that are in different forms. These techniques entail analysing and assessing the content of jobs so that they may be classified in an order relating to one another and to the marketplace.

COMMON FEATURES OF JOB EVALUATION TECHNIQUES

- Job evaluation is concerned with differences in the work itself, not in differences that are found between people.
- Reference is made to the 'content' of the job, i.e. what the work consists of, what is being done, what skills are deployed and the actions that are performed. This is normally discovered by job analysis.
- There are predetermined criteria, or factors, against which each job is measured. These may be descriptions of the whole job, or of its component parts.

- The practice of involving those who are to be subject to the job evaluation at an early stage helps to ensure both accuracy in job analysis and a commitment to the job evaluation scheme.
- The outcome of a job evaluation should be wage and salary scales covering the range of evaluated jobs, setting out the pay relativities and pay structures.
- All systems need regular review and updating, and have to be flexible enough to be of use for different kinds of work, so that new jobs can be accommodated.

WHAT DO WE MEAN BY THE WORD 'JOB'?

This may seem to be a silly question to ask, but we must remember that 'jobs' have no physical bounded existence. There is no way of 'seeing' or using any of our senses to comprehend the 'whole' of a job. The idea of 'job' is an analytical one, it enables us to describe a set of actions that are associated with the execution of a range of tasks. 'Tasks' consist of a number of elements that are actions (that is, intended behaviours), which are both observable and measurable. In thinking of tasks we have to think of people performing them, and therefore the major difficulty experienced by the job analyst who wishes to describe a 'job' is to be able to divorce the essential nature of the job from the people performing the job.

Jobs are now often regarded as less important than the skills and competencies employees possess, which can be used competitively in a number of ways. In this flexible world, the apparent bureaucracy of job evaluation sits uneasily with its emphasis on job descriptions and procedure. People often now work in teams, in matrix structures where accountability is spread between posts. Organizations change quickly, putting demands for flexibility on all roles. Job evaluation, however, is a process, not a single technique, and can be applied in any work situation where it is necessary to have a rational basis for rewards.

PROBLEMS OF MEASUREMENT

As people are at the centre of all 'jobs', either in the perceptions of others or in the written descriptions of jobs deriving from observations of how they are done, the evaluation is of human activity, not of some kind of impersonal operation. This is our first problem of measurement. It is the problem of the inherent subjectivity contained in the discriminatory judgements of the work of others. Our second problem of measurement emerges here also, because the criteria or benchmarks on which evaluation will be made are based on aspects of human action. We may illustrate this last point by thinking about the amount of discretion involved in any job. People seem to want to make choices about their work, and typically seek to extend the areas of discretion they already possess. Even the most routine job contains choices; sometimes about rest pauses, the amount of work or its quality. Even if, according to the operator's manual, the sequence and timing of actions are preset, there are always other aspects of the total job (such as collecting materials, reading drawings, talking to the supervisor) when the worker can exercise some freedom of action.

Job evaluation requires the acceptance of the assumption that there is sufficient typicality in the way the work is performed to make comparisons between groups of jobs worthwhile. The differences between people and the consequences for the way the work is done may not be significant. It is not until job evaluation has been undertaken that we can see what the differences are. The changing activities of an organization have to be put into an ordered context for pay purposes. Change emphasizes the need to conduct evaluation on a continuous programme, to update rewards and keep the balance in our rewards in the direction that best suits the organization's objectives. The problems and advantages of job evaluation can be summarized as set out below.

THE PROBLEMS OF JOB EVALUATION

- Schemes take time to establish and involve some formalization of rules regarding job hierarchies.
- The measures that are selected determine the outcome. The decision of what to measure, therefore, partly preconditions where the job is to be placed in the hierarchy of jobs that is being constructed.
- Job evaluation committees, where they exist to reconcile interest groups, have to reach compromises over what is 'politically' acceptable within the organization. Trade-offs can occur between the interest groups.
- Job evaluation introduces structure into pay systems, and reduces the opportunity for managers to exercise complete discretion.

THE ADVANTAGES OF JOB EVALUATION

- Some form of evaluation is necessary to introduce rationality into pay scales, thereby enabling comparison to be made on an explicit basis. This reveals where the differences in rates are a consequence of tradition or custom rather than for economic reasons (see Chapter 25 on 'equal value' legislation). Pay equality may be claimed by women or men if they are doing work of equal value as men or women, even if they are performing a totally different job (e.g. cooks (female), compared to carpenters (men)). The question is: What are the demands made on the worker, for example in terms of effort, skill, knowledge, etc? This means job evaluation factors must be non discriminatory, and the weightings given to each factor should be justifiable in relation to the importance to the job, not due to historical or other precedents.

- Any inherent bias in the process can be recognized, and partly dealt with, by using committees to help in the evaluation, and perhaps outside analysts to describe the jobs.
- Job evaluation can be applied to different situations – it is a process that can be adjusted to the requirements of the organization (its size, the kind of work, etc.).
- By involving employees at an early stage in establishing the system, it is possible to draw on their own feelings of fairness, their concepts of what should be rewarded, and to gain their commitment to the reward system. As a result, the reasons for pay differences are understood and agreed.
- Job evaluation helps organizations to create salary structures and pay levels that can be compared with market rates.
- There are considerable sums of money allocated to pay budgets. The control of costs introduced by job evaluation rules helps financial control and budgeting.
- Gender discrimination should be reduced, since the basis for pay scales is made explicit, is based on rational systems and can be challenged under the equal value legislation.

The argument that organizations want total flexibility is rather spurious. In reality, whilst there may be flexibility within some job families (jobs that share common basic skills, purpose and activity), there is little movement across job family boundaries, and specialization is still regarded as very important where there are individual skills and competencies (for example, the different hospital consultancy specialisms, camera crew in television production, airline pilots, chefs, etc.). Job evaluation can, therefore, be used to establish the benchmarks for job families, which can then act as control points for other job family members, for example, for production jobs, clerical jobs, warehouse jobs, to cite three kinds of job families.

Computer-aided job evaluation (CAJE) can also remove much of the bureaucracy and the time-consuming processes of comparison. There are two ways in which CAJE can be used:

1   As a software system, giving a data management service (e.g. in whole job ranking schemes).
2   As a rapid evaluation process, by computing the output from completed question-naires using predetermined criteria (e.g. in a points rating scheme).

A job description and a person specification are essential first stages to job evaluation. The procedure is the same as we described in Chapter 9, the person specification being an outline of the qualifications, experience and other attributes needed to do a job. The person specification should show the job factors. Both the description and the specification should be summarized into a 'job profile', recording the responsibilities, skills, competencies- in other words, the factors on which the job is to be evaluated.

DIFFERENT KINDS OF JOB EVALUATION SCHEMES

Broadly speaking, there are two main dimensions on which job evaluation can be delineated: whether they are quantitative or qualitative in the schemes' treatment of job factors; and the extent to which they are analytical of a job's content. A brief description of each of the most well-known schemes is given below.

WHOLE JOB RANKING

This is a non-quantitative and non-analytical method. It is a technique in which jobs are placed in order of importance or value relative to each other. The main guide is usually the amount of responsibility in each job or the importance of the job to the organization. This method looks at the whole job, not its component parts, and is concerned with the rank order of jobs (i.e. the relative position of jobs to each other), rather than differences in any absolute sense.

The procedure to be followed is:

1   Benchmark jobs are identified. These are jobs that are 'yardsticks' or standards against which others can be compared. They should be chosen because they are representative of job requirements, and there should be no controversy about their content, value or importance.
2   The benchmark jobs should be drawn from various levels in the organization.
3   Each job to be evaluated is compared with the benchmark job and a judgement is made to determine its relationship with the benchmark job.
4   As the number of ranked jobs increases, we can compare new jobs with those that have already been ranked.
5   In large organizations, we can use 'job families', where there are similarities, as finite populations – for example, accounts department staff.
6   It may be easier from an administrative point of view to use a computer program to make the comparisons.
7   A further refinement is the paired comparison method, where each job is compared with all the others in turn, until a consensus is reached among the assessors on the ranking. This should improve the reliability of the ranking, but the number of comparisons increases exponentially (from 1225 comparisons for 50 jobs to 4950 paired comparisons for 100 jobs).

Generally, the whole job-ranking method is thought to be appropriate for small organizations. There are problems in handling the number of comparisons if the number of jobs is larger. It is also difficult to choose benchmark jobs that do not have some flaw as yardsticks if a number of different departments and specialisms are involved.

CLASSIFICATION OR GRADING SCHEMES

This is also a qualitative and non-analytical method. It is a centralized approach that may best be seen as part of the design of the organization to which it is applied.

This approach requires the examination of jobs in the light of predetermined definitions of the grades, as part of a planned organization structure, where the level of work in each grade is founded on what is thought to be appropriate functionally. New jobs are then compared with the predefined grade descriptions to indicate the placing of the job in a relationship with other graded jobs.

Assuming that the grading scheme is to be integrated with the design of the organization, the following steps should take place:

1   The shape and size of the organization's hierarchy has to be determined. This becomes a question of how many levels there should be in the hierarchy, and the span of control (the numbers reporting to each supervisor) at each level.
2   The job hierarchy is divided into a number of grades, with written definitions for each.
3   The definitive grade descriptions are associated by outside analogues with appropriate pay rates, and effectively become the benchmarks against which other jobs are graded.
4   The broad differences that management wish to apply are written into the grade descriptions, often being in terms of the level of skill or responsibility.
5   Jobs are fitted into the structure by evaluation committees, who arrive at a consensus by comparing the ungraded jobs with the grade descriptions.

There are similarities between whole job ranking and grading schemes, in that jobs are taken as wholes. The hope with a classification system is that it will produce a planned organization. There are benefits in the approach to staff budgeting and career planning. However, there can be problems in making comparisons where an in-house scheme is used. If the categories or grades contain a wide range of skills or job requirements, this reduces the usefulness in discriminating between jobs. Non -analytical schemes are more likely to be discriminatory, and to fall foul of the Equal Value Regulations.

POINTS RATING

The points rating technique entails the analysis and comparison of jobs according to common factors, which are represented by a number of points, the amount of points depending on the degree of each factor present. Jobs are then placed in order of their total points rating. Pay is usually determined by reference to benchmark jobs. Points rating is therefore both a quantitative and an analytical technique.

The technique requires a number of steps that must be undertaken with care:

1   'Job factors' are discovered by an examination of the most essential elements in the job. Common job factors need to be present in all the jobs to be evaluated. This is accomplished by taking a significant sample of jobs for which complete job descriptions and person specifications should be prepared. The factors selected from the descriptions and specifications should be those that are critical for differentiation between jobs.

2   The factors that are categories such as 'engineering knowledge' required to do the job, or 'physical effort', are sometimes taken to be at a broad level and can be termed 'generic factors'. There are then a number of specific subfactors that comprise the 'generic' factor, for example: 'engineering knowledge' could be broken down to different aspects of mechanical engineering, or in the case of 'physical effort,' the physical demands can be qualified more precisely.

3   The subfactors should then be weighted according to the degree of importance they have in each job. This is done by dividing each subfactor into a number of 'degrees'. The degree or extent of the subfactor (and therefore the number of points awarded) increases according to the quantity of the subfactor in the job, or to the amount of difficulty the subfactor brings to the job, or the degree of importance of the subfactor for the performance of the job.

4   In order to resolve the problem of how to award points to each factor, and degree, it is useful to begin by assuming that the value of all factors present in any job will add up to 100 per cent. The evaluation committee can then give relative values of each factor in each benchmark job so that the generic factors are given a percentage that totals 100 per cent, and each subfactor a percentage that adds up to 100 per cent of the generic factor. The evaluation is of each subfactor, so that each subfactor should be broken down into degrees. At this stage we have an indication of the relative importance of each generic factor and each subfactor.

The number of degrees used should not go beyond what is likely to be recognizable, up to five degrees of a subfactor being the maximum for most purposes. Definitions of each degree used for each subfactor are required. The total number of points can be any number, but the maximum number for all factors must add up to this total, and therefore the number of points is dependent on the number of factors, and evaluators should allow room for the maximum combination of points. An appropriate number which offers enough scope could be 500 points.

Since acquired 'skill and knowledge' is rated relatively high in the example in Table 15.1, and training and previous experience is rated high on this, we may grant the highest degree of this subfactor, 100 points, of the 500 points total possible (that is, 40 per cent of 500 = 200, 50 per cent of 200 = 100). The number of points in each degree can be an arithmetical or a geometric progression, and the subfactor's degrees need definitions. For example, 'Experience':

- 1st degree (up to one month)   20 points
- 2nd degree (over one and up to four months)   40 points
- 3rd degree (over four months but less than 12 months)   60 points
- 4th degree (12 months to 18 months)   80 points
- 5th degree (over 18 months)   100 points

using an arithmetic progression.

5   A chart should then be drawn up, which shows the values for each subfactor, broken down into degrees present, with clear, agreed definitions of the subfactors and degrees.

6   Each job is then evaluated, preferably by a committee that will arrive at a consensus on the total number of points for the individual jobs being evaluated. From this process, the jobs may be placed on a range or scale.

TABLE 15.1 POINTS RATING SCHEME (THE FACTORS ARE DRAWN FROM THE BIM 'JOB EVALUATION' SCHEME)

Generic factor	Importance (%)	Specific subfactors	Importance (%)	Maximum points
Acquired skill and knowledge	40	Training and previous experience	50	100
		General reasoning ability	20	40
		Complexity of process	20	40
		Dexterity and motor accuracy	10	20
Responsibilities and mental requirements	30	For material equipment	5	7.5
		Effect on other operations	40	60
		Attention needed to orders	40	60
		Alertness to details	10	15
		Monotony	5	7.5
Physical requirements	20	Abnormal position	60	60
		Abnormal effort	40	40
Conditions of work	10	Disagreeableness	90	45
		Danger	10	5
Total				500

Although the points scheme may seem complicated, this technique has been widely used in Britain and the USA since its invention in the 1920s. There are a number of variations on the method outlined here, which indicates the flexibility of the points scheme. The use of points should not be seen as a sign of scientific objectivity, as the points system relies on judgements by evaluation committees. Nevertheless, the technique is useful in comparing many different jobs that contain the same job factors, and has been developed into tailor-made schemes to fit the specific requirements of companies.

PROPRIETARY SCHEMES

A good example of a variation on this approach is the PwC/Monks 6 Factor System. This is a competency-based analytical job evaluation system. It sets out to measure the levels of skill or competency required to perform the roles covered by the scheme. The factors are: knowledge, specialist skills, people skills, external impact, decision-making, and innovation/creative thinking. Each job is scored on each factor, with scoring based on assessment of the relative values of the competency in the labour market. The idea of relating the scheme to competencies, and the direct connection to pay, are the unusual features of the scheme.

GUIDE CHART PROFILE OF HAY MSL LIMITED (NOW HAY/MCBER)

The guide chart profile method was developed by management consultants Hay MSL Limited by using a factor comparison method, but it has evolved into a variant of the points rating technique. The scheme provides a total wage/salary package, and the widespread use of the scheme globally permits direct comparisons with other organizations to establish the market rate for particular jobs. A summary of some of its main aspects shows the *modus operandi*.

Following the scheme's extensive use, the consultants have identified three generic factors, and further subdivisions into subfactors. No doubt there may be further adaptations to the scheme as it evolves. The generic factors and subfactors are defined in Table 15.2.

Accountability and know-how are evaluated on a points scale with varying degrees and problem-solving shown as a percentage of the know-how required for each job, the final results being converted into a geometric scale of scores under the three generic factors.

Job profiles are produced to show the different aspects of each job, under each of the factors, and help to reveal the relationship between the required performance and the organization's objectives, and show where the main job demands are, whether in taking actions or advising.

TABLE 15.2 GUIDE CHART PROFILE FACTORS

Accountability (a) Freedom to act (b) Magnitude of accountability	Dependent on the job's purpose, which should be related to the organization's goals
Know-how (a) Skill, education, training (b) Breadth of knowledge, including planning, organizing, etc.	
Problem-solving (a) The 'thinking environment' (constraints) (b) The 'thinking challenge' (how creative, routine, etc.)	Dependent on frequency and importance of problems

There is a point value in a pattern of numbers for each factor, depending upon a definition given in the guide chart, with 15 per cent intervals in progression, this being the step change that indicates a significant difference in job content. A judgement is made about the balance between each of the three factors in the job under consideration.

One of the benefits of this scheme is its recognition of the variable nature of managerial jobs that cannot be classified without taking the person specification into account in an individual way. However, the method seems to be favoured in tackling the job evaluation for white-collar and executive rewards.

The HayXpert software can be used to conduct a benchmark evaluation which is then a basis for the remaining jobs in the organization. Hay believe that their scheme can be revised at middle to senior management levels to make more use of the Hay method's capacity to provide a profile of a job's 'shape', according to the level of the work and the nature of the work. They believe this can be reduced to five levels: 'enterprise', 'leadership', 'strategy formulation', 'strategic alignment' and 'strategic and tactical implementation'. They examine these in relation to three types of managerial work, from planning and policy, coordination and commercial business and operations, in a matrix. This simplification may be a useful way to extend the benefits from the job evaluation scheme, which is otherwise a very time-consuming method, and to integrate job evaluation and competency assessment (Cohen and Wethersell 2004).

FACTOR COMPARISON

Factor comparison is another analytical technique that uses some of the ideas of both the points rating and the ranking methods. One version of factor comparison, illustrated here, is a 'direct to money' approach. This system entails evaluating jobs in terms of each other, on

TABLE 15.3 FACTOR COMPARISON

Generic factor	Rank order for secretary (£505 total)		Rank order for data entry clerk (£345 total)	
Acquired skill and knowledge	1	£155	2	£100
Responsibility and mental requirements	2	£205	1	£135
Physical requirements	3	£80	4	£35
Conditions of work	4	£65	3	£75

a basis of a certain limited number of factors, and reconciling these rankings with money values for each factor derived from benchmark jobs. Out of the first stages of the exercise comes a table of factor rates for the benchmark jobs against which all the other jobs can be evaluated. There are two parts to the early stages, therefore: factor ranking and factor evaluation.

The method is more involved than the others described, as there are difficult judgements to be made at each juncture:

1 The first step is to agree on the factors that are found in each of the jobs to be evaluated, so that these can be defined. The number of factors chosen is usually limited to a few broad factors, not less than four or more than seven.

2 Early studies suggested: mental requirements, skill requirements, physical requirements, responsibility and working conditions, but the factors chosen will need to be those that are appropriate for the jobs.

3 The next stage is to choose benchmark jobs, which must contain all these broad generic factors. These benchmark jobs must clearly be representative of the factors, and, there should be an unambiguous wage or salary for the job in question.

4 The payment for the benchmark jobs can be either the current rate (if this is thought correct) or the intended rate for the job, based on evidence from salary surveys or negotiated agreements.

5 The evaluation committee then ranks the factors contained in each benchmark job. Taking the four generic factors we used in our previous example (Table 15.1), we can follow the factor comparison procedure for two jobs, say, a secretary and a data entry clerk concerned with computer input (see Table 15.3). It must be appreciated that full job descriptions and person specifications would be needed for these two jobs before evaluation, and we will assume for the sake of simplicity that these have been prepared.

6 The committee must approach the benchmark jobs also from the perspective of factor evaluation, when money values are given to each factor. Given that the total job is

worth 100 per cent of the composite wage, a percentage of the wage can be attributed to each factor on a basis of its importance in the job. In Table 15.3 we have shown money values against each factor.

7   The reconciliation between the factor rankings and the factor evaluation is a crucial stage for resolving any differences. Because two different scales are being applied and there are not necessarily equal intervals, it is possible that there could be wide variations. Thus, 'acquired knowledge or skill' is worth much less for the data entry clerk than for the secretary, although there is only one difference in rank. Problems such as these would need some compromise solution by the committee.

8   A pilot study would help to resolve any serious difficulties in reconciling the factor rankings with the money evaluation and, should the factors or benchmark jobs prove unsuitable, then the whole process must be restarted.

9   The remainder of the jobs to be evaluated can be dealt with more speedily once this early work has been done and, as each job factor is ranked and then evaluated, the network of values and rankings should reveal a pattern on which decisions can be reached more easily. Full descriptions of all the other jobs to be evaluated need to be prepared, of course, and the pay for each factor after the job has been analysed can be settled by reference to this table of rates for the key jobs that has been constructed.

Factor comparison schemes are often treated with suspicion by employees, and are not as popular in the UK as the other three methods we have outlined so far.

The benefits of the scheme are that in the early stages, when benchmark jobs are being evaluated, two different approaches to the same job are reconciled to produce a practical compromise on the relative value of the job. This is likely to result in greater accuracy than the ranking method as far as management or the evaluation committee is concerned.

TIME SPAN OF DISCRETION

This is a somewhat theoretical approach to job evaluation, developed by Elliott Jaques (1964). It borders on being a social philosophy. The assumption is made that individuals have a subconscious awareness when their work, payment and capacity are all approximately at an acceptable level of demands and rewards. When a person's work and capacity are equally matched there is, according to the theory, an amount of payment (including salary and benefits) of which the individual is aware that matches the work and capacity level. Thus, people can feel underpaid or overpaid, worked or utilized.

A second aspect of Jaques's theory is the view that the discretionary work activities that an individual performs can be measured in terms of the time that elapses before a manager is aware that his or her subordinate has performed this discretionary element satisfactorily, in balancing the pace and quality of his or her work.

These two aspects of the theory are related, in that what people feel is 'fair' pay is understood by individuals in conformity with the time span of discretion that their work demanded. The pay norms which are felt to be fair are intuitive understandings by people of the rates that others receive for similar work, their own standard of living, and conceptions of equity, all conditioned by their feeling of the extent to which their capacity is being used or developed.

Research in the UK and the USA has indicated that there is a high correlation between felt fair pay and time span measures. The implications are that at each level in the organization there are time span measures that should, therefore, correspond to pay levels. Jaques also claims that individuals have 'capacity growth curves', these being the rates at which an individual expects his or her capacity to grow in the future and, therefore, the salary progressions that he or she would anticipate. Salary scales could be constructed, it is argued therefore, using this information.

The theory has aroused a great deal of interest, and has informed discussions on rates of pay and questions of social justice. However, its practicality as a proposal for the evaluation of jobs remains in doubt. There is disagreement over the validity of the research where such vague concepts as subconsciously held pay norms are used and where there are different interpretations of what is discretionary. Because of the tendency for people to draw on their own experience, there must be a bias towards maintaining the *status quo* in any organization, that is, the time span approach does not make clear which is the dependent and which the independent variable. Do people believe that they have a certain time span of discretion because they are paid at a certain level in relation to others? If so, the theory becomes a self-fulfilling prophecy. Finally, there are difficulties in obtaining acceptance of these ideas by those in industry and commerce.

DECISION BANDING

This method starts with the premise that all organizations tend to reward their members in terms of the decisions they make. This is similar to the time span of discretion, where the quality of the decision varies at each level of the organization. Paterson, who invented the decision-banding method, postulates six basic kinds of decision:

Band E: Policy-making decisions	(top management)
Band D: Programming decisions	(senior management)
Band C: Interpretative decisions	(middle management)
Band B: Routine decisions	(skilled workers)
Band A: Automatic decisions	(semi-skilled workers)
Band O: Vegetative decisions	(defined by others – unskilled workers).

All bands except O can be divided into two grades, upper and lower, thus giving 11 grades.

The stages recommended by Paterson are:

1   The establishment of job bands according to the kinds of decisions.
2   An analysis of the content of the jobs, from which jobs can be put into the appropriate subgrade for Band B, using points rating, and by ranking for Bands C and D into the agreed band.
3   Monetary values are assigned to each level. The increase between grades for pay rates is exponential, requiring equal distances between the midpoints.

Paterson claims that his method can be used for all jobs in the company and that, given proper consultation, it is possible to achieve a consensus on the difficult question of differentials. The phrase 'vegetative decisions' also seems not to be a valid or worthy description of decision-making by those at the lowest level in the organization. There are choices to be made about work even at the lowest level of jobs. Among the possible problems that can be envisaged with the decision-banding approach are the rigidity of the bands, the reliance on the job analyst's descriptions and the difficulty of convincing employees that this rather perplexing scheme has initiated an accurate rate of pay.

DIRECT CONSENSUS METHOD

The direct consensus method is another derivative of the time span of discretion theory. Again, there is an assumption that a consensus of opinion will be found in any working group concerning the relationship between jobs. It is argued that a wages structure will be acceptable to employees if it embodies their conventional wisdom.

The method is simple, but for most practical purposes requires the use of a computer program, both to produce the ranking of jobs and to calculate the variations of assessors' opinions:

1   Job descriptions are prepared from a representative sample of jobs. The number of jobs should be a 'prime number' between eleven and seventy-nine.
2   A representative committee is established with a sufficient number of assessors to make it possible for each one to rank an equal number of jobs, using a standard form for the computer input.
3   The jobs are ranked as 'wholes' using the question of how important is the job (presumably to the organization) in relation to each other job.
4   Jobs are ranked using the paired comparison method. All possible pairs of jobs are compared; the total number of comparisons is:

$$\frac{N(N-1)}{2}$$

where N = the number of jobs.

5   Reconciliation between job rankings is usually left to a computer, which will also calculate the variation between the assessors' ratings.

Ranking jobs as wholes can lead to rather difficult ranking decisions, and it is possible that, given computer facilities, jobs could be ranked under the broad factor headings that is one variation of this approach. The direct consensus method is expensive as regards assessors' time. Since job content is likely to change, a comparison of factors would probably help to make the method flexible. Multiple regression can be used to weight factors relative to what is thought appropriate.

THE INTRODUCTION OF JOB EVALUATION SCHEMES

We have devoted a proportionately large amount of space to the description of various forms of job evaluation because it is an essential first step towards the creation of a salary/ wage structure that has a rational basis in the eyes of both management and workers. However, the way job evaluation is applied will be of fundamental importance in the acceptance of a scheme as a rational instrument.

Job evaluation committees have already been mentioned. Employee involvement is a part of the overall sharing of power. How management ensures the representation of the different interest groups is dependent on organization structure, size, the current state of union/management relationships and existing relationships among the groups of employees affected by the evaluation. Job evaluation committees are less used at present, reflecting the stronger sense of managerial prerogatives.

Where they are formed, as a general rule small rather than large committees are recommended and they should reach decisions by consensus. 'Consensus' here means that each member of the committee should be allowed to express an opinion, and where there are genuine differences the reasons for the differences of view should be argued out until a broad measure of agreement is found, even though there may be minor objections. The chairperson's role is obviously important in directing these discussions. Whoever fulfils the role should be capable of balancing judgements and drawing together disparate outlooks, and should command respect from both employees and management. Whatever approach is adopted, senior line managers must be represented.

PAYMENT SYSTEMS ARISING FROM JOB EVALUATION

The outcome of a job evaluation scheme is an ordered and accepted pay structure, where there is a logical relationship between the amounts paid and the job factors and where the differentials between jobs fit into the structure and are approved. In practice, this is difficult to achieve. If there are committee meetings, interest groups will achieve the redefinition of certain factors and will manage to push up or down the relative worth of some of the jobs, on the grounds of what is acceptable, comprehensible and traditional. The fitting of the results of the evaluation to the market rate prevailing may, therefore, be a result of negotiation.

The same job evaluation schemes are rarely used for both blue-collar and white-collar employees. Jobs that are highly technical in content, or scientific and professional, do not fit easily with administration, sales or managerial jobs. This imposes further constraints on each group, as the salary and wage structures that emerge are related in the minds of employees, but not through job evaluation, so the final structures will have to be convincing.

The provisions of the Equal Value Amendment Regulations mean that employers should ensure that the factors used do not discriminate in favour of one sex. There is potential for an equal value claim if there is a special scheme for lower-level employees if they are mostly female, while more senior employees covered by a different scheme are mostly male, for example.

We have already mentioned some of the techniques of putting a money value on a job. In the factor comparison example, this is intrinsic to the technique. From the points system, a salary band can be defined by plotting the values on a scattergraph. From such a scatter, a line of best fit can be drawn through the midpoints to help create the grades. The cut-off for each grade will always be a matter of judgement. To fit market rates to jobs requires a survey of the comparative data, including employee benefits. Job evaluation provides the database on which judgements can be made, but we must turn to the problem of devising salary/wage scales for the important stage of setting up and administering scales.

QUESTIONS

1   What are the advantages of job evaluation in establishing a reward structure?
2   Describe the methods adopted in an *analytical* job evaluation scheme.
3   How does job evaluation benefit the cause of gender equality of rewards?
4   Discuss the proposition that job evaluation schemes should reflect organizational needs for flexibility and diversity. What types of job evaluation scheme are suitable for these purposes?

REFERENCES

Cohen, P. and Wethersell, G. (2004). 'More to job evaluation that meets the eye'. *IDS Executive Compensation Review 286*. 21–24.
Jaques, E. (1964). *Time Span Hand Book*. Heinemann.

16 PAY SYSTEMS

INTRODUCTION

Pay policy and the technicalities of pay structures and systems need to be understood before we can go on to consider the broader strategic issues related to rewards. In this chapter, the practical issues about pay systems are discussed and explained. Reward policy, like any other policy, is about what actions should be taken by the organization in response to different organizational and individual needs.

The typical objectives of a policy towards pay and benefits could be best described as 'to remain competitive for labour whilst rewarding good performance and adopting a position on pay which controls costs and is felt to be fair by all employees'. Of course, policies also reflect the company's philosophy and reward strategy (for example whether the company should have a single status with the same benefits for all levels and occupations of employees), which provide the context for the policies on pay and benefits. These strategic matters are discussed in the next chapter on 'Total rewards', in which the linkage between HR strategy and reward strategy are explored.

Reward policy issues have to be considered in the current context of recession and the early recovery, but there are also some universal issues that have to be decided and which are not so context dependent. These are listed below.

1   Where the company wishes and can afford to be in the labour markets (e.g. whether or not to follow a 'high wage' policy, demanding sustained effort of a high standard for large rewards, by positioning the company in the top quartile relative to competitors). This question also relates to recruitment policy (see Chapter 10) in so far as the costs of labour are an important part of total costs.

The answer to the question affects other major issues such as the competitive position of the business, the 'grow your own' versus buy issue and also informs debates on, for example, 'offshoring' or outsourcing.

2   What kind of total remuneration package the organization wishes to offer (for example, whether or not to give a range of 'perks', such as cars, inflation-proof pensions, etc., or whether to let employees make their choices through a flexible benefits policy).

3   A further question is whether or not to trade off benefits against wages. Consideration will have to be given to the consequences, for the retention of employees, for the kinds of people who work for the company and for their motivation to work.

4   Profit share bonus schemes and share ownership schemes also have to be thought through, to see whether they reflect an incentive element in the employee's wage, and whether there will be any real feeling of participation as a consequence of the profit share.

5   The policy on variation of pay has to be resolved. The questions here are: whether or not pay is to be regarded as the main incentive for good performance; what job families are to be identified; how new jobs are included; and what kind of job evaluation scheme to adopt and how to run it.

6   To what extent will company policy on pay be delegated to local managers, and how does the degree of autonomy fit in with policies on profit centres and management accounting?

7   The frequency of pay reviews, who is to be consulted, what kinds of evidence will be sought and the negotiation posture of the company have to be decided.

These are some of the policy options available, the choice of what is suitable being dependent on individual company circumstances, trends in reward, labour market conditions and the philosophy of management espoused.

WAGE STRUCTURES

Most employees are now paid monthly directly into their bank accounts, although hourly rates are sometimes quoted. Whatever the pay interval, sometimes pay includes a proportion that is calculated on the individual's output. The various terms used are described below.

The basic or flat rate

This is the amount of money paid for an hour's work. It is also sometimes called the 'hourly rate'. The basic rate may refer to a daily or weekly or monthly amount. Time rates are predetermined rates per hour paid at the end of the week or month. The flat rate is often used where the work does not lend itself to any kind of measurement. Sometimes, in addition to the basic rate, an individual bonus payment may be made.

Payment by results systems

Piecework originated as the estimated time a worker would take to make a piece of work, the 'piece' being whatever the product or item the employee was expected to make.

Piecework systems are either of the following kinds:

1 *Straight piecework*: this is the system whereby the employee is paid according to output. The method is either to agree a fixed amount of money for the production of each item, or a period of time is allowed for making the item. In the latter scheme, sometimes called the 'time allowed' system, if the employee completes the work in less time than planned, he or she is still paid for the original time and thus is able to increase earnings by completing more of the pieces, the calculation of the bonus being based on the difference between the time allowed and the actual time expressed as a percentage of his or her wage.

2 *Differential piecework*: this is similar to the 'time allowed' system of piecework, except that the amount of the bonus earned (which stems from the time saved) is shared between the company and the individual, the wage cost being adjusted with output, so that the company takes a proportion of the bonus as production increases. Schemes of this sort may be known under various names, such as 'premium bonus schemes'.

The employee has a degree of choice with piecework on the level of output he or she wishes to achieve.

Measured daywork

The pay of the employee is fixed on the understanding that he or she will maintain a specified level of performance. This level of performance, known as the 'incentive level', is calculated in advance and the employee is put under an obligation to try to achieve the level specified, as his or her pay does not vary in the short term.

There are individual rates and bonus systems. In addition, there are bonus schemes that aim at providing a group incentive, either to a work group or factory or unit-wide.

SMALL GROUP INCENTIVE SCHEMES

Typically, a bonus is given to group members when their output targets are achieved or exceeded. There are numerous schemes, which vary according to the timescale adopted for measuring output, the size of the group and the intergroup competitiveness that they encourage. Payment of the bonus may be equal among the group's members, or proportionate to an individual's earnings or status.

Advantages of group schemes

1   They draw on the natural tendencies of working people to develop norms based on what the group believes is an acceptable and 'comfortable' level of production, thereby harnessing the team spirit.
2   They are administratively simpler than individual schemes; the cost savings come from less clerical and inspection work, and savings on time study.
3   'Indirect' production workers, such as cleaners, stores assistants, etc., who also contribute to the production process can be included.
4   Flexibility within the group is encouraged and one might anticipate that workers would be anxious to help remove production bottlenecks and to encourage training.

Disadvantages of group schemes

1   The impact of group pressures on the less efficient individual may not be beneficial where he or she needs advice and help in order to work up to the target.
2   Holidays and sickness may upset the working of the scheme. Special arrangements may have to be made to stagger holidays carefully and a shutdown may result in lower pay for the holiday weeks.
3   Variations in production targets due to problems of supply, or a sudden fall in demand, can be a cause of complaint and disillusionment with the scheme could set in.
4   Members of large or scattered groups may not respond to the implicit appeal to group cohesiveness that is at the heart of these schemes.
5   Group norms of production may not be adequate and, if translated into official 'targets', will then not create any real increase in production. If a level is set that is too high, the group scheme will be a non-starter. It is, therefore, very dependent for its success on the targets being achievable but also very worthwhile for the company.

Bonus schemes stand in different ratios to the base rate and a guaranteed or fallback rate is frequently part of the wage for pieceworkers. There are agreements and legal require-ments concerning lay-offs and short-time working in the UK (see Chapter 26).

LONG-TERM, LARGE GROUP SCHEMES (GAIN-SHARING SCHEMES)

The main difference between these schemes and those outlined above is that they apply on a long timescale, usually across the whole unit, and are often seen as an attempt to involve the staff in the organization of operations. They are sometimes called gain-sharing schemes. The bonus calculation would typically be made monthly, and would be based on changes in the value of goods produced, or improvements in the actual output per person/hour against the standard.

There are many variants of these schemes. For example, the Scanlon plan (which originated in 1947) was both a suggestion plan and a collective incentive scheme. The suggestion scheme was part of a system for drawing on ideas from the workforce about improvements that could be achieved jointly by management and union. It operated a bonus depending on reductions achieved by the workforce in labour costs compared with the sales revenue. Reductions in sales revenue could result in no bonus, however, although employees worked just as hard.

Another old established system with different variations, the Rucker Plan (in 1955) used 'production value' (or added value) as a basis for a collective bonus scheme. This value is defined as the difference between the sales revenue and the cost of the raw materials and supplies (that is, the inputs to the production process).

'Added value' bonus schemes make use of the idea that if the ratio of total employment costs to sales revenue falls below the level it has been, then the improvements in productivity this represents should be shared by granting a bonus to the people who have produced the change. A scale of bonus payments (as a percentage of basic pay) may be calculated. This approach is less susceptible to market forces.

Advantages of long-term, large group schemes

1   The long-term aspect should provide steady earnings.
2   Employee participation through production committees helps to overcome the 'them and us' attitudes that can be destructive, and employee involvement helps to build trust.
3   There is a wide range of applications to different businesses.
4   Value added schemes can be adjusted more readily to the company's trading position than those that use simple numbers of items produced.

Disadvantages of long-term, large group schemes

1   If applied across a whole factory or unit, there may not be a sufficient sense of identity from the scheme to help create teamwork.
2   For the schemes to have any incentive value, a bonus of at least 10 per cent would be expected by employees to make it worthwhile. The larger the numbers covered, the less the percentage amount to each employee, hence reducing its motivational potential.
3   It is questionable whether individuals see how their own particular effort will contribute to the achievement of the target over a long timescale. Here, it is worth remembering the many variables that can intervene (changes in personnel, supervision, customer requirements, machinery, etc., a list that increases as time passes).

Gain-sharing schemes can be designed with a variety of objectives, measured by indices besides output or revenue growth. Cost reduction and performance measures may be a significant part of the gain-share, but to these objectives can be added customer retention, safety, environmental impact, customer satisfaction and profitability, amongst many others. For example, in addition to its normal business measures, BP Exploration had safety and environmental goals. Each of its oil and gas rigs in the North Sea (managed separately as 'assets') were on separate gain-sharing schemes. Whilst this brought benefits, there was also the effect of discouraging staff transfers between the rigs, deriving from this approach.

Design features of gain-sharing schemes include the following:

1   The basis for the calculation – company-wide, team or individual measures.
2   If a team approach (often favoured) is adopted, then team goals are needed.
3   What triggers the pay out, for example, whether the team has to pass a profitability gate before any payout is made? Are there variable shares according to participation in the scheme, the amount of profitability achieved, length of service, grade, occupation or other variables? Will the amount be a percentage of pay, or an equal amount for all team members?
4   The 'gain-share' bonus may also vary according to the issue (e.g. 2 per cent for safety targets, 5 per cent for productivity targets). Very often the scheme produces a pool of money over time from which employees share according to a predetermined policy.

Choices over these design features can only be made according to the context. There is no one best practice, therefore.

SALARY STRUCTURES

The salary administrator's objective is to retain consistency in approach, to keep the rationality of scales whilst keeping sufficient scope to be able to reward outstanding performance, and to ensure the process and outcome are proofed against any local challenge, for example in terms of discrimination.

Most scales relate salary to the grade of the job. Following a job evaluation, a series of job grades may be constructed, using any of the methods we discussed in the previous chapter (not only as an outcome of the classification method of job evaluation). If the scales are drawn on a diagram, with grades lettered A–E (A being the lowest), a salary scale could be as shown in Figure 16.1.

Clearly, one of the questions to be decided is whether the scales for each grade overlap (as in Figure 16.1) and, if so, by how much? Related to this is the question of what the range for the scales should be.

The overlap needs careful thought because of the implications for transfers between grades and promotions. To determine the range of the salary, as a rough guide, an overlap of 10–20 per cent is usual between associated grades, the salary level at the top of the range being 20 per cent to 50 per cent higher than at the bottom of the range. Higher percentage spreads for higher-grade jobs are normal.

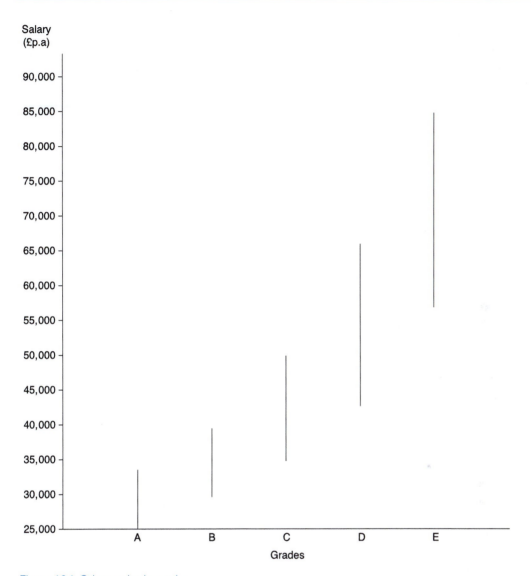

Figure 16.1 Salary scales by grade

Broadbanding

The need for flexibility at work, the flatter organization structures and the pace of change have resulted in a move away from the large number of individual grades. Increasingly, careers are lateral rather than vertical, and employees work in many different teams, often within matrix structures.

Broadbanding is one suggested response to these new pressures. Broadbanding means collapsing numerous grades or salary ranges into a few wide bands. These bands cover a number of job families that formerly would each have had their own pay ranges. Companies using broadbanding usually reduce the number of salary ranges or bands by a half or two-thirds of their previous number in the traditional structure. These new broadbands may not use the same salary points as the old bands.

CREATING SCALES FROM JOB EVALUATION RESULTS

In our discussion of job evaluation, the various techniques are all seen to have as their outcome an ordered positioning of jobs relative to each other. The result will be a list of job titles placed in order, but they will still need to be placed into specific grades (unless a classification scheme has been used).

Creating a scale

1   The list of jobs is placed in order, together with the associated salary and, if a points scale has been used, the points value. We will then have to decide the number of grades required. This will be dictated by the size of the organization and, in a traditional structure, the percentage salary difference between the midpoints of the grade. If we take the average salary for those ranked lowest, and the average for the highest, we can get some idea of the spread of salaries and the step intervals will then have to be decided taking the job evaluation results into account, using the principles on overlap between rates outlined above. It would be as well to aim for only as many levels as is consistent with the evaluation results.

2   As a matter of policy, it may be that more than one set of grades is thought necessary. In this case, the top group of grades will have different criteria applied from those at lower levels.

3   When there is a points scheme we can allocate an equal span of points to each grade. The 'classification' techniques of job evaluation will provide a predetermined list of grades, but in the ranking methods some kind of arbitrary cut-off point for each grade will be needed. Jobs that fall on the boundary of two grades will have to be looked at carefully, to ensure that a correct decision on the grading has been made, looking, for example, at the salary progression implications of the grading decision.

4   Finally, we need to show the relationship between the jobs on the new scale, by plotting the relative position of jobs that can be listed along the horizontal axis with their grades, whilst salary per annum is shown on the vertical axis, as in Figure 16.2. From this, the midpoints of the new scales can be calculated and the range of the scale then decided, in a traditional salary structure.

In a broadbanded system, the midpoint will not be a significant control point. The salary ranges are usually too great for that purpose and the job families are related in a different way to the marketplace. The options are to maintain the job-evaluated results and the marketplace relationships based on these (for example, to keep the points rating as in the Hay system) and to introduce the broadbanded scales at a second stage, or to use two or three control points in the band that are related to market rates.

Assuming that a salary survey has been undertaken, or that information is available to deal with the question of what is the new market rate for jobs of each category, existing scales will need to be updated. The design and interpretation of salary survey information is rather a specialized task and details of how to tackle that problem are given later in the 'wage/salary survey' section below. A new line will have to be drawn on a graph similar to Figure 16.2, which will be the new midpoint for the updated scale (see Figure 16.3). Such

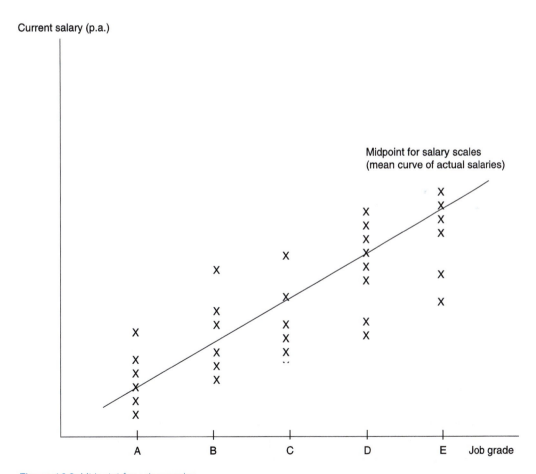

Figure 16.2 Midpoint for salary scales

Salary £p.a.

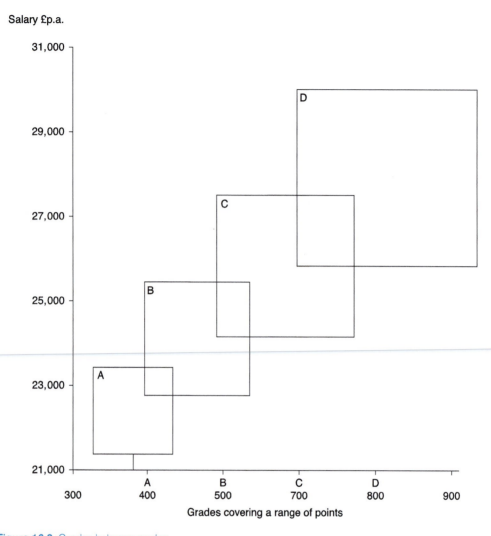

Figure 16.3 Overlap between grades

an important policy step has enormous policy implications for costs, recruitment and existing relationships, since it will form the basis for the new scales.

Scales may have to be adjusted and any anomalies identified. There will almost invariably be a few people who do not fit easily into the salary bands and, once identified, plans for the individual's increments to bring him or her into the scale will be required, for example by 'red circling' those paid over the rate and holding their increases down until the scale increases bring them into line, or 'green circling' those who are underpaid against the market rate, who would receive accelerated increments to bring them in line.

VALUE/COST ANALYSIS

Outsourcing market testing and 'best value' principles have now become common ways to reduce costs and to check the value of internal service provision. This approach can also be used to establish benchmark jobs or service values. For example, cleaning and catering services that are labour-intensive can easily be priced by reference to outside contractors. The analysis may be conducted by, first, calculating the impact on profit of the costs of replacing employment with an outsourced service and, second, comparing with this figure the costs of employment as a percentage of salary for the same service. These latter costs would need to include total compensation costs and all the 'on costs' (National Insurance Contributions, recruitment, training, support staff, sickness/holiday cover costs, etc.).

SALARY ADMINISTRATION

How the policy is operated within the agreed structures is a matter of salary administration. Large companies will usually have a specialist salary administrator and in the small- to medium-sized organization the task will probably fall on the HR manager, or could be performed by the chief executive, company secretary or chief accountant.

There are two types of scale to administer. There are those that have scope within each range for rewarding varying levels of performance differently, and there are those that grant automatic increments up to a maximum, according to some other criterion, for example, the qualifications attained. There are sometimes scales that give a mixture of the two.

The aircraft manufacturer Airbus UK, for example, introduced a generic job description to support a broadbanded structure, but retained its job levels for technicians, advanced technicians and professional levels. Pay progression was guided by the creation of three pay zones for each level, these being the 'incremental zone' for new starters, the 'target zone' that reflects the external market rate for the job (by size of job), with progression based on the acquisition of additional skills and responsibilities, and an 'enhanced zone' – the upper part of the salary band, for those performing a significantly larger job than the target level (IDS May 2005: 11–12).

The type of scale that provides for varying levels of performance over time can be shown as a 'box' on the graph, with overlaps between the grades (Figure 16.3).

The issues for administration are how to move individuals through these scales, and how to shift the scales themselves.

WAGE/SALARY REVIEWS

The impact of inflation and the annual cycle of wage negotiation have made an annual review of salaries and wages normal practice in many organizations. The distinction between different employee groups is often made with different review dates. This can lead to serious problems when trying to maintain a rational basis for salary/wage differentials, which is evidenced when hourly rated employees transfer on to the monthly payroll and when increases for monthly paid supervisors or indirect workers such as stores staff are considered in isolation from their hourly rated fellow workers. It is strongly recommended, therefore, that the same review dates for both groups are used.

Preparatory work on the reviews should be started well in advance, at least three to six months beforehand, depending on the size and complexity of the organization. Wage and salary increases can be for one or more of the following reasons:

■ cost of living (measured by the consumer price index (CPI) for example). The CPI is a measure of inflation, which is internationally recognized
■ merit
■ market shortages (in skills, for certain groups)
■ the correction of anomalies
■ consolidating bonus or overtime, or other restructuring.

Managers should be involved at various stages in the reviews. If the increases are to be negotiated, the preparatory work will include the development of a negotiating strategy and much supporting evidence will be required, together with the financial consequences of various prospective agreements.

Assuming either that negotiations agree the new scales and the criteria for merit increases, or that there are no union negotiations for the salary review, the following procedure is consistent with good practice:

1 HR department initiates and pilots through a job evaluation (may take some months to complete).
2 HR department undertakes salary surveys of local companies, or obtains national survey data.
3 Estimates of costs are prepared for new scales that are constructed using the data of the survey. These are submitted to the board for approval.
4 Once approved, senior line managers are given guidelines for recommending increases for merit, and an indication of the cost-of-living increase that has been incorporated in the new scales.
5 Line manager recommendations, confidential at this stage, are vetted by the HR manager.
6 HR manager refers back any problem cases, taking particular note of the costs and trends, notably the effect on relativities, progression policies and recruitment.
7 HR manager summarizes costs and presents consolidated list to the board (this may not include details of individual cases, but should be a breakdown of the costs into

different groups). The report should include an outline of any trends and the likely effects of the increases.

8   Once approved by the board, notifications are sent to individuals through their managers, and to payroll. The information is entered on personnel records. The new scales are then published.

The same procedures can be followed for hourly rated or monthly paid staff.

COST-OF-LIVING INCREASES

Inflation ran at double figures in the UK for most of the 1970s, although it fell in the 1980s. Other Western European countries were similarly afflicted, as were the USA, Canada and many Third World countries. Real wages (the amount of goods and services that monetary wages will buy) would therefore fall unless maintained by cost-of-living increases. It is argued that this in turn fuels inflation, producing a cost push for prices to rise, rather than a demand pull. The pressure from groups of employees to gain cost-of-living increases and the practice of incomes policy norms in the UK that set out expected percentage rises resulted, during the 1980s, in all wages being under upward pressure on an annual cycle. Although inflation has subsided, there is still a residual effect as employees often anticipate cost-of-living increases in their demands. Awards are often made according to the overall index (CPI) and have been running at around 2–3 per cent per annum for the early part of the twenty-first century. For a long period during the recession inflation has been running ahead of wage increases, although the position is likely to be reached where wage rises in the private sector will overtake the inflation rate.

When a scale is revised upwards, employees will expect to rise to at least the same position relatively on the new scale. However, it is possible, with the employee's agreement, to use the increase as a means of lowering the relative position in the grade (as discussed above) where an employee is being downgraded, for example, or where job evaluation and comparison with market rates has shown the employee to be overpaid in relation to the job. In these circumstances, rather than lower the pay the employee is best kept on a 'standstill' rate until the increases in the new grade affect the salary (so-called 'red circling'). This reflects a convention that wages are rigid downwards (see also the section on constructive dismissal in Chapter 24).

PERFORMANCE-BASED PAY/COMPETENCE-BASED PAY

One of the tests of a salary scale's adequacy is its efficiency in matching ability, potential and current performance with satisfactory rewards. To retain employees, the recognition of their performance must occur on time and equate with their own sense of what is fair.

Following Elliott Jaques we might expect individuals to have a preconceived notion of what is a 'correct' salary for the work they perform. This is also supported by social comparison theory, according to which employees are more concerned about differentials in pay between themselves and others than they are about absolute amounts of pay.

Merit increases are therefore given to show recognition and to imply the kinds of actions and attitudes that the company wishes to reward. This has a bearing on how other employees define success in that organizational context, and thus merit increases are an essential element in the drive towards the company's objectives. There is increasing interest in performance-related pay, through merit increases tied closely to objectives. This places greater emphasis on appraisal schemes. Merit pay is now often described as contribution-based pay.

To summarize, performance-related pay can be given as a bonus, or as a consolidated sum as a form of merit or contribution-based pay. Contribution-based pay focuses on the 'how' of performance, as well as what performance has been achieved. Contribution-based pay is contingent for its success on the appraisal mechanisms. Thus, most practitioners stress the significance of training appraisers in the system. Movement between scales is increasingly according to merit. Processes vary. For example, Rolls-Royce Defence Aerospace uses points rating to show achievement against objectives, in the civil service judgements about performance are linked to a competency system and departmental pay committees make judgements on line managers' recommendations. Airbus, mentioned earlier, has a matrix of performance ratings based on objectives on one side of the matrix, with behaviours on the other side of the matrix, assessed according to a key set of behaviours, and the resulting points are turned into pay.

Competence-based reward programmes use improvements in competence or job-related skills as criteria for increases. Other performance-based systems relate salary increments to performance against objectives.

The main criticism of competence-based pay is that it is centred on the inputs to the organization, rather than the outputs. Skill acquisition is only valuable if it can be converted into outputs that generate profits/sales or reduce costs. The combination of competence and objectives as criteria for increments are, therefore, to be recommended. Skill-based increments can fit readily into a broadband salary structure, where the intention is to encourage flexibility and the deployment of a range of skills. In total compensation schemes, where there is a total value placed on the job including benefits and other costs, a core standard value is the proportion of total job value that relates to competence, which usually includes the core salary (that which it is felt should not vary with performance), as well as pensions and social security benefits. (See below for a discussion on total compensation.) Pay increases using skill or competence criteria are designed to improve an employer's skill base, to improve flexibility and to assist in the implementation of technical change. When this has been achieved, new priorities may emerge, with a consequential change to reward policy objectives. The problem remains of what happens if skills acquired have been rewarded by an increase in the person's base pay, but the skills become obsolete over time? This leaves the individual on a higher rate than others but for no good reason.

The debate on performance-based pay has intensified recently, as schemes have spread up the managerial hierarchy and from private to public sector. There is no evidence that performance improves in the long run purely due to performance-based pay. The issues raised by Herzberg are still valid today. People are less likely to be motivated by money than they are by challenge, personal development, good supervision, feedback and a sense of achievement deriving from the work itself.

The arguments for and against performance-based pay can be summarized as follows.

Against

- Does not motivate (the Herzberg theory).
- After initial improvements, there is diminishing marginal utility to the organization as job holders have less and less that can be done to improve their work.
- It is inappropriate for some jobs, for example, where quality and personal service are important.
- Objectives change too quickly to be used annually in performance reviews.
- The variable element would have to be considerable to have an effect, but if the rewards are highly volatile individuals are unable to plan financially (e.g. regarding their mortgage payments).

In favour

- In a period of low inflation, when zero increases are the norm, the only possibility for increases in pay is through productivity improvement.
- Compensation has a high symbolic value. It symbolizes achievement and attracts peer group approval and has a wider meaning in society.
- If rewards can be linked to objectives, it will help to drive the objectives.
- By basing reward on competence acquisition, there can be a coherent recruitment, appraisal and development policy.
- There is clarity about rewards and, since all staff can have objectives, all can participate.

To summarize, performance-based pay can be useful, provided objectives can be easily set and there is good communication about the scheme. In addition, the amounts of the increases must be significant and be related to organizational objectives.

Table 16.1 is an example of a performance-based pay scheme in a large financial services company. All employees are appraised and an overall performance level is agreed for each employee:

TABLE 16.1 RELATING PERFORMANCE TO PERCENTAGE INCREASE

Performance level	Multiple of increase (decided each year)	% amount of increase company can afford (decided each year)
1	2.0 ×	
2	1.5 ×	e.g. 5%
3	1.0 ×	
4	0 ×	

Performance levels

1 Excellent – has exceeded all objectives and made an outstanding contribution.
2 Good – has achieved all objectives.
3 Average – has achieved most objectives.
4 Not rated/unsatisfactory – has not been in job long enough to be assessed, or has not met most objectives.

A multiple of the increase is then awarded and applied to the general company increase, this being the amount the company can afford, given the distribution of performance amongst employees. Sometimes, a forced distribution is created with a consequential rise in performance standards or changes to the multiple. The reward decision is made after the appraisal review.

DISCRETIONARY INCREMENTS

A further method is to make judgements at the stage of starting (or being promoted) as to how long it will take for an individual to perform the full range of duties satisfactorily. If this is, for example, four years, then the difference between his or her starting rate and the top of the grade is divided by four years to give an even rate of increases. Should performance change during the four years, then the remaining difference between his or her current salary and the top of the scale can be made divisible by a smaller or larger number.

THE DIVIDED BOX

The salary box (that is, the range over time) can be broken down into sub-ranges that show appropriate rates for performance predictions on a basis of previous experience

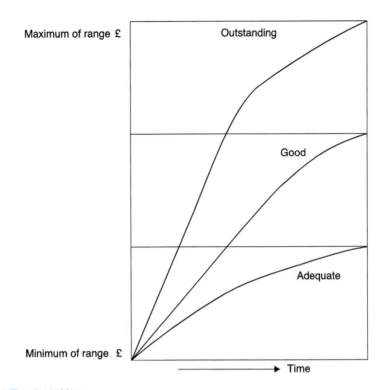

Figure 16.4 The divided box

and evidence of track records. Again, an individual can be switched from one salary progression line to another if his or her performance warrants it. An example of the divided box is shown in Figure 16.4. This shows three performance levels, namely outstanding, good and adequate, with three different progression curves through the range.

GRADE FUNNELS

This is a way of describing minimums and maximums of a range, which can change with the length of service of those in the grade. The placing of the individual's salary between these parameters would, therefore, give room for high levels of performance at any age, reduce the uncertainty on where to place the new starter or those who were promoted, whilst giving room for changing the line of the salary progression if performance changes. An example of the grade funnel is shown in Figure 16.5.

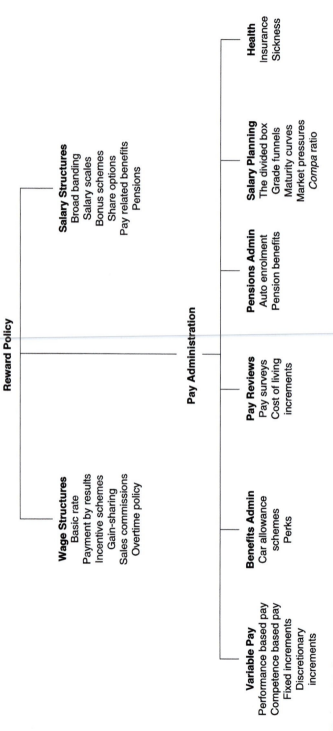

Reward Policy

Wage Structures
Basic rate
Payment by results
Incentive schemes
Gain-sharing
Sales commissions
Overtime policy

Salary Structures
Broad banding
Salary scales
Bonus schemes
Share options
Pay related benefits
Pensions

Pay Administration

Variable Pay
Performance based pay
Competence based pay
Fixed increments
Discretionary
increments

Benefits Admin
Car allowance
schemes
Perks

Pay Reviews
Pay surveys
Cost of living
increments

Pensions Admin
Auto enrolment
Pension benefits

Salary Planning
The divided box
Grade funnels
Maturity curves
Market pressures
Compa ratio

Health
Insurance
Sickness

Figure 16.5 Pay systems

MARKET PRESSURES

The reaction of managers to market rates and pressures is partly a problem of how to cope with short-term changes in market rates owing, for example, to a temporary skills shortage, without upsetting an agreed grading scheme that has arisen from job evaluation. Alternatively, market rates can vary owing to major economic change. If the change is not temporary (for example, a shortage of various kinds of computer specialists) the benchmark jobs will reflect the importance and rarity of the skills when the next job evaluation takes place, and a nego-tiation for a new pecking order will occur when the job evaluation committee meets. In prac-tice, in the example cited, it means the organization has to place a higher value on computing or system skills because of their scarcity.

During and in the aftermath of the recession, the approach to pay increases changed. In spite of serious economic difficulties, the need for talented people has been undimin-ished. Generally, companies sought to retain their skilled staff. Notably, in the UK, the USA and in Germany there were movements of employees onto different work arrangements found in the contingent labour force of part-time and temporary staff, often encouraged by the state – as in Germany's mini and midi jobs, where unemployment benefits were paid to part-time workers. There were pay freezes, especially in the public sector, and a fall in real wages in the UK. As the recession came to an end, private sector pay rose, whilst public sector pay rises were capped at 1 per cent, in view of the UK's massive deficit.

In the case of recruitment difficulties, short-term (say, up to two years) fluctuations may be met by considering a market rate supplement, which gives the shortage jobs a temporarily higher rate, which is recorded separately on their documents and records. It should be explained to the people concerned that such high percentage increases will not always be given. When market pressures abate, the salary will be brought back to the place on the salary curve that has been projected. Special bonus payments and other premia are sometimes used to retain staff, but the use of special payments outside the scales is to be avoided, as these anomalies create precedents for other groups, distort existing relativities and, if allowed to persist, make a total nonsense of the scales.

The impact of a 'pay freeze', commonly adopted in the recession, can bring longer term problems. The difficulty following a pay freeze is that all plans on pay changes are typically put on hold. This leads to individuals on pay rates that cannot be adjusted, which is de-motivating and can result in recruitment difficulties. To bring new people in at higher rates is detrimental to morale. Ending a pay freeze raises questions about the extent to which the organization can afford rises to the pay of the groups of staff who were penalized.

OVERTIME PAYMENTS

Overtime is most frequently paid to hourly rated employees; the premium may be time and a quarter, time and a half or double time. Overtime is yet another 'plussing-up' tendency that needs careful control. The concept of overtime is usually seen as a means of overcoming a short-term requirement for longer hours. Where companies have started to rely on overtime, either because of labour shortages or because it is a way of increasing earnings without revising scales officially, there is every likelihood of serious problems in the offing. A time will surely come when an employee does not wish to work 'compulsory over-time', or there will be a lull in orders, or a new manager will be appointed who does not agree to the 'blind eye' overtime, which is not really overtime at all but just an excuse to increase earnings. There are now legal restrictions on the number of hours an employee can be expected to work in a week. If expectations are not met, there is the making in all those situations of an industrial dispute.

A few simple rules for the control of overtime may help:

■ Overtime should always be authorized in advance by a senior manager (not the immediate supervisor).
■ A return showing the number of hours worked and the reasons should be made and statistics of overtime by department kept.
■ Some allowance should be made in the wage/salary budget for overtime when it can be projected (e.g. during holidays or at peak periods).

SALARY PLANNING

To carry through a policy necessitates planning for both the individual's salary and for the groups of people under review. Piecemeal salary decisions are likely to result in distortion to the overall policy unless careful planning takes place. For example, there is a steady attrition of salaries when a high labour turnover brings in new employees at lower rates than existing staff to the extent that the salary mean for the grade is reduced. Although this does afford opportunities within the overall salary budget for adjustments to other salaries, the global effect is to distort differentials and to make reviews more crucial. Salary administrators can turn to a number of devices for planning salaries.

The high costs of employment and the variety of additional benefits, perks and incentives are such that companies wishing to manage their human resources efficiently seek to control their total employment costs and to ensure that these expenditures are put to best use.

MATURITY CURVES

Projections of salary curves for groups of staff can be plotted to establish future trends. This is simply achieved by recording the salaries of people within the group on a graph, showing salary against time. The median salary of the group is usually taken to be a good enough measure for planning purposes. Future trends can be plotted using regression techniques. The benefits of planning a group of salaries, as distinct from individual salaries, are in the build-up of data concerning performance by the group – how long do they typically take to reach maximum for their grade and at what stage in their careers would you expect the increases in salary to level off? – are two of the questions this approach helps to answer. The more stable and career-minded the group is, the greater the benefit from this kind of planning. As far as actual salaries are concerned, one can either make allowances for inflation, or predict salaries at present levels, assuming constant price/wage levels, and adjust later.

COMPA RATIO

The *compa* ratio is a measure of the general level of salaries in a grade compared with the midpoint. It is calculated by applying the following formula:

$$\frac{\text{Average of all salaries in the grade} \times 100}{\text{Midpoint of the salary range}}$$

This can reveal that the salaries in the grade are unusually high if the ratio is over 100, for example, or that attrition in the salaries for the grade has taken place when it is low. It is sometimes useful to calculate the *compa* ratio for each of the grades in a department at the time of the salary/wage review so that, in discussions between the department manager and the HR manager, an overall view of the salaries for the department can be taken into account. The HR manager, or salary administrator, may also wish to use the *compa* ratio in comparing the recommendations for merit increases between department/line managers by calculating *compa* ratios for the different departments. Further useful comparisons can be made across the whole company to see how the salaries for each grade stand in the structure and thus what actions are needed to correct anomalies.

WAGE/SALARY SURVEYS

Where the company stands in relation to the wage/salary rates being paid in the labour markets is a question that exercises all those concerned with recruitment and with pay negotiations.

There are many published sources that one can draw on. In the UK and in other countries the state publishes statistics regularly, with tables of current earnings and comments generally on the prices index as well as on wage rates, overtime and hours worked. The major reward consultancies all publish data to their clients on reward package trends in the UK and internationally. Another useful source is the information supplied by Incomes Data Services, which disseminates details of wage settlements, surveys, trends and also comments on a wide range of matters related to employment.

In spite of all these secondary sources, up-to-date information is often needed quickly, and the HR manager frequently has occasion to conduct his or her own survey. Details of local rates and salaries for specialist groups may not be available from anywhere else.

If the company is well known in the locality, or if there are good personal contacts with colleagues at other companies, a quick telephone survey will give a general indication on salaries. However, to establish accurate comparisons, something of a more formal nature has to be done.

A postal or email survey will require careful preparation and will also require much effort in the analysis of results. A quick guide on conducting a survey is given on the companion website to this book: www.routledge.com/cw/tyson.

EXPATRIATE REWARDS

The management of expatriate pay and benefits revolves around the type of expatriation – whether these are people who will remain on post in a foreign country for a long period, or whether the individuals concerned are better described as frequent flyers, who go out to make short visits and there are no issues relating to family or home commitments. For expatriate salaries and benefits there is a strong argument for the use of specialized consultancy help from a reward consultancy with a track record in this aspect of its portfolio.

Although there is now freedom of movement for labour among the European Union (EU) Member States within Europe, in practice there are wide variations in conditions, hours, holidays, social security payments and benefits, including health and state regulations, so that comparison is difficult. One of the biggest problems in comparing pay internationally is the variability of exchange rates. Although the use of the Euro across most of the EU has helped, the UK remains on sterling, and there is still the need to make comparisons of costs with countries such as China and India, given the global nature of businesses, the trend towards offshore working and interdependence, for example, in energy production and consumption.

Since the value of money is dependent on the goods and services it can buy, comparisons of earnings must also include some kind of weighting according to the level of prices in each country. However, this in itself is not enough, since there will be different patterns of purchasing between countries. Assuming that a representative range of goods and services can be found in each country, the ratios of the costs of these between countries can be determined. These ratios are referred to as 'purchasing power parities'. However, if exchange rates and purchasing power parities are taken into account, the results of a comparison of salaries between countries will be more accurate, although there is bound to be a margin of error because of the non-salary elements in the total remuneration, because exchange rates are volatile and because patterns of consumption in such matters as transport and housing may not be comparable at all.

For the long term expatriate the key issue is whether he or she will be paid allowances or will be put on local terms and conditions with some help on accommodation and family issues, such as children's education, the spouse's own career and any dependent relatives. Pension arrangements are also a point of potential problems. The decision here is whether the person concerned should remain on home country terms in this aspect, or whether there should be a special expatriate scheme. Here, it is worth noting the trend towards so-called third country expatriates, whose home terms may not be very advantageous, for example where a US company sends one of its staff from India to the UK on an assignment.

There has been a steady growth in global cross-border mobility. Travel between EU Member States is common, and the increasing attention paid to emerging markets has increased the flow of travelling, often for short visits (Medland 2013). This has resulted in the appointment of global payroll officers, in an attempt to deal with the complexities of different tax and social security systems. Even short visits can render the individual liable for tax and social security payments.

ADDITIONS TO BASE PAY

Profit share

We have already described some of the schemes operated for employees that are typically related to output. There are other schemes based on company profits, where the level of net profit determines the bonus. The intention behind profit share schemes is to make the employee feel involved and to give him or her a sense of participating in the company's future growth.

A number of schemes exist. To give one example, the employees may receive a number of ordinary shares each year after the annual dividend has been calculated. The number of shares can be determined by translating the money set aside for the bonus into shares purchased at the current rate and then issuing these to employees. The number of shares and the cut-off point of the scheme may include qualifications of service, grade level, etc., and a clause stipulating that the shares should not be sold for a fixed period after the bonus. Some companies retain the shares for a time after the bonus, only issuing them to employees after a year or, if the employee leaves, the bonus may be paid out in cash. Employees would need to be well advised on the variable value of shares, and the fact that they would normally have to pay tax on dividends at their normal rate.

Sales commissions

There are some groups of employees for whom commission payments represent their main earnings, such as sales staff, sales managers and various kinds of representatives.

Questions about the usefulness of self-employed agents are beyond the scope of this book. However, it is worth considering the impact on relationships of a high percentage of commission earnings. If a small basic salary is supplemented by high commission, or bonus earnings, the sales staff can become almost self-employed agents. Commission earnings not only provide an incentive, but also give employees a choice about the work they do, where they concentrate their efforts and how they plan their time. Whilst this is necessary for the typical sales job, it does entail a loss of control and a lack of stability in earnings. Some kind of balance is necessary. To provide an incentive, at least 10 per cent of earnings should be in commission, but more than 30 per cent of earnings as commission provokes a heavy reliance on immediate performance, which is inimical to training and development and gives an instability to earnings. This might encourage the employee to supplement his or her income by working for other companies at the same time, or to regard themselves as self-employed.

Among the topics on any checklist for commission schemes are a number of items worth evaluating in advance; the check list produced by Keith Cameron gives a good guide:

Type of target:	Number of products; sales revenue, etc.
Targeting:	Who is responsible, what target?
Eligibility:	Sales staff, internal, external, management.
Assessment intervals:	How often assessed (monthly, weekly, etc.)?
Payment intervals:	How often paid?
Threshold:	Minimum sales before commission is triggered.
Ceiling:	Maximum amount of commission (per week, month, etc.).
Accelerator/decelerator:	According to profitability of different products, percentage increase or decrease in commission.
Returns:	What happens if product returned (defective) or if deal falls through?
Controls:	Who checks, what is checked? Paperwork?
Communication:	Telling people *what* the scheme is for and why. Communicating changes.
Time span:	Life of scheme.

Company car or car allowance

Policy on company cars will need to be laid down at the same time as the salary scales. Here the choice is whether or not company cars should be provided for use by employees privately as well as on company business, or to pay a car allowance, for the employee to use their own vehicle, and for whom this is essential. For some companies, a car goes automatically with the level of the job and, in some cases, two cars are now provided, one for the manager, the other for the manager's spouse.

The main consideration here is to ensure that there are rules that govern the use of a company car and that these rules should refer to the job content. If the use of a car is essential for the job, then it is easy to justify, both to the rest of the employees and to the Inland Revenue.

Alternatives to this approach include car allowances or company car purchase schemes, which allow the employee to own the car by granting a loan that is repaid over a period. Maintenance, petrol and running costs are borne by the company.

PENSION SCHEMES

With the demographic changes taking place, the topic of pensions has come under greater scrutiny. The problems in providing care of the elderly and the failure over many years for employees to provide for their future, and for employers to offer sufficient pension provision, have brought a flurry of pension reform proposals and schemes over the years, such as stake-holder pensions and changes to pension age, with the move for women and men to the same retirement age, as well as the raising of the retirement age. In fact, the 'retirement age', thanks to the age discrimination legislation, is of less relevance, as people are increasingly continuing to work beyond the notional retirement age, which is now simply the age from which the state pension is payable. The raising of the state pension has been an attempt to overcome the problems of poverty amongst older people because of the absence of personal provision.

The two types of employer-provided pension schemes are defined contribution and defined benefit schemes. The costs of providing defined benefit schemes, at a time of increasing longevity, have proved impossible to sustain. This is where the scheme contracts to pay out a defined amount of pension according to the number of years the employee has spent in the scheme, after the employee retires at ages 60 or 65. As a consequence, defined benefit schemes are disappearing, except for public sector schemes, and some few remaining larger employers, and organizations such as the university scheme. In the private sector, most defined benefit schemes are closed to new members.

In both types of scheme, the employer deducts contributions and makes a contribution itself. However, in a defined contribution scheme, there is a fixed amount of contribution in the contract between the employee and the provider but, at the agreed retirement date, the employee receives a lump sum and invests at their own choice, for example in an annuity or in some other income generating investment, so that there is no guaranteed amount of pension provision at the time the employee joins the scheme. The government in the UK has established the National Employment Savings Trust (NEST) as a defined contribution scheme for lower paid employees, run as an independent organization.

To improve pensions in the UK, in 2012 the government introduced auto-enrolment, so there is a compulsory approach for all employees, which is intended to benefit those who have no other pension provision except that of the basic state pension.

The new approach has automatic enrolment as the main lever to ensure people make provision and save for their retirement. From 2012 onwards, employers are obliged to offer a qualifying pension scheme to their employees. All employees who earn above a threshold amount – £10,000 a year in 2014/15 – are automatically enrolled into the scheme. This is being phased in with large employers obliged to participate from 2012; medium and smaller employers must have enrolled all staff by 2016. Employees can opt out of the scheme, but only after they have been made a member. Minimum contributions from employees for 2012–2017 are: 0.8 per cent plus 0.2 per cent tax relief; and for employers 1.0 per cent, making a total minimum contribution of 2 per cent. This rises in 2017/18 to a minimum employee contribution of 2.4 per cent, plus 0.6 per cent tax relief and an employer contribution of 2 per cent, making a total minimum contribution of 5 per cent. From 2018 onwards, employees will have to make a minimum contribution of 4 per cent, plus 1 per cent tax relief and for employers of 3 per cent, making a total of 8 per cent minimum contribution.

In 2013 there was evidence cited that only around 10 per cent of employees were opting out (Jones 2013), indicating that employees would probably continue in their schemes, perhaps out of inertia. The wider problem is the casual, temporary nature of work and the growing trend for periods of self-employment, so that the insecurity of some people in a very flexible labour market means they may have a lack of continuity in their pension arrangements.

SUMMARY

The next chapter on total rewards looks more broadly at benefit packages and flexible benefits, and considers how rewards can be envisioned in a strategic sense. However, the processes of managing reward require a thorough knowledge of the detail of any scheme introduced. This chapter has provided sufficient detail so that readers will understand the main technical matters and can follow up with more detail in specialized texts.

QUESTIONS

1   How do the objectives of a salary policy help to control costs?
2   What, if any, are the advantages of group base incentives over individual incentives?
3   What are the advantages of using broad-banded salary structures?
4   How can we introduce flexibility into salary structures without losing control of costs?
5   How can we ensure that any incentives we provide for employees are motivational and are considered to be fair?
6   Which non-pay benefits are important to employees and why?

REFERENCES

IDS (2005). 'Research file 69', *Incomes Data Services*. May.

Jones, G. (2013). 'Time to deliver'. *Pay and Benefits Magazine*. May 23–24.

Medland, D. (2013). 'Rise in mobility is a business risk'. *Financial Times*. 28 February 2013. Executive Appointments Supplement 1.

17 TOTAL REWARDS

INTRODUCTION

In a rapidly changing context, organizational agility is sustained by HR strategies, policies and programmes, adapted to provide an environment where employees feel a strong sense of attachment, and are motivated to give their best performance. As in the case of 'talent management', where we discussed in Chapter 13 how the phrase 'talent management' covers a whole bundle of policies, so the ideas behind 'total reward' cover all those areas in HR policies and practices that seek to reward, to motivate and to retain employees. This is intended to produce a strong culture at the centre of organizational identity, enabling constant adaptation by employees to market needs.

TOTAL REWARD STRATEGY

The psychological contract between employer and employee is the basis for the individual's relationship with the organization. The mixture of legal contractual terms, employer and employee expectations, and the values collectively espoused by the company are all captured under the heading 'total rewards' (TR). TR approaches are a way to express the linkage between employer and employee needs. TR can best be seen as a 'bundle' of policies and practices. These include but go beyond, pay and benefits, to broader non-contractual aspects of engagement and development, and embrace the espoused values and organization culture expressed in the style of working, the quality of work, the life style choices available, plus the careers and the work satisfaction provided for employees. These aspects of the psychological contract – the deal proposed by the employer – are intended to elicit reciprocal behaviours, shown in the efforts and attitudes of employees. In particular, the employer's need is for what are sometimes called 'organizational citizenship behaviours', these being behaviours where the individual engages in positive discretionary behaviour, designed to help the organization to be successful (Organ 1988).

The typical compensation package has multiple objectives, such as attracting employees, ensuring a long term perspective, encouraging high performance, retaining employees and giving employees a sense of identity. Multiple purposes often seem contradictory to employees and managers alike. For example, rewarding high performance might be best for those working in a job where performance is measurable, and retention might be more relevant in roles where a high labour turnover is likely. There is an advantage therefore for the employer to strengthen the coherence of the package. TR gives a strategic purpose to the bundles of policies, and formalizes some of the choices often left unsaid, but tacitly agreed in the psychological contract.

Much of what can be achieved through total reward is intended to improve performance. The TR approach therefore is an HR strategy, where certain policies are configured to generate positive employee responses and an organization culture consistent with the business strategy. The business case for TR is therefore based on an assessment of the range of options available to ensure a 'best fit' of the HR strategy to the organization strategy.

The current economic and social pressures on companies have lead to uncertainty, and the necessity for continued downward pressure on costs. In this context, where cost pressures prevent expenditure on new, highly attractive pay policies and benefits, TR offers the possibility for leveraging existing reward programmes and the non-financial aspects of the psychological contract. Those organizations introducing TR achieve this by establishing an internal coherence around organizational values and the corporate brand. For this to be successful, employees must feel and witness the organizational values and vision in action, as an authentic experience. The choices offered for the reward specialist to adopt are in the reward package mix. There is a creative tension for the organization to resolve in the reward package, a tension that is present in the roles of reward to support the business strategy on the one hand, and the need to respond to the pressures in the labour market on the other.

The probable benefits accrued from a TR strategy can be summarized as follows:

■ TR creates a linkage into HR strategy, providing a competitive advantage (as per the RBV).
■ TR provides choices to employers and to employees, through the large range of elements in the package.
■ TR supports organizational values and culture in a tangible way, emphasizing the authenticity of the brand and the brand values.
■ The coherence of the TR programme means the employer is able to define the employee experience of work.

- TR motivates positive discretionary effort – it appeals to employees' hearts and minds.
- TR encourages loyalty.
- TR helps to provide a measurable return on the investment in human capital, through costed TR packages.
- In TR employee choice sits well with employee involvement and engagement policies.
- TR helps to create a positive image of the organization in the labour market, with consequential benefits for recruitment and retention policies.
- There are possible positive spill-over affects from TR to customer and supplier relations, through the interactions with staff.

THE MAJOR ELEMENTS OF TR PACKAGES

The choices available to the organization relating to the content of TR packages are many and varied. Typically, they fall under the following five headings:

The contractual area

- pay systems
- market related pay and benefits, including pensions and conditions of service (e.g. holiday entitlement)
- variable pay, bonus and commission schemes
- employee share-ownership schemes
- fairness of reward policies, and use of reward levels (e.g. single status, or highly differentiated hierarchy).

Physical aspects of the work environment

- type of work space
- modern equipment and technology
- social space for interacting with colleagues
- facilities
- catering arrangements
- ease of access to public transport, parking facilities
- security of the working environment.

Leadership style espoused

- relationships encouraged on a friendly/formal level with colleagues and boss
- degree of autonomy
- pace of work.

Job satisfaction attribution

- perceptions of the job's value
- motivational tasks
- degree of challenge/interest in the work
- extent of recognition for effort.

Development opportunities

- learning and development opportunities available, on the job and off the job
- emphasis placed on work improvement through constructive feedback, financial reward and recognition.

Life style choices available

- work–life balance
- recognition of duty of care
- sense of belonging encouraged
- stress and health policies.

From this list, we can see that the areas of life style and work style, leadership, job satisfaction and development are important as are the tangible aspects of reward. The degree of importance of policies and practices in these areas is dependent upon the impact of these matters to the individual, at the stage they have reached in life and work.

As an illustration of the possible advantages to the company and to employees from the elements in the reward package, employee share ownership in the company they work for is a good example. One sign of the move towards the adoption of TR is in the growing popularity of employee share ownership schemes, encouraged by governments and companies. The notion that employees will become more engaged if they have a financial stake in the business is well established.

The Nuttall Review of Employee Ownership (2012) in the UK reviewed the evidence on employee share ownership, pointing out that research had shown that employee owned companies created jobs faster and were more resilient through the recent economic downturn. The review had received evidence that shareholder employees feel more committed, and are more involved. The business case was also set out for different ownership models, providing improved resilience to economic downturns, more choice for investors and for consumers. The figures quoted in the review showed that employee owned companies created more jobs during the recession in the period 2008/2009, where the growth in employee numbers per annum was 12.91 per cent, whereas in non-employee owned companies, the number of employees grew by only 2.70 per cent (p. 23). There was a similar pattern in sales growth, which was 11.08 per cent in 2008/2009 in employee owned companies, but only 0.61 per cent in non-employee owned companies for the same period (p. 24–25).

A new UK Employee Share Ownership Index (EOI) has been created with the support of the London Stock Exchange, which measures the performance of the share prices of FTSE All Share companies, where employees own more than 3 per cent of the total equity. This index shows that the shares in the 69 companies that met the share ownership criteria in the index in 2013 had produced total returns of 53.3 per cent on average, compared to 20.9 per cent from the 623 companies in the All Share Index (Moules 2014).

The advantages for creating an organization culture and a leadership style that help to improve performance are clear. A culture made real by the coherent reward strategy reduces uncertainty, helps to build trust between management and employees, as well as amongst customers who see evidence for this in their interactions with the company. This is a culture that nurtures engagement, builds commitment, encourages organizational citizenship behaviours and is developmental. These attributes, one might expect, would foster the dynamic capabilities needed for organizational agility.

MARKETING APPROACH TO REWARDS

The TR strategy is an ideal vehicle through which to apply marketing techniques. The psychological contract has aspects of employer branding, because, like the psychological contract, brands have transactional and relational aspects. Transactional contracts are concerned with pay, benefits and performance-based pay, whereas relational contracts are about longer term relationships (Martin and Hetrick 2006; Panczuk and Point 2008). There are three aspects of marketing that have been developed, which operate in conjunction with HR strategy (Parry and Tyson 2014).

First, internal marketing takes place when the company engages in brand awareness, sales and marketing programmes for employees, and launches new products and services. There is also internal marketing when an employee joins and is inducted, and when there are internal communications about organizational changes as well as the reporting of the corporate results. The objective of internal marketing is to ensure employees align their behaviour with the organization and its brands. The intention is to present to the customer a coherent and embedded understanding of the corporate brand and the organizational values. The view of internal marketing is that to set up a culture where 'organizational citizenship' behaviour is the norm will strengthen the corporate brand, and will prove to be a source of competitive advantage.

Second, the HR strategy links into the marketing strategy through the concept of the employee value proposition (the EVP), which sets out the benefits of working for a specific employer. The TR strategy outlined here is a way the employer can express the EVP. TR can also be used in the context of internal rather than external labour markets. Line managers can be seen as customers whose main interest in rewards strategy is its cost-effectiveness.

Employees within the internal labour market are the equivalent to consumers (who see TR as a set of products to meet their own motivational needs). TR as an EVP shows how competitive the package is within the sector, and why the proposition should attract the best applicants.

The third way in which marketing brings useful tools to TR, is in the concept of market segmentation. Marketing strategies are adapted to the different characteristics of the target customers (the different segments of the customer base). Reward managers also need to recognize the different needs, values and life styles of the different groups of employees. In the case of TR market segments, the following are typical groupings that are of interest in the reward field.

- *Occupational or sectoral groups.* For example, in health care, where there may be different needs for front line staff, compared to administrators, security staff, catering staff and so on. However, these other staff may have major differences in many cases than similar employees in different sectors; for example catering staff may need specialized dietary knowledge, not required by those working in highly commercial restaurants. So market segmentation requires differentiation to be used to inform how different groups would perceive the EVP.
- *Generational differences.* Where there are workplace traits attributed to different generations these could be worth using to produce a different value proposition. For example, for Generation X, opportunities to be creative and to work in an informal, direct work style and to have learning opportunities could be important differentiators for an EVP. However, care should be taken not to discriminate against employees because of their age, so any targeted benefit would have to be available to all employees.
- *Geographical differences* in employment are also important. For example, in multinational business, not only are there differences in the reward packages to reflect differences in taxation, living costs and social security in particular countries but there are also differences in the value placed on various items in the package, based on cultural diversity.

CREATING TR STRATEGY

A TR strategy cannot be introduced overnight. The inclusive nature of the TR approach means the strategy has to be introduced in stages. The three key features of TR that are prerequisites for a sustainable TR approach are:

1   An agreed HR and business strategy linked together, which sets forth the essential values and cultural underpinning that are a vital part of the strategic objectives of the business. The 'fit' between HR strategy and business strategy, is described in

Chapter 6. There has to be a genuine business need for a TR strategy as part of the HR strategy, and the organization culture should be established and be communicated across the organization.

2   A process whereby managers and employees espoused values would need to have been developed in order to understand the behaviours and attitudes, including organizational citizenship behaviours, which are an essential part of the TR approach. There would need to be a long-term development programme to sell in the attitudes and behaviours to be internalized by managers and employees alike. Resource and time to achieve this would need to be provided. The process would best be run as an organization development programme.

3   It is essential that there is a clear articulation of the elements of the TR strategy, as described earlier, and of the ways by which the decisions on how aspects of the psychological and legal contract are to be brought together in the package.

INTRODUCING TR

The practical steps to change the way the contractual relationships are brought into line with the requirement of TR are as follows:

1   Annual reward statements for employees should be produced and distributed to all employees. These statements should contain all the elements of the reward package and cost them, including pension, life insurance schemes and share schemes. These statements should be provided to each employee.

2   The introduction of flexible benefits as a subsequent step would be helpful, so that within a stated cost, employees can choose the mix of pay and benefits they find suitable, with opportunities to change the mix periodically (including salary sacrifice schemes).

3   Following the OD exercises with managers there would need to be departmental discussions with managers and their staff on the specific cultures and styles of working preferred in their departments that are consistent with sustainable high performance. Agreement, with help where necessary, from OD consultancy, would be useful in generating the departmental style of working, the options for employees and the process by which the work style, the quality of work and careers can be evolved and the opportunities for employees to make choices decided.

4   HR policies are needed to allow employees systematically to make choices on flexible rewards and benefits and to articulate the various total reward 'products' so that the employees understand what is available and how to maintain coherence in the EVP.

EMPLOYER INTEREST IN TR

The Towers Watson Global Workplace Survey of 2012/13 was based on 1605 responses from all industry sectors and regions of the world, the majority of respondents being from manufacturing, financial services, IT and telecommunications. This survey examined the move towards TR and the use of the EVP as a strategic tool in engaging and motivating the workforce in an increasingly competitive market place.

This survey showed that workforce segmentation brought better employee engagement, and better design and delivery of TR. The introduction of more coherent and integrated reward programmes is aided by clearly articulated EVPs, so that companies that adopt these practices are better at attracting and retaining competent employees than those companies that have not yet achieved this kind of clarity in their EVPs.

The report (at 4) goes further, and states:

> Organizations that have segmented the workforce, and that deliver customized EVPs for critical employee segments are nearly twice as likely as companies with more tactical and less integrated EVPs (27.6 per cent versus 14.5 per cent respectively) to report financial performance substantially above their peer group. (p. 4)

We know also that flexible benefits have been increasingly popular in UK organizations for the last 10 years, except during the recession in 2010, reaching 40 per cent of companies reporting using this approach by 2012 (People Management 2013, November: 62). One of the reasons for the adoption of TR strategies is the need to bring rationality and coherence to the ever-expanding number and types of benefits utilized by companies in a bid to attract and retain high quality employees. This expansion, and the increases in health care and life style type benefits, all seem likely to be reasons for the expanding definition of reward into TR.

In the USA, health care insurance costs have been rising dramatically, prompting employers to find ways to shift some of these costs onto employees. However, if employees were to be responsible for the costs, they also would expect to have more responsibility for taking decisions about these benefits (*HR Magazine* December 2012: 49). This pressure may also account for the rising popularity of flexible benefits, which is often seen as a staging post to moving on to TR as an HR strategy.

A good early example of flexible benefits as a step towards TR is the case of Nationwide, a bank and building society in the UK. This is a 'mutual' society, run on cooperative society principles, employing around 15,000 people.

Nationwide

The remuneration mix has three elements: fixed pay (basic plus progression 66.8 per cent), flexible benefits (22.2 per cent) and variable pay (11.2 per cent). There is a system of 11 job families spread over five different responsibility levels from clerical to director, and progression is dependent on performance. There are various bonus schemes, including a company-wide employee bonus scheme as well as a personal performance bonus for managers. In addition, there is a recognition scheme through which around 0.5 per cent of the base salary is awarded by a recognition team and line managers to employees for exceptional conduct and loyalty. The awards are made in vouchers and gifts as well as cash. The flexible benefits package includes buying and selling holidays, private health care, child care, discount card, and additional pension.

Under the system, employees can construct their own packages online, within predetermined limits, by mixing and matching the three elements according to their own choice.

Flexible benefit packages normally operate under the following conditions:

1   There are certain core elements in the package that cannot be traded or changed, e.g. a significant proportion of base pay, pension, life insurance and medical insurance.
2   There are rules concerning how much of the perks and benefits can be changed, e.g. the extent to which the model of a company car can be traded up or down, the maximum amount of additional contributions to the pension scheme, etc.
3   There is a finite list of benefits/perks in the scheme.
4   Employees are only allowed to make changes, to exercise their flexible options at set times (e.g. on appointment, promotion, when the car is due for change, etc.).
5   Employees receive a detailed statement showing the value of the benefits and sometimes free financial counselling periodically.

FLEXIBLE BENEFITS

There are a number of different variations in flexible benefits, with different degrees of choice for the employee. These range from core benefits only (no choice, but basic benefits including car, pension, etc.), to 'core plus' schemes where the standard benefits given to all employees are augmented with a few limited optional extras (e.g. private health insurance) to modular schemes where, as in a cafeteria, employees are able to choose a selection of benefits from a choice of set menus. The final version is either total choice of all benefits or ultimately all benefits paid in cash for the employee to use on benefits or not, according to choice.

Table 17.1 is an example of a flexible reward structure (closest to a 'core plus' scheme) from a large retailer which shows a summary of benefits.

TABLE 17.1 SUMMARY OF BENEFITS (UK, LONDON-BASED) AND THEIR VALUE/CASH ALTERNATIVE

Benefits	Value	Cash alternative	Trade-up/value to buy	Comments
Company car	Maximum leasing allowance according to grade	1. 'Trade out' – the amount of your annual leasing allowance	As required within limits	
			2. 'Trade down' – the difference between your annual leasing allowance and the actual cost of the chosen vehicle (with extras)	
Fuel card (private petrol)	*	*	Not available to buy	
BUPA	*	*		You will be able to rejoin at any level, but obviously fore-going the cash alternative
Oyster Card	*	*	*	
Dental plan	*	*	As required	Additional cover can be bought for your partner and/or children
Optical plan	Depending on chosen cover	n/a	Depending on cover chosen	
Financial services	Depending on option(s) taken	n/a	Depending on option(s) taken	
Overseas holiday travel insurance	Depending on cover chosen	n/a	Depending on cover chosen	

Note: *Values in £ to be shown, according to the amounts/rates prevailing, dependent upon premiums or contract.

SUMMARY

This chapter has described the HR strategy of 'total rewards', which is becoming a useful method for encapsulating the policies that link the hearts and minds of employees in the search for competitive advantage. The marketing techniques of segmentation and the EVP have proved a practical way to focus on the range of tangible and intangible rewards and benefits that are designed to attract, retain and motivate employees in the search for competitive advantage.

QUESTIONS

1   What are the strategic reasons for creating a total reward approach?
2   What do you see as the linkage between marketing and HRM that find an expression in total reward?
3   What are the useful steps that should be taken in preparation for total rewards?
4   What is the definition of the EVP?

REFERENCES

HR Magazine (2012). '2013 Benchmarks'. December. 49. Alexandria, VA, USA: Society for Human Resource Management.

Martin, G. and Hetrick, M. (2006). *Corporate Reputations, Branding and Managing People: A Strategic Approach to HR*. Oxford: Butterworth-Heinemann.

Moules, J. (2014). 'Fresh index shows value of employee ownership'. London: *Financial Times* 10 January. 20.

Nuttall, G. (2012). 'Sharing Success: the Nuttall Review of Employee Ownership'. *Dept for Business Innovation and Skills*. Ref.BIS/12/933 London: HMSO.

Organ, D. (1988). *Organizational Citizenship Behaviour: 'The Good Soldier Syndrome'*. Lexington MA: Lexington Books.

Panczuk, S. and Point, S. (2008). *Enjeux et Outils du Marketing RH*. Paris: Eyrolles.

People Management (2013). 'The Five Ages of Reward'. November. 62 (quoting Thomson online benefits). Wimbledon: CIPD.

Towers Watson (2012). *The Next High Stakes Quest: Balancing Employer and Employee Priorities 2012–2013 Global Talent Management and Rewards Study*. London: Towers Watson. towerswatson.com.

18 CORPORATE GOVERNANCE AND HRM

INTRODUCTION

The major global recession in the period 2009–2012 was a watershed for institutions of all kinds, and initiated a period of review and change. These effects were not just in financial services, but also in most aspects of the economy and society, as reflected in formal enquiries and institutional reform. The recession signalled an end to the complacency that had characterized regulatory institutions around the world, and presented the sharp choices for economic survival in the economies of Europe and US. Financial regulation weaknesses were seen as being at the heart of the problems. One outcome of the institutional reviews has been a new emphasis on corporate governance and what that means for the private sector, the public sector and for the 'third sector' of charities. The watchwords of 'accountability', 'transparency' and 'honesty', as well as the recognition of the importance of social responsibility for governments, companies and individuals express the general desire for a change to our relationships in society.

CORPORATE GOVERNANCE AND HRM

Black and others (2007) examined the proposition that job tenure would be affected by levels of equity market and merger and acquisition (M&A) activity, that investment in human capital would be inhibited by high levels of equity market and M&A activity, and that pay determination would be affected by high levels of equity market and M&A activity. This last point concerned the proposition that greater equity market and M&A activity would result in more decentralized pay setting, more employee share ownership and wider pay differentials, owing to more alignment at the CEO level, but the fragmentation of internal labour markets as a consequence of company restructuring. The results did show lower job tenure (higher labour turnover) associated with high levels of equity market and M&A activity.

As far as pay determination was concerned, equity market activity was negatively associated with bargaining decentralization, and employee stock plans were strongly associated with M&A activity. There was no significant relationship with training – the indicator of human capital investment that was taken. Clearly from this research, there is some evidence that there are impacts on HR policies and processes from the changes to ownership, and the volatility of equity share markets. How corporate governance is managed, therefore, is important for HRM.

There is a literature that shows the importance organizational stakeholders have in the development of corporate governance. Armour and others (2003) conclude from their study that hostile takeovers and the changes to corporate governance in the 1980s and 1990s were associated. They claim this resulted in what they describe as 'shareholder primacy' in UK corporate governance development. Given that there is ample evidence that shareholders were not involved sufficiently during the run-up to the recession, when unjustifiable risks were thought to have been taken by banks on both sides of the Atlantic, and where risky decisions may well have been encouraged by the reward systems of directors and senior managers in the financial industries, the concept of 'shareholder primacy' may be less important than the governance regulations.

The question of the effect of corporate governance on HRM is frequently addressed by using stakeholder analysis. This means examining the functions and accountabilities of those people involved. Konzelmann and others (2006) take a stakeholder perspective when looking at the stakeholder relationships in organizations, and the impact on HRM, in a study based on the UK's regular 'Workplace Employment Relations Survey' of 1998. They describe corporate governance as being the way ownership and control of organizations are regulated. They go on to say that corporate governance: 'sets the legal terms and the conditions for the allocation of property rights among stakeholders, structuring their relationships and influencing their incentives and hence, willingness to work together' (p. 452). They distinguish between internal and external stakeholders, arguing that different degrees of commitment are needed from the two different kinds of stakeholders – with shareholders (external to the company) having less commitment than manager/owners, or managers and workers (who are internal to the company).

The role of HRM is seen as being required to deliver strong commitment from the workforce, with a long timeframe, whereas shareholders may have a shorter time horizon for their financial interest. Whether such an adversarial view is helpful or not, the idea that different stakeholders in the corporate governance processes may well have different objectives seems a good starting point. There are other stakeholders within the corporation who have an interest in corporate governance issues, who may have different perspectives. Spitzeck (2007) sees the corporate governance processes as touching upon broad issues on corporate responsibility, which draws in a wider number of different stakeholders, for example those with an interest in environmental problems, those with an interest in human rights and those with a concern for local communities. This means corporate social responsibility (CSR) is integrated into corporate governance issues. As a consequence, Spitzeck's study looks at how decisions with an impact on CSR are integrated into the company's decision-making structures. This study argues from the evidence that CEO leadership is critical, since CEOs take the lead on corporate governance issues. The number of firms with a corporate responsibility committee, which includes a number of board members and others, increased from 15 per cent in 2002 to 60 per cent in 2008. There is also some evidence that firms with a CR Committee outperform those without such a committee on the Corporate Responsibility Index.

The HR activities of organizations that impinge on the company's societal role are perhaps the most significant. Even before the recession there were aspects of corporate governance that were becoming critical for organizations, most often seen in controversies over the environment or over executive pay. Increasingly, these seem to be more about the responsibilities organizations have to society, rather than merely the laws relating the firm.

CORPORATE SOCIAL RESPONSIBILITY FUNCTIONS OF HRM

Carroll and Shabana (2010) describe the origins of the term CSR. They quote the CSR definition of Davis (1960) as being the: 'decisions and actions by business "taken for reasons at least partially beyond the firm's economic or technical interest"' (p. 70). This is later taken to include the responsibility of business to society.

The four different categories of CSR in the definition of CSR are stated as: 'The social responsibility of business encompasses the economic, legal, ethical and philanthropic expectations that society has of organizations at a given point in time' (Carroll 1979: 500).

From the literature above on corporate governance, we can see that a stakeholder approach is suitable for examining HR's role and relationships, and from the CSR literature there are clear indicators of which particular stakeholders are important within the four categories of CSR. Five types of stakeholder relationship to the firm and to society are shown in the framework of HRM functions for responsibility to society set out below.

A functionalist perspective on HRM is useful in setting out the specific stakeholder groups that are important for HRM. The term 'functionalist perspective' means one of the functions the stakeholders perform for social responsibility to the rest of society. These are:

■ Those with a shared responsibility for economic performance and success in the countries where the company operates.
■ Those whose function is to take a shared social responsibility in the countries where the company operates. Included in the above two categories but with legal or other functions imposing responsibilities on them to society are the following:

- government and regulators, local and international
- individual employees
- owners/shareholders.

Examples of the kind of HR corporate social responsibility firms are expected to have are provided in the section below.

THE CSR FUNCTIONS OF HRM

The HR economic functions that are social responsibilities

- ensure the cost effectiveness of labour market processes
- ensure high levels of productivity in their organizations
- assist economic growth of the business
- help organizations to adapt to economic change
- train and develop the workforce
- ensure the fair distribution of rewards to employee groups
- ensure fair distribution of dividends to shareholders.

The aspects of the HRM function that have the most effect on the economy are those which concern the use of the labour market, whether it is to find and recruit suitable people or to make use of 'contingent' labour (the part-time, casual and sub-contract labour available on less permanent terms than other employees). HR also has a significant role introducing productivity schemes, helping line managers with their reorganization and reskilling of employees in order to improve output and to control the costs of labour to remain competitive. In a global economy, the availability of skilled labour and its price are major determinants of success for all in the nation, which makes this a wider economic aspect of social responsibility. The training and development of employees, including apprenticeship schemes, are vital functions of companies. Whatever is done in colleges or other off the job training, it is the on the job development that plays both a social and an economic function – providing self-esteem, the means to competition and success, which leads to the advancements in knowledge from one generation to the next.

Social corporate responsibility of HRM

- managing diversity
- encouraging social cohesion in society
- ensuring the company participates positively in local community activities
- offering flexible working policies, especially in cases of child care and elder care
- dealing fairly with employees and their representatives
- helping young people to adjust to the world of work

- ensuring high levels of trust in the organization
- creating approaches such as a total rewards philosophy, which offer decent and socially acceptable benefits, including pension arrangements, suitable for all levels of employees
- ensuring healthy and safe working conditions.

Businesses have social functions as well as economic functions. HRM is actively involved in promoting these social functions, for example through a general objective in encouraging social cohesion, removing discrimination in employment matters and participating in the various local communities where the company trades. One of its most important practical social functions is to create working conditions where flexible working is possible, for example to suit the needs of parents and carers, as well as to provide working opportunities for those who need to augment their earnings with part-time or casual work.

Although the social functions are subordinated to the economic functions of organizations, because without economic success the organization will not survive, the importance of the contribution of the social function resides in its long-term effects on communities, and on learning and personal development. It is a socializing, civilizing function, which reinforces how relationships should be conducted, based on trust, fairness and honesty.

Government and regulatory bodies as stakeholders place certain duties on HRM, both at the board level, and in the HR function of management, which includes line management as well as HR specialists. Their functions include:

- obeying all the legislation relevant to HRM, for example health and safety laws and codes of practice covering employment relationships
- ensuring corporate governance regulations regarding executive level rewards are followed
- protecting the rights of the 'whistle blowers'
- providing information and training to managers and others on management topics and corporate governance issues and relevant laws, e.g. bribery, corporate manslaughter.

Much of the social functions of HRM described above are also covered by laws and regulations, which prescribe what is acceptable (for example, on diversity issues). In this sense, the legal function of HR is to translate laws and regulatory codes into the rules of work in their organization and, in that sense, HRM acts on behalf of both the state and the employer. However, the function of HRM is not merely engaged in imposing the laws of any given country. The intention must be to embed the required behaviours in the work environment (for example on diversity and equal opportunity). There is also an element of self-interest for the organization here, since to disobey the law is socially and morally unacceptable and has penalties in loss of corporate reputation, as well as a loss of confidence in the management, which is potentially far more damaging than any fine or other legal penalty. The HR regulatory function extends to advising employees of their rights.

The HR responsibility for individual employees includes:

- discharging the duty of care to all employees
- dealing with all employees honestly and truthfully
- ensuring the rules of natural justice are applied in any conflict situations
- ensuring there are no instances of discrimination, harassment or bullying experienced by employees
- providing up to date information and advice where necessary to employees on topics such as pension arrangements, further education and other learning opportunities, personal problems and issues
- ensuring there are appropriate welfare services made available to employees in difficulty, in particular for any young or vulnerable employees.

All organizations owe a duty of care to employees, much of which is covered in the health and safety legislation, but includes not exposing employees to unnecessary risks. This duty extends to mental as well as physical health. There is a paramount need to ensure there is no discrimination, bullying or harassment. Dealing with employees in an open, fair and honest way brings potential benefits to the employer, in that this set of behaviours is associated with reciprocal higher levels of trust. We have already commented on the performance benefits that accrue to the organization from organizational citizenship behaviour (OCB) by employees. The reciprocity shown by employees to the CSR function of HRM could be one reason for their adoption of OCB.

Owners/shareholders also have responsibilities to society:

- ensuring, along with all other managers, wise use of resources, and protecting shareholder investments.
- ensuring honest reporting of activities as part of management's responsibilities.
- representing shareholders/owner's interests in responding to social needs.
- ensuring prevention of fraud or dishonesty or criminal activity at all levels in the company.
- maintaining good public relations.

The HR responsibility to shareholders that impinges on CSR is about the way resources are used, in this case, human resources. This has the advantage to the organization of helping to fulfil the economic aspects of CSR, just as the function of reporting honestly on HR matters to shareholders is consistent with the regulatory aspects of CSR. Honest dealing benefits the PR image of the company, and provides shareholders and employees with transparency.

There are a number of conclusions that can be drawn from looking at the different CSR stakeholder demands from HR management. These it is argued, show how HR performs a number of functions in its CSR role (see Figure 18.2). This shows four CSR aspects of the HR function:

1   There is an overlap between the stakeholder demands, so that by satisfying one set of demands, other functions of HRM are also reinforced.

2   That there is a mixture of regulatory, behavioural and organization cultural activities through which HR performs its CSR functions.

3   At this broad, overview level, the functions seem to be mutually supportive rather than contradictory. This does not mean that there are no conflicts when one comes to the detail of particular issues as shown below.

4   Similar functions are performed by other senior managers with different portfolios (e.g. marketing, finance), but what is special to HR is its coverage of all these other functions that also have an HR dimension.

SENIOR EXECUTIVE REWARDS AND CSR

The example of senior executive rewards is an ideal case to examine in detail to illustrate the issues of corporate social responsibility and corporate governance that are faced by HR managers. Director level reward packages typically consist of the elements shown in Figure 18.1.

Base Pay	Bonus (short and long term bonus)	Benefits	LTIPS	Perks

Figure 18.1 Elements of a typical director level reward package

The design questions relate to the proportions of these elements, the creation of an attractive EVP (compared to competitors in the industry concerned), the nature of the pension benefits, the design of bonus and long-term incentive plans (LTIPs), including any stock options. CEO and director level rewards are often based upon profit targets for directors and personal objectives (e.g. market share achieved, launch of new products and similar aims), earnings per share (EPS) and return on capital employed (ROCE). A frequently adopted target for directors is earnings before interest, tax, depreciation and amortization (EBITDA).

Share options are popular and are seen to attach the director's fortunes to the company owners in a tangible way, ensuring there is a joint interest: 'A stock option is the right (not obligation) to purchase a quantity of stock at a stipulated price (the strike price) over a given period of time (exercise period) following certain eligibility (vesting) requirements' (Milkovich and Newman 2005: 458).

Background

The principal reasons for the long-running debate about executive rewards are listed below. The separation of ownership (shareholders) from control (directors) means there is always some doubt about the extent to which there is an alignment of interests between the two groups As Black and others (cited above) have pointed out, there are differences between the insiders' type of commitment and that of the outsiders. Owners are looking for returns (increases in share price and dividends) on their investments and the security of their invest-ments, whereas managers may share some of these objectives, but who are also looking to maximize their own earnings, and who may be prepared to take risks to do so.

Shareholders have proved themselves lax in policing the rewards paid to board members, partly because they do not want to upset or destroy value in the business, and as long as they are seeing good returns, would be reluctant to demotivate or to force the resignation of a CEO or board chair, and so are reluctant to challenge large remuneration packages, if there is a persuasive reason provided to them. In any case, institutional shareholders would probably prefer to talk off the record to the chair or the remuneration committee, so we do not always know when they have intervened.

There is evidence that even in businesses that have been failing, directors who leave in these circumstances often receive reward packages that are often excessive. This has prompted a backlash from governments against 'golden farewells', arranged by the individual's friends on the board, who are laying down the precedents for big payouts when it is their turn to go. This feeds a popular belief that directors' decisions on rewards are self-serving and, even if the perception is unfounded, each report in the press increases the pressure on the corporate governance arrangements.

For some years, attempts at reforming corporate governance arrangements have been made in the UK, as evidenced in the recommendations from the Cadbury Report (1992), the Greenbury Report (1995) and the Hempel Committee of 1998. These reports recom-mended numerous changes for companies to adopt voluntarily, and there had also been attempts at reforms to the Companies Acts and persuasion by investors' organizations, such as the British Association of Insurers, to give more power to shareholders in order to separate the role of the chair from that of CEO, to involve non-executive directors more in the control of the business and to regulate board and senior executive pay through remu-neration committees. The Combined Code of the London Stock Exchange (1998) was a voluntary response to the pressure, which incorporated many of these recommendations and which all listed companies were expected to follow.

In 1999, the UK's Department of Trade and Industry issued a consultation document on director remuneration. This recommended that all quoted companies should have remuneration committees, with access to expert advice and that there be a general framework linking performance to pay, which should be disclosed, as should any gains made when exercising their share options. The recommendations also stated that the linkage of performance to pay should set out the long-term objectives in relation to board performance, the criteria for performance measurement, the comparator companies on which recommendations for pay changes were based and the relationship between firm performance and director rewards. Disclosures should include details of contracts and compensation arrangements.

The Directors' Remuneration Report Regulations (DRRR) 2002, were introduced following the DTI consultation, and enacted the recommendations already laid down. The Regulations apply to all companies incorporated in the UK that are listed on the London, New York or NASDAQ Stock Exchanges, or in the Member States of the European Economic Area. They do not apply to companies listed on the Alternative Investment Market (AIM).

The DRRR required that companies should establish a remuneration committee, which must produce a report as part of the annual reporting cycle, to shareholders and disclose details of individual directors' reward packages and the company's remuneration policy. A resolution on the report has to be put to the shareholders' annual general meeting for a vote. The results of the vote are not binding on the company. The shareholders are voting to reject or to accept the remuneration committee report, not on the amounts in the reward packages of individual directors. Remuneration committees are constituted to review the remuneration of the board, and the other senior executives within its remit. The members are non-executive directors, and are serviced by specialist compensation advice, either from HR and/or from external reward consultancies. The main purpose behind these reforms has been to promote transparency and more disclosure, and to encourage shareholders to have more control. As a consequence, HR directors on main boards will typically advise major institutional shareholders in advance of any potential reward changes in order to discuss their views before putting proposals to the shareholders' AGM, explaining the reasons behind the plans.

As an illustration of the kinds of rewards paid to directors at this time, in FTSE 100 and Fortune 500 companies, in 2003 CEOs of companies were being paid amounts including bonuses stock options of £4 million–£5 million per annum. For companies outside the FTSE 100, the amounts were much smaller (the median of FTSE 350 companies was around £1 million per annum). In the USA at the time there were CEOs receiving US$200 million per annum or, for some, as much as US$700 million per annum (Tyson 2005: 21–22). Comparable developments in corporate governance were taking place in Europe and the USA (for example in France, Germany and Sweden) and in the Sarbanes Oxley Act in the USA, which prevents companies from taking compensation advice from the consultancy department of their auditors (Tyson and Bournois 2005).

The financial crash of 2009/2011 raised issues about whether risky decisions were to blame for the financial crash, owing to the large amounts of bonuses, which it is argued encouraged unnecessary risk-taking. The 'bonus culture' – as it has been called – was thought to have had a corrosive effect on the quality of management and supervision. The debates about the role of bonus payments and risky behaviour have kept alive the ongoing controversies about executive rewards. The media began to take up the cause of the widening differentials between those at the top and those employed lower down, at a time when politicians were suggesting that all were sharing the problems of austerity. FTSE 100 directors received average increases in total earnings of around 49 per cent in the year 2010/2011, compared to average employee pay increases of 3 per cent per annum (Parry and Tyson 2014: 131, quoting figures from IDS 2012). At this time, some CEOs were being paid 100 times average pay. In financial services, to give a flavour of the rewards, asset manager CEOs were earning base pay of around £500,000, with an annual bonus of £4 million, and bonuses of around £1 million–£2.6 million for fund managers were not unusual (Oakley and Barker 2013).

Bankers' variable pay in the EU

The political response from the European Union has been to introduce new EU rules on bankers' pay, including a cap on bonuses paid. On 16 April 2013, the European Parliament approved the move, which imposes a number of measures.

These are quite detailed. The main terms are:

1   A cap on bankers' bonuses – the maximum amount allowed will be a ratio of 1:1, of fixed to variable pay.
2   This may be increased up to 1:2 with shareholder approval. Up to 25 per cent of the bonus can be paid in long-term schemes, valued on a discounted basis (which may produce a ratio of more than 1:2). If more than 25 per cent of the bonus is paid through these long-term schemes, any amount over 25 per cent would not benefit from the discount.
3   The rules apply to EU banks operating in the EU (even if their employees are based outside the EU, and to non-EU based banks, if they operate in the EU.
4   Those in scope are senior managers, those with a risk element in their work, those with control functions, and those whose professional work has a material impact on the risk profile of the bank or financial institution. The criteria here are those with annual earnings of £500,000 plus.
5   All the variable pay must be subject to clawback (a refund by the person concerned if there is a reason, e.g. because there is a loss or some other factor which may not have been apparent at the time).
6   At least 50 per cent of the variable pay must consist of shares or other ownership interests.
7   At least 40 per cent of the variable pay must be deferred over a period of not less than three to five years. If the variable amount is high (the UK the limit is £500,000), 60 per cent must be deferred.

These rules, which may be subject to further amendment as Member States get to grips with the implications, are due to be introduced on 1 January 2015, applying to remuneration based on performance achieved in 2014.

CONCLUSIONS

What can we say about corporate governance and CSR in the light of the above description of issues in executive reward? Corporate governance in the UK and Europe has come to the fore recently because of excesses in pay and the risks associated with what is perceived to be a 'bonus culture' in financial services. There are also changes to social norms, which are signalled by the increased prominence of 'whistle-blowers' as citizens who have a right and a duty to report wrongdoing, and the legislation on bribery, as well as the duty of care to employees (see Chapters 24–26). The growing interest in environmental issues and climate change are also examples of the pressures for change. Much in CSR seems to depend on the organization culture that has been created. HRM has a large responsibility in this area.

The case of corporate governance and executive rewards demonstrate the way regulation develops. The stages are:

1   Management and stakeholders come to be aware of an issue, from failures and from the press.
2   Industry leaders/professional associations debate the best way forward, often prompted by government to do so. A voluntary code is set up.
3   Broader public awareness of the issue is generated from the media, which leads to publicity about the failures in the voluntary code.
4   Lobby groups, customers and other stakeholders begin to press for more formal regulation.
5   Governments establish official and public inquiries.
6   Reports suggest some basic regulation, probably reinforcing informal or voluntary codes.
7   Regulation is imposed nationally and then amended to deal with avoidance.
8   There is a recognition that, because of the international nature of business, there need to be international accords on the subject.
9   There are regional, i.e. Europe-wide solutions, with legislation across countries with some local variations.
10 Full blown international agreements are made, and there is acceptance of the standards required internationally.

For the financial services' variable pay and risk issue, we appear to have reached stage 9. However, this has been accelerated by the international crisis. Similarly, with the issue of carbon emissions and the green agenda, there is a struggle to get to stage 10, and inevitably with different interests, any attempt at global agreement is difficult to achieve.

HRM is involved in the detail and in the regulatory role itself in some CSR issues. However, HRM has a role to play in all the economic social, individual employee and control CSR matters, as discussed earlier. The ownership versus control debates are connected to the long-term arguments found in discussions about executive rewards. In these cases, HRM can be caught in the middle, trying to exert control in a regulatory fashion on behalf of shareholders and regulators, but having to persuade and help managers to understand the long-term benefits to the company of shifting the culture to one of self-control, rather than

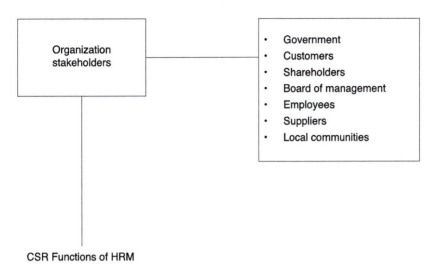

CSR Functions of HRM

Economic	Social	Regulatory	Employees	Shareholders
Labour market access Productivity Growth Adapting to change Training Fair rewards ROCE	Diversity Social cohesion Community participation Flexibility Fair dealing Trust Health/safety	Employment laws Corp. Gov. Regulations Protecting whistle blowers Provision of information	Duty of care Honesty in relationships Natural justice Fairness Welfare Provide information	Use of resources Future capacity Honest reporting Prevention of fraud Public relations

Figure 18.2 Corporate governance and HRM

relying on external controls. These issues are explored further in the chapters on employee relations and employment law.

For a summary of the chapter, Figure 18.2 shows the CSR functions of HRM.

QUESTIONS

1   Why do HR departments have such a wide range of corporate social responsibilities?
2   Why is there an increasing interest in CSR?
3   What is the main reason for the social functions HR has a leading role in discharging?
4   What attempts have been made to reduce excessive bonus payments to senior executives, especially in the banking sector?

REFERENCES

Armour, J., Deakin, S. and Konzelmann, S. J. (2003). 'Shareholder primacy and the trajectory of UK corporate governance'. *British Journal of Industrial Relations* 41, 3: September 531–55.

Black, B., Gospel, H. and Pendleton, A. (2007). 'Finance, corporate governance and the employment relationship'. *Industrial Relations* 46, 3: 643–50.

Carroll, A. B. (1979). 'A three-dimensional conceptual model of corporate social performance'. *Academy of Management Review* 4: 497–505.

Carroll, A. B. and Shabana, K. M. (2010). 'The business case for corporate social responsibility: a review of concepts, research and practice'. *International Journal of Management Reviews* 12, 1 March: 85–105.

Davis, K. (1960). 'Can business afford to ignore social responsibilities?' *California Management Review* 2: 70–76.

IDS (2012) 'The Director's Pay Report 2011/2012'. London: *Incomes Data Services.*

Konzelmann, S., Conway, N., Trenberth, L. and Wilkinson F. (2006) 'Corporate governance and human resource management'. *British Journal of Industrial Relations* 44: 3 September 541–67.

Milkovich, G. T. and Newman, J. M. (2005). *Compensation.* 8th Edition. New York: McGraw Hill.

Oakley, D. and Barker, A. (2013). 'Fund managers wary of restrictions on pay'. *Financial Times.* 19 March 17.

Parry, E. and Tyson, S. (2014). *Managing People in a Contemporary Context.* London: Routledge.

Spitzeck, H. (2009). 'The development of governance structures for corporate responsibility'. *Corporate Governance* 9, 4: 495–505.

Tyson, S. (2005). 'Fat cat pay' in Tyson, S. and Bournois, F. (eds) *Top Pay and Performance.* Oxford: Elsevier Butterworth-Heinemann, 12–28.

PART SIX

EMPLOYEE RELATIONS

19 THE DEVELOPMENT OF TRADE UNIONS

This chapter is a very short summary of the development of trade unions in Britain, and goes on to examine the role of the different parties involved in collective bargaining. Our intention here is to set out the history of trade unions only in relation to three main areas: trade unions and the law; the political consciousness of trade unions in the UK; and the main changes that have occurred in unionization.

THE EARLY HISTORY OF TRADE UNIONISM UP TO 1914

In the early history of trade unionism we should distinguish between unskilled unions and the craft societies. The craft societies were unions of workers who had served an apprenticeship, which was seen by the craftsman to give him a right to a customary wage, control of entry, the maintenance of standards and the general regulation of the craft. Craft societies set down rates and offered their members friendly society benefits, notably benefits in cases of sickness, accidents and retirement.

Local control of rates was soon augmented by national organization in the mid-nineteenth century, so that the engineers, iron-founders, boilermakers, carpenters and joiners each formed amalgamated societies out of local or regional societies, which gave sufficient local autonomy in custom and practice, while providing standard minimum rates, hours and benefits to members. Trades councils also developed in the towns from the mid-1850s, representing all trades in one district, and were a forum for ideas on unionism to spread.

The political ideology of the craft societies was based on an individualistic doctrine represented by the liberal cause. The artisans believed that self-help and the freedom to associate with their colleagues to further the aims of the craft were not incompatible objectives, since it was through hard work and sacrifice that the tradesman learned his craft, and the benefits granted by the union were based on the insurance principle through contributions.

The industrial revolution fundamentally changed employment conditions. Some of the newer industries adopted apprenticeship schemes; others relied on training through experience.

One of the features of early trade unions was the discontinuity of their organization. They rose and fell in strength and influence with the trade cycle, growing in booms and falling in slumps. Cuts in wages were not unusual, since employers regarded labour as a variable cost that should be subject to the same principle of price determination as other 'commodities'. The casual nature of the employment contract, together with the large pool of unskilled, poor people anxious for work, made the organization of unions difficult. Unions possessed little in the way of financial reserves. Until the 1880s, there were many small unions with localized membership.

There are few statistics, but by about 1890 union membership is thought to have covered approximately 5 per cent of the working population, that is, 10 per cent of adult male workers. Half the membership was in the north of England, and the density of member- ship (the proportion of actual to potential members) varied across industries, the largest numbers being in metals, engineering, ship-building, mining, quarrying, the building trades, printing, textiles and wood-working.

The mid-Victorian period of unionism was characterized by a rather pragmatic non- militant approach, deriving from the policy of a 'Junta' of union secretaries based in the London Trades Council. The opposition to the Junta's domination of policy, and emerging working-class radicalism, led to a counter-movement. A Trade Union Congress was organized in Manchester in 1868, and in Birmingham in 1869, by the provincial trades councils. After 1871, there were annual TUCs that conferred on questions of importance to unions and working people. The TUC has never sought either to control individual unions or to be a federation of unions. One of the main information-gathering arms of the TUC was its Parliamentary Committee, which also sought to influence ministers and Members of Parliament.

In the late 1880s a new unionism emerged. This was the start of large-scale organiz- ation of unskilled and semi-skilled workers on a national basis, pursuing claims for better wages by hard-fought strikes, as exemplified by the famous London Dock Strike of 1889, the seamen's strike in the same year and the improvements gained by the gas workers. These 'general' unions owed their stability and growth to their success in a few large indus- tries and the larger works, where the strength of the leadership could exert an influence. These general unions had a more militant outlook on collective bargaining, and put forward a broad socialist doctrine on the redistribution of ownership and the removal of the worst abuses of capitalism.

The legal status of trade unions has always been uncertain. The law has frequently been used to repress groups of workers. In the early nineteenth century there were the

Combination Acts, and it was not until 1871 that the position of the unions was clarified by the Act, which established that members were not liable to prosecution as criminal conspiracies because they were in 'restraint of trade'. The Act also sought to make unions responsible for their own internal organization, whilst granting them protection for their funds and allowing them to register as friendly societies. Unfortunately, the contemporaneous Criminal Law Amendment Act made most of the actions of a union in dispute subject to severe penalties, and it was not until 1875 that a new law, the Conspiracy and Protection of Property Act, permitted peaceful picketing and strike action. Similarly, the 1875 Employers' and Workman's Act made breach of contract a purely civil matter.

The union cause received a further setback from the *Taff Vale* judgement in 1901, when the House of Lords held, on appeal, that employers have a right in law to sue trade unions in the courts and to obtain damages from their funds for the actions of their officials during disputes. The judges found that, although trade unions were not corporations, the rights granted to them in the earlier legislation gave them a corporate character so that they could be sued for damages. In 1906, the new Liberal Government reversed the effects of this judgement by passing the Trade Disputes Act, which again made peaceful picketing legal and gave trade unions and their officials immunity from any claim for damages caused by actions in furtherance of a trade dispute

1919–1939

Unions were more militant and sought long-term benefits in negotiation immediately after the First World War, when labour was scarce. This was a period of amalgamations between unions, which resulted in the formation, for example, of the Amalgamated Engineering Union, the Transport and General Workers' Union and the Amalgamated Union of Building Trade Workers. Financial problems were one reason for amalgamations. The small local unions could not compete, and were soon to disappear. The combinations of employers into employers' associations who faced the unions were another major reason for seeking to present a united front.

Towards the end of the 1920s, unemployment rose and trade unions went on the defensive, aiming to protect jobs rather than to increase wages. Employers sought to cut wages and to restore wages to a supply and demand basis. This was the time of the famous 'triple alliance' between the miners, transport workers and the railway workers – an alliance in areas of policy and for mutual support at a time of difficulty and confrontation. The attempts by the unions to maintain their socialist gains from the wartime economy were opposed by the employers and the government, which sought to disempower the mines and the railways.

The General Strike of 1926 lasted nine days and was a result of a breakdown in the negotiations between the Miners' Federation, the coal-owners and the government over the employers' demand that the miners should work longer hours for less pay. The TUC was not a 'revolutionary body'. It would appear that all the TUC wished to do was to put pressure on the government by the threat of a general strike, and it was quick to call off the strike when it was pronounced illegal.

The result of the General Strike was the Trade Union Act of 1927. This made all sympathetic strikes illegal, and state employees were prohibited from joining any union whose membership was open to workers in other occupations and 'contracting in' to the political levy was made necessary. Large-scale unemployment, together with the draconian approach of the 1927 Act, resulted in less militancy by the unions by the end of this period.

The General Council of the TUC was concerned to reduce the problems of inter-union clashes over the recruitment of members, and in 1924 the congress approved an inter-union code of conduct. More precise and binding rules were laid down by the TUC in 1939, when meeting at Bridlington. The 'Bridlington Agreement' stipulated that where a union already represented and negotiated on behalf of a group of workers at an establishment, no other union should attempt to recruit members there. Although restricting choice, this agreement helped to introduce order into collective bargaining.

1939–1951

In the Second World War, as in the case of the First World War, there was cooperation between unions and government. This 'total' war involved everybody, and from the perspective of trade union development was significant for two reasons. First was the need for local control and cooperation in production, which assisted the growth of the shop steward movement. Managements needed stewards as much as the union did as a vital communication channel with working people. The large-scale and increased pace of work made communications even more important. Second, with the changed role of the state and with a Labour Government (initially as part of a coalition during the war), elected with a large majority to carry through reforms, union leaders felt that the tide of history was with them. The welfare state and the nationalization of basic industries brought socialist aims nearer. Indeed, one of the first steps of the new Labour Government was the repeal of the 1927 Act, making sympathetic strikes legal and returning the position on the political levy to 'contracting out'.

1951–1970s

The membership of trade unions grew mostly in the white-collar area (see Table 19.1), although during this period the density of white-collar membership did not increase dramatically until the 1970s.

TABLE 19.1 INCREASE IN TRADE UNIONISM 1948–1974

	Membership %	Density %
White-collar	+ 117.1	+ 9.2
Manual	+ 0.1	+ 7.2

The reasons for the growth in white-collar union membership were as follows:

1. There were more white-collar jobs owing to changes in the occupational structure. The growth areas in the British economy were the service areas and process industries. More women joined unions as a result.
2. White-collar unions achieved a higher density, possibly as a result of incomes policies and a need felt by their members for professional negotiation on their behalf.
3. White-collar jobs emerged in large concentrations – 'clerical' factories, especially in the public sector. The standardization of functions helped to create a common identity.
4. The duty imposed by governments on nationalized industries to bargain with the unions also encouraged white-collar union growth.
5. Most of the employment growth was in the public sector, and it was in this area that membership expanded sharply; so that local and central government became largely unionized.
6. Associated with the previous point, the impersonal relations and standardization of conditions of service stimulated the representation of interests through union officials.

Having achieved a good penetration of most sectors (including junior and middle managers) and increased their density, white-collar unions were more militant in pursuit of wage claims, as was seen during the winter of 1978/79.

One of the major areas for confrontation between unions and government was over the issue of pay controls. Since 1945 there have been numerous attempts to control inflation by some form of prices and incomes policy. There have been two main effects of incomes policy and price rises:

1. A 'threat effect' caused employees to join unions to protect themselves against falling living standards.
2. There was also conflict over pressure for local-level bargaining against incomes policies, which were readily applied at national level.

The 1960s were years of low unemployment and union militancy. There were large numbers of unofficial strikes, and it became common for Britain's economic problems to be blamed on the union movement. A Royal Commission under Lord Donovan investigated some of these issues, and its report was published in 1968. It concluded that management should assume a more direct responsibility for industrial relations and that, among other improvements, bargaining should be at a local level.

This, in fact, has been the trend. We will discuss the emerging role of the shop steward more fully later. Here, it may be noted that shop stewards, encouraged by the size of companies and their independence from employers' associations, had come to fill a vital place, both for management and workers.

The advent of incomes policies and the 'social contract' slowed down the movement towards local autonomy in bargaining. It was clear, however, that the greatest difficulty with incomes policy was for the union leaders to obtain the agreement of the members.

The growth of employment legislation since the 1960s is discussed in later chapters. Both Labour and Conservative Governments sought to introduce some kind of legal framework within which trade unions should operate. The Labour Government's White Paper, *In Place of Strife*, was never translated into legislation, but the Industrial Relations Act of 1971 under the Conservative Government provoked an enormous wave of protest over its attempt to make collective agreements legally binding on the parties, and the extension of controls over union affairs. With the defeat of the Conservative Government following its confrontation with the miners over pay, the new Labour Government repealed the 1971 Act.

INDUSTRIAL RELATIONS IN THE 1980s

The industrial relations scene changed in the 1980s. Some previous trends, such as the move to company-level bargaining, continued, and the individualistic ideology evidenced in the 1970s grew in the 1980s, finding political expression through government policies. A new climate for relationships at work emerged. What caused these changes?

1   High levels of unemployment reduced trade union militancy.

2   The move from 'smoke-stack' industries to a service-based economy meant that unions lost support in their traditional areas, especially in the nationalized industries.

3   The changes to the occupational structure, blue-collar to white-collar jobs, affected the number of trade union members.

4   New technology changed jobs and working practices. There was now more competition between unions for members (as, for example, in the printing industry and in the active recruitment at that time by the then Electrical, Electronic, Telecommunications and Plumbing Union – EETPU).

5   There were more women in the workforce. Approximately 5 million people (mostly women) now worked part-time. It is always difficult for trade unions to organize part-time employees.

6   The Conservative Government elected in 1979 introduced legislation which removed the possibility of secondary action, and forced unions to ballot before strikes. One

of the aims of the Thatcher Government policy was to reduce trade union power. Managements showed themselves ready to obtain court injunctions against unions.

7   New approaches to industrial relations were brought to the UK from Japan. There were in the mid 1980s more than 70 Japanese companies operating in the UK, their preferred approach being one union, with a single-status for employees with emphasis on employee involvement.

8   The recession caused managers to act more strategically in the way they handled industrial relations. This entailed managers opening up parallel communication channels to the unions, seeking longer-term agreements, bargaining for gains in productivity and looking for quality improvements.

These trends therefore had an effect. During this period, trade union membership fell by over 3 million people, and the number of days lost through strikes also fell. Some trade unions, notably the Amalgamated Union of Engineering Workers and the EETPU, sought ways to modernize the movement with new approaches. Trade unions were merging in an attempt to pool their financial strength and to obtain economies of scale. 'No strike' deals with employers, single-union agreements and strong local involvement of employees in the company were some of the threads which emerged as a basis for the new approach.

However, during the 1980s recession, productivity improved. Output increased by 12 per cent between 1983 and 1986. Inflation at that time was running at around 3.9 per cent per annum, whereas wage settlements were on average 7 per cent per annum, showing that some of the productivity gains were shared by the workforce. In spite of the loss in membership, the number of trade union members held up as a proportion of full-time employees represented, given that almost half of those working in the UK were employed as part-time, casual workers, self-employed or unemployed or on various training schemes.

FROM INDUSTRIAL RELATIONS TO EMPLOYEE RELATIONS

During the 1980s the trade unions were put on the defensive. Union membership fell, and a range of laws was passed to make unions more accountable to their members, in order to outlaw closed shops and sympathetic strikes, as well as to institute the ballot box as a key control on union leaders.

The increased incidence of derecognition by employers, and the lower recognition rate among newer workplaces in the 1980s, were attributed by Millward (1994) to the removal of statutory support for recognition in the 1980s and the higher rate of turnover among establishments in the 1980s. New offices, factories and warehouse units were being rapidly set up, just as others were closing. Other reasons included changing occupation and employment structures, the use of the secondary labour market of part-time, sub-contract, temporary and casual workers, and the increased trend towards outsourcing. In the period 1984–1990, the number of workplaces with recognized unions fell from

66 per cent to 53 per cent, and from 1990 to 1998 to 45 per cent, and the number of employees who were trade union members in those workplaces had fallen to 36 per cent in 1998, many of these changes being caused by derecognition.

At the same time, employers have been increasing direct communication with the workforce and have put the work group, with the supervisor as a central figure, as a focal point for human resource policies. First line supervisors now undertake most communication with the workforce, but there has also been an increase in the use of multimedia techniques, corporate PR, business television, with live interaction between workers and chief executives, and attitude surveys.

The broader term 'employee relations' is coming to be used more frequently to describe the relationships at work, intended to encompass both union and non-union members, and to include all those policies adopted by employers towards managing the relationships with the workforce. The second recession to hit the UK in the 1990s reinforced the changes occurring in 'industrial relations'. Large-scale European unemployment kept wages down and maintained pressure on prices. Big companies as well as small were hit by this second recession, which affected the service industries as well as manufacturing, and the south and south-east of England as well as the Midlands, the north of England, Scotland, Wales and Northern Ireland. This recession has resulted in greater attention to organization restructuring and to the delayering of organizations. 'Empowerment' became a term in common usage. Given flatter structures, there were wider spans of control, and it was now necessary to give the work group a high degree of autonomy. Semi-autonomous work groups have been used since the 1950s; however, as we discussed earlier, what was different in the 1990s was a raft of HR policies in development and rewards and business process redesign policies aimed to move organizations towards a process rather than a functional base. Total quality management policies were introduced to support this new approach.

The early 1990s was a period when trade unions began to see the need to change and to address the problems of the new industries, new occupations, new contractual arrangements and the diversity of the workforce. Much of the history of trade unions had pushed them towards a strategy of dependence on the return of a Labour Government. When that happened, in 1997, it became apparent that times had changed, and that they were more likely to be successful in following what has been described as a 'British version of social partnership' (Lloyd 1997).

The early part of the twenty-first century saw a number of trends emerge. Responding to falling numbers of members, especially in the private sector, unions sought mergers or the transfer of their members in a transfer of engagement. Under a transfer of engagement the members of one union vote to transfer to another, whilst in a merger, two or more unions merge to form a new entity. There were 37 of these mergers and transfers during the period from 1999 to 2005, the largest being the merger between the AEEU and MSF in January 2002, forming AMICUS. This was the largest merger since UNISON was formed in 1993, and created the second largest union in the UK.

The 1999 Employment Relations Act encouraged recognition agreements, both as a result if the legislation itself, and also because the Act encouraged employers and trade unions by creating a statutory procedure. The extensive employment law developments have not necessarily encouraged trade unions to flourish. Many issues such as unfair dismissal and grievances are covered by statutory procedures giving the individual employee rights to take a case to the Employment Tribunal. In practice, there may be benefits to both management and trade unions in these trends, since trade union members may prefer to take issue through the support of the trade union, and managers have the possibility that experienced employee representatives will discourage futile claims. Formal grievance and disciplinary policies gave employees the right to be accompanied at hearings by their trade union representative. The significance of the legal framework by which relations between employers and their employees is regulated is even more apparent in the twenty-first century. For trade unions this offers new opportunities and new challenges.

THE FINANCIAL CRASH AND THE RECESSION 2009–2013

Most trade unions have shown a strong desire to maintain the *status quo*. The history of trade unions has seen attempts to adjust changes so that there is the least negative effect on their members. In the recession, this has revolved around the opposition to reductions in public sector employment, and to trying to retain the employment of members in the private sector by accepting pay freezes and seeking safeguards and time for members to find other work, where companies are in difficulty, or going through mergers or closures.

TU membership in the UK and over much of Europe is in decline. In the period 1993–2003, aggregate TU membership fell by one-sixth in Europe (Carley 2004), in Germany it fell by 23 per cent and in the UK by 12 per cent. Comparing the two major recessions, that of 1989–1992, there was a reduction of 7 per cent, whereas in 2008–2011, there was a fall of 7 per cent. TU density declined during the period 1995–2007, but this was a consequence of increases in the total number of people in employment.

Although TU density in the UK remained unchanged in 2008–2009, this is because the total number of people in employment fell during this period, offsetting the fall in TU membership. There are big differences between the TU density of the public and private sectors. The Labour Force Survey of 2011 showed that 67.8 per cent of public sector workers were covered by collective agreements, compared to 16.7 per cent of private sector workers. In 2011, TU membership fell, at a time when the number of members and non-TU members fell in the public sector.

Typically, TU members receive higher pay than non-union members: this is known as the 'union wage premium'. It is calculated as the percentage difference in hourly earnings of union versus non-union members. In 2011, union wage premiums were much larger for public sector employees than for those union members in the private sector: 18 per cent for public sector workers; 8 per cent in the private sector.

In 2011, 54.7 per cent of union members were female. Older workers and those with longer service were more likely to be union members and union density was highest amongst full-time employees and those in professional occupations.

TRADE UNION ORGANIZATION

From the history and development of TU described above, trade unions cannot be classified as 'craft' or 'industrial' or 'occupational' any more. In practice, TUs are not organized on these principles, deriving as they do more from historical precedents.

Shop stewards

One of the most important matters to be clear about is the significance of 'lay' as opposed to 'official' representatives of TU. The most important role here is that of shop stewards. Shop stewards are not only representatives of the working groups, but also are frequently active in the local union administration, as one might expect. In some cases, the branch and district committee representatives are shop stewards, strengthening the steward's role in grass roots administration.

Shop stewards were simply described as 'trade union lay representatives at the place of work' by Lord McCarthy in his research for the Donovan Commission. The title of worker representatives varies according to the industry and trade; for example 'works representatives' or 'staff representatives', and there are variations in the size and nature of the constituency the steward represents.

Shop stewards are usually elected by a show of hands, and their representative functions are conducted in informal meetings with members, and in meetings with management, arranged through local procedures. In multi-union environments, their meetings will probably be between the management and a joint shop steward committee. This latter body may be elected or appointed by the shop stewards, and where there is a large number of stewards there is likely to be some form of seniority granted to facilitate organization. Shop stewards may represent workers from other unions where it is impractical for a separate steward to be appointed. The extent of management recognition of stewards varies according to whether or not the company or an employers' association negotiates pay and all the terms with the unions at national level, and also on the extent to which there are local negotiating procedures even where national agreements exist.

The practice has emerged, therefore, for shop stewards to occupy positions of power at the focal point of collective action in the daily interface with first-line supervisors. There is a difference between the *de jure* and the *de facto* rights and duties of shop stewards. Although few union rule books contain specific references to shop stewards, their performance of the duties summarized below has granted them a vital place at the centre of British industrial relations. Their functions have extended to the negotiation of terms and conditions, pay, piecework rates, overtime and hours of work, the regulation of work rules and staffing levels, and together with stewards from other unions they influence inter-union relationships.

The duties a steward would be expected to perform are:

1   Recruitment of new membership, seeing new starters and explaining the union's activities to them.
2   Maintaining membership, through the inspection of union membership cards, and by keeping the interest in the union alive.
3   Collecting subscriptions. This is now often arranged through the company, who collect for the union (a 'check-off' system), but stewards do still collect in some establishments.
4   Operating at the heart of the communication network between management, union and members, collecting views, passing on information, and sometimes determining the position which the membership should take up. The steward represents this to management, union officials, and passes back to members the management response.

The official organization of trade unions

Many unions have local branches that are organized into districts and/or regions. The members of the union elect the executive committee or council, which is responsible for administering the union's activities, and for conducting agreed policy. All unions have general secretaries, who are full-time officers, and who are responsible to the executive committee. Large unions have presidents. The general secretary and, where applicable, the president, share responsibility for the day-to-day business, and are responsible for the work of the other full-time officers, for example at regional or district level. The policy of the union is decided by the representative conference, the delegates to which are elected by the membership, voting in their branches. In many unions, this conference elects the executive.

There are a number of checks to the power of the leadership, which prevents an autocracy developing: for example, the local autonomy of district committees, the trade group structure of some unions and the balances within unions' constitutions. Such constraints may make for less decisive leadership, so there may be delays in handling disputes. The requirement for secret ballots for elections, and for industrial action, means there is a need for a democratic mandate, and one should therefore be cautious about ascribing militancy to any particular member of the leadership.

The trend towards 'professional' HR management has provided a counterweight to professional union negotiators.

EMPLOYERS' ASSOCIATIONS AND MANAGEMENT

Employers' associations

The members of employers' associations consist of large and small organizations ranging from self-employed members to public companies and large conglomerates, which may cover several associations in different industries. They seek to regulate the relations between employers and workers, or trade unions, and to lobby governments on behalf of members, in such matters as trade, national and international economic policy, and on policies affecting their industries, including employment legislation, and health and safety.

Management

Employment relationships are an integral part of the management of any business. Throughout this book, an emphasis has been placed on managerial roles in ensuring the satisfactory nature of such relationships, and therefore the relevance of good communication practices and consultation.

The management role begins with the recognition of the implications of any decisions taken for relationships at work, for example, when deciding on corporate strategy, or the acquisition or disposal of assets, when planning new products, investment in new machinery, or changes to the size or composition of the work force. In Chapter 21, there is a discussion about employee engagement, and in our previous chapters on change management, there is an emphasis on understanding the various interest groups in the organization, so that there can be a plan for incorporating concerns, involving people where possible, and negotiating solutions.

THE INTERNAL BARGAINING PROCESS

Too little attention is paid to the internal bargaining process within companies, and the assumption that there are two power groups, managers and unions, is misplaced. Just as in trade unions, where there are different groups – shop stewards, officials and groups of militant members, forming a loose coalition – so on management's side there are interest groups. Local level managers, for example, may not agree with the overall corporate policy, or supervisors who may have an identity of interests with the shop stewards, may try to frustrate any deals which lead to extra work, and HR staff may have a wider strategic aim, such as a long term pact with the trade unions in mind.

Management organization is not a monolith, therefore, and the informal processes that occur include attempts by boards to control their negotiators, and the marshalling of workshop pressure against the union. What happens on the 'shop floor' or the 'office floor' is what ultimately matters. This is where the internal bargaining process is utilized to maintain order and to control and change working practices.

DIFFERENT APPROACHES TO BARGAINING

Collective bargaining comprises the settlement of wages, terms and conditions, and procedures by bargains expressed in the form of an agreement made between employers' associations or more frequently, single employers and trade unions. The objective of all bargaining is to find an agreement. Agreements may be conveniently divided into procedural and substantive agreements. Procedural agreements set out the rules by which the formal relationships between the company and the union will be regulated. These could include disputes procedures and procedures by which substantive agreements are to be interpreted.

Substantive agreements are agreements about the terms, conditions and pay of a group of workers. These include the hours of work, holidays and the rules governing how work is to be done. A further sub-division is into bargaining at industry and at domestic level. At the industry level, bargaining between employers' associations and a confederation of trade unions settles both broad procedural and substantive areas. In the domestic bargaining of particular companies with the union representing their work force, the rates paid for specific jobs, and the regulation of the work, as well as local procedures for dealing with discipline and grievances are negotiated. These procedures would have to provide at least the same protection as the ACAS grievance and discipline procedures. Examples of this fourfold classification are given in Table 19.2

CONCLUSIONS

The ebb and flow of power in industrial relations over the centuries has pushed the frontiers of control back and forth between management and workers. From this abbreviated history of trade unions in the UK, we can see how they play a part in the political processes of the nation. Conflicts with the law have been a feature of their relationship with the state. Unions are democratic movements, and their power is dependent upon the support of ordinary working people. The emergence of shop stewards, and the move to local-level bargaining,

TABLE 19.2 SUBSTANTIVE AND PROCEDURAL AGREEMENTS

Agreement	Domestic	Industrial
Substantive	Wage agreements, productivity agreements	Hours of work, apprenticeship schemes, holidays
Procedural	Local disputes, discipline and grievance procedures	Industrial procedures (applied through various joint councils, for example)

leads us to the conclusion that it is at the company level where industrial relations policies and strategies can forge productive relationships. Increasingly these relationships are seen as part of a wider strategy and agenda from management towards an engaged work force through good employee relationships.

The bargaining processes which take place between the two sides are such that neither side can always be sure of support from those they represent. There are factions on both the union and on the management side. One issue which is emerging as an issue for the future is how trade unions can adjust to a social partnership role, and how mature is our industrial relations system? Is it capable of responding to the pressures from overseas, low wage economies, and the pressures of social change? Above all, the fragmentation of the labour market, due to pressures for flexibility, means there has been a major shift to types of employment (characterized by casual, part-time, zero hours and similar types of contract) which presents a challenge for TU who have difficulty in organizing this type of contingent labour.

QUESTIONS

1   To what extent do trade union relationships with governments over the years represent conflicting interests?
2   How did the two world wars affect trade unions?
3   What happens to TU membership during recessions?
4   How different are the modern TU from their predecessors in the early years of the twentieth century?
5   Are the big, long-term, set-piece strikes of the past ever likely to return?
6   What are the current key issues for TU?

REFERENCES

Carley, M. (2004). *European Industrial Relations Observatory on line.* ID No. Document TN 0403105u.
Labour Force Survey: Quarterly Labour Force Survey (2012). (QLFS) Office of National Statistics.
Lloyd, J. (1997). 'Industrial relations in Britain'. In Tyson, S. (ed) *The Practice of Human Resource Strategy.* Pitman. 51–72.
Millward, N. (1994). *The New Industrial Relations.* Policy Studies Institute.

20 DISPUTES AND WAYS OF RESOLVING CONFLICT

INTRODUCTION

The approach managers take to managing relationships with employees is critical to their success. The approach necessarily depends upon their values, deep set beliefs about the legitimacy of managerial authority and their view of how power should be distributed in organizations. Fox (1966) has suggested that the 'frame of reference' that managers adopt conditions their response to the issues they face and how they define these issues.

The frame of reference is a term coined to describe their typifications and tacit understandings that are founded on their values and deep set beliefs. Fox characterizes managers' frames of reference as falling into two categories: the 'unitary' and the 'pluralistic'. The unitary frame of reference sees all the people in the organization working towards the same goal, where there is one source of authority-management, and conflict is anathema. Managers often see themselves as leading a 'team' and they expect all those who work for them to take the same view. The pluralist frame of reference, on the other hand, sees organization members as part of a plurality of differing interest groups, with differing and sometimes competing interests, which may come together from time to time, and who have sectional interests in the pursuit of power and resources. The manager's role in this regard is to balance the varying interests, including those of customers and share-holders, and to create an open climate of relationships where disagreements can be more readily resolved.

The reality of most organizations is that people hold a multiplicity of personal objectives. There would seem to be some truth in the claim that most employees really work for the material and psychological satisfaction they can achieve, and that their work is therefore an instrument used towards their own ends. In addition to this instrumental attachment to work, interest groups form in organizations, where individual interests coalesce. These groups seek to achieve their ends through alliances and by following group strategies.

A number of sociologists have suggested that our attention should be addressed to the explanation of 'order', or lack of 'conflict', which is perceived by some to be unnatural, the normal pattern being one of disagreement, conflict and often violence. One outcome of such a view is that 'political activity' is necessary to avoid a state of anarchy. This political activity includes the formation of alliances, the representation of interest groups in consensus decision-making and mechanisms for containing and canalizing opposition.

The values of managers govern their attitudes towards workers taking action in pursuit of claims and condition the manager's response to 'industrial action'. Whether such action is regarded as a legitimate part of the bargaining process will depend on a manager's view of conflict in organizations as a whole. Important questions we must face are: can we expect to have the total commitment of people to their tasks? Do groups of workers have the right to express their disagreement and to use their power in confrontation? In this chapter the answers to these questions will be explored and the nature of industrial conflict and its resolution will be examined.

THE CONFLICT CYCLE

There are a number of distinct phases in a conflict cycle. The cycle begins with substantive or emotional issues being triggered by an event, which seems to focus attention on what are regarded as the underlying issues. Tension escalates to the point where sides are drawn and each side makes judgements on the opposition's power and goals. Those involved in the situation experience fear at the confrontation according to the risks they are taking with family, income, job, prestige, etc. There is negotiation or a series of meetings where both sides work through their disagreement. The outcome either will be a resolution by compromise or the conflict cycle will start again.

Conflict takes place at different levels. There may be a 'running fight' between management and workers over a period of months or even years, with occasional outbreaks of overt conflict in the form of 'wildcat' strikes, or the conflict could be at a national level, as in the famous miners' strikes in the 1970s and 1980, or an event such as the disputes and one-day strikes on the London Underground in 2013/14 to resist the closure of ticket offices, so that ticket machines could take over issuing tickets to customers. In the recent past, there have been industrial disputes in the fire service, airlines and one-day stoppages in schools and universities and various parts of the public sector, over redundancy and reorganization, which the unions have often interpreted as cost-cutting in order to meet budget targets rather than to improve efficiency or give a better service.

DIFFERENT TYPES OF DISPUTE

There are signs of disaffection with organizations, which are explicit, such as strikes, confrontation leading to lock-outs and various forms of withdrawal of cooperation by workers in furtherance of their claims. High labour turnover, absenteeism, high accident rates owing to inattention, poor training and customer complaints could also be regarded as implicit conflict in the sense that they are indicative of at least a lack of interest or motivation to work and, at worst, animosity towards the company and what it represents. Strikes are, therefore, not of themselves an indicator of low productivity (except, of course, for the period of the strike itself). A study of coal-mining, for example, revealed that pits with few strikes were not outstandingly productive. Apathy and a low level of energy at work are probably more damaging than outright confrontation over differences.

Industrial conflict takes a variety of forms. Overtime bans, working to rule and refusal to use new machinery have all been seen in different industries over the past decades. The draughtsmen's union invented an ingenious form of pressure on management: 'working without enthusiasm'. White-collar workers and managers who are unionized have considerable scope for this type of action since their work frequently requires them to use their initiative and creativity.

Apart from sanctions against management, workers sometimes take action against those of another union, or employer, by 'blacking' the goods they produce; that is, refusing to use or handle them. Sanctions against individual workers who do not obey the majority decision also occur. Unofficially, these may include 'sending to Coventry' (that is, a form of ostracism, by not communicating with the offender at work), and physical sanctions have been known, although never officially approved by unions. We may recall here the way in which offenders who broke group norms were struck on the upper arm, as recounted in the Hawthorne research.

STRIKES

A strike is not the only type of sanction that workers can apply. It is, however, one of the most effective. Withdrawal of labour puts pressure on an employer immediately, and although there are costs to employees in the form of loss of pay, the employer faces an immediate need to negotiate so that a return to work and a resumption of business can take place. Other forms of industrial action can become a 'running sore', and may cause as much difficulty for employees as for management. Overtime bans are only effective when overtime is regularly expected, and 'working to rule' can be inconvenient for the workers as well as for management and customers. The 'lock-out' by an employer is not so frequent nowadays, this being where the employer refuses to allow a group of employees to return to work unless they accept management's terms.

Strike action on a selective basis has been used to minimize the cost to the union and to maximize the effect on the employer. This is exemplified by the withdrawal of a small number of key workers, such as those operating a computer installation. For a strike to be effective, the employer's business has to be stopped, and thus strikers place great emphasis on solidarity and regard picketing as an essential element in their tactics. The use of pickets on the premises of employers not directly related to the dispute, but who can bring pressure to bear on the employer who is engaged in a dispute (secondary picketing), has been banned (see Chapter 26).

Strikes and other forms of industrial action are not always sanctioned by the union. We can, therefore, differentiate between official and unofficial strikes, the former providing the benefit of strike pay to those on strike and the use of the union organization. Matters are not always so clear-cut. Strikes that start as unofficial are often made official as they progress.

The classification of strikes for comparative purposes is, therefore, problematic because each strike is a complex phenomenon in which people with different and changing motives are acting out the various stages in the conflict cycle. As there are many other forms of industrial action, statistics on strikes cannot be taken as a definitive measure of industrial unrest. There are also serious difficulties in collecting strike statistics. It is probable that many small strikes are unrecorded, and the different methods of recording in each country make international comparisons imprecise. Strike statistics are usually kept on the total number of stoppages beginning in a year and the aggregate number of working days lost owing to stoppages in progress during a year. The caveats extended above counsel caution when interpreting these statistics. The benefit gained from studying the statistics is to derive a general impression of signs of militancy, and to see which industries are strike-prone.

Until 1926, the pattern was for large numbers of working days to be lost from a relatively small number of strikes. After the General Strike in 1926, until 1956 the number of days lost was not typically so high, but the number of strikes increased. The late 1960s saw an increase in militancy; from 1968 to 1977 the average number of working days lost for every 1000 workers was 452, which was nevertheless better than the record of Italy, Australia, Canada and the United States. The number of strikes starting each year was around 2000 from 1957 to the late 1970s, except for 1970 when almost twice that number started. In 1957, the engineering strike pushed up the number of days lost to 8.4 million and there have been four particularly bad years since then: in 1972, 24 million working days were lost; in 1974, 15 million days; in 1979, 28 million days; and in 1984, 27 million days (owing to the miners' strike).

During the 1980s, the strike weapon came to be used less: the number of stoppages fell from 1348 in 1980 to 701 in 1989, and down to the 600 level in the early 1990s. By the end of the 1990s, the number of recorded strikes was negligible.

Strike activity in 1997 was the lowest since records began in 1891, according to the Office for National Statistics. In 2012, 248,800 working days were lost owing to disputes, compared to 1,389,700 in 2011. There were 131 stoppages of work because of disputes in 2012 compared to 149 stoppages in 2011 and 92 in 2010. The majority of working days lost (79 per cent) were in the public sector, and about half of the 131 stoppages were in the public sector (52 per cent). Sixty-eight per cent of working days lost were owing to wage disputes. The duration of disputes was short: 76 per cent of days lost in 2012 were for one day. (The source of the statistics in this section of the chapter is the Office of National Statistics. Labour Disputes. Annual Article 2012.)

This reduction in trade union militancy may be the result of a number of factors. First, high levels of unemployment are associated with reduced militancy. Second, the Conservative Governments during the 1980s and on into the 1990s expressly sought to reduce trade union power by introducing legislation that made the unions liable for damages caused to employers in a dispute in a wider number of situations. The introduction of the need for a ballot of members before any action is taken gives time for management and unions to reach a compromise on issues in dispute. Third, the collapse of Britain's old industrial base in the mining, heavy engineering, ship-building and some manufacturing sectors changed the occupation structure and labour force characteristics. Many jobs have become part-time, often occupied by women, and are in the service sector of the economy. In manufacturing and construction there has been more sub-contract and non-union labour. These changed features of the labour force may also have reduced the propensity to strike.

When militancy was higher, economic reasons accounted for 80 per cent of stoppages and 90 per cent of person days lost. In 2011 and 2012 combined, 92 per cent of days lost in disputes were concerned with pay issues. However, in the face of the recession and austerity, only 24 per cent of days lost were over pay. Instead, in 2009 to 2010, 72 per cent were over redundancy. However, the restructuring of organizations, redundancies, pension arrangements, outsourcing, mergers and the need expressed by management for greater flexibility have become potential reasons for conflict. There have been various disputes, for example the teachers' unions, in the NHS and in other areas. Strikes have often been threatened (for example in the Prison Services), but not always put into action.

Most strikes are short, sharp affairs, where the employees walk out when an event triggers the examination of a number of underlying problems over which there has been frustration and annoyance, for example, over grading decisions or work rosters. The set piece, long drawn-out battles in steel, transport and the mines, for example, came at a stage when negotiations had broken down. The trend will probably be towards more official disputes, since in the growth area of unionism, the white-collar area, the members are more prone to strike on union instructions.

From research completed by the former Department of Employment, we can see a profile of a strike-prone industry:

■ labour-intensive
■ high union density
■ the average size of the units managed is large
■ high-paid, skilled labour force
■ majority of labour force is male
■ industry is subject to fluctuating market pressures.

PROCEDURES FOR CONFLICT RESOLUTION

Discipline procedures

In the past there were many disputes each year owing to management's disciplinary actions. Dismissal and suspensions occur for breaches of rules (such as sleeping on the job, negligence, breach of safety regulations) and for more general problems of conduct, including absenteeism and bad time-keeping.

Discipline procedures may be local procedures devised by management, sometimes negotiated and agreed with the unions concerned. Shop stewards and/or local union officials may take part by representing their members at any hearings or appeals against management's decision. The advent of unfair dismissal legislation (see Chapter 24) and the use of ACAS-based disciplinary procedures and grievance procedures in employment may reduce the incidence of disputes in these areas (ACAS 2009). Under the 1972 Contracts of Employment Act, employers were obliged to provide written information for their employees about the disciplinary rules that are applicable to them, and details of the person to whom they should apply if not satisfied.

The following prescription for a discipline procedure is drawn from the ACAS Code. Discipline procedures should:

1   Be in writing.
2   Specify to whom they should apply.
3   Be quick in operation.
4   State the disciplinary actions that may be taken.
5   Specify the levels of management with the authority to dismiss (usually those at senior manager or director status).
6   Give the individual details of the complaints.
7   Give individuals a right to be accompanied by a trade union representative, or by a fellow employee of their choice, at any disciplinary hearing or interview.
8   Unless it is a case of gross misconduct, no employee should be dismissed for a first offence.
9   Disciplinary action should not be taken until a case has been carefully investigated.
10 Individuals must be given an explanation of any penalty imposed.
11 Employers must provide a right of appeal with an established procedure. The employee has the right to be accompanied by a trade union representative, or an official employed by the trade union, or by a fellow employee at the appeal.

This leaves a number of questions to be resolved. How should a manager decide whether or not a subordinate's action is misconduct? What is serious misconduct? How and when should action be taken on cumulative problems such as lateness or inefficiency? How many warnings should be given, and who is to be involved in the discipline process?

Let us start to deal with these questions by saying that the purpose of discipline at work is to improve performance/change behaviour. If an employee behaves in such a way that he or she shows he or she has no intention of being bound by the contract of employment, then the employer can regard the contract as broken. There should be no moral purpose behind disciplinary action, and it is not the responsibility or the right of the manager to impose his or her own moral code. If it is possible for the employee to change his or her behaviour or performance, then the manager has a responsibility to offer an opportunity for improvement and to help the employee to progress.

We can distinguish between four different kinds of problems that result in disciplinary action of some sort, sometimes resulting in the termination of employment:

■ inefficiency or performance issues (failure to perform up to the required standard)
■ absence owing to sickness and unavoidable personal problems (e.g. serious illness)
■ cumulative discipline problems (e.g. repeated incidents such as absenteeism, bad time-keeping)
■ immediate discipline problems (e.g. theft, fighting).

Inefficiency/performance

The performance problems of a subordinate are initially a problem for the immediate supervisor and, before any disciplinary action is taken, the procedures outlined in our sections on appraisal, induction and training should be followed. This will involve a careful and complete enquiry into the evidence that there is a performance problem. Only when these have failed to improve the performance of the individual, and development or other assistance has been provided, and the possibilities of transferring the person to a more suitable job have been exhausted, should a discipline procedure be instituted. Having tried all these possibilities, managers should move to Stage 1 of the discipline procedure outlined below and give the employee a formal warning.

Sickness/unavoidable personal problems

The first step is to spend time on investigation of the problem through sick-visiting or a counselling interview. It is important to ask the employee whether or not he or she is able to return. For most organizations, there should be a referral to the doctor at the occupational health service to which the organization subscribes, for an occupational health assessment. The requirement for a referral at the behest of the organization should be contained in the employment contract, since otherwise it may be difficult to require the employee to attend, and to consent to the report from the Occupational Health Service being sent to both the individual and the organization. The decision on termination of employment will depend on the length of the absence and the needs of the work. It may be necessary to terminate the employment if a long absence is likely and there is urgent work to be done. This decision must be taken only as a last step, of course, and employers should show compassion in dealing with sickness. If the employee would be capable of performing another type of job, a transfer should be examined.

Cumulative discipline problems

The stages in the discipline process are:

1   The immediate supervisor should interview the employee to discover the cause. The union representative should be advised and asked if he or she would like to be present, or a friend/colleague of the employee may come to the discussion.
2   The supervisor issues a verbal warning, recorded on the file by the HR department, and the employee must be told in what ways he or she can improve, what help is available and over what time period the improvement is expected.
3   If there is no improvement, a further interview is necessary and a written final warning should be given (either by senior management or by the HR department). The steps that are to take place if he or she fails to improve should be explained, and the employee should be given every assistance to improve and extra efforts should be made to help, including formal training if necessary, with a time limit by which an improvement should be made. The union representative should be informed.
4   If the final warning is not heeded, the employee should be told that he or she will be dismissed, with a provision for an appeal to the HR director or managing director if the employee has reason to believe that there has been any unfairness. While such an appeal is taking place, the employee should be suspended from duty on full pay. The appropriate union official should be informed.

Immediate discipline problems

1   An interview should be held to establish the cause of the problem. By the nature of these problems it may be necessary to institute an inquiry, with other employees called in to give their accounts of the incident. When the 'offender' against the rules is asked for his or her version, he or she must be allowed to call other witnesses and to be accompanied by a trade union representative or a friend.
2   If the investigation is likely to take days to complete, it may be wise to suspend the employee on full pay during this time. Suspension under these circumstances should be distinguished from suspension as a penalty imposed as a consequence of a hearing.
3   When the investigation is complete, the employee should be interviewed again and advised of any action that is taken. If a penalty is proposed, written particulars ought to be handed to the employee concerned and a copy given to the union representative. If a warning is proposed, then the manager should continue from Stage 3 of the procedure for cumulative problems as outlined above. There should be provision for appeals against any penalty in the way already suggested.

Provided management follow an appropriate procedure and the grounds for dismissal are fair, mistakes that could result in an unfair dismissal, with the attendant tribunal problems, can be avoided. We set out reasons for dismissal that are fair in Chapter 24.

GRIEVANCE PROCEDURES

Grievance procedures are necessary to ensure that employees have a recognized channel through which they can bring their grievances to the attention of management. The objective of grievance procedures is to grant employees the right to have their grievances heard, investigated and, if proved justified, remedied. No matter how good the procedure is, the maintenance of good communications is only possible where the climate of relationships favours open criticism, honesty and fairness in dealings between people. A grievance procedure that is simple, and which is respected by employees and management, should help to continue such a climate.

We can draw a distinction between individual grievances, which should be handled by the grievance procedure, and group grievances, which would normally be the subject of negotiation, joint consultation or a formal disputes procedure. The stages of a grievance procedure are represented in Figure 20.1.

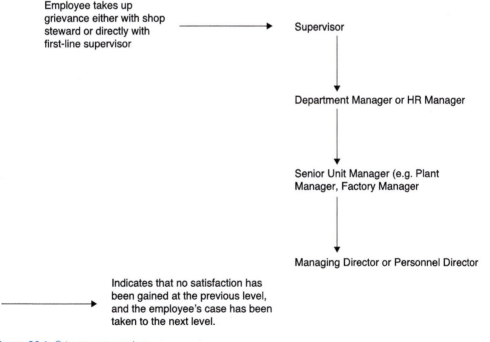

Figure 20.1 Grievance procedure

There are variations in the role that the HR manager can play in grievance procedures. The HR specialist should not be called in at once, and there are advantages in HR managers being at the end of the procedure, to avoid clashes over authority among line and 'staff' functions and to help preserve the status of HR as the last 'court of appeal'.

The time that must elapse before an employee can move on to the next stage of the procedure should be stated. Grievances should be dealt with quickly. If a delay is unavoidable before a manager can get the answer, he or she should make sure that the employee knows why and what the timescale is for a resolution of any difficulties.

The clear-cut distinction between individual and group grievances becomes blurred in some circumstances. Although applying to one person, grievances may be seen as representative of the actions by management, such as changes in work rules that a group of people oppose.

SETTLEMENT AGREEMENTS

In the changes to the Employment Tribunal Regulations in 2013/2014, new rules were introduced that allowed either employers or employees to initiate off-the-record conversations about terminating employment at any time, to enable a negotiated settlement. Effectively, these conversations are, in the legal parlance, 'without prejudice', that is, the discussions cannot be used by either party in any subsequent Employment Tribunal hearings. The benefit of the process is in those situations where both parties feel the relationship between management and employee cannot realistically continue, and there is a desire to have an arrangement and time to fix a mutually beneficial settlement, which means the two sides may part company amicably. The employee can be accompanied in any discussions either by a trade union representative, trade union official or colleague employee. These conversations existed before, but were not regulated, and it was difficult for an employee to initiate them. There are penalties to organizations that fail to follow the ACAS guidelines on the process. We will look at mediation in the chapter that follows. The objectives of the settlement options are designed to reduce legal action and the number of Employment Tribunal hearings.

DISPUTE PROCEDURES

There are dispute procedures that operate at a local domestic level and procedures at an industry-wide level. In some industries, the industry-wide procedure will only deal with disputes about the interpretation of national agreements, whereas in others, any type of dispute, substantive or interpretative, can be put through the recognized industry procedures. Where industry procedures will only accept interpretative disputes, any other form of disagreement has to be handled at the local or domestic level.

At the domestic level, procedures work through local committees. Shop stewards (where there is unionization) take part in the procedures in joint consultative and works committees, and in combined committees with management. Local disputes are usually taken up with management by the local employee representatives as part of their normal bargaining. Long-term questions may overcome the more pressing disputes and the immediate issue is incorporated into a longer-term strategy, sometimes by the union.

Large organizations have formal procedures at the local level. There are different levels of conflict settlement offered by a series of committees in tiers. A failure to agree at a local level results in the dispute being passed to district or company level, and so on upwards to national or industry level.

ENGINEERING INDUSTRY PROCEDURE

This is a good example of an industry-wide, employers' association procedure. Works committees with a maximum of seven representatives of the management and up to seven shop stewards meet regularly and will consider complaints from individuals or groups of workers. If no settlement is reached, a further meeting of the works committee may be held with the union district officer and the employers' federation representative present. If there is still failure to agree, the disagreement may be referred through the procedure's 'provisions for avoiding disputes'. The objective is to avoid either a partial or a full stoppage of work until the procedure has been exhausted.

The stages are:

1   Either party may bring a problem before the local conference held between the local employers' association and local union officials.
2   If no settlement is reached at the local conference, either party may refer the disagreement to a central conference (held monthly), with a panel of employers and national officers. The central conference tries to reach an agreement.

If it is not possible to arrive at a mutual recommendation, then the whole matter will go back to the shop floor for settlement by the normal means of collective bargaining.

There are a number of different procedures operated by different joint industrial councils, such as those in gas and electricity and in chemical and allied products. In the building industry, there are four stages:

1   A site meeting with union and association officers.
2   A local joint committee meeting.
3   Regional conciliation panels are held.
4   National conciliation panels are the final stage, with the provision that further disagreement can be referred to arbitration, and there is an emergency procedure that is used

for urgent problems when, for example, a stoppage is imminent. Under this emergency procedure, the national officers can refer the dispute directly to a regional joint emergency disputes commission and, finally, to a national emergency body.

ARBITRATION

There is nothing to stop either or both sides in a dispute seeking arbitration. Some procedures for settling disputes have built-in clauses concerning arbitration. These are mostly in the public sector, including the civil service and local authorities.

Public inquiries have been used to settle disputes where a long strike is thought to be damaging to the public interest. The Advisory, Conciliation and Arbitration Service (ACAS) is an independent, state-backed body that seeks to conciliate and to offer advice to either or both parties whenever requested to do so. When it is impossible for employers and unions to agree through collective bargaining, ACAS may appoint a mediator from outside, or a board of arbitration if both parties request this. Any attempts by ACAS at arbitration do not have any binding force on the parties.

In addition to ACAS, there is the Central Arbitration Committee, which can hear claims for improvements in terms and conditions of employment if the union is not recognized by the employer.

Within the union movement, arbitration in the settlement of disputes between unions can be provided by the TUC, which has the power to suspend a union and to recommend its expulsion from the Congress.

INTERPERSONAL RESOLUTION OF CONFLICT

Conflict and problems in relationships are sometimes more susceptible to less procedural solutions. There are conflicts that are a consequence of interpersonal relationships, for example, when an individual has problems in integrating into a larger unit. Managers in these circumstances need to adopt a style that keeps communication flowing. This may entail:

1   *Supportive behaviour on the manager's part*: supporting and counselling the individual with the problem. 'Difficult' behaviour by subordinates may be a cry for help rather than a challenge to managerial authority.
2   *Work group problem-solving*: using the resources of the group to resolve the problem. This means opening up a dialogue between members of the group and persuading them to be open about any problems that they experience. This is a strategy that requires a high-trust relationship, and the manager must be prepared to take criticism of his or her own performance.
3   *Job design techniques*: the objective is to design jobs that both give satisfaction for individuals and opportunities for improving performance.

CONCLUSIONS

Conflict resolution starts with a careful diagnosis of the causes of the problem. It is then the responsibility of the manager to apply an appropriate procedural, structural or personal solution, or a combination of all three (see Figure 20.2). The manager's greatest assets in

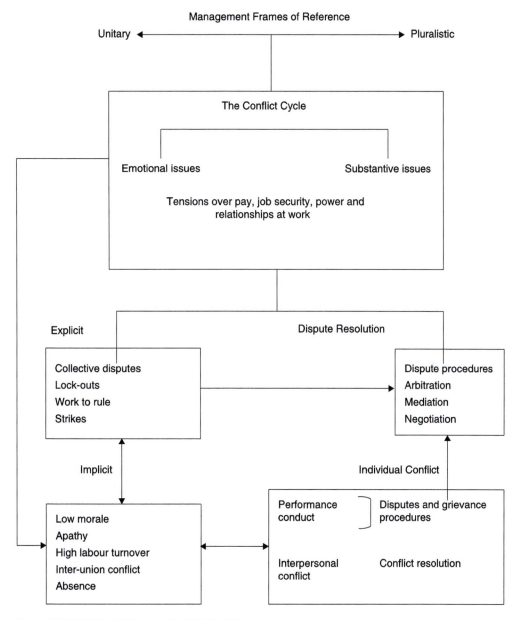

Figure 20.2 Disputes and ways of solving conflict

resolving conflicts will be his or her own preparedness to adopt a pluralist stance, and the interpersonal skills that he or she can bring to bear – supplemented by perseverance, honesty and pragmatism.

QUESTIONS

1   What is the difference between a unitary and a pluralist frame of reference?
2   Why has the number of TU members been declining in the last decade or more?
3   Does this account for the reduction in the number of official disputes, or are there other factors?
4   Set out the main steps in a discipline procedure. What are the different approaches towards cumulative and immediate discipline problems?
5   What are the stages in a grievance procedure?
6   What are the benefits of a formal disputes procedure? At what stage would you expect there to be arbitration?
7   When conflict is a consequence of interpersonal relationships what sorts of solutions are available?

REFERENCES

ACAS (2009 and subsequently). *Disciplinary and Grievance Procedure*; and *Discipline and Grievance at Work-The ACAS Guide*. Norwich: TSO (The Stationery Office).

Fox, A. (1966). Industrial Sociology and Industrial Relations Research Paper No. 3. *Royal Commission on Trade Unions and Employers Associations*. HM Stationery Office.

Office of National Statistics (2013). Labour Disputes. Annual Article 2012. Released 4 July 2013. UK National Statistics Publication Hub www.statistics.gov.uk/hub/labour.

21 CONSULTATION, PARTICIPATION AND ENGAGEMENT

INTRODUCTION

The width of interpretation we can give to the idea of participation is reflected in the many levels at which employees participate in a modern democracy. There is participation through national institutions, through industry-wide bodies, and at company and sometimes department or section level. Collective bargaining in its many forms could be said to be employee participation in the distribution of wealth in society. The current interest in the idea of employee engagement is a stage further on this theme, which seeks an organizational culture solution to the issue of how to create an identity of interests between management and employee attitudes and interests.

DESCENDING AND ASCENDING PARTICIPATION

One way of distinguishing between different forms of participation was described by Walker in 1977, when he differentiated between 'descending participation' and 'ascending participation'.

Descending participation includes schemes for enlarging and enriching the employee's job, so that some of the functions of the next level up of supervision become part of his or her work, and this approach to participation can also be found in forms of supervision where decisions are made by the work group acting with the manager by problem-solving as a group. In this latter case, the manager becomes very much the representative of the group that operates its own control and discipline functions. In the former instance, job enlargement schemes seem to some supervisors to be threatening because they tend to squeeze the middle and junior levels of management. To be successful, therefore, they have to be applied from the top of the organization so that power and responsibility are devolved downwards.

Ascending participation is characterized by joint consultative committees and arrangements that recognize the employee's demand for more information from management and for involvement in decision-making. This is now often termed the demand for employee voice.

There has been a tradition of joint consultation in the UK since the end of the First World War. The advent of both world wars reinforced the need for cooperation between employers and their workforces to achieve the production targets essential for victory. The early experiments in joint industrial councils, which the Whitley Committee advocated in 1919, eventually faltered in most industries, except in the public sector. Nevertheless, the idea has blossomed at a local level in industry, and a number of organizations have maintained joint consultative committees through the years. The principles behind joint consultation have also been influential in the training of HR managers. Other forms of participation, for example, through 'empowerment programmes', quality circles and through financial participation such as employee share ownership plans, seek to engage the commitment of employees. Even organizational surveys, focus groups and 'intranet' communication can be seen as at least some attempt at listening to employees' voices. As is often said, employees only value such techniques if their voices are also valued.

The advent of the internet with social media and twitter means information is no longer under the control of management. How management can influence the types of views about the organization is no longer a matter for public relations. Management must now present authentic accounts of the reality of organizational life, rather than partial narratives in order to present corporate reputations accurately to customers, suppliers and prospective employees. This would best be achieved if employees are fully involved through surveys and various forms of participation.

JOINT CONSULTATIVE COMMITTEES

Joint consultative committees (JCCs) usually operate at company level. They are committees of managers and workers, with a formal constitution, which meet regularly to discuss problems of mutual interest that are outside the normal area of negotiations. Employee members of such committees are elected and serve for a fixed term. The arrangements can apply to any form of organization structure, irrespective of whether or not the employees are members of a trade union.

The principles on which joint consultation is based are those we have outlined in our comments on problem-solving. The approach to employee relations is integrative rather than distributive, and could be summarized as follows:

1   For employees to be concerned about the achievement of the organization's object-
    ives, they must be made aware of the objectives and understand the reasons for the
    policies that are followed.
2   Good communications between management and the workforce are vital. Employees
    should be advised in advance of areas under discussion so that they can express their
    views and contribute to the thinking that goes into the decision.
3   Problems that stem from the application of rules to local situations, and matters that
    are of direct concern to the employees in their working lives such as working methods,
    attendance at work, catering, welfare arrangements and conditions of service, are
    best dealt with by management and staff representatives meeting regularly to talk and
    put forward solutions.
4   A reservoir of goodwill and interest should be built, to be drawn on when unpopular
    decisions have to be accepted by the workforce. One of the benefits of the JCC meet-
    ings is that employee representatives receive training and experience in how to present
    cases at meetings, to report to their constituents and to research into problems.

Whilst there is already provision for recognized trade unions to have access to information
from the employer so that collective bargaining may proceed, under the Trade Union and
Labour Relations (Consolidation) Act 1992, regulations on consultation have been brought
forward. The Information and Consultation of Employees Regulations 2004 (ICE) give
employees a right to be informed about the activities and the economic circumstances of an
undertaking, and to be informed and consulted about employment prospects. The
Regulations were introduced over time. ICE now applies to public and private sector organizations that have a registered office or principal place of business in the UK.

There is flexibility in the ICE Regulations as to how employers introduce and use the
consultation process. The onus is on the employees to ask for the consultation arrangements to be agreed, the threshold being 10 per cent of the workforce requesting these
arrangements. Pre-existing arrangements, including various forms of collective bargaining
may be sufficient, and where there are already obligations under, for example, TUPE, there
is no requirement to consult again.

There are a number of issues to be decided, including the constitution of a JCC; an
example is given below:

1   *The scope of the JCC.* The areas which fall within its scope should include the overall
    business strategy as well as the more everyday needs, such as working arrangements,
    information about products/services, the organization's financial position, future
    employment prospects, security, suggestion schemes, physical working conditions,
    catering, etc. These ought to be set out in general terms.
2   *The relationship between the JCC and other bodies*: these ought to be agreed and
    stated, notably any committees which are concerned with negotiation, or with the flow
    of information from management to work people. If there is more than one JCC, the

areas each is to cover should be set out and the procedure for referring matters to the next level up (e.g. from company to division to group level) should be specified.

3   *The intervals at which the JCC meets.* For example, meeting monthly or bimonthly would probably be sufficiently frequent to prevent the JCC from being bypassed with urgent problems and its consequent relegation to a 'talking shop'.

4   *A list of the officers of the committee*: such as chairperson, secretary and their deputies, together with their functions. At least one of these officers should be representative of the workforce. The method of electing the officers should be set out.

5   *The arrangements for the election of representatives to the committee.* This would normally be achieved by obtaining nominations and then holding a ballot, jointly supervised by management and by the unions or other worker representatives. In some companies the shop stewards may automatically serve on the JCC, or representatives of the stewards may be voted on to the JCC by the stewards voting as a whole.

6   *The length of time members should serve on the committee*: and what to do if members leave in mid-term (e.g. through illness, resignation, etc.). Management members may be coopted on to the committee.

7   *The agenda should be prepared in advance*: by the JCC Secretary, with the items submitted by any member of the committee. The secretary should be responsible for the minutes and their circulation to senior management and notice boards. Minutes should be brief and be quickly produced.

Some critics of joint consultation see it as merely a device for preventing militancy by union representatives, as a trick to gain consent. Another criticism is that JCCs become bogged down in trivia. It is sometimes suggested that the meetings are rituals and that no real change occurs as a consequence of them. When JCCs *do* become influential, the argument runs, then they become negotiating bodies.

As a counter to these points, if a JCC is operated as intended, that is, as a forum for a discussion of the matters that are of importance to the workforce, then there is no reason why a JCC should not be an extremely effective way of achieving consensus decisions that resolve problems for the organization as a whole. Much will depend on the qualities of the chairperson and the impartiality and real interest in joint consultation that he or she brings to the role. Trade union criticism of joint consultation is often motivated by the vision of one communication channel between management and workers, which the union controls and which is primarily a channel for negotiation.

THE DEBATE ON PARTICIPATION

In the 1970s there was a push for 'industrial democracy' built on attempts by previous governments to bring together the government, the Confederation of British Industry and the TUC in long-term planning, through the National Economic Development Council and its offshoots. 'Tripartism' spread into the control of quasi-governmental organizations such as ACAS, the Manpower Services Commission, the Health and Safety Commission, etc., while the 'social contract' between the Labour Government and the unions in the mid-1970s allowed the unions to trade pay restraint in return for agreement by the government to put some of their political objectives at the top of the policy agenda.

From 1976, the fourth medium-term economic programme of the EEC encouraged participation in management's decision-making, and sought greater capital accumulation by workers. This led to the Bullock Report in January 1977, which contained a number of recommendations on participation in decision-making.

MEDIATION

Mediation, in which trade unions and management work together to solve problems, leads to a situation where the joint process can have beneficial effects on work relationships. As Saundry and others (2011: 38) comment:

> . . . the greatest value of mediation could lie in its ability to provide a basis for the renegotiation of working relationships. At a micro level this may mean restarting communications between colleagues in conflict with each other, but at the level of the organization it could recast the traditional adversarial roles adopted by stake-holders within traditional resolution processes.

THE SOCIAL DIMENSION OF THE EUROPEAN UNION

The programme to complete the European internal market aims to remove all the remaining barriers to trade between the members of the EU.

The Single European Act, ratified in 1987, added three obligations to the Treaty of Rome. These covered the harmonization of national provisions to improve the functioning of the labour market, improvements in health and safety of workers, and Article 118B, which stipulates: 'the Commission shall endeavour to develop the dialogue between management and labour at European level'. The Social Dialogue was started in 1987 between the Union of Industries of the European Community (UNICE) and the European Trade Union Confederation (ETUC).

The objectives of the ETUC are to influence governments and European institutions in protecting and furthering workers' interests, which are pursued through the twin routes of collective bargaining and legislation. Formed in 1973, in April 1995 the ETUC had approximately 46 million affiliated members in 22 countries, through national bodies such as the British TUC. The ETUC was an influential body in the discussions that resulted in the Social Protocol at the Maastricht meeting.

The arguments that have been deployed have centred on the need for a 'level playing field' if competition is to be fair. There is a view that poorer Member States might avoid improvements to working conditions in order to take advantage of low wage costs, and that a plinth of social rights is necessary to avoid social dumping. A price competition spiral might ensue, when companies in the richer countries might be tempted to try to reduce costs by reducing pay and social benefits. From this destabilizing price war there would be no winners.

The British Conservative Government was vociferous in opposing the idea of the Social Charter; largely, it seems, for ideological reasons. Having 'freed up' the UK labour market, there was a desire by the British to keep it free of restrictions imposed by what was seen as the Brussels bureaucracy.

The Community Charter of Fundamental Social Rights, published in September 1989, contained 12 sets of 'fundamental rights'. These included, inter alia, rights to social protec-tion, to freedom of association, to vocational education and training, to equality of treatment between men and women, to information, consultation and participation, as well as to health protection.

However, these proposals were not acceptable to the British at the European heads of state meeting in Strasbourg in December 1989, and the original ideas were 'watered down' to become more a matter for guidance than a mandate for action. In practice, many of the proposals (such as equality of treatment between men and women) were already enacted in British law.

At Maastricht, Britain negotiated an opt-out from the provisions of the Social Charter on the grounds that flexibility in the labour market was necessary in order to encourage inward investment and thereby to reduce the massive unemployment in the EU (which was standing at around 18 million people in 1998 from a figure of around 20 million at the time of Maastricht).

Some increases to employees' participation in decision-making have been brought about through the health and safety regulations, where the statutory rights for health and safety committees and the free flow of information to employees was accepted as important; more so, than the enforced adoption of German-style 'co-determination', which was once feared by employers. Irrespective of the objections to formal participation schemes, large modern companies accept the necessity to obtain the agreement of employees to change.

As a result of the opt-out, British employers were originally not required to obey the European Works Council Directive in respect of their UK employees. Following the election of the Labour Government in 1997, the new government decided to end the British opt-out from the Social Charter and to accept the European Works Council (EWC) Directive. Many companies had, in any case, already negotiated EWCs. At least 430 EWC agreements had been concluded by September 1996. For example, United Biscuits, BP, Marks & Spencer had all concluded agreements, the main reason for which being that they had employees working across Europe and therefore not to create an EWC would have resulted in consulta-tion only with their staff based elsewhere in Europe.

It is worth noting here that statutory works councils were already required prior to the directive, in Belgium, France, Luxembourg, the Netherlands, Germany, Greece, Portugal and Spain, and some form of employee representative on most company boards of directors in Denmark, Germany, France, Finland, Luxembourg and Sweden. These representational arrangements do not necessarily have an impact on trade union membership, which varies considerably between countries.

The EWC Directive only applies to undertakings with at least 1000 employees in the EU, and at least 150 employees in at least two countries, whilst central management is responsible for setting up an EWC or a special negotiating body. To establish such a body would require the support of at least 100 employees or their representatives, in two undertakings or more, or from establishments in at least two or more countries.

Those companies that have established EWCs report a number of benefits, in particular greater awareness of business strategy and priorities, an improved understanding of what is happening in different counties, increased trust, encouragement for higher standards in training, communication and consultation, according to research by the IPA, which conducted research in companies including Henkel, Zeneca, ICI, Kone and Générale des Eaux.

A variety of selection procedures are used to find delegates to the EWC, including selection by the union, or through election or some combination of selection and election. The EWCs are allowed to invite experts to their meetings (for example, in connection with health and safety matters).

In the IPA's research into 26 companies, the researchers asked what measures for success they use for EWCs: on both sides, the most common answer was that the EWC could be considered a success if they considered that there had been a real exchange of views in terms of frank and full disclosure of information, informed discussion and executives had listened to and taken on board opinions. Many also hoped that the EWC would break down barriers and improve employee relations.

Revisions to the original directive were made possible under Article 15 of the 1994 Directive. In April 2004 the Commission consulted the EU social partners on measures to enhance the effectiveness of EWCs. The ETUC was in favour of revisions, but Business Europe (previously known as UNICE) was not. Following negotiations, the Commission proposed changes aimed at improving the definitions of 'information' and 'consultation', in order to overcome legal uncertainties, for example, when businesses were being restructured, and to harmonize directives on employee representation. These amendments were adopted by the European Parliament in December 2008.

The new 'recast' directive more clearly defined the information rights of EWCs, differentiated the requirements for information and consultation for EWCs and national bodies, provided a new definition of the transnational matters covered by EWCs, gave a greater role to trade unions, entitled EWC members to training without loss of pay and contained rules on adapting EWCs to structural change in the multinationals concerned.

New EWC agreements declined during this period. This may be because of the recession. Approximately 70 new EWCs were set up each year from 1997–2001, but this number has declined to 30 per year in the 2000s and only 15 were signed in 2010. As at 2012, 1214 EWCs had been established, some at a divisional level. Around 931 multinational companies had an active EWC by the end of 2012.

Because of the increasing pace of change, the consequential importance of gaining commitment is essential. Many large companies have consciously adopted a more participative style, sometimes announced in a statement of the company's philosophy. For example, GEC, GKN and United Biscuits have developed their own ways of dealing with the participation question, through such means as communications exercises, autonomous work groups and committee structures.

PARTNERSHIP

In addition to formal participation or consultation systems, managers also encourage direct forms of participation. The former is seen in the JCC or the EWC, the latter in cases where the manager maintains some control of the decision-making process, for example by delegation, empowerment and involvement schemes.

The notion of 'partnership' has come to be used as a way to describe an approach characterized by a unitary frame of reference, and a strong desire to harness the energy and commitment of employees to the flexibility and change orientation necessary for business survival. The IPA defines the partnership approach as consisting of three elements: a commitment to working together to make the business more successful, understanding the need for both flexibility and security, with policies to address these needs, and relationship-building with the workforce. They cite companies such as Elida Gibbs, Boots, Rover, Blue Circle, John Lewis, Transco, Scottish Power, Thames Water and Welsh Water, as cases where the partnership approach has been developed (IPA 1998a).

The CIPD sees partnership as being 'about particular processes of management, rather than about structures' (CIPD 1997: 8), and argues for a mixture of direct and representational participation. The concept of partnership can be taken further: suppliers and customers could be involved as partners, and the idea of the stakeholder organization implies a long-term agreement to work together for mutual success.

EMPLOYEE SHARE OWNERSHIP

According to the European Federation of Employee Share Ownership (EFES) Survey (2013), the capital held by employees in European companies rose by 32 per cent to €267 billion, this being the same level as just before the financial crash. This increase is slightly misleading, since it is attributable to increases in share price, rather than to any increase in employee share ownership.

However, in 2013, around 30 per cent of all large European companies launched new employee share plans. The survey showed that in 2013, 85 per cent of all large European companies had employee share plans (presumably including share option plans for directors), and 53 per cent had 'broadband' plans for all levels of employees. The UK Government has increased the amounts employees can invest in SIP employee share plans from £500 to £1800 per year, and government approved (Save As You Earn) SAYE employee share plans have also increased the amount that can be invested. The sale of Royal Mail gave employees around a 10 per cent share in the company.

ENGAGEMENT

Much of this chapter has focused on formal mechanisms for achieving participation by employees in the way the organization is run. As modern work life is no longer so dependent on large masses of work people, and the nature of work itself has changed through new technology, there is a search for a more unitary way to ensure a sense of engagement in the work of all in the enterprise, which is less reliant on procedures and gives more emphasis to the sense of attachment to work held by employees. Competitive pressures, it is argued, make a sense of engagement in work by employees essential for corporate performance.

The origins of this concern have already been discussed in Part One of this book, and later in Chapter 17. The ideas behind engagement include the sociological literature on 'attachment to work', for example, in which researchers sought the nature of attachment to work.

For example, Goldthorpe and others (1968: 174) researched whether the behaviours and attitudes of workers were conditioned by the features in the job itself or were more a consequence of their orientation to work. They concluded that workers' attitudes and behaviours were more a consequence of their definition of their own work situation, rather than a response to it. That workers defined 'their work in a largely instrumental manner; that is essentially a means to ends which are extrinsic to their work situation'. This is the backdrop against which employers try to inculcate 'organizational citizenship behaviours'.

The debate on employee engagement has been dogged by the absence of a commonly agreed definition for the term. In their research, McLeod and Clarke (2009) came across 50 different definitions. The Institute for Employment Studies' definition is often quoted as a basis for discussion of the topic:

> A positive attitude held by the employee towards the organization and its values. An engaged employee is aware of the business context, and works with colleagues to improve performance within the job for the benefit of the organization. The organization must work to develop and nurture engagement which requires a two-way relationship between employer and employee.

> (Robinson and others 2004: 2)

There are a number of measurement methods to establish what the engagement status is of the employees in the organization, and what can be done to improve the situation. In the USA, Gallup uses a well established survey tool known as Q12 for this purpose.

Balain and Sparrow (2009: 5) deconstruct the ideas behind the concept of employee engagement. They see the concept of employee engagement deriving from internal marketing, as a means to communicate the need to change, from the performance improvement position, by employees 'self-management' of their activities, and from the understanding of the relationship between employee attitudes and customer service. The significance of understanding the mechanisms by which engagement occurs, and how this influences performance is, they suggest, 'because HR Directors need to "reverse engineer"' what happens in order to create the necessary behaviours to deliver performance.

The concept of engagement seems to be so inclusive that it lacks the specificity needed for HRM to act to create the engagement they desire. The two way aspects of engagement mean the HR director can only create the conditions for engagement to thrive, and start the process off by involving employees through surveys, using their priorities, work shops and designing jobs with them and their managers. The rest will require the company and the workforce to come to understand the value of their work, their work relationships, and to see clearly the mission in which all are engaged.

CONCLUSION

Cooperation between management and workers is essential for success in business, and the way that this is achieved will vary according to the organization, the employee relations situation, the HR strategy, and the attachment the employees have to their employer and their work. There are requirements for formal mechanisms to be adopted across Europe, and the need to share information is increasingly accepted. Engagement offers the possibility that employees can come to adopt organizational citizenship behaviours, with potential performance benefits to the business. This may be seen as part of a wider agenda where management and the workforce act in partnership, according to the principles of democracy in society at large.

QUESTIONS

1   To what extent has the form of participation moved from ascending to descending participation?
2   What are the benefits from joint consultation in companies?
3   Has the social dimension of the European Union introduced useful ways to involve employees in organizational decision-making?

4   It is often argued that employee engagement is an important ingredient for creating a successful business, but do all employees want to be engaged?

REFERENCES

Balain, S. and Sparrow, P. (2009). *Engaged to Perform: A new perspective on employee engagement.* White Paper 09/04 Centre for Performance-Led HR Lancaster University Management School.

Goldthorpe, J. H., Lockwood, D., Bechhofer, F. and Platt, J. (1968). *The Affluent Worker: Industrial Attitudes and Behaviour.* Cambridge University Press.

IPA (1998a). *Sharing the Challenge: Employee Consultation.* A guide to good practice. IPA.

IPA (1998b). *European Worker Councils.* A guide to good practice. IPA.

McLeod, D. and Clarke, N. (2009). *Engaging for Success: enhancing performance through employee engagement.* A Report for Government. Department of Business, Innovation and Skills July. Crown Copyright.

Robinson, D., Perryman, S. and Hayday, S. (2004). *The Drivers of Employee Engagement.* Institute of Employment Studies Report 408.

Saundry, R., McArdle, L. and Thomas, P. (2011). *Transforming Conflict Management in the Public Sector? Mediation, Trade Unions and Partnerships in a Primary Care Trust.* Research Paper Ref: 01/11 London: ACAS.

Walker, K. (1977). *Worker Participation in Management: problems, practices, and prospects.* Bulletin of the International Institute of Labour Studies. Geneva.

22 WELLBEING AT WORK

INTRODUCTION

This chapter concentrates on the 'human' aspects of human resource management. This is taken to be at the heart of the subject, as has been shown throughout this book. In the last chapter, we examined the growing interest in the idea of employee engagement, and early on, the importance of leadership, team working, organizational citizenship behaviour, the psychological contract and the employee value proposition. In this chapter, the focus is on the employee's sense of wellbeing within the context of relationships and the work arrangements where the employee is located. The importance of the topic of wellbeing at work stems from the significance of how people feel about their managers, supervisors and colleagues, all of which is affected by the employee's sense of wellbeing.

We will begin by defining 'wellbeing', before going on to consider the significance and impact on HRM, the extent to which there is a sense of wellbeing at work, and the HR policies which are used to influence this aspect of working life.

DEFINITIONS OF WELLBEING

The World Health Organization (WHO 1948) defines health in the preamble to its constitution in a broad way, encompassing all aspects of physical and mental health: 'Health is a state of complete physical, mental and social wellbeing and not merely the absence of disease or infirmity'. The realization that health and wellbeing are integrated topics is already established, therefore. One should also note that the implications from the WHO definition are that perceptions of the person's own state of wellbeing are central to understanding their health.

In Cynthia Fisher's (2010) review of the notion of 'happiness at work', she argues that happiness at work goes beyond job satisfaction, and that a more comprehensive picture is necessary, which should include organizational commitment, job involvement, engagement, morale and task satisfaction. The use of phrases such as employee 'mood' and 'enjoyment' are seen as an aspect of happiness at work. Happiness and wellbeing amongst employees is seen as depending upon employees experiencing what she describes as a positive affective experience of work, a sense of 'thriving and vigour', 'vitality and energy'. From her analysis of a number of measures of intrinsic motivation, she includes mood-based measures, for example, 'anxiety versus contentment' and 'depression versus enthusiasm' (Warr 1990: 397). She points to the significance of organizational context, and to the personal agendas of individual employees, which are very likely to influence mood and any sense of vitality. As regards the work context, she states: 'Individuals are happier when embedded in a work environment that matches their values and goals, and that meets their needs and preferences'.

THE SIGNIFICANCE OF WELLBEING FOR HRM

Much of what has been covered in this book seems to be consistent with the explanations of wellbeing found in the literature. In particular, the ideas of employee commitment, engagement and job satisfaction are all seen to enhance employee wellbeing, provided the context is supportive, and always subject to the effect of individual differences and group processes, as we discussed in Chapters 1 and 2. In addition, in the UK employers owe their employees a common law duty of care. This means that employers must take reasonable care to safeguard the health, safety and wellbeing of their employees.

However, we should be careful not to jump immediately to the conclusion that a sense of wellbeing naturally results in high performance. Nor is it possible to ensure the organizational context automatically favours the values and preferences possessed by all employees. Organizational stakeholders include a range of people, with their own needs and preferences. Creating cultures to order is a tough assignment for any HR function since cultures emerge from the interactions between the people in the company, and the contextual variables which are dependent on structure, size, customers and the priorities of the times. Designing a culture is as much a matter of circumstances and 'the hand of fate' as it is a social science task. HR policies and practices can and do create the context, but the meaning of that context is for the employees to interpret. Even if the company wanted to socially engineer the cultural context, such an approach would be inimical to policies and the values associated with participative management approaches, employee involvement, upward communication and any attempts to deal with the various interests pluralistically. Nevertheless, companies are proud of their cultures and do have values that underpin their brands and their style of working, which are one aspect of their competitive advantage over other rival companies.

THE REALITY OF WORKING LIFE

To what extent are organizations creating a sense of wellbeing for employees? Recent evidence seems to indicate that there are differences between the perceptions of employees and those of management. One online survey of 200 HR managers showed that 66 per cent of employers made the connection between wellbeing and employee engagement, and 33 per cent said they had a wellbeing strategy. However, although 47 per cent thought the health and wellbeing of their employees were both good, 40 per cent of employees scored low on health and levels of energy at work (Newcombe 2012). In a large-scale survey in 2013, the CIPD showed the proportion of UK staff who felt engaged at work to be 55 per cent in the voluntary sector, 37 per cent in the private sector, and 33 per cent in the public sector (Stevens 2013).

In the same article there are examples of well known companies acknowledging their understanding of the importance of employee engagement. The stories of how engagement is related to organizational performance are also here, in companies such as Marks & Spencer, Whitbread and Sainsbury. If the levels of engagement in UK companies were typically below 50 per cent as stated, then we must presume these are atypical organizations.

One reason behind the differences between the rhetoric and the reality of working life resides in the changing nature of work. The last few years have seen a massive increase in what is sometimes called 'contingent labour'. As we described in Chapter 8, these are the part-time, casual, temporary and sub-contracted jobs, which have increased dramatically, partly because of the growing number of low level service sector jobs and also as a consequence of the drive to reduce costs and to outsource such jobs if this is a cheaper option. This is also because modern ways of working lead to employers requiring some parts of their labour force to be available instantly, in response to customers' demand. The number of people on zero hour contracts has grown to around one million people (Churchard 2014).

In their study of flexible working practices and performance, de Menezes and Kelliher (2011) showed that different flexible working arrangements had different performance effects. For example, they showed that flexible arrangements may reduce turnover rates, but this depends on the circumstances of the individual employee (for example, post-natal retention in employment was improved through more flexible working arrangements). Flexible working arrangements are associated with reduced levels of absenteeism, but the linkage to improved productivity is not always found. There seemed to be some evidence that the greater the number of flexible working arrangements available, the less stress there was amongst the workforce. However, remote working was associated with stress, but even this is not straightforward (for example, the stress of travel to work is reduced by the opportunity to work more flexible hours, and to work at home, but role conflict in remote working results in stress). Some aspects of stress arising from working reduced hours arise because women working reduced hours feel guilty with increased anxiety. Scheduled flexibility resulted in improved employee wellbeing, but this may depend on whether variability is under company control, or if flexibility is under the control of the worker.

Research by Cambridge University showed that flexible working practices could damage employee health (Churchard 2014). The study, based on UK and US supermarkets, showed that part-time contracts, including zero hours contracts, provided no security of guaranteed working hours, and this forced workers to undertake overtime in order to survive. According to the report, the system of 'labour matching' meant managers rearranged shifts to meet customer demands so that staff who normally worked 'key time' (a limited core of hours) were asked to work extra hours at only 24 hours' notice. This unpredictability resulted in uncertainty and anxiety about hours and income.

Call centres have also been cited as work contexts where stress and anxiety are generated by the working arrangements. Although there are, of course, different kinds of call centres, including those where there are staff involved in problem-solving using expertise, it is the more routine type of centre dealing with routine transactions where there is likely to be a stressful working environment. In these call centres employees are engaged in transactional activity, with little discretion: for example, work is closely monitored and workers follow a standardized script. There are targets and sometimes group or individual bonuses adding to the pressure. The studies have shown that in addition there is often abuse from customers, and workers had to act out their calls to customers from the script, to appear genuine, causing further anxiety (Russell 2008).

These detailed examples can be seen as cases of work intensification. In addition, the casualization of work for some occupations has produced a growing underclass of people moving in and out of work, so they and their families feel a degree of impermanence, affecting their income, status, housing and the education of their children. These conditions may well lead to family breakdown. In the UK, the 'Living Wage Commission' was set up by the Joseph Rowntree Foundation (a charity), to monitor the amount of poverty associated with low pay. They claim there were 5.2 million jobs in the UK paid less than the living wage of £8.80 per hour in London, and £7.45 per hour elsewhere in 2014.

Many of these people were receiving welfare benefits, although at work in low paid jobs, so that the state was effectively subsidizing the employer (Living Wage Commission 2014). The difficulty then becomes what is known as the poverty trap, where the person is unable to increase earnings without losing benefits and, unless the increase in earnings is substantial, would also lose out to the tax increase. People in these circumstances often resort to short-term loans at very high interest rates from money lenders, which increases the individual's vulnerability.

During the recessionary years, following the financial crash of 2008/10, there were reports of increased levels of stress, clinical depression, increased bullying and heart attacks (Parry and Tyson 2014). The CIPD (the UK professional association of HR specialists) and the Society for Human Resource Management (the US association for specialists in HRM in the field), reported record levels of stress in the work place. Sickness absence levels fell during the recession, and 'presenteeism' was said to have risen. HRM has a range of policies that are designed to influence these aspects of working life, which are considered in the next section.

HR POLICIES RELATED TO ILLNESS INCLUDING STRESS

Sick pay

The fear of losing earnings through sickness absence haunted workers until social security and sickness schemes were introduced.

The main rules regarding statutory sick pay (SSP) are that employers pay SSP where there is an entitlement for up to 28 weeks to employees who are sick for at least four days consecutively (including weekends and bank holidays). Entitlement is determined by the following:

1   SSP is paid for whole days (not parts of days).
2   Employees must comply with the employer's rules regarding notification of absence.
3   Payment is only made for the fourth and any subsequent qualifying days.
4   A period of entitlement begins with the first day of incapacity to work and ends when the first of any of the following events occurs: SSP is exhausted, the incapacity period ends, the employee is in prison, the contract of employment ends, or the maximum period of entitlement (three years) is reached.
5   There are special rules regarding pregnancy, invalidity pensions and trade disputes.

Absenteeism

Unscheduled absences from work give rise to serious management problems. Planning is brought to nothing by the absence of a significant number of the workforce.

The costs of absences in the public sector in the UK were brought to the public notice in the Chancellor of the Exchequer's Spending Review in 2004. This invited the Department of Work and Pensions to examine the management of long-term sickness absence. The figures showed that the public sector lost around 10/11 days per annum, compared to the average for the private sector of around 8.5 days, costing the tax payer around £4 billion a year.

The private sector has also taken absenteeism seriously. Tesco, for example, reported that in 2002 average absence ran at 7.2 per cent per annum. Missing employees were putting extra pressure on those who did attend. Consequently, a new programme was introduced: 'supporting your attendance' aimed at giving managers the leadership skills to manage relationships and the absence process, as well as how to be more flexible in planning time off with staff, and in job design, and to involve staff in absence reduction. Policy initiatives included 'welcome back meetings' and 'attendance review meetings'. Whilst management initially took a flexible approach to each case, a harder line would be taken if absences continued.

Sick-pay schemes are sometimes blamed for influencing those who are not genuinely ill to stay at home, because the threat of loss of earnings has been removed. However, the subject is more complicated than it may appear. There may be more illness among certain groups of workers because of the nature of their work. The more junior personnel may have to take days off for spurious illnesses, since, unlike their senior counterparts, they are more stringently supervised and can only attend to personal problems in this way. Although it is easy to accuse someone of malingering if he or she takes a number of single days off for rather unconvincing reasons, the person concerned may be under some form of stress or simply has a general feeling of unease, tiredness and fatigue. Absenteeism may also be a safety valve preventing serious industrial unrest, as it allows individuals a way of expressing a token protest.

There are more clearly identified trends in absenteeism. Alcoholism is a significant cause of absences on Mondays. There are occupational reasons for illnesses, drivers often suffer from ulcers and digestive complaints and 'jet lag' has come to be accepted as a reason for absence for globe-trotting executives, for example. The stress of each job is not obvious to outside observers. The overall effect of these factors is to put pressure on employers to curb sickness absence.

Alongside welfare reform the Coalition Government in the UK, in the period 2010–2015, produced an initiative: 'Coordinating Health and Work and Well-being Initiative', which was aimed at helping people with a health condition to stay in work or to return to work. This was to be achieved by the creation of a new health and work service. After four weeks of sickness absence, the employee will be referred by the doctor (GP) for an assessment by an occupation health professional. There will also be occupational health advice to the GPs.

Stress

'Stress' is a genetic term for a whole area of problems arising from physical and psychological reactions to perceived challenges or threats to wellbeing, which are beyond the subject's normal capacity to meet. There are physical symptoms of stress, such as high blood pressure, eating disorders, sleeplessness, irritability and so on. The extent to which the person affected is feeling adverse reactions to a stressor will be mediated by the perception of the stressor, the individual's personality type, the degree of control over the situation felt by the subject and the coping style adopted.

Many people will experience some mental difficulties in a lifetime. It is estimated that around 20 per cent of people will suffer a major depressive episode in their lifetime (that is, lasting two weeks or more), 15 per cent will suffer from some kind of anxiety disorder, 33 per cent have had at least one panic attack and 11 per cent have suffered from some kind of phobia. There is growing evidence that illnesses such as immune system problems (for example, opportunistic infections and allergies), some cardiovascular disease, memory loss and even sexual dysfunction have a stress-related element. 'Burn out' symptoms, such as irritability, persistent sense of failure, blame or guilt, feelings of discouragement, lack of concentration, rigid thinking, suspicion of others and social isolation can be traced often to a long exposure to stressful situations.

Those with mental ill-health problems are often frightened to reveal their difficulties to others, so great is the stigma and, where stress is obvious, research has shown that 38 per cent of people with mental health problems reported being teased, harassed or intimidated at work (Reed and Baker 1996). Work intensification has recently been seen as one cause of increasing reports of stress. The most highly rated causes named often are time pressures, tight deadlines, work overload, threat of job losses and lack of consultation (Cooper/TUC 1997).

There is now a legal requirement to deal effectively with work-related stress (as demonstrated in *Walker v Northumberland County Council* [1995] IRLR 35 (QB)) and millions of working days are lost each year due to stress-related illness.

Corporate reactions to these kinds of problems include employee assistance programmes, which are run by external organizations and are entirely confidential, where employees can talk to counsellors who are independent of the company. These are run in such a way very often that there is a system whereby serious issues such as harassment can be brought to senior management's attention without any middle management blocks. Best practice in encouraging employee wellbeing includes better occupational health policies and health education relating to eating, exercise habits and stress reduction, often conducted in workshops (see the companion website for more details: www.routledge. com/cw/tyson). A number of companies have developed extensive and well regarded programmes (for example the Astra Zeneca 'Calm' programme, and the Marks & Spencer 'Managing Pressure' programme).

OCCUPATIONAL HEALTH

There have been occupational health initiatives since Dr Thomas Legge's appointment as the first Medical Inspector of Factories and Workshops in 1898. These include the following:

- comprehensive health and safety legislation, which has also been actively promoted by the European Union
- concept of risk assessment firmly established in practice
- increased professional standing and organization of occupational health disciplines, including medical (organized through the faculty of occupational medicine, as a part of the Royal College of Physicians) nursing, ergonomics, etc
- greater expansion of the general bio medical science base
- widespread public and media interest
- greater access to sources of information, including via the internet
- widespread use of employee assistance programmes.

The Health and Safety Commission is constantly pushing forward the frontiers; witness the code of practice on stress at work. Nevertheless, organizations do not often invest in their own medical officer, so there is a danger that HR staff may not always have access to medical opinion trained in employment matters if they rely on reports from the person's doctor (GP), rather than use specialist occupational health advice.

If managers are fretting about malingering, they must separate out the genuinely sick from those who are not genuinely ill. Illness has no precise definition; it is, therefore, best left for managers and supervisors to deal with individual cases with the help of occupational health specialists and HR managers if necessary. Perhaps the most useful approach is to try to create conditions under which employees want to go to work and look forward to the experience rather than fear or dislike it.

OUTPLACEMENT

There is now extensive use of outplacement for those made redundant. This consists of the provision of special counselling and help through the transition, as well as the creation of a job search strategy for the individual affected. Approximately 75 per cent of companies in the UK use either external (consultancy-based) outplacement or internally provided outplacement services. These are in various forms, from one-to-one counselling and help (often for executives) down to group schemes for shop-floor workers. There is a burgeoning outplacement industry in the USA, as well as in other parts of Europe and the UK. The objective, from the employer's point of view, is to ease the pain of redundancy by including outplacement in the package, and also to demonstrate to the 'survivors' (those who remain after their colleagues have been made redundant) an acceptable level of care in order to maintain the motivation and morale of the survivors who are a key group in any restructuring.

WELFARE POLICIES

Personnel management originated, in part, from the early welfare workers of the 1890s to 1918. With the growth of employment management from the 1930s, specialist welfare departments have become only adjuncts to the main HR department. The welfare role has moved into specialist services, and has also become more diffuse in its general applicability.

The management of people now brings managers into contact with a huge variety of personnel problems and organizational issues, ranging from drug abuse, alcoholism and AIDS, to overwork, stress and problems arising from single parenthood, care of the elderly and interpersonal disputes.

Drug abuse is becoming a major problem. Specialist assistance and care is needed to help people with a drug addiction but, before that can be provided, line managers and HR staff have to manage the referral of employees to the appropriate agencies, as well as manage the communications issues with the people in the organization about the absence in such a way that this does not make a return to work difficult.

THE WELFARE ROLE OF THE MANAGER

All managers have a welfare role to perform for their staff. The immediate line manager or supervisor will be first to notice the signs that an individual has a problem, for example poor performance, absence, sickness and difficulties in relationships will be seen by the perceptive manager, who should be conscious of the importance of a sense of wellbeing for the achievement of results.

Such an approach by managers does mean that they see themselves as helpers to their staff. Helping in this sense is being supportive, problem-solving with subordinates and constantly seeking ways to make the employee successful. In the case of such a manager–subordinate relationship, personal problems and sickness, for example, will be problems the subordinate will want to share and, if it is feasible, to seek help in solving.

There will be occasions when expert assistance is required. The skill for the manager in his or her welfare role, therefore, has two aspects. He or she must be able to diagnose with the employee what the problem is and, if possible, help to solve it, and he or she must be able to persuade the employee that expert help is required where necessary.

COUNSELLING AT WORK

The first stage in seeking help is the 'counselling interview'. This kind of interview requires a problem-solving approach. To apply this technique, experience and training are needed, but the following outline gives an impression:

1   *The identification of the problem*: this requires a non-directive approach, using open-ended questions which allow the problem holder to explain his or her problem, listening and *not* offering advice or evaluative comments. The manager or welfare officer must remain neutral at this stage. To allow the employee to talk about topics that are highly sensitive, it is important that he or she be given time to think and express him or herself thus silences should be allowed, and techniques for opening up the problem should be used, for example, 'reflecting back' key phrases to elicit some further expansion of the issues raised.

2   *The conditions under which the problem occurs*: by exploring the conditions under which the person experiences the problem, the 'boundaries' of the problem can be found. If the conditions changed, would the problem change? The 'conditions' include the feelings of the person whose problem it is. These feelings are facts. By allowing problem holders to reveal what their own feelings are, they will come to accept their own part in the problem. Active help that a supervisor might contemplate to alleviate problems could include changes within the job, relieving pressures for a temporary period, getting the subordinate to use his or her workmates in helping to resolve a problem.

3   *Solutions to problems will only be real solutions if the person who believes there is a problem also believes in the solution*: it is most likely that people will believe in the solution if they put it forward. They should therefore be encouraged by the manager to do so, and a useful role for the manager is to get the subordinate to evaluate his or her own solutions rationally.

4   *Where a problem is identified which requires expert help*: this switches the focus to the problem of how to achieve a fruitful conjunction between the problem holder and the expert agency (e.g. drug addiction centres, marriage guidance, etc.). Various types of supportive behaviour will assist, for example, giving time off, respecting confidentiality, accompanying a nervous person on the first visit, in some cases, or at least ensuring the person has a friend to support them.

It is clear from the above rather brief account of counselling that there is a difference between 'counselling' and 'discipline'. The distinction is in the concept of discipline that the manager possesses. If he or she believes that the employee can change him or herself then the counselling role is appropriate. Only when this has been tried and failed should he or she move into the discipline procedure (see Chapter 20).

SPECIALIST WELFARE ROLES

Specialist welfare officers can offer a unique role. Where they are neither part of senior management nor within the employee groups, they can portray a kind of neutrality which makes them valuable as helpers in the wider social problems that society faces. The personal problems experienced are sometimes so serious that they need to be discussed with someone outside the chain of command. For the person with problems of alcoholism, or whose children are in trouble, for example, the neutral welfare officer may also have useful contacts with outside help. Their specialized experience will also enable them to recognize problems more readily. The most productive arrangement is where there are well trained, sympathetic line supervisors and an experienced welfare officer. Given a mutual desire to help employees, much can be accomplished by these two working together.

'ORGANIZATIONAL HEALTH' STATISTICS

Organizational statistics serve two very important functions: they provide essential information about main areas affecting the general state of the organization at a particular time; they also indicate trends that need to be made apparent, so that timely measures may be taken to improve conditions of work and performance. The main statistics that normally need to be kept are briefly described below:

1   *The state of the labour force*, that is, the number actually employed as against the budget, or establishment, figure. This needs to be for a specific period, and we will assume that this is *one year* in the ratios below. We discussed labour turnover in Chapter 7 on workforce planning. In addition, statistics on labour stability and on a variety of other indicators should be routinely examined.

2   *Timekeeping/attendance*: ratio:

$$\frac{\text{Number of person hours lost} \times 100}{\text{Total possible person hours worked}}$$

3   *Accidents* (including types): ratio for frequency:

$$\frac{\text{Number of lost time accidents} \times 100}{\text{Number of person hours worked}}$$
(There are 100,000 total of hours in an average working life.)

4   *Health* (including types of illness): sickness statistics, showing average length of absence.
5   *Records of reports of bullying, harassment* or similar incidents, by department.

These statistics need to be broken down into departments, locations, occupations, grades, sex, age groups and, where applicable, causes. The requirements of the Data Protection Act 1998 should be kept in mind.

CONCLUSIONS

The issues raised by employee wellbeing policies and the HR activities in response to cope with the effects of work intensification, and the demands of the 24/7 society mean that HRM has to ensure there are policies and practices to reduce anxiety, to treat stress and to institute an organization culture which enables high performance. The EVP, talent management and total rewards, employee engagement and coherent industrial relations policies are all aiming to construct such an enabling culture. The tension HR has to deal with, between the content of HR policies and the processes for embedding them in the culture are critical for success. Introducing changes into an organization without trying to socially engineer this in an age of engagement, with a participative approach is the task.

To do this, HR managers need to produce an outline content of policies and to agree a process for bringing change about, whilst allowing full participation of the work force in the process. This approach allows the details of how to create a resilient and supportive culture to be worked through, whilst setting out with clarity the purpose.

QUESTIONS

1   How is the concept of wellbeing different from the concept of employee welfare?
2   Why is the wellbeing of employees considered an important topic in managing people?
3   How is employee 'stress' defined, and why has it become such an important issue in the wellbeing of employees?
4   What kinds of policies are considered useful in dealing with stress?
5   Is there a link between the employee sense of wellbeing and employee engagement?

REFERENCES

Churchard, C. (2014). 'Zero hours "tip of iceberg" of flexible working abuse'. *People Management Magazine online*. 22 April 2014.

Cooper (1997). In Arnold, H. (ed) 'Crisis talks'. *Personnel Today*. October, 29–32.

Fisher, C. (2010). 'Happiness at Work'. *International Journal of Management Reviews* 12, 4: 384–412.

Menezes de, L. and Kelliher, C. (2011). 'Flexible working and performance: a systematic review of the evidence for a business case'. *International Journal of Management Reviews* 13, 4: 452–74.

Miller, D. M., Lipsedge. M. and Litchfield, P. (2002). *Work and Mental Health – an Employers' Guide*. Gaskill & Faculty of Occupational Medicine. The Royal College of Psychiatrists.

Newcombe, T. (2012). 'Companies failing on employee well-being strategy'. *HR Magazine* www.hrmagazine.co.uk.

Parry, E. and Tyson, S. (2014). *Managing People in a Contemporary Context*. Abingdon, Oxford: Routledge.

Read, J. and Baker, S. (1996). 'Not just sticks and stones'. *Mind*. November.

Rowntree Trust (2014). *Living Wage Commission*. Interim Report.

Russell, B. (2008). 'Call centre: a decade of research' *International Journal of Management Research* 10, 3:195–219.

Warr, P. (1990). 'The measurement of well-being and other aspects of mental health'. *Journal of Occupational Psychology* 63 193–210.

World Health Organization (1986). Constitution of the World Health Organization. In *Basic Documents*, 36th edn WHO Geneva p. 1.

PART SEVEN

EMPLOYMENT LAW

23 INSTITUTIONAL FRAMEWORKS FOR EMPLOYMENT LAW

INTRODUCTION

Legal rules represent the power of the state, acting through the institutions that sustain society. The growth of employment law as a significant topic in human resource management reflects the way that regulation has entered into most aspects of the employment relationship. Employment laws underpin many aspects of HR policies. The way the employment relationship is managed is at the heart of the employment contract between employer and employee. Employment law plays an important role in protecting the legitimate interests of individuals and of organizations, in ensuring fairness in treatment, protecting individuals and their representatives from harm as a consequence of their work, stipulating the responsibilities of employers and of employees and embodying social values. Legislation is devised in a particular historical context to meet the challenges of the time. It must, therefore, always be subject to review and there will always be new interpretations made by courts and tribunals. In this chapter, the institutional framework of regulation in the UK is set out, including the role of the relevant European institutions, and there is some exploration of the concept of an international convergence in laws and of the complexities involved.

Laws are made by Acts of Parliament (statutes) and by statutory instruments (regulations) where there is enabling legislation. In addition, the UK is subject to the Treaty of Rome and to the delegated legislation of the European Commission and the Council of Ministers. European law is given precedence over the laws of individual Member States in the European Union. The European Court of Justice (ECJ) defines European law. The final court of appeal in a Member State can refer cases to the ECJ for interpretation, and individuals or groups can challenge Member States about their interpretation of European law in the EC.

A number of institutions have come into being in the UK to help the interpretation and to administer the law and give advice to management, workers and trade unions.

ADVISORY, CONCILIATION AND ARBITRATION SERVICE (ACAS)

ACAS promulgates codes of practice and offers an advisory service and researches employee relations, and offers training seminars and conferences. It aims to improve organizations and working life through better employment relations. The possible forms of intervention by ACAS include:

■ conciliation (attempts to get both parties together)
■ mediation (offers grounds for settlement)
■ arbitration (assists in appointment of one or more arbitrators).

ACAS is also involved in individual cases of conciliation, before complaints by individual employees are heard by a tribunal and, where the parties agree to their involvement, settle disputes by arbitrating in unfair dismissal, and other types of employment claims, under the Employment Rights (Dispute Resolution) Act 1998.

CENTRAL ARBITRATION COMMITTEE (CAC)

The CAC was established under the 1975 Employment Protection Act. The Committee has, in addition to the chair and 11 deputy chairpersons, 23 employer and 21 worker representatives. It replaced the old industrial court, and is a permanent tribunal which deals with referrals on voluntary arbitration in trade disputes, trade union recognition, disclosure of information to trade unions for collective bargaining purposes, resolving complaints under the Information and Consultation Regulations 2004 and from the disputes procedures of a number of organizations. The CAC can play an important role in arranging trade union recognition agreements under the Employment Relations Act 1999. Central Arbitration Committee awards are published and take effect as part of the contracts of employment of those employees covered by the award.

EMPLOYMENT TRIBUNALS

The industrial tribunals were renamed 'employment tribunals' in 1998, and exist throughout the UK to deal with most of the cases that are brought under the statutes relating to employment. Tribunals also have jurisdiction in employment-related contractual disputes, but can only award up to £25,000. These tribunals are intended to be informal, consisting of a legally qualified employment Judge and two members, one selected from an employers' panel, the other selected from a trade union panel. Evidence is given on oath, witnesses are called and legal representation of the contending parties is permitted. The decision by the tribunal is legally binding. However, tribunal decisions can be challenged either by reconsideration (within 14 days of the decision being sent out, or 14 days of the date on which written reasons were sent out, if later) or by appeal (within 42 days of the decision, containing written reasons, being sent out. Where the decision does not contain written reasons, they must be requested from the tribunal within 14 days of the date on which the judgement was sent out and an appeal must then be lodged within 42 days of the date on which the written reasons are sent out).

The power of review enables an employment tribunal to rehear the whole or part of a case if there has been some administrative error leading to the wrong decision by tribunal staff, or if a party did not receive notice of the proceedings, or a decision has been made in the absence of a person entitled to be heard, or there is important new evidence or, more generally, 'in the interests of justice'.

Following the growth of the number of tribunal cases, the Employment Tribunal System Task Force was set up in 2001 to review the way tribunals operated. The Employment Act 2002 contained statutory dismissal and disciplinary procedures (DDP) and statutory grievance procedures (GP), which were later modified, and replaced by an approach which was aimed at encouraging potential claimants to use internal procedures before taking cases to a tribunal. The repeal of statutory grievance and discipline procedures followed the Gibbons Report of March 2007 and the Employment Bill of December 2007. This repealed the statutory procedures, placing reliance on the ACAS Statutory Code, which emphasizes written policies, prompt consistent action, unbiased investigation and decisions.

Both of these reviews have been mostly aimed at encouraging potential claimants to use internal procedures before taking a case to tribunal. Statistics from the tribunal system show a reduction of 26 per cent in claims, from 2004 to 2005, which has continued, so that during 2011/12 there was a 15 per cent fall in claims, partly as a consequence of the accent on conciliation, and perhaps also as a side effect from the recession. In 2012/13 there was roughly an 80:20 split between non-discrimination cases and those alleging some form of discrimination. Of the non-discrimination cases, 19.61 per cent were about unfair dismissal, 18.74 per cent breach of contract, and 10.55 per cent failure to pay redundancy pay. Of all cases 18.77 per cent were allowed, others either not proceeding for some reason or being dismissed. Around one-third of all cases were resolved by conciliation.

An employment Judge may make a default Judgement if the employer (or other respondent, which in discrimination claims can be an individual employee of the employer) fails to comply with the relevant time limit for making a response (28 days from the date on which the tribunal sends a copy of the claim to the respondent(s)), or if a response is not accepted, and no application for the decision to be reviewed has been made. In the circumstances, the default Judgement may decide liability.

Tribunals have been granted case management powers to require the attendance of witnesses, for documents to be produced, to extend time limits or for witness statements to be prepared. Employment Judges may hold a preliminary hearing, which includes types of hearings that were formerly known as case management discussions (to deal with these timetabling and case management issues) and pre-hearing reviews to determine preliminary matters, for instance to order a deposit against a party continuing a case despite their case being considered weak, to consider any oral or written evidence and to strike out a claim considered to be 'scandalous, or vexatious or has no reasonable prospect of success'. Under the current Employment Tribunals (Constitution and Rules of Procedure) Regulations 2013 (see below), the scope of preliminary hearings is dealt with under rule 53.

A further review of tribunal rules and consultation led by Mr Justice Underhill (a former President of the EAT), produced more changes to the tribunal rules effective from July 2013. These regulations replaced the Employment Tribunals (Constitution and Rules of Procedure) Regulations 2004. The overriding objective of the new rules is to enable employment tribunals to deal with cases fairly and justly. Dealing with a case in this way includes:

- ensuring that the parties are on an equal footing
- dealing with cases in ways which are proportionate to the complexity and importance of the issues
- avoiding unnecessary formality and seeking flexibility in the proceedings
- avoiding delay, so far as compatible with proper consideration of the issues
- saving expense.

Those involved in proceedings are advised that: 'the parties and their representatives shall assist the Tribunal to further the over-riding objective and in particular shall co-operate generally with each other and with the Tribunal'.

The parties are also encouraged wherever it is practicable and appropriate to use the services of ACAS or by agreement. Two or more claimants may make their claims on the same claim form, provided their claims are based on the same set of facts.

There are provisions covering irregularities, non-compliance and reasons for rejecting claims at the outset. There are conditions under which claimants and respondents can apply for a 'reconsideration' of a decision not to accept a claim or a response by the tribunal. There is also a mechanism within the tribunal rules for applications for extension of time for presenting the response.

Once the claim and response have been lodged, there is an initial process of sifting, when the employment Judge may order a party to provide more information if needed. Some claims (or parts of claims) may be struck out at this stage, for example if there is no reasonable prospect of success or the claim is outside the jurisdiction of the tribunal (for instance, because it has been presented outside the statutory limitation period). If part of the claim or response is permitted to stand, the Judge will make a case management order. If a party gets through the sift stage, and an allegation either in the claim or response has little chance of success, that party may be ordered to pay a deposit not exceeding £1000, as a condition of continuing with the case. If the fee or deposit is not paid, and no remission application has been presented, the claim will be dismissed.

The tribunal is not bound by any rule of law concerning the admissibility of evidence in court proceedings. A hearing may be conducted in whole or in part by electronic communications, including by telephone, provided the public attending can hear the evidence also. Tribunals may order that a preliminary hearing be treated as a final hearing, or vice versa. Where a claim has been withdrawn, the tribunal issues a judgement dismissing it, so that the claimant may not commence a further claim based on the same or substantially the same complaint, unless the claimant reserves the right to bring it later for a legitimate reason or the tribunal believes that such a continuance would be in the interests of justice. Agreement may be by the consent of the two parties.

A tribunal may reconsider it on its own initiative, or after a request from the Employment Appeal Tribunal, or on the application of a party, in the interests of justice.

Parties may be represented at a tribunal by a lawyer or by a lay person. The costs incurred are defined as fees, charges, expenses, including witnesses' expenses incurred in attending a tribunal hearing. Tribunals may make cost orders or a time preparation order. A tribunal may decide that a party is entitled to one order or the other, but may defer until a later stage in the proceedings to decide which order to make where it considers a party has acted vexatiously, abusively, disruptively or otherwise unreasonably in bringing the proceedings or in the way they were conducted. As regards amounts:

1   A costs order may be made to pay the receiving party the whole or part of the costs, not exceeding £20,000, the amount being decided by the county court, or its equivalent in Scotland, or by an employment tribunal Judge.
2   The Judge may order the reimbursement of all or part of the tribunal fee, and a specified amount of expenses, or if the two parties agree, to a specific amount.
3   The Judge may order the paying party to pay another party or a witness a specified amount in respect of necessary and reasonably incurred expenses.
4   The costs of the lay representative's fees must not exceed £33 per hour (to be increased by £1 per hour each April).

Amounts charged to the paying party for 2–4 above may be in addition to the £20,000 maximum.

EMPLOYMENT APPEAL TRIBUNAL

Appeals against a tribunal's decisions are permissible on points of law to the Employment Appeal Tribunal (EAT), which also has the same review powers as an employment tribunal. Employment Appeal Tribunal appeals are normally heard by a High Court judge and two or four lay persons (although a judge may sit alone if the appeal arises from an employment tribunal decision where only the employment Judge was involved). The EAT may also hear appeals on fact under the Trade Union and Labour Relations (Consolidation) Act 1992 concerning entry on the list of trade unions and issues related to the certificate of independence of trade unions. The EAT has also adopted more stringent rules concerning documentation, and a process for quickly disposing of unmeritorious appeals, in the interest of their overriding objective to ensure cases are dealt with justly, saving expense, dealing with cases expeditiously and fairly.

INTERNATIONAL DIMENSIONS

Law in the UK is influenced by membership of the European Union. The European Court of Justice (ECJ) is the Court where day-to-day issues of justice would be referred. The European Court of Human Rights (ECtHR) deals with applications that affect national judgements, concerning the European Convention on Human Rights (ECHR), to which the UK along with other governments, is a signatory; for example Article 11 of the Convention, which protects the right of an individual to freedom of association.

The account of employment law here is largely in the UK context. However, the internationalization of business and the complexities arising from trading across geographical boundaries mean there is a need to understand employment law in the overlapping jurisdictions where people work. The institutions that administer the law are no longer necessarily in the single country where work is done.

Recent disputes between European institutions and British courts are a sign of this trend. Amongst a number of cases, there are the instances where individuals have sought redress when they believed their human rights were violated in some way by their employer. Here, the employer is arguing that certain actions of the employee are in contravention of a corporate rule, or will negatively affect the relationship between the company and its customers. For example, in the case of an airline employee, in which a Christian woman wished to display a crucifix to show her religious belief whilst wearing her uniform. Management said this was in contravention of its rules. Here, the ECtHR had to balance the individual's rights to freedom of conscience and religious belief, which were weighed against the potential impact on customers, their perceptions of service providers, and the impact on other team members. The ECtHR ruled that what is protected is the right to manifest religious belief in the work place. 'Manifestation' was defined as 'the public display of emotion or feeling or something spiritual or theoretical made real', to determine whether or not what is being manifested is a genuine religion or belief, which is a weighty and substantial aspect of human behaviour. The belief must have attained a certain level of seriousness, cogency and importance and be worthy of respect in a democratic society. It must not be incompatible with human dignity, and not conflict with the fundamental rights of others. The manifestation of the belief must be intimately linked to religion, even if it is not mandated by it. From these reasons we can see how the criteria for making management decisions on employee behaviour are predetermined from European decisions.

Drawing conclusions from comparisons between countries is of necessity imprecise. The context of jurisdictions is complex and particular to the histories and societal, economic and institutional differences of countries. This no doubt pushes international courts to find rationales for decisions that are as context free as possible.

This is well illustrated in the USA. The mixture of federal and state laws on HR issues adds enormously to complexity and compliance difficulties for multi-state employers in the USA. There are many areas where it is possible to fall foul of a state law whilst being in compliance with a federal law (*HR Magazine* May 2013: 69–72). For example, although the Federal Family and Medical Leave Act does not require employers to provide paid time off for leave taken in the circumstances covered by the Act, California and New Jersey do, as do San Francisco and Washington DC.

States are adopting their own laws on wages and on hours of work rules, and on the verification requirements to establish nationality in regard to immigration laws. There are 41 states (plus the District of Columbia and Puerto Rico) which have their own state income tax laws. There is a US Supreme Court ruling that a state may tax all the income of its residents, even if the income is earned in another state, posing problems for employers on what taxes they should withhold.

Are there converging trends in employment laws? Perhaps the strongest pressures for convergence come from the needs of governments across the world to react to common trends. Examples include: the impact of new technology on employment practices, resulting in data protection laws and data privacy; social trends for shorter hours; more flexibility and parental leave, owing to social changes and changes in the labour market, as well as the global pressures from multi-nationals; and common systems for quality control, for logistics and the needs to collaborate as required by trading conditions from the great trading blocs such as the European Community and the USA. Whilst there are trends towards convergence, therefore, there are also significant institutional, political, economic and cultural reasons for divergence in law and practice, not only between countries, but also within states.

24 CONTRACTS OF EMPLOYMENT

The focus of this chapter is the employment relationship as it affects the individual. The chapter describes aspects of employment law relating to contracts of employment, types of employment such as part-time and fixed-term contracts, how to change contracts of employment and the termination of employment, including redundancy, pay, time off work, and paid annual and sick leave.

CONTRACTS OF EMPLOYMENT

A contract of employment exists when one person engages another to perform a particular task as part of his or her business, in a manner that he or she dictates in return for payment. The relationship will then imply certain duties on the part of the employer: for example, to pay National Insurance contributions, to deduct income tax and to conform with the requirements laid down in employment legislation.

The contract may be formed by conduct, by a document or orally, or by a combination of these methods. All that is required to establish that a contract exists is the agreement of the essential terms by the parties.

WRITTEN PARTICULARS OF A CONTRACT

Employers must provide all employees (full- or part-time) with certain written particulars of their contracts. These must be supplied within two months of starting work, or after a month if the employment ends in that time or, if the employee is going overseas for more than one month, before the employee leaves to travel (sections 1–7 of the

Employment Rights Act 1996). Existing employees who have not received particulars must be provided with them within two months of a request. It is important to check that the particulars are correct. Changes to written particulars of the contract must be notified to the employee as soon as possible, and in any case within one month.

The following information must be supplied in one document (the 'principal statement'):

1   The names of the parties to the contract.
2   The date the employment started and the date the statutory continuity of employment started (if different).
3   Remuneration scale or rate and method of calculation.
4   Payment intervals.
5   Hours of work.
6   Holiday entitlement, including any roll-over holiday rights from one year to the next.
7   Job title or brief description of the work. (For the sake of flexibility, it is better to use generic job titles.)
8   Place of work, or the employer's address if the work is itinerant.

The employer must also supply up-to-date information in the following areas (which may be in a separate document and may be referred to in the principal statement but which must be accessible), and there must be an opportunity for employees to read these:

1   The rules concerning sickness or injury, including any entitlement to sick pay.
2   Pension arrangements.
3   Notice provisions, referring to statutory minimum notice periods or whatever has been agreed contractually, or to collective agreements where these are stipulated.
4   Expected duration of the work if employment is not permanent or fixed term.
5   Disciplinary procedures, showing the stages and to whom and how the appeal is to be addressed, for both discipline and grievance procedures.
6   For overseas employees, the duration of overseas employment expected, the currency to be used for pay purposes, any additional benefits, expatriate terms and the conditions on return.
7   Any collective agreements into which the employers have entered covering this employment must be explicitly stated.

If there are no specific elements to be supplied in the list above, the employer must state that fact in the written statement of particulars.

There is no stand-alone monetary remedy for failing to provide written particulars of the information in the above list. However, a declaration of terms by an employment tribunal can be sought by an employee, which may be unfavourable to the employer. However, if an employee brings successful tribunal proceedings in relation to certain other matters (e.g. redundancy) and the employer was in breach of the requirement to provide written particulars when the proceedings began, then the tribunal has the power to make an award against the employer of at least two (and up to four) weeks' pay.

EXPRESS AND IMPLIED TERMS OF CONTRACT

Express terms are those that the parties specifically agree upon, and these terms of contract will typically include many of the items mentioned above, such as rates of pay. The express terms may also include a description of the nature of the work itself. An agreement between the employer and a trade union may be referred to as containing certain of the terms of the contract.

Implied terms are those which are not expressly stated, but which nevertheless impose obligations and duties on both parties. For examples of implied terms we may quote the employer's duty to give the employee reasonable notice in the event of the parties not having agreed the length of notice, for example, where an employee has not yet served for four weeks.

One of the most practically important implied duties is the duty on both the employer and the employee to maintain the relationship of trust and confidence between them. The other important implied duty is the employee's duty of good faith and fidelity while in employment, which extends to a duty of confidentiality during employment.

UNLAWFUL CONTRACTS AND RESTRICTIVE COVENANTS

Any contract which is unlawful, or which is contrary to public policy and restrictive, cannot be legally enforced.

Under circumstances where an employer is anxious that former employees might set up in opposition, make use of the former employer's trade secrets or in some way damage the employer's legitimate business interests, recourse is frequently made to some form of restrictive covenant in the contract, forbidding the employee to engage in a competitive business within a specified period after leaving (sometimes this is coupled with a geographical limitation).

Restrictive covenants are unenforceable if they are considered to be in undue restraint of trade, that is, unreasonable in the interests of the parties and the public. Attempts at removing competition by preventing former employees from exercising their skills may be considered to be against public policy, the test being whether the employer is protecting a legitimate business interest versus the right of the individual to earn a living. However, if the employer merely wishes to protect business secrets he or she might be able to justify a restrictive covenant.

It is difficult to distinguish between the two purposes, but the courts have decided in the past about confidentiality clauses on the basis of whether or not the employer was trying to preserve 'objective knowledge', which is the employer's property, or if it is the employee's skill and expertise or mental/manual ability, which is the property of the individual and should be transferable to other businesses without hindrance. Legal advice is necessary before drawing up a covenant of this kind, in order to ensure its validity. It may be enforced by the employer applying to the court for an injunction to restrain the employee's breach or anticipated breach. The employer can also claim damages for losses suffered, and may be able to claim against any new employer if such an employer 'induced' the employee to breach his or her contract.

An unenforceable covenant does not invalidate the remainder of the contract, although if an employer breaks the contract, a restrictive covenant that would otherwise have been acceptable would not be enforceable. In short, an employer cannot seek to enforce the provisions of a contract which the employer itself has breached. An example of this is where an employer commits a breach by dismissing an employee in breach of contract (e.g. by not giving proper notice) and then seeks to enforce a post-termination restrictive covenant. The employer would not be able to seek enforcement in these circumstances.

PART-TIME WORKERS DIRECTIVE

The purpose of this directive, adopted by the European Union in December 1997, is to remove discrimination against part-time workers, and to improve the quality of part-time work. The directive passed into UK law in 2000. The directive states that part-time workers must not be treated 'in a manner less favourable than comparable full-time workers', in regard to their employment conditions. Comparisons to full-time workers should be to another employee of the same employer, under the same contract and performing similar work, requiring similar levels of qualification, skill and experience. If a full-time employee reduces hours of work to become part-time, the previous full-time terms and conditions can be used for comparison. If someone returns to the same work with an absence of less than 12 months, the previous full-time employment can be a comparator.

Comparisons apply to all employment conditions, including pension benefits, as well as pay rates, overtime, sickness and maternity rules. Employees can ask employers for a statement explaining the reasons for any differences in treatment and can make a claim to an employment tribunal if not satisfied with the grounds offered for less favourable treatment.

Wherever possible, part-time workers' terms should be calculated on a pro rata basis. Moreover, employers must consider requests for part-time work, and movement between full-time and part-time is to be permitted, unless this is established as not practicable by the employer.

CHANGES IN A CONTRACT'S TERMS

If the parties to the contract agree, the terms may be changed. Unilateral attempts to change the terms to the disadvantage of either party would be ineffective and may result in the contract being broken (for instance by breaching the implied duty of trust and confidence). Changes to written particulars referred to earlier in this chapter must be communicated to the employee within one month after the change. This can be done by giving the employee written particulars of the change, or by making the amendment available for inspection. Changes to a contract's terms, if to the disadvantage of the employee or owing to the behaviour of the employer, may constitute 'constructive' unfair dismissal if the employee leaves. Best practice is for proposed changes to employment terms and conditions to be agreed with employees or their representatives through consultation. Whilst this approach helps to maintain good employee relations, it also has the benefit of providing employers with a reasonable defence in the event that an individual claims that the change to terms amounts to a constructive unfair dismissal. Where the old contract is going to be terminated and substituted with a new one (also known as dismissal and re-engagement), employers would be wise to give employees full contractual notice of that fact or risk claims for wrongful dismissal, which is effectively a breach of contract claim.

Where there is a business need to change contractual terms, there are two types of change where the employer will not need to vary the contract:

1   Where the change does not affect a term of the contract of employment.
2   Where the contract itself already authorizes the change that the employer wishes to make.

In the situation where the changes proposed are to non-contractual provisions, for instance a policy, an employer can modify non-contractual provisions without the employee's agreement. These may be announced or notified through such means as staff handbooks, company manuals and the procedures or policies on the intranet.

One way to avoid problems arising from changes to a contractual term which can be foreseen, as in a fast moving business, is to ensure when drafting the contract that the existing term can be interpreted to accommodate changes in the future, including the requirement within the contract for employees to be flexible within certain limits, for example about location of work or times of work.

When obtaining agreement by employees to changes to the employment contract, this should be in return for some financial consideration. Employees can notify their agreement to change in writing or verbally, but must not be put under duress.

Although an employer could terminate employment, and offer re-engagement on new terms, this would be risky and would open the way for wrongful dismissal to be claimed. Therefore, procedure has to be carefully followed, with consultation, transparency and a sound business case to justify the approach.

FIXED-TERM CONTRACTS

A fixed-term contract is one where there is a fixed end date from the outset. It is advisable to give fixed-term contracts in writing for even the shortest periods of time. All fixed-term contracts should ideally be for specific duties or projects, and there should be a good reason for giving one.

For fixed-term contracts, once the person has been continuously employed for two years or more, unfair dismissal may be claimed (one year's employment if the person was engaged before April 2012). If short-term employment can be justified by the employer, the termination may not be unfair. It may be justified as a redundancy dismissal if the temporary post has to come to an end. Since 2002, employees entering into, renewing or extending a fixed-term contract can no longer waive their rights to a statutory redundancy payment. A similar right to waive unfair dismissal protection was abolished in 1999. With effect from July 2006 an employee retained on successive fixed-term contracts for four years automatically becomes permanent, unless the employer can justify a continuation on a fixed-term basis. This may apply even if there are gaps between contracts, if the period adds up to four years.

It would be wise for an employer who is contemplating offering a fixed-term contract to seek legal advice beforehand.

AGENCY WORKERS

Agency workers can claim to be an employee of the agency or of the employer where they work. Various tests have been applied by courts and tribunals to determine who should be regarded as the employer in a particular case. These tests include whether or not there are mutual obligations to carry out the work, as well as a promise of future work, whether or not the work is controlled, and the payment system for the work. The Conduct of Employment Agencies and Employment Business Regulations 2003 require employment agencies to state whether or not a person who obtained work through the agency was employed or self-employed, together with a written notice of the terms and conditions.

THE TERMINATION OF A CONTRACT

The Employment Rights Act 1996, which followed the Act of 1978, lays down minimum periods of notice. For the employer this is one week's notice after four weeks' continuous employment, and then increases after two years' continuous employment to two weeks, by one week for each year of continuous employment between two and 12 years, and is at least 12 weeks' notice if the period of continuous employment is 12 years or more. The employee must give at least one week's notice after four weeks' service. The employer's and employee's period of notice may be extended beyond that by agreement expressed in the contract. Payment in lieu of notice (PILON) may be made by agreement (although this does not deny the employee the right to claim unfair dismissal or redundancy) and, unless stated to the contrary, notice may be given on any day of the week.

An employee with one year's continuous service has a right to a written statement giving particulars of the reasons for dismissal (in some cases, no period of service is necessary). These reasons must constitute a full explanation, not simply abbreviations such as 'misconduct'. The employee's request, which can be oral or written, must be met by the employer within 14 days, or a claim to a tribunal may award up to two weeks' pay as compensation. Employees with more than two years' continuous service (one year if in the employment commenced before April 2012) can claim against their employer if they believe they have been unfairly dismissed, although there are a number of circumstances in which there is no qualifying period to claim; for example, where it is claimed that the reason or principal reason for dismissal is pregnancy or 'whistle-blowing'.

DISMISSAL

Wrongful dismissal

We should distinguish between wrongful dismissal and unfair dismissal. It is still possible for an employee to claim that he or she has been wrongfully dismissed in an ordinary common law action for breach of contract in the civil courts or in an employment tribunal. This applies where the employee claims that the employer did not dismiss him or her in accordance with the terms contained in his or her contract. Claims under £25,000 are generally heard in an employment tribunal; otherwise the more appropriate forum would be the High Court or county court.

This might arise, for example, where the employer had failed to give proper notice as stated in the contract or where the dismissal breaches terms of the contract, such as contractual disciplinary or redundancy procedures. The amount of the compensation or damages awarded would normally aim at placing the employee financially in the position in which he or she would have been had the wrongful dismissal not taken place. There is no qualifying period of service. The employee would not be entitled to reinstatement or re-engagement. A wrongful dismissal can have other consequences, however, such as rendering restrictive covenants unenforceable.

Unfair dismissal

Since the Trade Union and Labour Relations Act of 1974, as amended by the Employment Protection (Consolidation) Act 1978 and the Employment Rights Act 1996 and subsequent legislation and case law, employees have had the right not to be unfairly dismissed. There are two aspects to 'unfair' dismissal:

1 The manner of the dismissal must be fair, that is, the tribunal must be satisfied that the employer has acted reasonably and fairly, in all the circumstances, in the manner of the dismissal. Whilst the original legislation stated that the tribunal will decide this 'in accordance with equity and the substantial merits of the case', following the 2002 Employment Act, new dispute resolution regulations were introduced in October 2004 which included a statutory grievance procedure and a statutory disciplinary procedure with which all employers had to comply. Although these are no longer statutory procedures, the employer would be at a disadvantage if the ACAS procedures were not followed, resulting in a claim that the dismissal is unfair because the employer failed to follow the relevant procedure.

2 The legislation lays down a number of reasons for dismissal that might be considered sufficient if the manner of the dismissal is fair. These reasons are:

   (a) Redundancy.
   (b) Ill-health or lack of capability or lack of qualifications for the job in which the employee was engaged: capability is to be assessed according to skill, aptitude, health or any other physical or mental quality (including the employee's adaptability and flexibility). Employers should provide proper induction and any necessary training and establish performance standards.
   (c) Misconduct: this must be sufficiently serious to warrant dismissal or could be a culmination of a series of less serious matters.
   (d) Where the employee could not continue to work in the position without breaking the law (for example, driving while his or her licence is suspended for a long period or the expiry of a work permit entitling an employee to work in the UK).
   (e) Some other substantial reason of a kind such as to justify the dismissal of an employee holding the position which that employee held, commonly referred to as 'SOSR'.

With regard to point (e), a number of reasons have been used to justify dismissal under this heading, including an irreconcilable conflict of personalities, caused by the dismissed employee; and an ultimatum from an important customer which forced the employer to dismiss the employee. However, the manner of the dismissal must be shown to be fair, so for instance, in cases of redundancy the employer should make efforts to search for vacancies or try to transfer the employee to a job where he or she will be successful.

A minimum of two years' service is normally required (unless the employee was in the employment prior to April 2012) in order to qualify for the unfair dismissal protection. However, there are a number of circumstances where the dismissal would be deemed to be automatically unfair, irrespective of the length of service of the employee. These special cases are listed below.

UNFAIR DISMISSAL: SPECIAL CASES

An individual has a right not to be dismissed because he is, or is not, a member of a trade union or a member of a particular trade union (Trade Union and Labour Relations (Consolidation) Act 1992). Employees should also not be subject to any detriment on grounds of union membership or activities, and employers should not select people for redundancy because of their union membership or because they are not members of a trade union. Mass dismissals for industrial action are unfair (assuming the action has been properly balloted and limited to action within the authority of the ballot). Commercial contracts stipulating that contractors should employ union-only labour, or that require the contractor to consult with trade unions, are outlawed.

Statements within the written particulars given to employees that they are encouraged to join a trade union are not of themselves unlawful. However, the legislation is clearly aimed to establish the absolute right of individuals not to belong to a trade union, and there is no length of service requirement in this case of unfair dismissal.

Under the Employment Rights Act 1996 there is no length of service requirement in situations relating to health and safety complaints, where an employer must not act to the detriment of the employee for reporting an unsafe practice. This is intended to prevent victimization, and also covers occasions where the employee carries out duties preventing or reducing risks to health and safety, or leaves the employer's premises in the event of imminent danger. There is no limit to compensation for unfair dismissals of those people raising health and safety issues, or for whistle-blowers, in accordance with the Public Interest Disclosure Act 1998. The two year minimum service requirement also does not apply in discrimination cases (see below). However, cases must be brought within three months of the dismissal taking place.

Dismissals where the reason is pregnancy, or the principal reason is connected with pregnancy, are automatically regarded as unfair. It is also automatically unfair if the reason is that the employee took part in industrial action. Similarly, dismissal is automatically unfair (with no service qualification) where the dismissal is victimization for exercising rights to representation at disciplinary or grievance hearings or in regard to TU recognition claims, or for asserting other statutory rights such as working time rights, etc. Similarly, asserting the right to be paid in line with the national minimum wage legislation or in some cases relating to a transfer of employment, or if dismissed because of a spent conviction, are all situations where no service requirement is needed for the employee to be able to claim unfair dismissal.

REDUNDANCY

Definition of redundancy

An employee may be redundant if:

1   The employer ceases or intends to cease carrying on the business for the purposes of which he or she was employed (sometimes known as 'role' redundancy).

2   The employer has ceased or intends to cease to carry on business in the place where the employee was employed (sometimes known as 'place of work' redundancy).

3   There is a diminution (or expected diminution) of the requirement for employees to carry out work of a particular kind.

4   There is a diminution (or expected diminution) of the requirement for employees to carry out work of a particular kind in the place where the employee was employed by the employer.

5   There is a dismissal for reasons not related to the individual, e.g. reorganization of work.

If the selection for redundancy is for some reason other than a diminution in the amount of work, or the circumstances applied equally to one or more other employees in the same undertaking in similar positions but who were not made redundant, or the selection for dismissal contravened a customary arrangement or general principles of fairness and reasonableness, then the employee may claim that he or she was unfairly dismissed.

Where an employer wishes to offer alternative employment, he or she should do so in writing before a new contract is due to start. The written particulars of the agreement between the employer and the employee should state the terms and conditions of the new employment, rates of pay, location and duties, etc. If the employee does not believe that this is a suitable alternative offer, he or she may apply to a tribunal for redundancy pay.

If there is to be a trial period in the new employment, the trial period will begin with the ending of the previous employment and should not last for more than four weeks unless a longer period is mutually agreed for retraining purposes. Such an agreement must be in writing, and must state the date of the end of the trial period and the terms and conditions of employment during the trial period.

A renewal of contract or a re-engagement should take effect within four weeks of the termination of the old contract. Where the employee accepts the suitable alternative offer, his or her employment is deemed to be continuous.

Rights to a redundancy payment

Employees who are made redundant are entitled to a payment from their employer. The right to receive a payment depends on a number of conditions:

1   Employees must have been dismissed because of redundancy.

2   Some employees may be entitled to a redundancy payment if they are laid off or kept on short time.

3   The employee must have served for at least two years.

Dismissal due to redundancy

Irrespective of whether the employee is given notice, or in cases of redundancy constructive dismissal, leaves, the termination will count as a redundancy if the definition outlined above is met. The date of the dismissal is the date on which the notice expires or the termination takes effect. If the employer, after giving notice, substitutes a shorter or longer period of notice, the date will be the new substituted dismissal date. Employees who refuse to work to the later date may lose the entitlement to the full redundancy payment, depending on the circumstances of the case.

If the employee anticipates the expiry of the employer's notice by indicating his or her intention to leave earlier than was originally agreed, the employee will still be taken to have left due to redundancy, and the effective date will be the new date the employee gives. If the employer objects, he or she can write to the employee, requiring him or her to withdraw notice and to continue in employment until the original notice of the employer has been served, and stating that, unless he or she does so, the liability to a redundancy payment will be contested. The issue might have to be resolved by reference to a tribunal. This is true of dismissals owing to misconduct during the notice period, when the employer may withhold redundancy pay, but may equally have to fight out the case at a tribunal hearing.

Tribunals are often asked to decide whether the selection for redundancy is fair. Here the tribunal will take into account the reason for the redundancy, the basis for the selection (for example, last in, first out – LIFO), how this principle was applied in fact and the extent to which reasonable efforts were made to find alternative employment.

Lay-off and short-time working

If an employee is 'laid off' or put on short time, he or she may be entitled to a redundancy payment.

Where there is a diminution of work of the kind the employee is required to perform under his or her contract, and because of this the pay for any week is less than half a week's pay, he or she is legally regarded as on short time. Should he or she be on short time (or laid off altogether) for four or more consecutive weeks, or have been on short time or laid off for a series of six weeks or more in a period of 13 weeks, then the employee can claim redundancy pay if he or she gives the employer proper notice of his or her intention to do so. If there is a reasonable expectation that, no later than four weeks from the termination date, the employee would enter a period of 13 weeks without short time or lay-off, then the employer must notify the employee within seven days that he or she contests the redundancy payment, as the employee would not under those circumstances be entitled to it. An employee is only entitled to a redundancy payment in these circumstances if he terminates his employment.

Length of service

The two-year minimum service must be continuous, and if any re-engagement has taken place, whether or not the service was broken will depend on the re-engagement, the length of the break being crucial (see above on re-engagement within a four-week period).

The amount of the payment

The amount of the redundancy payment to which the employee has a legal entitlement is as follows. The following list gives the amount of pay for each year's service in the relevant age bracket:

age under 22 = half a week's pay
age 22–40 = one week's pay
age 41 and over =one and a half weeks' pay.

This is subject to a maximum of 20 years' service, that is, only the previous 20 years will count. The amount may also be reduced if the employee has a gratuity or pension from the time he or she leaves.

Pay

Methods of payment

Following the repeal of the Truck Acts, manual workers do not have to be paid in coin of the realm, and payment is increasingly made by electronic funds transfer direct into a bank account.

The National Minimum Wage Act 1998

For all employees (with the exception of those listed below) the Act prescribes minimum rates of pay. These are (as at October 2013): for those people aged 21 years and over, £6.31 per hour, for those 18–20 years of age, £5.03 per hour, for those under 18, £3.72 per hour and for apprentices under 19 years, £2.68 per hour. Apprentices over 19 years of age are paid the amount that is applied to the relevant age.
Exceptions are listed for whom there is no minimum as follows:

■ workers on sandwich course secondments, work experience or similar training schemes
■ prisoners and voluntary workers
■ a homeless person given shelter and other benefits in return for work
■ nuns and monks working for religious orders
■ *au pairs* and family workers.

Calculation of the wage payments for national minimum wage purposes is based on a method that, for most practical purposes, is the base rate plus any non-premium overtime, that is, gross pay before tax. Allowances such as shift allowances or London allowance are disregarded, as are benefits. The method to be adopted is to include:

1   Total remuneration (gives sum before income tax, National Insurance and compulsory stoppages such as attachment of earnings orders or Child Support Agency payments).

2   But excludes benefits in kind, advances or loans, retirement allowances, redundancy payments, suggestion scheme rewards and vouchers (e.g. Luncheon Vouchers) or stamps.

3   If free accommodation is provided, a notional rate of £3.90 a day is included.

4   Reduction cumulatively from the figure of pay for absence periods which were not part of the working time.

5   Overtime allowances (e.g. for unsocial hours, or London allowance), tips and gratuities from customers paid by the customer in cash (i.e. those paid through the payroll would be included), reimbursement of expenses, amount of any payment made by the individual to the employer (except fines for misconduct paid under contract, repayments of advances or loans, payments for goods and services bought from the employer, which are included, unless these are part of a contractual obligation as with compulsory deduction for staff canteens, which would be excluded).

The 'reference period' is the pay period (a maximum of one month). Working hours for the reference period are calculated differently according to the four categories of workers defined. These are:

Category	Defined
Time workers	Paid for hours worked; pieceworkers who have a set number of hours.
Salaried hours workers	Paid a stated annual salary for a number of hours in a year, (including annualized hours).
Output workers	Workers paid piece rates or on commission, with no fixed hours.
Unmeasured workers	Any worker who does not fall into any of the other three categories.

The amount paid must be at least the minimum amount required under the national minimum wage legislation during the reference period.

Working time includes time spent working, time spent at or near the workplace and when the worker is required to be available (except when the worker is required to sleep on the premises), travel for purposes of work (except between home and work) and time spent on training. Working time excludes rest breaks, industrial action and absence which affects pay.

Employers must keep 'sufficient' records, which must be available for inspection by employees as well as by the Inland Revenue, which is the enforcing authority.

ITEMIZED PAY STATEMENTS

Where an employer employs more than 20 people, the employees have a right to receive an itemized statement of pay that shows:

- gross amount of pay
- variable deductions (such as income tax)
- fixed deductions (such as pension contributions); if the employer prefers, a statement can be issued annually showing the aggregate of fixed deductions and net amount of pay.

RIGHT TO TIME OFF FOR STUDY OR TRAINING

Under sections 63A–63C of the Employment Rights Act 1996 there is a right to paid time off for study or training. Any employee aged between 16 and 17 years of age who has not reached a specified standard is entitled to paid time off to study for qualifications identified in the regulations. These qualifications include five GCSEs, Scottish Qualifications Agency award (SQA) in five subjects, Business and Technology Education Council (BTEC) and vocational qualifications. The courses do not have to be related to the employee's current job.

GUARANTEE PAYMENTS

Employees with at least one month's continuous service have a right to a limited amount of pay if laid off or put on short time. The conditions under which this is granted to an employee are:

1 He or she must not unreasonably refuse suitable alternative work and must comply with a reasonable attendance requirement.
2 He or she must make him or herself available for work.
3 The lay-off or short time must not be a consequence of a trade dispute involving his or her own employer. Thus, if there is a strike in the company that is not associated with his or her own employer, then guarantee pay would apply if the employee was laid off.

The amount of guarantee pay is limited to a maximum of five days within any three-month rolling period and there is a statutory limit.

The formula for calculating a day's pay is:

$$\text{Number of normal working hours} \times \text{Guaranteed hourly rate}$$

$$\text{The guaranteed hourly rate} = \frac{\text{One week's pay}}{\text{Normal working hours per week}}$$

If the hours per week vary, the average over the last 12 weeks is taken as representative. Where the employee has less than 12 weeks' service, then the average for similar workers of the same employer is taken.

COLLECTIVE AGREEMENTS ON GUARANTEE PAY

Where a collective agreement exists which would result in the employee receiving more than the minimum guarantee pay under the Employment Rights Act 1996, then the employee receives the larger amount. Whether or not the legal minimum gives more than the collective agreement depends on how many days are involved, and on whether or not the collective agreement guaranteed a proportion of a week's pay instead of a day's pay as a basis for calculation.

The parties to an agreement on guarantee pay may apply to the Secretary of State for exemption from legal obligations, provided their scheme is as beneficial to employees as the state scheme.

SUSPENSION ON MEDICAL GROUNDS

There are situations where the employee may be suspended on medical grounds because of a health hazard at his or her place of work or because of a recommendation contained in a code of practice. Employees with a minimum period of one month's service, who are not absent for a personal health reason, are entitled to payment for up to 26 weeks of suspension. Employees must not unreasonably refuse offers of alternative work during this time.

A number of state payments are now made through the payroll. These are presently statutory sick pay and statutory maternity pay.

STATUTORY LEAVE AND SICK LEAVE

Statutory annual leave accrues during sickness absence. On termination, payment must be made in lieu of any accrual. Employees can carry over statutory leave entitlement to the next holiday year, if prevented by illness from taking statutory holiday leave. Employees must request holiday; they cannot claim it was refused unless a request has been put in at the appropriate time. Employers need to manage absence, and to provide a clear policy on holidays, for example to allow employees to take alternative dates if they are sick during their holiday.

BRIBERY ACT 2010

This Act came into force in April 2011 and created new bribery offences, repealing existing laws on bribery. The Act applies to public and private sectors. The Act created four basic criminal offences:

- bribing – to give or offer a bribe
- being bribed – to request, agree to receive or to accept a bribe
- bribing a foreign public official
- bribery as a corporate offence.

As a corporate offence this is where a commercial organization fails to prevent persons performing services on its behalf from committing bribery. A business can be found guilty of an offence if a person associated with it bribes another, and the bribe is for the benefit of the company. Although there is no need to prove negligence or direct involvement, association can cover employees, directors, subsidiaries, joint ventures, partners, agents and suppliers.

One limited defence is that the company has, for example, penalties, anti-corruption training or whistle-blowing procedures. The penalties if found guilty are up to 10 years in prison, and/or unlimited fines. For companies, penalties include unlimited fines, director disqualification and debarment from tendering for public contracts, as well as reputational damage.

25 THE LAW ON MANAGING DIVERSITY

In this chapter we describe the main statutes and regulations that are designed to manage relationships at work, reflecting the growing diversity of modern society. These laws are a guide for policies on the conduct of employers and employees, representing the way people should be treated and protected.

COMMISSION FOR EQUALITY AND HUMAN RIGHTS

The Commission for Equality and Human Rights (CEHR) was created in October 2007 as the independent regulator for equality and human rights in Britain. Its mission goes beyond the need for equal opportunities, which is seen as only one aspect of the promotion of human rights, but also encompasses the need to promote good relationships among different communities, to protect people from unlawful discrimination and harassment, and to encourage good practice on equality and diversity. To quote the CEHR remit: 'It has a statutory remit to promote and to monitor human rights and to protect, enforce and promote equality across nine "protected grounds": age, disability, gender, race, religion and belief, pregnancy and maternity, marriage and civil partnership, sexual orientation and gender reassignment'.

It also runs the Equality Advisory Support Service for those who need advice and support on discrimination and human rights issues, although this service does not provide legal advice on particular cases.

EQUALITY ACT 2010

The Equality Act consolidated 22 pieces of legislation on discrimination, and aims to provide a simple and accessible framework, and thereby to promote a fair and more equal society. All the protected characteristics listed above are protected in their own right. There is no defence to direct discrimination (save for cases of direct age discrimination, where an objective justification defence is available), and the Act has a wide interpretation covering conduct related to discrimination. Perception is also included, for example, when a person is less favourably treated or is harassed because he or she is perceived to have a disability or other protected characteristic; the discrimination is still unlawful. Association is also covered, for example, where a person is less favourably treated because the individual has a partner or other relation in one of the protected categories; this counts as discrimination.

Harassment is now defined as 'unwanted conduct related to a relevant protected characteristic'.

Disability is defined as a physical or mental impairment. The disability would need to be one that had a substantial and long-term effect on a person's ability to carry out normal day-to-day activities. There is no requirement for an individual to demonstrate that impairment affects something on the list of capacities – mobility, speech, ability to understand, etc. The Act covers discrimination arising from disability and indirect discrimination. For employers to use a defence of 'justification' they would 'have to show a proportionate means of achieving a legitimate aim'. In disability cases where the employer has failed to make reasonable adjustments, no defence is available.

Enquiries about health at the recruitment stage are included within the scope of the Act to prevent employers from screening out disabled applicants. Prospective employers must not enquire in pre-employment questions about the health of applicants for work. Health questions can only be raised after an offer of employment has been made. There are one or two exceptions: permissible health questions may be made pre-offer if the issue is intrinsic to the function of the job, or for monitoring diversity, or if disability is a job requirement, and if reasonable adjustments are required for applicants to be assessed for the job.

In the rest of this chapter we will include many of the earlier laws to ensure coverage of discrimination legislation.

EQUAL PAY

The Equal Pay Act 1970 was designed to stop discrimination in the contractual area of terms and conditions between men and women. It applies to both sexes and to employees of any age. There must be no difference in the pay, benefits and conditions of service for women or men in 'like work', or work which is rated as equivalent. The comparisons made are between people working for the same employer or at the same establishment (where there are differences based on location), or at an establishment observing the same terms and conditions. A 'benefit' has been defined by the European Court of Justice as pay if there is an entitlement based on the employment relationship.

Exceptions are in maternity provisions, and when there is a statutory reason as, for example, where pregnant women are forbidden to carry out certain work in factories on health and safety grounds. An employer must be able to prove that any difference between the pay of men and women is a result of a material difference in the work. Work that is 'broadly similar' is regarded as the same for the purposes of the Act. Job evaluation schemes that use non-discriminatory factors show the value of different jobs in relation to each other, indicating that no discrimination has occurred.

EQUAL VALUE

Following a case brought by the European Community against the UK Government, which succeeded in showing that the Equal Pay Act did not fully conform to the Treaty of Rome and the EC's 1975 Equal Pay Directive, the Equal Pay Act was amended in 1983 to ensure that the principle of equal pay for work of equal value, compared between men and women, was included in the equal pay legislation.

There are three ways in which a claim (by a man or a woman) may be made in respect of pay, terms and conditions of service:

1   Where she (in the case of a woman making the claim) is employed on 'like work' to that of a man.
2   Where she can show that she is employed on work rated as equivalent to a man under a job evaluation study.
3   Where she can show that the work she does is of equal value to a man's work in terms of the demands made upon her in such areas as effort or skill, etc.

A claim under the Act is made to an employment tribunal. Tribunal panels with specialist knowledge in equal value cases have been established. If no conciliation is possible, the tribunal will examine any job evaluation scheme to see if it is valid. Where no job evaluation scheme is operating, the tribunal may still reject the claim if it thinks there are no reasonable grounds for the claim. Where there is a job evaluation scheme and the employer can show that there are no grounds for the scheme to be regarded as sexually discriminatory, the claim will not succeed. However, unless the employer is able to show that there are no reasonable grounds for saying that the work is of equal value (for example, by showing that there is a genuine material factor which proves that the difference in pay or conditions is due to reasons other than sex differences), the tribunal must commission a report from an independent expert. This report will be considered when it is completed (usually within 42 days) and the tribunal, at its resumed hearing, will make a decision. Tribunals can require information to be given to the independent expert, and there are safeguards if the report is inadequate. Employees can also issue questionnaires to obtain data on pay in the organiz-ation before tribunal proceedings are commenced. The employer must respond to the questions within eight weeks. If the employer does not furnish a response, a tribunal cannot order it. However, a tribunal would be entitled to draw an adverse inference if an employer does not respond.

In 2003 the Equal Opportunities Commission introduced a new Code of Practice on Equal Pay, which suggests a way for conducting an equal pay review.

The six month time limit for bringing an equal pay claim is relaxed where the employer has deliberately concealed relevant facts, or where the woman was under a disability during the six months. Back pay may be paid, if successful, for up to six years. A single claim can be made if there has been a stable employment relationship, even if there have been a number of separate employment contracts.

SEX DISCRIMINATION

The Sex Discrimination Act 1975 (now superseded by the Equality Act 2010) was aimed at removing discrimination in the non-contractual areas of employment and set up the Equal Opportunities Commission to oversee the working of the Act and the Equal Pay Act.

A distinction is made between direct and indirect discrimination, both of which are unlawful. Direct discrimination is where a person is treated less favourably than the opposite sex because of their sex (for example, the recruitment of all males in managerial jobs). Indirect discrimination occurs when, although the provision, criterion or practice is applied equally to men and women, the effect of the condition is to disadvantage one sex (for example, stipulating that all managers must be over 6 feet 3 inches in height, this being less likely as a female characteristic). Therefore, where the condition is irrelevant and where the number of women who can comply is fewer than the number of men (or vice versa), then there is indirect discrimination.

Similarly, discrimination against people on the grounds of their marital status is regarded as unlawful.

The only general exception to direct discrimination is where there is an occupational requirement. Examples of this can include:

- physiological reasons (e.g. a male actor)
- for decency or privacy (e.g. a lavatory attendant)
- where the employee is required to sleep on the premises
- where special care is provided (e.g. in prison)
- personal services for education, health or welfare
- where there are overseas restrictions and it is necessary for the person to work overseas (e.g. in some Islamic countries women might be restricted)
- where the job is for a married couple or a couple who are civil partners.

The main areas where HR managers must watch for discrimination are in:

1 *Advertisements*: these should not have any particular reference to sex. Job titles that have a gender included should be avoided (e.g. 'sales girl', 'office boy').
2 *Recruitment procedures*: these must avoid discrimination; notably the person specification must not show signs of direct or indirect discrimination.
3 *Promotion, training, transfer policies*: these should be sufficiently well known and obviously non-discriminatory so that accusations of unfairness can be avoided.

Complaints may be made (within three months of the discrimination) to a tribunal, which can award damages.

The burden of proof in sex discrimination cases is on the respondent (which is generally the employer, but can be an individual colleague), once the claimant has produced sufficient evidence to establish a prima facie case that, in the absence of an adequate explanation, unlawful discrimination has taken place. Then the respondent must show that the adverse treatment 'is in no sense whatsoever' tainted by sex discrimination (*Barton v Investec Henderson Crosthwaite Securities* [2003] IRLR 332)).

We have already referred to the issue of sexual equality and pension schemes. Following the case of *Barber v Guardian Royal Exchange Assurance* (1990), pension benefits in occupational pension schemes are treated as pay, and therefore men and women must be treated equally with regard to these benefits. The right to join a pension scheme (contributory or non-contributory), contracted in as well as contracted out, public and private sector, is equal for men and women. There is no obligation to equalize benefits for service before 7 May 1990. Effectively, men can now retire at the same age as women (but this is not mandatory). Claims can be brought against the pension fund as well as against the employer.

SEXUAL HARASSMENT

Amendments to the Sex Discrimination Act in 2005 include specific provisions prohibiting harassment, both sex-related and sexual harassment. These aspects are now dealt with under the Equality Act 2010.

Harassment on grounds of sex occurs where a person engages in unwanted conduct that has the purpose or effect of violating another's dignity or creating an intimidating, hostile, degrading, humiliating or offensive environment that that takes place simply because someone is a woman (or a man). But harassment can also occur where there is unwanted verbal, non-verbal or physical conduct of a sexual nature, which similarly affects dignity or creates such an environment (e.g. a person making unwelcome sexually explicit comments).

RACE DISCRIMINATION

The Race Relations Act 1976 (now superseded by the Equality Act 2010) followed the same broad principles in seeking to remove discrimination, and the distinction between direct and indirect discrimination exists in the context of race discrimination. The Commission for Racial Equality's role in promoting harmony between ethnic groups extends beyond employment.

Racial groups are defined by reference to race, and a person's racial group is a reference to a racial group into which the person falls. The segregation of racial groups is unlawful. The victimization of anyone who brings a complaint under the Equality Act is also unlawful.

Employers must pay particular attention to their recruitment procedures to ensure that no discriminatory practices enter into their decisions (for example, in advertising, screening applicants, etc.), and should ensure that their employees are treated fairly so that promotion, training and development opportunities are not forgone because of discrimination. Terms and conditions of employment must apply equally to all racial groups, there must be no discrimination during disciplinary action and, unless membership of a particular race is a genuine occupational qualification (for example, for a film or play), then there are no exceptions. The Equality Act applies to organizations of all sizes.

DISCRIMINATION BECAUSE OF RELIGION OR BELIEF

An extension of discrimination legislation arose from the Treaty of Amsterdam 1997. The Framework Equal Treatment in Employment Directive 2000/78/EC promulgated new measures aimed at preventing discrimination on the grounds of sexual orientation, religion or belief, disability and age.

The Employment Equality (Religion or Belief) Regulations 2003 (SI 2003/1660) were introduced in the UK on 2 December 2003. These made discrimination on the grounds of 'religion or belief' unlawful and have since been superseded by the Equality Act 2010. Courts and tribunals may consider when deciding what is a religion or belief by reference to issues such as whether there is collective worship and a profound belief affecting one's way of life. Beliefs do not necessarily include all philosophies unless they are similar to a religious belief. Protected beliefs are religions and religious or philosophical beliefs. Philosophical beliefs are defined as those which are:

- genuinely held
- a belief – not an opinion or viewpoint
- related to weighty and substantial aspects of human life and behaviour
- treated with cogency, seriousness, cohesion and importance
- worthy of respect in a democratic society.

ACAS has produced a guide entitled 'Religion or Belief in the Workplace' to help organizations to create policy, procedures and monitoring mechanisms. This is clearly an area where tribunals will refine and operationalize the law through judgements.

Discrimination because of a person's association with someone else is also covered by the legislation, as are people who are or were ordinarily resident in the UK, but who are working abroad for an organization based in the UK.

It is unlawful to discriminate against or subject to harassment someone because of his or her religion or belief. This includes applicants for work, employees, self-employed persons, workers supplied by a contractor or agency and ex-employees. HR policies covered include terms and conditions, opportunities for promotion, training or benefits, the termination of employment (including constructive dismissal) and the provision of employment references.

Claims must be brought within three months of the action, which is the source of the complaint. As with other anti-discrimination law, direct and indirect discrimination is taken into account. People who make allegations or bring proceedings must not be victimized. Similarly, those who support colleagues in their complaints of unlawful discrimination are also protected from victimization (e.g. accompanying a complainant at a grievance hearing to discuss a discrimination complaint or giving evidence on support of a claimant at a tribunal in a case of unlawful discrimination).

Harassment is defined as where, because of a person's religion or belief, they are subjected to unwanted conduct that has the purpose or effect of violating that person's dignity or of creating an intimidating, hostile, degrading, humiliating or offensive environment for that individual.

Exceptions to treating people differently because of their religion (but not to the harassment provisions) are made where there are genuine occupational requirements (for example employment in churches, and in denominational schools), or more general requirements such as a halal butcher who must be a Muslim.

AGE DISCRIMINATION

Legislation was introduced to outlaw discrimination from October 2006. The legislation follows similar principles as other anti-discrimination law: it applies to direct and indirect discrimination and is designed to prevent discrimination on a basis of age alone, applying equally to young and old. Indeed, research has shown that young people feel more discriminated against in employment matters than do older people.

The law covers recruitment, selection, development, reward, promotion and benefits (although containing special provision to account for the actuarial rules in regard to pensions). There has been lengthy consultation on the question of retirement age. The default retirement age of 65, which had applied in many organizations, was abolished from October 2011. Retirement is not a fair reason for dismissal, apart from some special cases where retaining a compulsory retirement age can be objectively justified by an employer. These include the following cases:

(1)   If it is necessary for the employer to encourage the recruitment and promotion of younger workers, in order to establish a balance between generations, and to avoid disputes relating to employees' ability to perform their duties beyond the age of 65. For example, see *Seldon v Clarkson, Wright and Jakes* [2012] (SC).

(2)   In the case of ECJ ruling in 2011, civil services retirement age of 65 has been upheld. As civil servants rarely resign, so a compulsory retirement age is the only means of ensuring employment is distributed among generations (and in the case of UK civil servants there is a substantial pension scheme, worth for some people up to 72 per cent of base pay, so financial hardship after retirement is unlikely).

(3)   In the case of airline pilots, air safety rules stipulate that pilots can fly aged up to 65 years. Therefore, the collective agreement between pilots and employers, which had retirement at 60, was not upheld in an ECJ case (*Prigge and Others v Deutsche Lufthansa* [2011] (ECJ)).

The legislation requires HR departments to make fundamental changes to policies. For example, age should no longer be a criterion for recruitment or selection and should not influence training or development decisions. Examples of the potential effects are the abolition of pay by age scales, minimum ages for specific posts and the avoidance of language that constitutes indirect discrimination (for example 'experienced', 'energetic', 'seasoned professional'). Employers will have to review person specifications to decide whether the criteria described are essential or are merely reproducing stereotypes and bias. Similarly, development opportunities need to be dealt with in a transparent fashion, so that decisions can be justified on business grounds.

Inevitably, there will be many challenges and refinements from precedents.

SEXUAL ORIENTATION

It is unlawful for employers to discriminate (either directly or indirectly) against or to harass (or allow the harassment of) a person because of his or her sexual orientation.

Sexual orientation is defined as 'a sexual orientation towards persons of the same sex, persons of the opposite sex or persons of the same and the opposite sex'.

DISCRIMINATION AGAINST DISABLED PEOPLE

This is covered in the Equality Act 2010. To be clear about the implications, prior to the Equality Act, the Disability Discrimination Act 1995 aimed to protect disabled people and those who have been disabled from discrimination in employment. It placed a duty on employers to make reasonable adjustments to any physical feature of premises occupied by the employer or any arrangements made by the employer to avoid causing a substantial disadvantage to a disabled person.

The Act (now superseded by the Equality Act 2010) also covered the recruitment system and process and the terms of employment, as well as the reasonable provision of suitable physical facilities, such as wheelchair access.

An employer discriminates against a disabled person if the employer, for a reason related to the disability, treats the disabled person less favourably than he or she would treat others, unless one or more of four reasons which may be entered as justification apply. These reasons include:

1   The disabled person is unsuitable for the employment.
2   The disabled person is less suitable than another person.
3   The nature of the disability would significantly impede the performance of the person's duties.
4   The disability would significantly reduce the value of training (either to the disabled person or to the employer).

After the Court of Appeal case of *Clark v Novocold*, it is very easy to show less favourable treatment; for example, any absences related to a disability have to be ignored in deciding whether to dismiss, even if a non-disabled employee absent for a similar period could have been fairly dismissed.

As stated above, the Equality Act defines 'disabled person' as a person with a 'physical or mental impairment which has a substantial and long-term adverse effect on his or her ability to carry out normal day to day activities'. The definition excludes substance addictions (unless prescribed), hay fever and disfigurements, such as tattoos and body-piercing. Physical or mental impairments, which are included within the meaning of disability, include sensory impairments (such as those affecting eyesight or hearing) and mental impairments. Long-term effects are those which have lasted at least 12 months, or are likely to last more than 12 months, or for the rest of the life of the person. Recurring effects such as epilepsy are included.

Typical reasonable adjustments that an employer might make include:

■   making physical changes to premises
■   allocating some of the disabled person's duties to another person
■   transferring to fill another job
■   altering working hours
■   modifying equipment, instructions or reference manuals
■   providing a reader
■   providing special training.

There are codes of practice to help employers to eliminate discrimination.

REHABILITATION OF OFFENDERS ACT 1974

This Act (which does not apply in Northern Ireland) means that convicted criminals who have completed their sentences, whether imprisonment or fine, have a period of rehabilitation after which the conviction should be regarded as spent. The period of time before the conviction becomes spent is dependent on the sentence. Thus, for example, for sentences of six to 30 months' imprisonment the period is 10 years before the conviction is spent and, at the other extreme, an absolute discharge is spent after six months. Further convictions during the rehabilitation period extend the time before the earlier conviction is spent so that both convictions are spent at the same time.

As far as HR managers are concerned, when interviewing applicants for employment they may ask about any previous convictions, but must not question the person about any spent convictions. If an applicant does not reveal a spent conviction, no action should be taken against the applicant and he or she must be treated as though the offence had not been committed.

A spent conviction is not grounds for dismissal, or for not recruiting or promoting an employee or in any way treating the employee differently from others. Certain professions, such as barristers, accountants, medical practitioners, etc., are excluded from this generalization, and spent convictions may be taken into account in their case. When giving references, no information should be disclosed about spent convictions. Such a reference would be slander or libel, and would also risk prosecution.

PUBLIC INTEREST DISCLOSURE ACT 1998

This Act seeks to protect 'whistle-blowers' whose disclosure is protected if the information shows criminality, any breach of a legal obligation, health and safety dangers, environmental danger or concealment of any of these. The employee is not protected if the act of disclosure involved committing a criminal offence. The disclosure is protected if made in good faith, although the requirement for a disclosure to be made in good faith will soon be removed and disclosures made in bad faith will, in future, be capable of being protected. Disclosure should be made to the employer, other responsible persons or to a third party in accordance with a procedure agreed with the employer. Employees who make protected disclosures are protected from dismissal or action short of dismissal, since such action by the employer would be automatically unfair, with no minimum qualifying period of employment being required.

DATA PROTECTION ACT 1998

This Act repeals and replaces the 1984 Data Protection Act, although a number of the provisions are similar, in regard to the need to be careful and to treat data confidentially. The

1998 Act gives the employee rights of access to most personal data that the employer holds on individuals. It implements the EU Data Protection Directive. The Act covers electronically stored and paper-stored information. It limits the type of information that can be processed and the purposes for which it is processed. Personal data is defined as any set of information about an individual either processed by a computer or kept manually, which forms part of a file. This covers personnel files and notes by managers.

Processing sensitive personal data is subject to more stringent controls, including information about a person's racial or ethnic origins, political opinions, religious beliefs, trade union membership, health, sexual life and actual or suspected criminal offences.

The processing of personal data includes all processes used in obtaining, recording and holding data, which covers the processes of organizing, altering, retrieving, consulting, disclosing and using data. Employers must appoint a data controller who will be responsible for determining the purposes and processes of data collection. The duty of the data controller is not to process the data unless certain conditions are met, such as that the data may only be held for specified, lawful purposes, and not be excessive in regard to purpose.

There are further conditions dependent upon whether or not the data is classified as sensitive personal data. The conditions for sensitive personal data revolve around the need for the individual's explicit consent, whether or not processing the data is in his or her interests, or if he or she has already made the data public. For non-sensitive data, many of the same conditions apply; for example, the processing is necessary for the purposes of exercising or performing any right conferred or obligation imposed by law on the data controller in connection with employment. In the case of non-sensitive data, legitimate reasons include if the data controller has to process the information in order to comply with non-contractual obligations such as health and safety requirements, or if the processing is necessary for the performance of a contract to which the individual is a party (for example, payroll).

Employers must ensure that the data protection principles are adhered to, for example, by asking the employee to give consent for different types of data processing.

We should note that the Human Rights Act 1998 gives effect to the European Convention for the Protection of Human Rights and Fundamental Freedoms 1950, under Article 8 of which 'everyone has the right to respect for his private and family life, his home and his correspondence'.

ACCESS TO MEDICAL RECORDS ACT 1998

There is a right for employees to access any medical records (whether or not kept on a computer) supplied by a medical practitioner for employment or insurance purposes. This is where the report is prepared by the individual's own doctor (either before or during employment) rather than the company doctor. The employer must obtain the consent of the individual concerned if a medical report is to be requested from that person's own doctor, or a doctor covered by this law, and must advise the person of his or her rights under the Act.

FAMILY-FRIENDLY POLICIES

Parental Leave Directive

This EU Directive (Council Directive 96/34/EC) was implemented in December 1999. In the UK, the Employment Relations Act 1999 implemented the Maternity and Parental Leave Regulations and in March 2013 the leave was increased, entitling a parent to a minimum of 18 weeks' leave (which may be unpaid) in order to care for a child, provided the conditions set out in the Regulations are met.

There is a minimum qualifying period of one year's employment. The directive and the Regulations apply to both parents and include adoption as well as birth, and are applicable for each child. The time may be taken in blocks or in multiples of one week. Only parents of disabled children can take parental leave in periods of less than a week at a time. Leave is available up to a child's fifth birthday or 18th birthday if the child is in receipt of Disability Living Allowance. In the case of adopted children, the limit is 18 years or the fifth anniversary of adoption, whichever is the earliest. The contract of employment continues throughout the leave, and parents taking leave have a right to return to the same job or, if this is impossible, the employer must offer an equivalent or similar job consistent with the person's employment contract. However, redundancy could occur. There are rules for employers to control the timing of the leave, if it causes difficulty, and there is protection against victimization for employees who seek to assert this right.

There is also a right to reasonable absence from work to take 'necessary' action to deal with particular situations affecting their dependents, for instance in cases of sickness or accident. This includes relatives (for example, elderly parents) as well as children and non-family dependents, and applies where it is necessary to have support or assistance from the worker at the time. This absence may also be unpaid. There is no qualifying requirement, nor a prescribed maximum limit on the amount of time off that can be taken. There is no requirement to give advance notice if it is not reasonable to do so.

Maternity provisions

A woman who is dismissed because she is pregnant will be regarded as automatically unfairly dismissed unless by continuing to work she was in contravention of a statute. In this case, the employer has a duty to offer suitable alternative work or, where there is none, to suspend the employee on full pay.

Maternity leave

All women are entitled to maternity leave, which is categorized under three headings:

Compulsory Maternity Leave (CML): Women are not allowed to work for an employer for the two weeks immediately after childbirth. This forms part of OML.

Ordinary Maternity Leave (OML): 26 weeks. To qualify, an employee must inform her employer, no later than 15 weeks before the Expected Week of Childbirth (EWC) that she is pregnant, the date of EWC and the date she wants to start her maternity leave, which cannot be before the 11th week of EWC.

Additional Maternity Leave (AML): Pregnant women with a minimum of 26 weeks' continuous service are entitled to a further 26 weeks' additional maternity leave (i.e. a total of 52 weeks' maximum).

OML is considered to have started on whichever is the earlier date of either the date notified, the date after the start of the fourth week before EWC when she is absent due to pregnancy or the day after childbirth (the start of compulsory leave).

An employee on OML is entitled to return to the same job, and for no change to be made to her terms and conditions. An employee returning from AML is entitled to return to her old job or, if it is not reasonably practicable to do so, to return to another job which is both suitable and appropriate in the circumstances. If redundancy has arisen during maternity leave, she is entitled to be offered any suitable alternative work and is entitled to receive priority for this over other candidates who are not on maternity leave. If a woman fails to return after a period of maternity leave, it should be followed up in the same way as an employer would do for any employee who fails to turn up for work.

Statutory Maternity Pay (SMP) is payable from the start of maternity leave for 26 weeks to pregnant women who have worked for that employer for at least 26 weeks continuously at the 14th week before EWC. SMP as a minimum is payable at 90 per cent of average weekly earnings for the first six weeks, and then at £136.78 (from 7 April 2013, but increased each year) for the remaining 33 weeks. The pregnant woman must receive the benefit of all non-pay terms and conditions during ordinary maternity leave, and also during maternity leave.

All the provisions about maternity leave, such as start of maternity leave and return to work rules are covered by regulations. The Employment Rights Act 1996 covers the overall statutory framework, as well as the Sex Discrimination Act 1975 (Amendment) Regulations 2008. An employer is required to give paid time off for ante-natal care as instructed by the doctor. There are special provisions regarding the rights of mothers breast-feeding babies, to avoid risks up to six months after birth, which oblige employers to transfer the mother to suitable alternative work or to suspend her on full pay if necessary.

Paternity leave

Statutory paternity leave (SPL) and adoption leave (AL) were introduced through the Employment Act 2002. SPL is available for an employee who is the father of the child, the mother's husband or partner, and who has the responsibility for the child's upbringing. A 'partner' in this sense can be of either sex. The employee must also have worked continuously for the employer for a minimum of 26 weeks by the 15th week before the expected week of the baby's birth, and give 28 days' notice of intention to take SPL. The SPL is for up to two weeks and is paid at the lower rate of SMP, and the employee has the right of return at the end of the leave.

Adoption leave

Adoption leave is a right for employees who adopt a child to have leave from work so that he or she can establish a relationship with the child. Either (but not both adoptive parents) can take leave. Following the same principles as maternity leave, there is a period of 26 weeks of ordinary adoption leave (OAL) for either parent, provided they have continuous service for a minimum of 26 weeks. Adoption leave can start at a predetermined date, which is no more than 14 days before the child is expected to be placed. Additional adoption leave (AAL) can also be taken at the end of OAL, according to the maternity provisions.

26 TRADE UNION RELATIONSHIPS, HEALTH AND SAFETY

Laws governing trade union activities have a long history in the UK. Back in the early part of the nineteenth century, Combination Acts were passed to try to prevent unions from organizing their members, and it was not until 1871 that the position of the unions was clarified by an Act which established that members were not liable to prosecution as part of criminal conspiracies, because unions had previously been defined as being 'in restraint of trade'. The Act also sought to make unions responsible for their own internal organization, while granting them protection for their funds and allowing them to register as friendly societies. Unfortunately, the contemporaneous Criminal Law Amendment Act made most of the actions of a union in dispute subject to severe penalties, and it was not until 1875 that a new law, the Conspiracy and Protection of Property Act, permitted peaceful picketing and strike action. Similarly, the 1875 Employers' and Workman's Act made breach of contract a purely civil matter.

DEFINITION OF TRADE UNIONS AND ROLE OF THE CERTIFICATION OFFICER

The Trade Union and Labour Relations (Consolidation) Act 1992 defined a trade union as an organization of 'workers ... whose principal purposes include the regulation of relations between workers ... and employers or employers' associations'.

An independent trade union is defined as one that is free from control or interference by the employer. The certification officer is responsible for certifying the independence of trade unions and for keeping a list of trade unions and employers' associations. The certification officer can hear complaints from trade union members concerning breaches of trade union rules on certain issues, for example, the election or removal of a person from office, disciplinary proceedings and any proceedings of the executive committee of a trade union.

EUROPEAN WORKS COUNCILS

The European Works Council Directive of September 1994 (94/45/EC) seeks to facilitate consultation and communication with employees in 'community scale undertakings'. It does not cover organizations that operate only in one of the EU countries. A 'community scale undertaking' is defined as any undertaking with at least 1000 employees within Member States and at least 150 in at least two Member States (see Chapter 21).

TRADE UNION RECOGNITION

Claims for recognition by trade unions are handled by the CAC. There is a tight time table with short deadlines for each stage, but the intention is not to be too formal. The Employment Relations Act 1999 provides a right (under certain circumstances) whereby a trade union may claim recognition by employers and a procedure for this to take place. The right to claim recognition is extended to any trade union or two or more trade unions acting jointly, where the employer has at least an average of 21 employees (including associated companies in the UK, employee numbers averaged over thirteen weeks), including part-timers, provided another union is not already recognized in the bargaining unit. The bargaining unit is to be chosen by the trade union or by employees, not by management. The detailed procedures to determine the unit are contained in the Employment Relations Act 2004.

In the case of a disagreement, the appropriate bargaining unit is decided by the CAC, which has to take into account the need for the unit to be compatible with effective management, the location of workers, the views of the parties and the need to avoid small fragmented bargaining units.

Recognition is automatic if the trade union can demonstrate it has a majority of the workforce in the bargaining unit in membership (or joint applicants have a majority). However, the CAC may consider a ballot is necessary if a significant number of members affected tell the CAC they do not want the union to be recognized, or the employer has doubts about membership, such as the circumstances under which people joined the union. In these situations, the CAC will order a ballot to be conducted by an independent party, where there needs to be a majority in the ballot, plus at least 40 per cent of the bargaining unit voting in favour for recognition to be granted. Employers must cooperate in this process.

If the trade union and the employer fail to agree recognition procedures voluntarily there is a fall-back procedure, which will be legally enforceable, based on a model prescribed by the Department for Business, Innovation & Skills (BIS).

Derecognition is dealt with by a similar approach. Applications for derecognition may be made by employers or by a worker or workers within the bargaining unit, and this would only apply if the recognition were awarded by the CAC or under the procedures of the CAC. However, there is a moratorium for three years after a recognition has been agreed, before any application for derecognition claim can be made. The grounds for derecognition are where the number of employees has fallen below 21 (where derecognition would be automatic), or if at least 10 per cent of the bargaining unit want derecognition and a majority will support derecognition. The issue would then be decided by a ballot, in which case 40 per cent of the electorate would have to support derecognition, and where the original recognition was based on majority membership, if the union no longer has a majority of members this would also result in derecognition.

TRADE UNION IMMUNITIES

The 1980, 1982 and 1984 Acts consolidated in the Trade Union and Labour Relations (Consolidation) Act of 1992 severely limited the immunities previously enjoyed by trade unions from tort liabilities, such as breach of contract, intimidation by threatening a breach of contract, interference with a contract or inducement to break a contract.

Immunity is now restricted to actions that are 'in contemplation or furtherance of a trade dispute'. The disputes to which this applies are limited to disputes between workers and their employers, which relate wholly or mainly to one or more of the following:

- terms and conditions of employment, or physical conditions of work
- engagement or non-engagement, termination or suspension of employment or duties of employment of one or more workers
- allocation of work or duties of employment between workers
- discipline
- membership or non-membership of a trade union
- facilities for officials of trade unions
- negotiation machinery, consultation procedures, including recognition issues.

Effectively, this prevents official secondary action and political disputes, stops sympathetic strikes and restricts disputes of an official nature to those involving the workers of the same employer. The TULR(C) Act (1992) removed immunities from trade unions which take industrial action without the support of a ballot. This does not prevent unions from threatening action without a ballot, but they cannot carry out the threat without one.

Under the 1992 Act, vicarious liability is defined. A union is only liable for acts 'authorized or endorsed by the trade union'. Examples are members of the union's executive committee and those empowered by the rules to act. Damages are limited according to the size of union membership. For trade unions of over 100,000 members, the maximum is £250,000.

TRADE UNION MEMBERSHIP

Every employee has the right not to have action taken against him or her which seeks to prevent him or her from joining an independent trade union or from taking part in its activities (that is, if the union is a party to an agreement with his or her employer).

It is unlawful for an individual's employment to be made conditional upon his or her union membership or non-membership of a trade union. Blacklists of trade union members used for recruiting purposes are banned. Individuals have the right to join the trade union of their choice, which may signal the end of the Bridlington principles because under the 1993 Trade Union Reform and Employment Rights Act it is unlawful for a trade union to expel someone unless for a permitted reason. These permitted reasons are mostly matters of personal conduct, or in cases where the rules restrict membership to those employed in a specific trade, profession, industry, occupation or with particular qualifications. The dismissal of an employee for failing to join, or for proposing to join, a trade union is unfair.

People have a right to join or not join a trade union. Members of trade unions may only be disciplined according to the rules of the unions (according to the 1992 TULR(C) Act). Disciplinary action is unlawful, inter alia, in relation to the following conduct:

■ failing to take part in industrial action, or criticizing such action
■ encouraging or assisting other people to perform their contracts of employment
■ alleging that trade union officials acted unlawfully
■ failing to agree or withdrawing their agreement to a check-off arrangement
■ working, or proposing to work, for an employer who employs or has employed people who are not members of the union or of another union.

Under the same 1992 Act any term of a contract which stipulates that a supplier of goods or services must employ union or non-union labour is rendered void. It is similarly unlawful to refuse to deal with suppliers on grounds of trade union membership.

RIGHTS TO TIME OFF

Trade union officials (shop stewards, trade union safety representatives, etc.) in recognized trade unions have a right to time off during working hours, with pay, to carry out trade union duties, including training in industrial relations. Members of trade unions have the right to time off to take part in union activities other than strike activities. This includes representing their members at disciplinary and grievance hearings and at meetings of the membership, but there is no obligation to pay for this latter time off.

A similar right exists for time off without payment for public duties, such as attendance as a justice of the peace or in local authorities.

DISCLOSURE OF INFORMATION TO TRADE UNIONS

Employers are required to disclose certain information to the representatives of an independent trade union that they recognize for collective union bargaining. This does not apply to employers' associations. The union representative (who could be a shop steward and/or a full-time official) can be required by the employer to put his or her request for information in writing.

The employer has an obligation to produce information only if:

1   It is in his or her possession.
2   It relates to his or her undertaking or that of an associated employer.
3   It is in accordance with good industrial relations practice (as per the ACAS code of practice).
4   The absence of the information would impede the trade union representative to a material extent in conducting collective bargaining.

There is no obligation to produce information relating to particular individuals, information given in confidence, or information which could cause substantial injury to the employer's undertaking, other than its effect on collective bargaining. There are similar exclusions regarding national security, information used in legal proceedings or if giving the information could break the law. The employer does not have to produce any original document or compile data where this would cost more than its value for collective bargaining purposes.

Trade unions may complain to the CAC when an employer fails to comply. In such circumstances, ACAS would normally try to conciliate, but if this fails, the CAC may make an award. To date, most references have been made by white-collar unions and most of them have been settled without a full hearing.

There is a discussion on the European Works Councils and the Information and Consultation Directive in the previous chapter on consultation. The European Directive on Workers Councils came into force in January 2000 and covered transnational operations. The Information and Consultation Directive 2002 sought to provide rights to employees on information and consultation within UK undertakings. This is a general statutory framework, aimed at encouraging employers to negotiate and discuss trends and changes with their employees.

Where there is a request from at least 10 percent of the workforce, employers must initiate negotiations. If there is already an agreement in place, the employer can ballot the workforce. If there is a failure to agree, the default position applies: the employer must inform elected representatives of business developments, consult with them on employment trends and inform and consult with a view to reaching agreement on changes in work organization. Complaints are investigated by the CAC and appeals can be made to the EAT. There are protections against unfair dismissal for those exercising their rights, there are confidentiality clauses, and employers may withhold information which could seriously harm their business, if disclosed.

ELECTION OF UNION OFFICERS

Part I of the TULR(C) Act (1992) requires a trade union to hold a secret ballot of its members to elect candidates to a union's principal executive committee, a procedure which must be followed at least every five years. All members of the union must have an equal opportunity to vote without any constraint. An independent scrutineer, with a right of access to the union register, will distribute voting papers and will count the votes.

POLITICAL OBJECTIVES OF TRADE UNIONS

Section 71 of the TULR(C) Act (1992) requires a union to ballot its trade union members at least once every ten years if it is to retain the authority to devote union funds to political objectives. This legislation was retrospective as far as the ten-year period was concerned. The rules for the ballot are similar to those for electing union officials, except that a wider constituency, embracing unemployed members, those in arrears, etc., is given. The same rules regarding the independent scrutineer apply.

CHECK-OFF ARRANGEMENTS

These are arrangements whereby employers deduct trade union subscriptions from a members pay on behalf of trade unions. The written (and dated) consent of each employee is required, and must be renewed every three years. An employee has the right to withdraw consent by writing to the employer at any time. Employers must notify those covered of any increase in subscriptions at least one calendar month in advance, unless the subscription is a percentage of salary.

STRIKE AND INDUSTRIAL ACTION BALLOTS

A union's call for industrial action of any kind against an employer will only be immune from tort proceedings if it is preceded by a full postal ballot. Unions must inform the employer about the ballot in advance and must inform any employers whose employees are affected of the result. If more than 50 people are to be involved in the action, the ballot must be subject to independent scrutiny. Whilst industrial action should take place within four weeks of the ballot, the ballot validity may be extended to eight weeks, by agreement, to allow negotiations.

If the vote is in favour of a strike, the union must give the employer seven days' notice of the industrial action, and must inform the employer of the dates and whether the action is to be continuous or sporadic.

It is unfair to dismiss employees involved in strike action for the first 12 weeks of any official strike. Thereafter it may be fair if the CAC agrees that all reasonable action has been taken by the employer to end the strike (Employment Relations Act 1999).

PICKETING

Picketing is only permitted legally where pickets seek, by peaceful means, to communicate with and to persuade workers to work or not to work in support of a trade dispute.

Preventing people from crossing the picket lines by physical means and picketing outside a private home are both unlawful. Picketing is permitted only where it is outside or near the employee's own place of work and is conducted by the employees in dispute or with their union representative. The Secretary of State has produced a code of practice on picketing which has to be taken into account by the criminal courts in any litigation. The code suggests that in general the number of pickets should not exceed six at any entrance to a workplace, and recommends liaison between the picket organizer and the police.

CARRYING OUT REDUNDANCIES

An employer proposing to make 100 or more employees redundant at one establishment over a period of 90 days should notify BIS of that proposal at least 45 days before the first dismissal takes effect. If 20 to 99 employees are potentially redundant, BIS must be informed at least 30 days before the first dismissal takes effect.

ADVANCE CONSULTATION WITH APPROPRIATE REPRESENTATIVES

Advance consultation with the appropriate representatives is necessary at the earliest opportunity when 20 or more redundancies are proposed from one establishment within a 90 day period. If there is an appropriate trade union, consultation must be with that union. The appropriate trade union is defined as the independent trade union that is recognized by the employer for bargaining or representation on behalf of that worker or group of workers.

If there is no appropriate trade union, consultation must be with employee represent-atives elected for this purpose. An employer has positive obligations in relation to that election process, including an obligation to ensure that the election is conducted fairly.

Employers must undertake consultations with a view to reaching an agreement with the appropriate representatives. Consultation for collective redundancy does not need to run for the full 45 days or 30 days, but should in effect be negotiation in good faith with the objectives of avoiding, reducing or mitigating the effects of redundancies (for example any severance package to be offered). Relevant cases here are Middlesbrough Council v. TGWU [2002 IRLR 332], Securicor Omega Express v. GMB [2004 IRLR 9]. As part of the consultation process, the employer must disclose the following information:

■ reasons for redundancy
■ numbers and descriptions of those to be made redundant
■ total number of the those employed in the establishment in question
■ proposed method of selecting who is to be dismissed
■ method and timing of dismissals
■ details of the method of calculating any redundancy payments other than those required by law.

Where an employer fails to comply with the statutory collective consultation obligations , a tribunal may make a 'protective award', which is an order that the employer must pay the affected employees for a protected period, which can be up to 90 days gross pay for each affected employee. The purpose of the award is not to compensate the employee, for any loss suffered, but to be a sanction on the employer. The Court of Appeal decision in the case of Susie Radin Ltd. V. GMB 2004 [IRLR 400] shows that tribunals should assess the extent to which employers have failed to comply with the legislation, and where that is found, to start at 90 days and to see if there are mitigating circumstances to reduce it.

TIME OFF TO LOOK FOR ANOTHER JOB

An employee who is to be made redundant (provided he or she has at least two years' service) must be allowed up to two days' paid leave of absence to search for other employment. When the normal hours differ week by week, the average weekly hours are taken over a 12 week period immediately preceding the day on which notice was given.

TRANSFER OF UNDERTAKINGS

Where a transfer in the ownership of a business is contemplated, and such transfer will involve actions (known as 'measures') that will affect the employees (for example a proposed post-transfer restructure or relocation of the business), then employers (either vendors or purchasers, depending on who proposes the measures) must follow a similar consultative procedure as specified in the earlier section on carrying out redundancies. Regulation 13 of the Transfer of Undertakings (Protection of Employment) Regulations (TUPE) 2006 states appropriate employee representatives (which must be a trade union if one is recognized for collective bargaining purposes) must be informed:

- the fact that the transfer is to take place, the date or proposed date and the reasons for it
- any legal, economic or social implications of the transfer for any affected employees
- whether or not any measures are intended with regard to the employees, either by the vendor or the purchaser
- suitable information relating to the use of agency workers.

Where measures are proposed, employers are required to consult with the appropriate employee representatives and to consider their representations. Where a reply is required, they must give reasons if they reject the representations. The representatives can complain to a tribunal about a failure to comply with these regulations. If a tribunal upholds the complaint, the maximum compensation is 13 weeks' gross pay for every employee affected. The Regulations apply to any type of business or undertaking, whether or not it is a commercial or public sector activity. The Regulations apply irrespective of whether or not property is transferred (for example, they include franchises) and where there are several stages to the transfer process.

Employees potentially gain a number of rights from these Regulations:

1 After a transfer, the new employer must honour all the existing contractual terms of the employees. Pension rights were previously excluded from a transfer but, since April 2005, there is now a minimum level of occupational pension protection in the event of a TUPE transfer.
2 Employees have the right to object to the automatic transfer of their contracts of employment. Such a refusal would not constitute a dismissal, and employees would not have to give notice. In these circumstances, the employee would not be entitled to any severance pay (e.g. notice pay or redundancy pay).
2 Any dismissal because of the transfer will be regarded as unfair, unless it can be shown that the main reason was not connected to the transfer itself or, if it was connected to the transfer, there was an economic, technical or organizational reason entailing a change in the workforce (known as an ETO reason).
3 Contractual redundancy rights can also transfer with the contractual rights.
4 Accrued pension rights up to the transfer date must be protected. The Pensions Act 2004 has now introduced a minimum standard of occupational pension entitlement to transferred employees who had such an entitlement prior to the transfer.
5 Employer liability for any past breaches of contract.
6 Employer personal injury liability.

Dismissal may not be automatically unfair if the employer can mount a defence that there are economic, technical or organizational reasons which entailed changes in the work force, but not in the terms of employment. Where there is contracting out in the public sector, TUPE often applies.

There is an ongoing consultation on some of the controversial areas as to what is being transferred, whether it is a service or a part of a business, as well as the wide variety of circumstances, such as outsourcing, insourcing or retendering for contracts. Cases such as the European Court of Justice decision in *Suzen v Zehnacker Gebaudereingung GmbH* (1997) emphasized that there needs to be an analysis of what transfers, which must be an economic entity, and that sufficient of its assets have been transferred such that its essential identity is preserved in the new organization to which it is transferred.

The transfer of the work can come some time after the dismissals, for example, the company can go into administration but be purchased by another organization later, when TUPE would still apply.

WORKING TIME REGULATIONS

The Working Time Regulations, dated 1 October 1998, were implemented into UK law by the EC Working Time Directive of 1993. These Regulations set out maximum working time, minimum rest periods and holidays and rules regarding night work.

Working time is defined as 'any period during which the worker is working, at his [*sic*] employer's disposal and carrying out his activity or duties'.

The Regulations state that workers are entitled to:

- daily rest periods of 11 consecutive hours in every 24 hour period
- uninterrupted rest break of at least 20 minutes during working days of more than six hours
- weekly rest periods of at least 24 consecutive hours in every seven days (this may be 48 hours in a 14-day period, by agreement)
- paid annual holiday entitlement of 28 days (5.6 weeks) (this can include eight bank holidays which, depending on the employer, may be unpaid)
- maximum working week of 48 hours, which for employees aged over 18 is averaged over a specified period (normally 17 weeks)
- limitation on the hours of night workers (not more than eight hours in a 24-hour period if special hazards, physical or mental strain)
- the holiday entitlement for part time workers is pro rata
- 16- and 17-year-olds are not allowed to work more than 48 hours in any week
- for trainee doctors, the 48 hours maximum is averaged over 26 weeks
- for offshore workers, the average is taken over 52 weeks
- there are a number of occupations and industry sectors where the rules on working time are specific to that industry, for example, the aviation industry and the road transport industry.

Formal written agreements between employers and trade unions or workers, may be made to restrict or amplify the above provisions, if the workforce comprises more than 20 workers.

There are also derogations for 'autonomous' workers and managing executives, these being people who determine their own working hours. There are further discussions on shift systems and working time flexibility in Chapters 8 and 22.

HEALTH AND SAFETY AT WORK

The Health and Safety at Work Act 1974 places a general duty on all employers to maintain standards in health, safety and welfare of people at work, to protect the general public and visitors against risks to safety and to prevent pollution of the environment. A Health and Safety Commission exists with a Health and Safety Executive to enforce the law.

Scope

The Act requires the employer to provide for his or her employees, so far as it is reasonably practical, plant, machinery, systems of work, handling, storage and transport that are safe and without risks to health. The employer also has an obligation, so far as is reasonably practical, to provide information, instruction, training and supervision on safety, to maintain any places of work in a safe condition, to ensure a working environment that is without risk to health, with adequate facilities, and a written safety policy. It should be noted that mental health as well as physical health is covered. Failure by employers to address the problems of stress at work, for example, can result in successful claims against employers. Employers must now conduct formal risk assessments and appoint competent persons to assist in compliance. The policy must state how it is to be carried out and who is to be responsible. Employers must not charge employees for the cost of safety equipment or for special protective clothing, such as goggles.

Sanctions for breaches of the Act are imposed in the criminal courts. The penalties are a fine of up to £20,000 and up to six months' imprisonment for every person guilty of infringement. Unlimited fines and up to two years' imprisonment may be imposed for some offences.

Employees also have duties, notably to cooperate with management on safety matters.

RISK ASSESSMENT

Employers must make regular assessments of the risks faced by their employees and non-employees at work 'arising out of or in connection with the conduct of their undertaking'. The purpose of the risk assessment is to identify the measures needed to comply with health and safety rules.

If there are five or more employees, a written record must be kept to show significant findings and any group of people who are particularly at risk. The Health and Safety Executive's *Five Steps to Risk Assessment* explains the process:

1   Look for hazards.
2   Decide who might be harmed and how.
3   Evaluate the risks arising from the hazards and decide whether existing precautions are adequate or if more should be done.
4   Record findings.
5   Review the assessment periodically and revise if necessary.

When evaluating the risks under Step 3 above, employers should assess whether the risk in relation to each hazard is high, medium or low, and then check to see if generally accepted industry standards/controls/measures are in place.

The regular reviews can be prompted by changes to machines, working practices, substances in use, etc. Even if no changes have occurred it is wise to review procedures on a regular basis (for example, annually) and to include non-routine operations in the assessment.

As we discussed in Chapter 22, stress at work is becoming a serious health issue. The approach to occupational stress which is taken by the HSE is to encourage better management rather than to rely on enforcement, to focus on prevention and to support risk assessments. With that in mind, management standards and an outline of the state to be achieved are being promulgated as part of the guidance provided. In the meantime, stress claims are increasing. Employers are only liable, it would seem, if they were on notice (directly or constructively) that there is a risk to the employee's health (for example *Best v Staffordshire University* ([2002] IRLR 190), *Wheeldon v HSBC Bank Limited* ([2005] IRLR 293) and *Sutherland v Hatton* ([2002] IRLR 263).

Under 1999 regulations, which were introduced to comply with EC directives, a range of responsibilities was placed on employers to ensure that all work equipment is suitable and well maintained, that workers are trained and given information on use, and employees are provided with protective equipment and are not obliged to undertake manual handling operations that involve a risk of injury where this can be avoided.

FACTORY ACTS

The 1961 Factories Act, which has over 200 consequential regulations and orders, details particular duties on employers, such as the fencing of machinery, and rules concerning the employment of women and young persons in factories.

For example, first-aid boxes and, where 50 or more persons work, a trained 'first – aider' are required. The temperature in workplaces should be reasonable and normally at least 16°C, and there must be adequate ventilation, etc.

Perhaps the most important provisions are those covering the fencing of machinery, guards being obligatory on all moving parts. Periodic inspections of hoists, cranes, boilers, etc., are expected. Accidents causing absence of more than three days must be reported to the enforcing authority, as must an explosion or fire which causes an interruption of work for 24 hours or more, or a death in the workplace.

In addition to any penalty for failing to comply with the regulations, there is the possibility of further civil action for compensation for a breach of statutory duty.

OFFICES, SHOPS AND RAILWAY PREMISES ACT 1963

This covers the same sort of issues as the Factory Acts but for the premises named in its title. It deals with such matters as sanitary facilities, cleanliness, overcrowding, ventilation, lighting, etc., and lays down minimum standards in these areas. (This legislation and the Factories Act 1961 have been largely superseded by the general requirements of Health & Safety at Work Act 1974 and subsequent regulations.)

REFERENCES

Health and Safety Executive. *Five Steps to Risk Assessment*. www.hse.gov.uk/risk/fivesteps.htm.
References to cases are in the IRLR (Industrial Relations Law Reports). ISSN 0307-5591. London: LexisNexis Butterworth.

INDEX

Page numbers in *italic* refer to figures and diagrams
Abbreviation: HRM = human resources management

203–4; case study 209–10; differing approaches *200*; fast track development 201, 203; human resources management 69; importance of 199–201; learning and development 212; performance appraisal 198; policies 201; potential assessment 201, *202*, 202–3, 206–9; promotions 201, 204–5; questions 211; succession planning 201, 205–6; workforce planning 107

Tannenbaum, R. 30

task: flexibility 125; fulfilment orientation 18; job satisfaction 11; nature of 18–19

task oriented behaviour 17–18; group functioning 27; leadership 28, 29, 30–1; systems theory 39

task time, flexible working 127–8

Tavistock Institute of Human Relations 19, 39

Taylor, F. W. 8, 38, 87

Taylor, G. S. 61

teams: competency 21–2, *23*; groups 20–1; job evaluation 236; leadership 141–2; learning and development 221; managing change 60; mental models 22

technology: historical perspectives 83, 308; impact on organizations 41–2; iPhones 153, 159 , 224, 228; learning and development 228; organizational structure 45, 47; web 2 developments 153; workforce planning 110. *see also* internet; social media

Teece, T. J. 91

Templeton, G. F. 61

temporary organizations 131–2

temporary workers, assessing cultural fit 169

ten point plan, human resource strategies 97–101, *100*, 107

tension-releasing humour 18

termination of contracts of employment 369–72

Terracciano, A. 4

terrorist attack, World Trade Centre 81

testing. *see* psychometric tests

Thatcher government: HRM 78–9; trade unions 309, 321

Thematic Apperception Test 176

theory of complex man 14

theory X/theory Y: motivation 12; performance appraisal 190–1

Thomas, P. 335

Thorpe, R. 32

3D printing 45, 83, 110

360 degree feedback processes: learning and development evaluation 229; performance appraisal 196–7, *197*

thriving employees 343

Thurstone, C. 5

tight-loose properties of organizations 44

time allowed system 253

time, flexibility 125. *see also* flexible working hours

time and motion studies 8–9, 87. *see also* work-study

time off allowances, trade union members 397, 401

time scales, workforce planning 109

time span of discretion methods, job evaluation 246–7

timekeeping statistics 352

top down learning 227

Torres, R. T. 221

total rewards (TR) 277, 287; corporate social responsibility 292; employer interest 284–5; flexible benefits 283, 284, 285, *286*; major elements of packages 279–81; marketing approach 281–2; Nationwide bank and building society 284–5; questions 287; strategy 277–9, 282–3

Towers Watson Global Workplace Survey (2012/13) 284

Trade Union Act (1927) 306

Trade Union and Labour Relations Act (1974) 370

Trade Union and Labour Relations (Consolidation) Act (1992) 333, 396, 399

Trade Union Congress (TUC) 304, 305–6

trade unions 303, 308, 394; industrial relations; advance consultation 400–1; check-off arrangements 399; definitions 394–5; disclosure of information to 398; historical

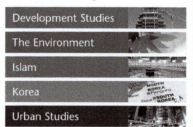